D0984098

ROME AND MEDIEVAL CULTURE

CLASSIC EUROPEAN HISTORIANS

A SERIES EDITED BY LEONARD KRIEGER

Ferdinand Gregorovius

ROME

AND

MEDIEVAL CULTURE

Selections from
History of the City of Rome in the Middle Ages
Translated by Mrs. Gustavus W. Hamilton

Edited and with an Introduction
by K. F. Morrison

THE UNIVERSITY OF CHICAGO PRESS
CHICAGO & LONDON

ISBN: 0–226–30749–2 (clothbound); 0–226–30750–6 (paperbound)
Library of Congress Catalog Card Number: 72–142863

THE UNIVERSITY OF CHICAGO PRESS, CHICAGO 60637
THE UNIVERSITY OF CHICAGO PRESS, LTD., LONDON

Contents

Series Editor's Preface

GREGOROVIUS's notable history of medieval Rome, published here in an abridged edition, has a special function in the series of *Classic European Historians*. The series is designed to serve both historiography and history by reproducing landmarks in the development of the one and lasting contributions to our knowledge of the other. Gregorovius and his work serve these dual purposes admirably, for he was an outstanding German representative of that pungent mid-nineteenth-century historiography which has helped so much to mold all subsequent approaches to history, and at the same time his history of Rome remains, as Professor Karl Morrison indicates authoritatively in his informative introduction, a standard work in a still underdeveloped area of medieval history. But what is particularly distinctive of Gregorovius in the context of this series is the connection between his historiography and his history. With a clarity rarely as visible in other historians, his writing reflects the running battle of the historian's own values with his historical conscience, and with an urgency equally rare his writing requires the reader's awareness of this battle and of its stakes before it can be understood. Moreover, with a success representative of the best historians, Gregorovius's writing shows the historical fruitfulness of this tension between the frank application of political or cultural values and the stubborn retention of the commitment to the truth of the past.

The reason for the uncommon transparency of Gregorovius's historical mentality lies perhaps in the overt contrast between the liberal nationalism of his values and the hieratic universalism of his medieval subject matter—a contrast which facilitates the tracing of each component. Gregorovius, like Macaulay, Michelet, Motley, Parkman, and Renan, belonged to the liberal wing of the romantic second generation. They viewed history as an art which both could and should be shaped by the historian's convictions, an art which could be amateur in the sense of being practised either by or for nonspecialists, but also an art which should be practised in conformity with the increasingly scientific standards of dispassionate truth set by their professional colleagues in the universities. To watch Gregorovius carefully balance, for figure after figure, for section after section, his condemnation of medieval authoritarianism, both ecclesiastical and political, against his understanding portraits of men and his perceptive descriptions of events is to watch the most typical of all historical dialectics at work—where partisanship does not merely alternate with understanding, but where partisanship spurs understanding, requires it, and creates a dialectical history that records the continuing interaction between the two. This integrated balance, indeed, reflects the deeper cultural ground which Professor Morrison shows to have underlain the liberal Protestant's original choice of the archetypical conservative Catholic subject: his recognition that the noblest, most spiritual, and most humane values of the civilization were transmitted from the ancient to the modern worlds by the fallible institutions centered in Rome, and his consequent need to understand the history of these institutions in order to chart the elliptical course of the cherished values.

There is also a second strand of historical dialectic in the book which should be even more relevant to present-day readers. Gregorovius's history of medieval Rome is an early example of urban history in the microcosmic sense that is now standard for the genre. Like the histories of cities being prosecuted today, Gregorovius's Roman history is an attempt to write general history by focusing upon a circumscribed, manageable framework which is either the embodiment or the crossroads of general movements.

For Gregorovius the city of Rome was precisely such a crossroads in the middle ages: as the seat of the papacy, as the basis of the Empire, and as the pivot of Italy, his Rome witnesses the crucial events of European history from the schism of east and west through the duel of pope and emperor to the end of the Italian Renaissance and the start of the modern age of liberty. These events, moreover, lose their abstract character and take on palpable and dramatic forms when they appear on the Roman scene. Gregorovius shows the big events in their local impact and he shows the expansive effects of superficially local events: but always what concerns Rome concerns the world at large. The choice of Rome as the urban microcosm was especially appropriate to the middle ages, when most men were vitally committed both to the local and to the universal, to the familiar and to the absolute, and only vaguely to the intermediate levels between them—and Rome was the one locality that was the home of both universal medieval institutions, papacy, and Empire.

Hence Gregorovius's work is one of the great general works of medieval historiography. But its implications are more far-reaching than its mere periodic achievement. Gregorovius was driven to microcosmic history because he was possessed both of the historian's passion for the concrete vitality of human existence as individuals actually live it and of the idealist's passion to comprehend the fate of humanity as the whole species has undergone it.

The lessons are clear. Partisan history can be great history if the partisanship is a troubled one. And the world can be seen in a grain of sand if the grain is nicely chosen.

LEONARD KRIEGER

Editor's Introduction

WRITING his *History of the City of Rome in the Middle Ages* took Gregorovius nearly seventeen years, but he conceived the entire work in one moment. Standing on the Ponte Fabricio early in the autumn of 1854 he suddenly saw in the buildings and ruins of Rome more than vestiges of one city's aspirations and failures. He saw Rome as a point of intersection for the great forces whose conflicts had generated European civilization. The bridge on which he stood witnessed to the heritage of classical Rome. Originally built by the Emperor Otto III, the Church of Santo Bartolomeo, at the foot of the bridge, represented the Germanic empire. Behind him, on the Capitoline, stood the Campidoglio, the stronghold of Roman republicanism in the Middle Ages. Up the Tiber rose Saint Peter's, an enduring moment of papal monarchy.

For Gregorovius, these buildings were relics, not simply of men, but of the spirit that had moved men, of ideas that had dominated the world. Beyond the plane of local politics, concerning the short-range fates of immediate issues and great men, Gregorovius detected a second level—that of universal history, the drama of mankind's advancement through increasingly complete stages of spiritual freedom. "In a flash," he grasped the inspiration for the history in these two aspects as "something great, something that will lend a purpose to my life."[1]

1. *The Roman Journals, 1852–1874,* ed. F. Althaus, trans. Mrs. G. W. Hamilton, 2d ed. (London, 1911), p. 16 (3 October 1854).

Eighty years earlier, almost to the day, Edward Gibbon had conceived his great work, *The Decline and Fall of the Roman Empire*, while, in Santa Maria Aracoeli, he "sat musing amidst the ruins of the Capitol," a few yards from the Ponte Fabricio. Gibbon was then twenty-seven years old. Gregorovius was thirty-one when he first envisioned the *History of Rome*. Gregorovius was aware of these coincidences, but he did not plan to repeat the performance of his predecessor. He intended to treat the city of Rome instead of the empire; and the burden of his work concerned the period A.D. 641–1453, which Gibbon treated cursorily. Gibbon's theme was the gripping spectacle of imperial decay, the triumph, as he put it, of Christianity and barbarism. Gregorovius's was the inspirational drama of the birth of European culture. Gibbon saw liberty as best exercised within the firm, if benevolent, military rule of the Antonine emperors; for Gregorovius, political and spiritual freedom alike were won by revolution.

The two authors confronted Rome at roughly the same stage in life. Gibbon chose the grandeur and disintegration of the ancient Empire; Gregorovius, the political chaos of an impoverished medieval city, a cultural backwater, of which he could write: "While other cities shone conspicuous by their weath and power, Rome's only glory was that she was Rome." (See below, p. 154.) The reasons for Gibbon's choice are clear. Those for Gregorovius's came from an intellectual catalysis caused by the events that he experienced in Rome.

Gregorovius was born in Neidenburg, East Prussia, in 1821.[2] Sensitivity to problems of legal order came to him from his father, who was a *Justizrat*, or state's attorney. Affinity to the medieval period came from the fact that his father's official residence was in the castle of the Teutonic Knights, at Neidenburg.

---

2. For biographical data, see the memoir by F. Althaus, as translated in F. Gregorovius, *History of the City of Rome in the Middle Ages*, trans. Mrs. G. W. Hamilton, vol. 1 (London, 1909), pp. xvii–xxx (also printed as part of the introductory material for the *Roman Journals*). Fuller discussion is in J. Hönig, *Ferdinand Gregorovius als Dichter* (Stuttgart, 1914), Breslauer Beiträge zur Literaturgeschichte, n. f., 39. Hft.; and by the same author, *Ferdinand Gregorovius der Geschichtschreiber der Stadt Rom*, 2d ed. (Stuttgart and Berlin, 1921, 1944).

Indeed, Gregorovius often observed to his friends that his history of Rome was a plain effect of passing his early years within the castle's walls. Religion was a third formative influence. His father served, not only as a lawyer, but also as a Lutheran pastor. He presided over the same parish as had his own father and grandfather, and he insisted that Gregorovius study theology at the University of Königsberg with a view to continuing the pastoral succession. Finally, as he came to adolescence, Gregorovius felt another influence. His sympathies were forcibly engaged by great struggles for national self-determination pursued under the watchword "freedom." In 1830, when he was nine years old, he saw hosts of refugees fleeing across the nearby Polish border from the ferocious military regime that followed a nationalist revolt against the Russian government.

The rigors of education at the gymnasium of Gumbinnen (1831–38) failed to stifle Gregorovius's idealism. When he matriculated at Königsberg (1838), he obediently studied theology, as his father wished, but his personal convictions had entered the state of religious agnosticism that he explicitly described in 1844.[3] He studied theology for its humane values, adding to that work extensive readings in philosophy. As we shall see, the influence of Hegelianism at this point gave a permanent form to Gregorovius's lofty aspirations for mankind and to his conceptualization of the past.

His dissertation at Königsberg, dealing with Plotinus's doctrine of the Beautiful, fell within philosophy rather than theology. But just as he had turned away from theology, he later left philosophy proper. While he made his way as a private tutor after receiving the doctorate (and wrote some poetry of a strongly romantic flavor), Gregorovius devoted much thought to questions of individual liberty and social cohesion. Two of the resulting works were published in the "year of revolutions," 1848–49: first, *Die Idee des Polentums: Zwei Bücher polnischer Leidensgeschichte*, and later, *Göthes Wilhelm Meister in seinem socialistischen Elementen entwickelt*. Other, shorter essays appeared during his career as jour-

3. Hönig, *Ferdinand Gregorovius als Dichter, op. cit.*, pp. 18 f.

nalist (1848–52), editor of the *Neue Königsberger Zeitung* and correspondent for the *Hartung'sche Zeitung*. His engagement with issues of freedom and social order had a distinctly historical cast, and as the revolutions of 1848 broke out, Gregorovius was completing his *Geschichte des römischen Kaisers Hadrian und seiner Zeit* (published only in 1851), a work which focused his historical and philosophical interests on Rome. The general failure of the liberal revolutions in Germany and, especially, in Poland, disheartened Gregorovius; in 1852, he left Königsberg for Italy.

He found Rome a profoundly troubled city. As sovereign ruler of the Papal States, Pope Pius IX (1846–78) inherited from his predecessors a distressed treasury and a disordered political system. The papacy had beaten back revolts early in the 1830s only by calling in French and Austrian troops, and the popes' continued reliance on the coercive force of foreign allies exacerbated legitimate grievances and outraged Italian nationalists. At the beginning of his pontificate, Pius launched a number of governmental reforms—such as relaxing the rules of censorship—designed to placate liberals. But he found it impossible to come to terms on two unnegotiable demands of the opposition: that clergy be removed from civil government and replaced by laymen in a representative system, and that the Papal States resign a measure of its sovereign rights in favor of a league of Italian states.

The reforms that Pius instituted (1847) for the municipal order of Rome and for the Papal States were condemned as empty, insincere gestures. The constitution that he promulgated the next year was in effect counteracted by violence in Rome supporting the Milanese revolt against Austria. Pius had inflamed the feelings of his hostile subjects by taking a stance of official neutrality in the struggle for independence from the Habsburg Empire. The chief of state in the new papal government, Rossi, was assassinated; and the radically democratic ministry of Galetti, who succeeded Rossi, disbanded even the pope's own military force and put a civil militia in charge of Pius's personal security. The pope considered himself powerless and a prisoner. He fled to Gaeta in the Kingdom of Naples. Early in 1849 a constituent assembly proclaimed a Roman republic. Pius condemned this revolution, again appealed to France and Austria for military assistance, and in 1850 reentered Rome surrounded by foreign troops. The revolution had forced him permanently into the camp of political archconservatives; he resolved to fight with all his strength against liberalism and nationalism, and he set reactionary measures in motion to revive conditions as they had been before 1848.

To be sure, Pius served Rome well by introducing modern amenities of a technical sort. He improved the city by new building programs, by bringing in the railroad and the telegraph, and by other important urban advancements. But public works formed the light side of the moon. Arrest without warrant; detention without charges or trial; cruelty in judicial process and sentencing —these were all aspects of Pius's repressive government. Along with this active destruction of "the rights of man and citizen" went irresponsible and corrupt financial administration and the revival of what would now be recognized as guerilla warfare in the countryside, the last resort of desperate resistance.

This was the city where Gregorovius conceived the plan of the work which was to give meaning to his life.

Verdi composed his early operas, such as *I Lombardi* and *Ernani*, as political analogues, using long-past events as a code in which Italian nationalists saw their own struggles against Austria. It is not surprising to find Gregorovius also writing of medieval Rome in symbolic fashion. He makes this explicit throughout, but especially in his concluding remarks. The conflict between Pius IX and republicanism that Gregorovius saw developing day by day was mirrored in the medieval controversies between the popes and various experiments in republican government. Pius's hostility to Italian nationalism had counterparts in papal opposition to movements that had culminated in the tribuneship of Cola di Rienzo in the fourteenth century. Austria's role as the foreign mainstay of papal government found parallels in some periods of the medieval empire.

This sort of identification between past and present gave bone and sinew to Gregorovius's historical writing. Its life came from a different source. The associations that Gregorovius consciously made were more than simple analogues. They were also stages in the same line of development, the same progress of "the universal civilization of mankind." The actors and the great ideas in the political drama of the mid-nineteenth century were, for Gregorovius, the same as those in the conflicts of medieval Rome, reawakened after a dormant period that began with the sack of Rome in 1527 and the Counter-Reformation.

In that space of about three hundred years, Rome ceased to be a mirror of Western culture; for the first time, the whole tendency of civil and intellectual life in the ancient capital—dominated as it was by the papal government—actively fought against all that was innovative and progressive. The struggle between Italy and Germany, represented in Gregorovius's view by the papacy and the empire, had ended; the generation of European culture by that enduring conflict was accomplished; the progress of mankind toward spiritual liberty now found multiple centers in the several nations and was no longer focused upon one geographical point.

The first decisive conflict between Italy and its antithesis, Germany, occurred during the barbarian invasions, which, Gregorovius argued, wrecked the Roman Empire. In the early Middle Ages, the popes exercised their spiritual powers unadulterated by lust for temporal government; and, Gregorovius wrote, Rome "rescued Europe from the chaos of barbarism and made it capable of receiving a common freedom and culture."[4] After this initial conflict, the Germanic peoples restored the empire that they had destroyed, though in its new life it took the form of feudal monarchy. Influenced by Rome's imperial past, by theological doctrines, and by the Germanic institution of feudalism, the papacy became an imperialized theocracy, a territorial government. The church betrayed its spiritual charge by falling into worldliness, and it even perverted the spirit by using religious sanctions to justify works of earthly passion.

The recurrent conflicts between empire and papacy—both

4. See below, p. 17.

claiming universal dominion—proved the lasting force of the Italian-German antagonism. These controversies prepared the way for the second decisive conflict between the German and the Latin worlds: the Reformation. The reformers, led by Luther, reaffirmed the integrity of spiritual freedom. The papacy had by that time become a retardant in mankind's advancement toward the liberty of the spirit. The Reformation broke down the barriers that the papacy had set in the way of progress and liberated reason, consciousness of the free spirit. The papacy's vital role in the genesis of European culture was at an end. Spiritually bankrupt, the papacy had only its temporal government—which it used for no good purpose—to impede the development of Italian unity and to repress advocates of civic republicanism in the city of Rome. As Gregorovius wrote triumphantly in the conclusion to his *History*, the events of 1869 and 1870 extinguished that vestige of papal greatness.

Even in this précis of a long and discursive work, the biases of Gregorovius's intellectual formation are clear: perceptiveness of the tension between public order and personal liberty; sensitivity to religious and, more generally, spiritual values; the impress of a half-discarded Lutheran bias against the Reformation papacy (given ceremonial recognition by Rome itself when the *History* was put on the Index in 1874); and, perhaps most important, a romantic idealism drawn from Hegelian philosophy. His acceptance of ideas as lasting and creative forces; his concept of mankind's progress through increasingly wide levels of spiritual freedom; his description of history in terms of a dialectic of thesis, antithesis, and synthesis (papacy versus empire producing European culture; papacy versus republicanism yielding Italian unity); and even his chronological divisions at the barbarian invasions and the reign of Charles V, with their supporting rationales, all stem perhaps indirectly from Hegel's treatise, *The Philosophy of History*.

In 1854, when Gregorovius described his plan for the *History* to a classicist at the German Archaeological Institute in Rome, his friend solemnly declared, "It is an attempt in which anyone must fail."[5] Indeed, errors of fact and emphasis mar Gregorovius's exposition, although he worked many years at his task and, like Ranke, had access—not to the Vatican archives, to be sure—but to the excellent private archives of some great noble families, particularly that of the Barberini. As examples of errors: Pope Leo III did not anoint Charlemagne and his son at the imperial coronation of A.D. 800. The antipope in 1084 was Wibert of Ravenna, not Cadalus of Parma. It falls rather far of the mark to say that Magna Carta was "the foundation of all political and civic freedom in Europe." The dispensations against which Luther protested were being sold for the benefit of the archbishop of Mainz, not to pay for building Saint Peter's in Rome.

The preeminent historians of Gregorovius's day took a dim view of such errors as these. Ranke held that the work was "more a history of the popes than of the city of Rome and its municipality" and that Gregorovius had often failed to master his voluminous material.[6] Sensitive to these criticisms, Gregorovius became acutely hostile to historians who held academic appointments, and when his renown later brought him invitations to assume professorships at Weimar and at Munich, he declined both in order, he said, to preserve his independence.

Although disparaged by learned critics, the *History* won an extensive public. Rome's municipal government conferred upon Gregorovius citizenship of the city and commissioned an Italian translation of the work. Translations into English and Russian subsequently appeared. Even on the scholarly level, the *History* has held its own as the chief survey of civic and cultural life in medieval and Renaissance Rome, an enduring landmark in urban, as well as cultural, history. It has outlasted its nineteenth-century rivals and has continued to have more appeal than later works because of its vivid descriptive passages and its development of one dramatic theme from beginning to end.[7]

5. See above, note 1.
6. Hönig, *Ferdinand Gregorovius als Dichter*, p. 281.
7. A fresh edition of the *History*, by W. Kampf (Darmstadt, 1953–1957) gives strong evidence of its continuing value. A number of histories of medieval Rome were current in Gregorovius's day—e.g., F. Papencourt, *Geschichte*

Gregorovius's literary production reached its peak during his
years in Rome (1852–74). Aside from the *History*, he published
an account of his travels in Corsica; a study of funerary monuments of the popes; *Lucrezia Borgia*; and *Euphorion*, an idyllic
poem of epic proportions. He also kept a diary, which he published in several editions (*Wanderjahre in Italien*).

When he completed the *History* in 1871, he felt that his reason
for staying in Rome had been exhausted. Two years later he
moved his permanent residence to Munich. During the rest of his
life he made long annual visits to Rome, and two journeys to
Greece and the Levant (1880, 1882) inspired him to write his
Geschichte der Stadt Athen im Mittelalter (2 vols., 1889), a work
which, in contrast with the Roman history, brought praise from
the academic establishment.

It is right to consider the *History of Rome* a statement of philosophical conviction, almost a personal confession, under the guise
of history. As such, the work represents a large and diverse family
of nineteenth-century historical thought. For example, Gregorovius's process of conceptualization had much in common with
those of his contemporaries Nietzsche and Marx. All three absorbed the Hegelian approach to the past as boys in Prussian

---

der Stadt Rom im Mittelalter (Paderborn, 1857); the relevant volumes of
Ludwig von Pastor's *History of the Popes;* and T. H. Dyer's *The City of
Rome: Its Vicissitudes and Monuments from Its Foundation to the End of
the Middle Ages* (New York and London, 1877); and H. Grisar set out to
cover much the same ground in his *Geschichte Roms und der Päpste im
Mittelalter* (Freiburg, 1901), only the earliest sections of which were ever
published. A. von Reumont ended his friendship with Gregorovius by publishing his *Geschichte der Stadt Rom*, 3 vols. (Berlin, 1867–1870).
  Curious to say, subsequent writings have not superseded Gregorovius's
book as a whole. Since 1938, however, the Istituto di studi romani has been
publishing its *Storia di Roma*, a series of monographic studies, and these
works together provide valuable revisions of some segments of Gregorovius's
History. See particularly: vol. 9, O. Bertolini, *Roma di fronte a Bisanzio e ai
Langobardi* (Bologna, 1941); vol. 10, P. Brezzi, *Roma e l'impero medioevale*
(774–1252) (Bologna, 1947); vol. 11, E. Dupré-Theseider, *Roma dal
comune di popolo alla signoria pontificia* (1252–1377) (Bologna, 1952); vol.
12, P. Paschini, *Roma nel Rinascimento* (Bologna, 1940); vol. 13, P. Pec-
chiai, *Roma nel cinquecento* (Bologna, 1948); vol. 27, F. Hermanin, *L'arte
in Roma dal sec. VIII al XIV* (Bologna, 1945).

schools—Gregorovius in East Prussia, Nietzsche in Prussian Saxony, Marx in Rhenish Prussia—and continued studies of Hegelian philosophy at a higher level. All came from Lutheran families. Nietzsche, like Gregorovius, sprang from a line of pastors; Marx's father had converted from Judaism. All did their major work outside the academic establishment (though Nietzsche briefly held a professorship at the University of Basle) and outside their native lands. They came to radically different conclusions, these demi-Hegelians and lapsed Lutherans: Gregorovius the humanist; Nietzsche, the nihilist; Marx, the Communist. But, true to the philosophy of romantic idealism, all saw in history the advance of mankind through dialectical conflict toward greater and greater freedom. All offered men revolution, liberty, and hope. In an address delivered in Munich shortly before his death in 1891, Gregorovius expressed their common prospect for the human race, the conviction that inspired and ran throughout the Roman *History*.

> The future belongs to future men. No Sibyl unveils to our view the roads which mankind will travel after us. As it advances in the mass, we will recede into the background. Today we look back upon the past's social and political culture forms as upon obsolete stages of spiritual development. In exactly the same way, subsequent generations will glance backwards upon the constitution which society, state, and church have achieved in our present. We know only this: that the synthetic spirit of man forms the world's panorama more splendidly and more uniformly with every day, and that every miracle of its inventive power opens an inconceivable series of miracles yet to come.[8]

The following excerpts have been selected to show how, in Gregorovius's view, the cosmic drama of this eternal progress was played out in the institutions and cultural achievements of medieval Rome.

The translation by Mrs. Gustavus W. (Annie) Hamilton is here reproduced without most of the footnotes, since their references

8. F. Gregorovius, "Die grossen Monarchien oder die Weltreiche in der Geschichte," in *Kleine Schriften zur Geschichte und Cultur*, vol. 3 (Leipzig, 1892), pp. 262–63.

to documentary and analytical materials are now out of date. It was published by George Bell and Sons, London, after Gregorovius's death. Mrs. Hamilton (d. 1919), the wife of a distinguished historian, frequently visited Italy, and, toward the end of her life, she moved permanently from London to Bordighera. Aside from the heroic work of translating Gregorovius's *History of the City of Rome*, she also translated two other works by him, *The Roman Journals* and *Siciliana: Sketches of Naples and Sicily in the Nineteenth Century*. Her last work, *Italy and the War*, was a translation of essays by Italian scholars published for the benefit of the Italian Red Cross.

The volumes of the *History* represented in this book appeared as follows: 1 (1909); 2 (1894); 3 (1895); 4, parts 1 and 2 (1896); 5, parts 1 and 2 (1897); 6, parts 1 and 2 (1898); 7, parts 1 and 2 (1900); 8, parts 1 and 2 (1902).

The map and the table of popes and emperors have been prepared especially for this edition, and all the topical headings are likewise new.

K. F. MORRISON

Popes and Western Emperors in the Period Treated by Gregorovius

Emperors	Popes
Honorius, 395–423	Innocent I, 401–17
	Zosimus, 417–18
	[Eulalius, 418–19, antipope]
	Boniface I, 418–22
Valentinian III, 425–454	Celestine I, 422–32
	Sixtus III, 432–40
Petronius, 455	Leo I, 440–61
Avitus, 455–457	
Majorian, 457–461	
Severus, 461–465	Hilary, 461–68
Anthemius, 467–472	Simplicius, 468–83
Olybrius, 472	
Glycerius, 473–474	
Julius Nepos, 473–475	
Romulus Augustulus, 475–476 (transfer of government over the West to the emperors at Constantinople)	
	Felix III, 483–92
	Gelasius I, 492–96
	Anastasius II, 496–98
	Symmachus, 498–514
	[Lawrence, 498–505, antipope]
	Hormisdas, 514–23
	John I, 523–26
	Felix IV, 526–30
	[Dioscorus, 530, antipope]
	Boniface II, 530–32

Emperors	*Popes*
	John II, 533–35
	Agapetus, 535–36
	Sylverius, 536–37
	Vigilius, 537–55
	Pelagius I, 556–61
	John III, 561–74
	Benedict I, 575–79
	Pelagius II, 579–90
	Gregory I, 590–604
	Sabinianus, 604–6
	Boniface III, 607
	Boniface IV, 608–15
	Deusdedit, 615–18
	Boniface V, 619–25
	Honorius I, 625–38
	Severinus, 640
	John IV, 640–42
	Theodore I, 642–49
	Martin I, 649–53
	Eugenius I, 654–57
	Vitalian, 657–72
	Adeodatus, 672–76
	Donus, 676–78
	Agatho, 678–81
	Leo II, 682–83
	Benedict II, 684–85
	John V, 685–86
	Conon, 686–87
	[Theodore II, 687, antipope]
	[Pascal I, 687–92, antipope]
	Sergius I, 687–701
	John VI, 701–5
	John VII, 705–7
	Sisinnius, 708
	Constantine, 708–15
	Gregory II, 715–31
	Gregory III, 731–41
	Zacharias, 741–52
	Stephen, 752
	Stephen II, 752–57
	Paul I, 757–67
	[Constantine and Philip, 767–68, antipopes]
	Stephen III, 768–72
	Adrian I, 772–95
Charlemagne, 800–814	Leo III, 795–816
Louis the Pious, 814–40	

Popes and Western Emperors

Emperors	Popes

Emperors

Popes

Stephen IV, 816–17
Pascal I, 817–24
Eugenius II, 824–27
Valentine, 827

Lothar I, 840–55
Gregory IV, 827–44
[John VIII, 844, antipope]
Sergius II, 844–47

Louis II, 855–75
Leo IV, 847–55
Benedict III, 855–58
[Anastasius III, 855, antipope]
[John IX, 855–57, antipope]
Nicholas I, 858–67
Adrian II, 867–72

Charles II, the Bald, 875–77
John VIII, 872–82
Charles III, the Fat, 877–87

Martin II, 882–84
Adrian III, 884–85

Interregnum, 887–91
Stephen V, 885–91
Guido, 891–94 (in Italy)
Lambert, 892–99 (co-ruler
Formosus, 891–96
with Guido)
Arnulf, 896–901

Boniface VI, 896
Stephen VI, 896–97
Romanus, 897
Theodore II, 897
John IX, 898–900

Louis III, 901–5 (928)
Benedict IV, 900–903
Leo V, 903
Christopher, 903–4

Berengar, 905(915)–24
Sergius III, 904–11
Anastasius III, 911–13
Lando, 913–14

Lapse of Imperial Title, 924–62
John X, 914–28
Leo VI, 928
Stephen VII, 929–31
John XI, 931–36
Leo VII, 936–39
Stephen VIII, 939–42
Martin III, 942–46
Agapetus II, 946–55

Otto I, 962–73
John XII, 955–63
Leo VIII, 963–64
Benedict V, 964
John XIII, 965–72

Otto II, 973–83
Benedict VI, 973–74
[Boniface VII, 974, antipope]

Emperors	*Popes*
Otto III, 983–1002	Benedict VII, 974–83
	John XIV, 983–84
	Boniface VII, 984–85
	John XV, 985–96
	Gregory V, 996–99
	[John XVI, 997–98, antipope]
Henry II, 1002–24	Sylvester II, 999–1003
	John XVII, 1003
	John XVIII, 1003–9
	Sergius IV, 1009–12
	Benedict VIII, 1012–24
	[Gregory VI, 1012, antipope]
Conrad II, 1024–39	John XIX, 1024–32
Henry III, 1039–56	
	Benedict IX, 1032–45
	[Sylvester III, 1045, antipope]
	Gregory VI, 1045–46
	Clement II, 1046–47
	Damasus II, 1048
	Leo IX, 1049–54
Henry IV, 1056–1106	Victor II, 1055–57
	Stephen IX, 1057–58
	Benedict X, 1058–59
	Nicholas II, 1058–61
	Alexander II, 1061–73
	[Honorius II, 1061–72, antipope]
[Rudolph of Swabia, 1077–80, antiking]	Gregory VII, 1073–85
[Herman of Luxemburg, 1081–93, antiking]	
[Conrad of Franconia, 1093–1101, antiking]	
	[Clement III, 1084–1100, antipope]
	Victor III, 1087
	Urban II, 1088–99
Henry V, 1106–25	Paschal II, 1099–1118
	[Theoderic, 1100, antipope]
	[Albert, 1102, antipope]
	[Sylvester IV, 1105–11, antipope]
	Gelasius II, 1118–19
	[Gregory VIII, 1118–21, antipope]
	Calixtus II, 1119–24
Lothar II, 1125–37	Honorius II, 1124–30
	[Celestine II, 1124, antipope]
Conrad III, 1138–52	Innocent II, 1130–43
	[Anacletus II, 1130–38, antipope]
	[Victor IV, 1138, antipope]

Popes and Western Emperors

Emperors	Popes
	Celestine II, 1143–44
	Lucius II, 1144–45
Frederick I, 1152–90	Eugenius III, 1145–53
	Anastasius IV, 1153–54
	Adrian IV, 1154–59
	Alexander III, 1159–81
	[Victor IV, 1159–64, antipope]
	[Pascal III, 1164–68, antipope]
	[Calixtus III, 1168–79, antipope]
	[Innocent III, 1179–80, antipope]
	Lucius III, 1181–85
	Urban III, 1185–87
	Gregory VIII, 1187
	Clement III, 1187–91
Otto IV, 1198–1212	Celestine III, 1191–98
Philip of Swabia, 1198–1208	
Frederick II, 1212–50	Innocent III, 1198–1216
	Honorius III, 1216–27
	Gregory IX, 1227–41
	Celestine IV, 1241
[Henry Raspe, 1246–47, antiking]	Innocent IV, 1243–54
[William of Holland, 1247–56, antiking]	
Conrad IV, 1250–54	
Great Interregnum, 1254–73	Alexander IV, 1254–61
[Richard of Cornwall, 1257–73, claimant]	
[Alfonso X of Castile, 1257–72, claimant]	
	Urban IV, 1261–64
	Clement IV, 1265–68
Rudolf of Hapsburg, 1273–91	Gregory X, 1271–76
	Innocent V, 1276
	Adrian V, 1276
	John XXI, 1276–77
	Nicholas III, 1277–80
	Martin IV, 1281–85
	Honorius IV, 1285–87
Adolf I, 1292–98	Nicholas IV, 1288–92
	Celestine V, 1294
Albert I, 1298–1308	Boniface VIII, 1294–1303
	Benedict XI, 1303–4
Henry VII, 1308–13	Clement V, 1305–14
Lewis IV, 1314–47	
Frederick of Hapsburg, 1325–30, coruler	John XXII, 1316–34

Emperors	Popes
	[Nicholas V, 1328–30, antipope]
Charles IV, 1347–78	Benedict XII, 1334–42
[Günther of Schwarzburg, 1347–49, antiking]	Clement VI, 1342–52
	Innocent VI, 1352–62
	Urban V, 1362–70
Wenceslas, 1378–1400	Gregory XI, 1370–78

Roman Line

Urban VI, 1378–89
Boniface IX, 1389–1404
Innocent VII, 1404–6
Sigismund, 1410–37 — Gregory XII, 1406–15
[Jobst of Moravia, 1410–11, antiking]

Avignonese Line: Antipopes

Clement VII, 1378–94
Benedict XIII, 1394–1424

Conciliar Line: Antipopes

Alexander V, 1409–10
John XXIII, 1410–15
Martin V, 1417–31
[Clement VIII, 1424–29, antipope]
[Benedict XIV, 1424, antipope]
Albert II, 1438–39 — Eugenius IV, 1431–47
Frederick III, 1440–93 — [Felix V, 1439–49, antipope]
Nicholas V, 1447–55
Calixtus III, 1455–58
Pius II, 1458–64
Paul II, 1464–71
Sixtus IV, 1471–84
Innocent VIII, 1484–92
Maximilian I, 1493–1519 — Alexander VI, 1492–1503
Pius III, 1503
Julius II, 1503–13
Charles V, 1519–56 — Leo X, 1513–21
Adrian VI, 1522–23
Clement VII, 1523–34

ROME AND MEDIEVAL CULTURE

Introduction

THE CITY OF ROME
IN ANCIENT TIMES
AND IN THE MIDDLE AGES

The City of Rome
in Ancient Times
and in the Middle Ages

THE aim of these volumes is to present a comprehensive history of the city of Rome in the Middle Ages; a subject which, apart from its connection with the papacy and the empire, has not hitherto been dealt with. The Romans themselves, upon whom the task of writing it should more especially have fallen, have been withheld by a variety of causes from making the attempt, and have only contributed a quantity of valuable material towards so truly national a work. Will it therefore be considered presumptuous in one not of the Latin race, but a German, to venture on this arduous undertaking? I do not fear the imputation; not only because the domain of knowledge is free territory, but also because, that next to the Romans and Italians, no other people in the Middle Ages had relations with Rome so close and so international as the Germans. Since the Goths of Theodoric, who first subjugated Rome and then reverently upheld her; since the Franks of Pepin and Charles, who freed the city from the yoke of the Lombards and Byzantines and again restored her to prosperity, for centuries, through the Germanized Roman Empire, Germany has stood in no ordinary relations to Rome. To the German nation Rome is an

From book I, ch. 1, sec. 1.

imperishable title of glory, and the mediaeval history of the city has become an element inseparable from that of Germany.

When I first conceived the thought of writing this work, my aim was as follows: that, from all extant and accessible material and with the aid of a many years' acquaintance with the monuments and topography of the city, I would trace the course of its history from the first fall of Imperial Rome under the power of the Visigoths of Alaric in the year 410, down to the last fall of the papal city into the hands of the troops of Charles V in 1527, when, at the beginning of the Reformation, the ancient alliance between Germany and Rome was forever sundered.

Throughout the long space of more than eleven hundred years, Rome is to the historian as a lofty watchtower, whence he can survey the movements of the mediaeval world, so far as that world derives from her its impulse or stands in active relation to her. For she is endowed with a twofold nature—municipal and cosmopolitan, neither of which is entirely separable from the other. Thus it was in ancient times, and thus it remained throughout the Middle Ages.

Three cities shine conspicuous in the history of mankind, by reason of the universal influence which they exercised upon it— Jerusalem, Athens, and Rome. In the course of the life of the world, all three are factors working with and through each other for human civilization. Jerusalem, the capital of the small and impotent Jewish race, was the center of that enigmatic theocracy from which Christianity emerged, and therefore the metropolis of the religion of the world. Long after its fall it maintained a second historical existence, by the side of, and in relation to Rome. The Romans had destroyed it in ancient times; its people were scattered over the world; its sanctity had passed away to Christian Rome; but in the eleventh century it again revived, and during the period of the Crusades was the goal of Christian pilgrims and the object of the great struggle between the nations of Europe and Asia. Then, together with the ideas of which it had been the symbol, it sank again into silence and obscurity.

Beside the city of the One Jehovah, polytheistic Athens shines on another summit of historic life, as the first center of Western genius, of its science, its philosophy, and its beautiful ideals. Then arises mighty Rome, the lawgiver of the political world. Athens and Rome are indissolubly united and correspond to each other, as mind to will and thought to deed. In them are embodied the classic forms of life. The intellectual power of Athens excites the enthusiastic love, the practical greatness of Rome the reverent admiration of mankind. All the creative work of thought and imagination was collected in the capital of Hellenic genius; and the little republic of Pallas Athene exercised an ideal dominion over the human race which still endures, and will for ever endure in the universal civilization of mankind.

The universal sovereignty of Rome, on the other hand, a unique, incontrovertible fact of history, rests on quite other foundations. Anyone who considers the existence of this wonderful city only from the outside, may assert that with unparalleled military skill, and with no less unparalleled political genius, she subjugated the world, and robbed, or destroyed, the flower of nations nobler than herself. In contrast to free and genial Athens, he sees only slavery and despotism. In Rome he discovers poverty in creative ideas of civilization; he sees only a great political impulse towards conquest, a great practical intellect with its accompanying wants, and the marvellous and gigantic structure of the political system of justice and of civil law. But everything which tends to raise the intellectual spirit to the higher regions of thought he finds either not cultivated at all, or only acclimatized from other lands. Even the wealth of noble works of art which beautify the city only seems to him the spoils of tyranny, behind whose triumphal car the captive Muses follow, forced to serve the prosaic Queen of the World.

This fact is undeniably true, but it is not the whole truth. The origin of Rome from her myth-shrouded germ, her growth, and finally her unrivalled supremacy, will, next to the rise and dominion of Christianity, ever be one of the deepest mysteries of history. And Christianity, which sprang up with the narrow confines of Jewish nationality, though cosmopolitan in its essence, was drawn to Rome, the capital of the world, as to a seat already prepared for it by history, where, from out the ruins of a political monarchy, it was destined to raise up a moral monarchy in the giant form of the church. The marvellous power by which one city obtained dominion in language, customs, and intellect over so many different nations cannot be explained. Its development can only be followed in a long chain of events, whilst the inner law, which governs the fact and which is called Rome, remains inexplicable to us.

It was not by the educating power of the intellect which emanated from the Acropolis of Athens that the world was conquered and governed, but, through streams of blood, by the all-devouring Jupiter of the Capitol. The city of Romulus, on the banks of the Tiber, inherited the treasure and the work of three parts of the world, in the midst of which she was built in the fairest country of the earth. In herself she had no creative genius either for religion or science; she incorporated and made them her own, and she was in the highest degree adapted to spread civilization abroad, and to give form and language to the spirit by which it was animated.

Cosmopolitan power makes its appearance with Rome. It becomes a system which embraces in a universal order all that had hitherto been developed and formed in the ancient world, which throws down the narrow confines of nationalities, and unites tribes and peoples under a central government as members of one great family. It is this principle which, when brought to bear on mankind, exalts it above the individualism which was the ideal of Greece. It is, in a word, the idea of the "imperium," or of the empire, which originated in Rome and gave its form to the world. It is the idea which has ruled the West as an inherent principle down to our own times. Its power and continuity have only been approached by the church, and the church in its visible shape is only the religious form of the ancient idea of the state.

Before the Romans the idea of the "imperium" does not appear in history. The principle, however, that the moral world is by the law of its being a unity (a monarchy), is involved in monotheistic Judaism. In the "chosen people" of Israel, and in their prophets, lies the first consciousness of a universal mission, and there the cosmopolitan idea of Christianity had its origin.

8

Introduction: The City of Rome

Among the Greeks no religious ideas of the kind are to be found. The Greek ideal rests in the universal culture of the free, all-searching intellect. The cosmos of the spirit was created by the Greeks, but politically it was only represented in a scattered colonial system, whilst the Hellenic state is an individual state or confederation. Beyond Hellas there was only the despised barbarian, just as beyond the Mosaic theocracy there was only the despised heathen. Even to Aristotle the non-Hellenic races were outside the law and destined by nature to servitude. If Alexander, who, in opposition to Greek ideas, wished to realise the idea of a universal Hellenic kingdom embracing the barbarian races, had turned his plans to the West, the course of the world's political system would have suffered no other change than that which followed in the Hellenized East. For, with the death of this enlightened ruler fell to pieces the universal Hellenic Empire which he had founded.

Rome at length achieved what Greece, fortunately for the complete development of her own genius, did not achieve; in the form of the empire she embraced civilization in a universal organism. The empire was the civilized world of an epoch, for which Greece had created intellectual culture, Rome had constructed civic laws, and Judaism had provided the universal religion. Virgil has expressed the full consciousness of the mission of the Romans to establish a cosmopolitan monarchy in the imperishable verses:

> Tu regere imperio populos, Romane, memento:
> Hae tibi erunt artes, pacisque imponere morem,
> Parcere subjectis, et debellare superbos.

> [Remember, o Roman, that you rule the peoples by your
>   military command.
> These will be your arts—to impose the habit of peace,
> To spare the subject, and to put down the proud.]

This high-sounding dictum, which so completely expresses the character and mission of Rome, impressed itself deeply on mankind; and the motto of the mediaeval empire, "*Roma Caput Mundi Regit Orbis Frena Rotundi* [Rome the head of the world governs the reins of the whole earth]," is nothing more than its echo. From Augustus downwards the belief was firmly rooted that the Romans were the nation elected to universal supremacy, and that the Roman Empire was the empire of the world, even as among the Jews the belief remained, that their nation was a divine nation, and their religion the religion of the world.

The line of demarcation which Greece and her greatest thinkers had drawn between herself and the barbarians, as Israel had done between herself and the heathen, disappeared in the cosmopolitan empire of the Romans, under which all forms of civilization were accepted, all religions enjoyed freedom of worship, and all nations rights of citizenship. Thus, in the Roman Republic was represented the unity of civilized mankind, of which the elected head was the emperor, and the capital "Rome, the Eternal," the miracle of the inhabited earth, the product and monument of the history of the world.

The majestic city grew, waxed old, and sank side by side with the empire, and its dissolution is a process as remarkable as was its growth; as vast an effort of time being necessary to destroy and lay low this colossus of laws and administration, of political institutions, of traditions and monuments of past centuries, as had been required to build it up. There is no spectacle in human history so tragic and so thrilling as the fall and final extinction of mighty Rome. Seven years before the incursion of the Western Goths, the last poet of the Romans stood on the Palatine; thence he surveyed the still unconquered city, and, filled with enthusiasm, he celebrated the indescribable splendor of ancient imperial Rome, her golden-roofed temples, her triumphal arches, her columns, her monuments, and the gigantic buildings in whose colossal foundations human art outrivalled nature. Scarcely two hundred years after Claudian, Bishop Gregory stood in the pulpit of S. Peter's, and in his gloomy sermon likened the once immeasurable city to a broken earthen vessel, and the once sovereign Roman people to an eagle, which, bereft of its plumage and enfeebled with age, droops dying on the Tiber's shore. Eight centuries after Gregory, Poggio Bracciolini stood amidst the ruins of the Capitol. Of ancient Rome he saw nothing but the remains of ruined temples, overthrown architraves, rent arches, and fragments of the splendors of the Forum, where cattle now grazed. He wrote his book on *The Changes of Fortune*, the doom which all that is great must inevitably undergo. The same sigh three hundred years later inspired the English Gibbon with the idea of writing the history of Rome's ruin, an idea which he subsequently developed in his immortal, *The Decline and Fall of the Roman Empire*. Though actuated by precisely similar feelings, it is needless to say that I do not for a moment aspire to rival such men as these. Deeply stirred by the sight of Rome, I resolved not only to depict the ruin of the city, but to follow it on in its reawakening to a new world-governing power. Rome alone amongst all the cities of the world has been honored with the divine title of "Eternal," and the prophecy of the poet [Virgil], "*Imperium sine fine dedi* [I have given empire without end]," in her attains reality.

The Roman Empire, sunk in the decrepitude of age, fell under the onslaughts of the vigorous German tribes. The majestic city of the Caesars fell of itself when the Roman state and its ancient worship perished. The Christian religion destroyed and transformed the pagan city of the ancient Romans, but she rose again from out the catacombs, her subterranean arsenal, a new Rome, veiled again in myth. For as Romulus and Remus had been the founders of ancient Rome, so now were two holy apostles, Peter and Paul, the legendary creators of the new city. This also grew slowly and amidst terrible changes, until, under a system unrivalled in history, it once more became the capital of the world. And since it was Rome that gave form to that great period in the life of the human race which we call the Middle Ages, just as she had already given form to antiquity, we shall do well to investigate the elements which combined to invest this one city, after so great a fall, with a second supremacy. Unlike the origin of her ancient dominion, this new birth of Rome presents no difficult enigma, being fully explained by the idea of the empire, which, firmly rooted in the West, now became bound up with Christianity and produced the Roman church.

That the Christian religion arose simultaneously with the foundation of the empire of the Caesars, is one of those great historic facts which we are accustomed to call providential. It permeated the ancient empire and blended with it, the cosmopolitan theory of Christianity being in perfect accord with the theory of a universal monarchy. Constantine recognized this. The new church adopted the administrative organization of the empire; she extended over the bishoprics and districts a network of administration which corresponded to the constitution of dioceses as fixed by Constantine. She was in her outward form a Latin creation, having the empire for her type. Gradually she developed into a spiritual power, but remained enclosed within the state, and was preserved by the empire so long as it endured. From the time of Constantine onward, the universal emperor was also the head of the Universal (Catholic) church, in which no bishop had precedence over another, while the Oecumenical councils, summoned under the imperial authority, gave it unity.

As soon as the Germans had overthrown the Western Empire, the Roman church, in her essence a still purely spiritual phenomenon, and, as such, unsusceptible of injury at barbarian hands, cast aside her wrappings and appeared as the universal authority in the West. She here usurped the place of the imperial power, the principle of which she preserved as a law in her Ark of the Covenant. Latinity and the ancient civilization which had passed over to her—or rather, the remnant of which she had taken into her keeping—were both saved. And here she stood—the only bulwark against which broke the surging deluge of barbarism. That she was already an immovable organization when the ancient empire fell, is one of the most important facts in history, for on the firm foundation-stone of the church the whole life of Europe was established anew.

The church therefore, which had arisen from the union of Christianity with the Roman Empire, drew from the empire the system of her centralization and the treasures of an ancient language and culture. The degenerate ancient races, however, could not provide her with the vivifying material necessary to her development; on the contrary, they it was who perverted Christianity, inoculating the new system with the ancient paganism. By means of historic ties, the church allied herself with youthful Germanism, and the union forms her second epoch

12

in universal history. The primitive races of Germany possessed only a religion of nature, which offered no resistance to the Christian religion, such as that presented by the paganism of the classic nations, deeply rooted as this was in the dominion of a thousand years, in literature and art, in ritual and the state. The Germans were, for the most part, already Christians when they gained possession of the Roman West. While actually overthrowing the empire, they yet bowed in reverence before the Roman church as before the Roman imperial ideal, the tradition of which had become the political dogma of the world. The church herself, in her essence the guardian of the theory of the unity of the human race, or the Christian republic, inculcated in them this Latin idea. She strove to Romanize them. The ecclesiastical creed of the Germans, their hierarchy, the language and ritual of their faith, their festivals, apostles, and saints were all Roman or grouped around a Roman center. It thus eventually came to pass that the Germans, the rulers of the Latin races with which they had become intermingled on the ancient classic soil, themselves restored the empire they had previously destroyed. The restoration, however, was essentially the work of the Roman church, which of necessity demanded the empire, her own prototype, as supplying the international form and the guarantee of the universal religion.

For this great achievement, the alliance of the old with the new, of the Latin with the German world, the continued existence of the city of Rome was essential. Rome, in truth, towered like an Ararat of human civilization amid the universal deluge of barbarism which followed on the overthrow of the Western Empire. The ancient capital of the world remained, or became, the moral center of the transformation of the West. But after the power of the political empire had fallen from her, she could no longer have retained this position, had not the bishops, who had taken up their seat within her, acquired for the church in the Roman city supremacy over every other episcopate. They attained to the high priesthood of Christianity. They made Rome the Delphi or Jerusalem of the new confederation of the peoples, and united to the original imperial idea of the Capital of the World the Jewish conception of a City of God. The supremacy to which, with Roman arrogance they laid claim, could find no basis in the unpolitical teaching of the Savior, nor in the fact of the equality which originally existed between all the apostles, all priests and all congregations, nor yet in the antiquity of the Roman bishopric, since the churches of Jerusalem, Ephesus, Corinth, and Antioch were all older than that of Rome. But the ancient tradition of the foundation of the bishopric of Rome by Peter soon endowed the claims of the Roman church with a victorious power, and already in the first century this apostle was esteemed head of the church, and the immediate vassal and vicar of Christ himself. For to him the Savior had said, "Thou art Peter, and on this rock will I build my church." On these words, which are to be found in only one of the four evangelists, rests the origin of papal domination. They are still to be read in huge letters round the frieze of the great cupola of S. Peter's, and they have been to the Roman church what those of Virgil were to the empire.

Not only was the doubtful, because unauthenticated, foundation of the Roman church by Peter disputed by the jealous East, but the consequences of her supremacy, which followed on the acceptance of the legend, were also contested. In the West the tradition grew with time firm as an article of faith, and the bishops of Rome called themselves the successors of Peter, the vicars of Christ, and therefore the heads of the Catholic church. If the power of a venerable tradition resting on the conviction of centuries appears strange, we must remember that, in every successful form of religion, tradition and myth constitute the basis of practical operations, and, so soon as the latter have been recognized by the world, are accepted as facts. This particular tradition would, however, have remained ineffectual with regard to any other city. Neither the sanctity of Jerusalem, where Christ taught and died, nor the undoubted foundation of the church of Antioch by Peter gave these cities any claim to ecclesiastical precedence. But the bishops in the Lateran, who did not recognize the political importance of the capital Constantinople as a measure of the position of the patriarchs there, successfully asserted the claims which the ancient capital of the world possessed to the reverence and obedience of nations. The nimbus of Eternal Rome reappeared, this time surrounding her priestly heads; they were the heirs of the Spirit, the discipline and ambitious instincts of ancient Rome reincarnate; and although the empire fell, its great, if lifeless, machinery still lived on. The provinces still bear the deep impress of the government and administration of Rome, and the rule of the ecclesiastical city soon began to flow through the provinces in the channels which pagan Rome had traced.

The Roman church gradually changed into the papacy the imperialism within which she had attained her development as a hierarchical creation. The organization of the empire was transformed into an ecclesiastical system, with the pope as its center. The old imperial Senate, in the form of cardinals and bishops, surrounded this elective spiritual monarch, in whose case, as in the case of the emperors, race and nationality were indifferent; but the constitutional principle which the Caesars had never recognized, was, on the score of the democratic theory of the equality of the priesthood, introduced in councils and synods, to which the provinces sent representatives to the universal senate-house, the Lateran. The governors of these ecclesiastical provinces were the bishops consecrated and controlled by the pope. The monasteries, scattered over all countries, resembled the ancient Roman colonies, and were strongholds or stations of the spiritual dominion of Rome, as well as of civilization; and, after the heathen or heretic barbarians in Britain and Germany, in Gaul and Spain, had been overcome by the bloodless weapons of Rome, the Eternal City again ruled and gave laws to the fairest portion of the ancient world. However we may regard the new centralization which emanated from Rome, it was based on the historic requirement of mankind; and the supremacy of Rome was necessary for rude and lawless centuries, since it alone upheld the unity of Christendom. Without an absolute church, without the Roman spirit of the bishops, who in the provinces suppressed, with the power of a Scipio or a Marius, every rebellious tendency to fall away from the orthodox faith, national imagination and traditions would have given birth to a hundred forms of faith. History repeated itself in the fate of Rome and the world; and in the end it

15

was again the Germans, who, a thousand years after the fall of the ancient empire, destroyed the universal supremacy of the second Rome, and by a great and creative revolution, won freedom of faith and knowledge for mankind.

During the Middle Ages the reverence of the nations for the city was unbounded. In her, as in the great Ark of the Covenant of ancient as of Christian culture, they saw united the laws, the charters, the symbols of Christianity. In the city of the martyrs and of the princes among the apostles, they beheld the treasure-house of supernatural graces. Here was the center of the divine administration of the human family; here was enthroned the high priest of the new covenant which claimed to represent Christ on earth. All the chief spiritual and temporal powers received their consecration in Rome; the sources of the priestly power, the power to bind and to loose, the fount of imperial majesty, finally, civilization itself, seemed to spring from the hills of Rome, and, like the streams of Paradise, flow to fertilize the four quarters of the world. All the institutions of mankind had originally sprung from this single city. Bishoprics, monasteries, missions, schools, libraries were all colonies of Rome. Like the praetors and consuls of former days, her monks and priests had been sent forth to the provinces and had converted them to faith in the spiritual power of Rome. The remains of Roman martyrs were brought over sea and land to be buried as sacred relics under the distant altars of Britain and Germany. The language of the faith, the schools of the barbarians, were derived from Rome, as were all literature, sacred or profane, music, mathematics, grammar, the arts of painting and architecture. Men in the obscurest borders of the north and west had all heard of Rome, and when her name, which had already thrilled mankind through so many centuries, fell upon their ears, they were seized with a mystic longing, and their excited imagination pictured, in the form of the Eternal City, an Eden of beauty where the gates of Heaven opened or closed. There were long centuries in the Middle Ages in which Rome was truly the law-giver, the instructress, and the mother of nations, encircling her children with a threefold ring of unity—spiritual in the papacy, temporal in the empire, the crown of which German kings came to receive in S. Peter's, and the unity of that general civilization which the ancient Romans had bequeathed to the world.

This should be sufficient to show the stature to which Rome had attained in the Middle Ages, as the dominating power in the Christian commonwealth of nations. The recollection of the mighty task, which, for the second time in the world's history, Rome took upon herself, should serve to soften the bitterness of the memory of those long centuries of suffering, during which the human race struggled to free itself from subjection to Rome, opposing to her discipline the light of that knowledge to which it had attained. The sins of the ancient despot must be weighed against the great ideas of universal citizenship which she represented, and by which she rescued Europe from the chaos of barbarism and made it capable of receiving a common freedom and culture.

I

FROM BISHOPRIC TO LORDSHIP

I

Byzantine Rome

*Gregorovius devoted the greater parts of books I and II to the history of Rome between the fourth and the sixth centuries. Though he described the administrative organization of Rome in the fifth century, the ecclesiastical regions superimposed on the civic districts, and architectural features, Gregorovius devoted most of these sections to the histories of church and empire. The three sacks of Rome (by the Visigoths in 410, by the Vandals in 455, by Byzantine-paid troops in 472) are treated as incidents in the dissolution of the Western Empire and the establishment of barbarian kingdoms. Toward the end of these sections, Gregorovius took up the restoration of imperial rule in Italy by Byzantine forces under Belisarius (in 536); Belisarius's subsequent retreat before the Ostrogothic King Totila; and the triumphant resumption of Belisarius's work by Narses.—*Editor.

THE victory of Narses was not yet complete. A frightful horde of barbarians suddenly descended upon the unhappy country and threatened to overwhelm Rome. Tejas had already sought, by promises of booty and of the treasures of Totila, to induce the Franks to invade Italy, and the Goths of upper Italy had sent them a still more urgent summons. The overthrow of the well-ordered

From book II, ch. 7, secs. 1 and 3.

kingdom of the Goths again set in motion the current of wandering barbarism which had been held in check by the vigilance of Theodoric. Italy, torn asunder by long wars and a thousand ills, appeared defenseless and an easy prey. More than 70,000 Alemanni and Franks crossed the Alps under the leadership of two brothers, Leutharis and Bucelin, and advancing through the northern provinces spread devastation indescribable. The feeble Greek garrisons made but trifling resistance. The general himself hastened from Ravenna to Rome, where he spent the winter of 553–54, and it was owing to the threatening attitude which he there assumed that the barbarians did not attack the city. Avoiding Roman territory, they entered Samnium, and there separated into two divisions. Leutharis advanced along the Adriatic as far as Otranto, Bucelin laid waste Campania; Lucania and Bruttium to the Straits of Messina.

The greedy hordes of robbers wandered through southern Italy with the speed and destructive force of the elements, their aspect terrifying the historian and lowering his conception of humanity. In truth this phenomenon, one of the most terrible in the history of Italy, resembled only too nearly some dreadful visitation of nature. Leutharis and his followers, laden with spoil, had already returned to the Po at the end of the summer of 554, when pestilence seized on the leader and his hordes. Bucelin, on the contrary, having turned northwards by Reggio, had reached the Capuan territory. Here, at a spot named Tannetus, on the banks of the river Casilinus or Vulturnus, he encountered Narses. After a battle as terrible as those of Marius against the Cimbri or Teutons, the half-naked barbarians succumbed before the military skill of the Greek veterans. Cut down like cattle, barely five were left to save themselves by flight.

Narses had thus become the liberator of Italy; and the annihilation of these hordes had given him a greater claim to the gratitude of his contemporaries than even his victories over the Goths. Laden with the plunder of the slain, the spoils of Italy, the Greek army entered with rejoicings the city they had saved, and the streets of deserted Rome glittered with the last triumphal pomp which her people were to witness. The triumphal procession of

Narses signified the subjugation of the German race in Italy, under whose rule the country had become free; it signified the restoration of the unity of the Roman Empire under the scepter of the Byzantine Emperor, and it further signified the victory which the Catholic church had gained over Arianism. Narses may well have been deemed worthy to follow the path of the Roman conquerors of old, the path which led to the Capitol; but the venerable Capitol was now nothing more than a pile of ruins haunted by great memories. And in harmony with the scene was the aspect of the Senate, a small band of nobles in purple-bordered togas, who, like a shade of the past, greeted the victor at the city gate. The triumfator, a pious eunuch, proceeded to the Basilica of S. Peter, where he was received on the steps by the clergy with hymns, and where he prostrated himself in prayer at the grave of the apostle. His soldiers, richly rewarded and laden with spoils, gave themselves up to sensual enjoyments, "exchanging the helmet and shield for the wine-cup and lyre." But Narses, who, as at least reported by the priests, was accustomed to ascribe all his conquests to prayer, assembled his troops and, exhorting them to moderation and humility, required them to subdue sensual instincts by constant military exercises. A last struggle still awaited them; 7000 Goths, companions of the Alemanni, had thrown themselves into the fort Compsa, or Campsa, and, under the leadership of the Hun Ragnaris, here offered an obstinate resistance. They were, however, at length overcome by Narses in 555.

Having reached the close of this long and terrible war for the possession of Italy, let us try to ascertain its consequences on the condition of Rome. The city had, within a short space of time, been five times devastated by war and five times conquered. Famine, pestilence, and the sword had mowed down the inhabitants by thousands. At one time driven forth one and all by the Goths, they had returned again, although not in like numbers, to be exposed afresh to all the vicissitudes of war. We cannot give the number of the population with any certainty, but according to the highest reckoning, it may have amounted to from 30,000 to 40,000 souls. The exhaustion and the misery of Rome could not at any time, even at that of the so-called exile of the popes to

Avignon, have been greater than at the end of the Gothic war. All characteristics of civil life were utterly destroyed. Private property, with the remains of such precious relics of antiquity as had escaped the Vandals and Goths, had disappeared, owing to the necessities of the siege and the extortions of the Greeks. The Romans who still remained were reduced to utter beggary, inheriting from their ancestors scarcely anything beyond bare and desolate dwellings or the right of possession over distant estates and farms on the Campagna, which, deserted as early as the third century, had now become an uninhabited desert. All traces of agriculture must long since have disappeared and every colony have been destroyed. Entire tracts were now reduced to swamps by the destruction of the aqueducts.

The condition of Rome at this time was reflected throughout the whole of Italy. In despair of being able to depict the universal desolation, we may confirm what a historian says concerning the period, that "the human mind is unable to conceive so many changes of fortune, so many cities destroyed, so many men driven into exile, so many people slaughtered, far less adequately to describe them." Italy, from the Alps to Tarentum, was strewn with corpses and ruins; famine and pestilence, following on the track of war, had reduced whole districts to deserts. Procopius undertook to reckon the numbers of those slain in the Greek war, but despaired of reckoning the sands of the sea. For Africa he reckons five millions, and, since Italy was three times greater than the Vandal province, he assumes that her loss was proportionately greater. The estimate, although probably somewhat exaggerated, since the Italy of that time could scarcely have numbered a population of five millions altogether, must have amounted at least to a third part of the population. Amid the frightful storms of the Gothic war classical civilization perished for ever in Rome and throughout Italy. In cities burnt, desolated, and mutilated, ruins remained the sole evidences of former splendor. The prophecy of the Sibyls was fulfilled. The night of barbarism had descended on the Latin world, a darkness in which no light was visible, other than that of the tapers of the church, and the lonely student-lamp of the monk brooding in the cloister.

Justinian regulated the affairs of Italy in his Pragmatic Sanction of August 13, 554—a celebrated edict in twenty-seven articles, called forth by the entreaties of Pope Vigilius. Uniting Italy again with the Eastern Empire, Justinian confirmed all the decrees of Athalaric, of his mother Amalasuntha, and even the appointments of Theodatus (thus recognizing the dynasty of the Amal), but declared void the acts of Totila. He sought to remedy the confusion with regard to property, while he protected the property of fugitives against seizure by claimants, and established the fixity of contrast from the time of the siege. In the nineteenth article of the Sanction the appointment of weights and measures for all provinces of Italy was made over to the pope and Senate, which not only shows the increased municipal importance of the bishop, but also bears witness to the fact that the Senate still existed in Rome. Henceforth the pope began to exercise the influence over the administration and jurisdiction of the city which the legislation of Justinian accorded to bishops in other cities. Bishops henceforward possessed not only jurisdiction over the clergy, but the right of supervision of all imperial officials, even the judex of the province. They interfered in the government of the cities, and the election of the *Defensores* [Defenders] and of the *Patres Civitatis* [Fathers of the City] depended more upon the bishops than upon the "primates" of the cities themselves. Justinian invested the Italian bishops with legal authority; and from the influence which they exercised on all branches of secular administration, the dominion of the pope within the city by degrees arose.

With regard to the Senate we know nothing. Historians, however, who have sought to prove the continued existence of the Senate through the succeeding centuries, have assumed that Justinian restored this august body, replacing the loss of its most illustrious members by new creations from plebeian families. Undoubtedly the ancient Roman race with its aristocracy must have been reduced to very small proportions during the Gothic war. In the meantime, however, a new population had arisen owing to the influx of natives of other districts. In the city, it is true, there remained behind a remnant of the state authorities, who continued to direct the administration and jurisdiction under the leadership of the *praefecti urbis,* until these authorities made way for the imperial magistrates. Justinian gave the senators full freedom to go and settle where and when they willed, did they wish to withdraw to their devastated estates in the Italian provinces, or to migrate to the court at Constantinople, an alternative which many naturally preferred.

The same Pragmatic Sanction contained resolutions in favor of Rome, apparently however to be regarded as nothing more than benevolent wishes. Under the twenty-second head it is enjoined that the public distributions (*annona*) given to the people by Theodoric, and which Justinian boasted to have revived— although the assertions of Procopius go to prove quite the contrary—should for the future be administered. It further decrees that even the grammarians and rhetoricians, the physicians and the learned in law, should continue to be paid the customary salaries, "in order that youth, trained in the liberal sciences, may flourish in the Roman Empire."

By this regulation was revived an edit of Athalaric, which had ordered that the salaries of the professors of grammar, eloquence, and law should be paid out of the state coffers. These payments, which had been introduced by the Emperor Hadrian, were discontinued when the empire fell into confusion. We have reason, however, for doubting whether these good intentions of Justinian were ever carried into effect. In the utter overthrow of all public and private relations, the schools, which had again flourished under Theodoric, had perished, and rarely was a rhetorician or grammarian heard in the ancient Athenaeum or the halls of the Capitol. Latin learning died. The Roman aristocracy who, in the time of the last emperor worthy of the name, and under the first Gothic king, eagerly, if perhaps unprofitably, had cherished literature, was now destroyed. The supporters of classic culture, the last Maecenas of Rome, had perished or had disappeared without leaving a trace. We look with grief on the dark or bloody fate of the last cultured Romans of ancient and illustrious houses, with whom the associations and traditions of Latin civilization come to an end; on Faustus and Avienus, Festus, Probus and

26

Cethegus, Agapitus and Turcius Rufius, on Symmachus, Boethius and Cassiodorus. The last of these great men retired to a cloister, a witness that henceforth the church should be the only asylum where the remains of pagan literature could hope for preservation. Moreover, the fall of the Gothic kingdom involved not merely the overthrow of schools, teachers and knowledge, but likewise the destruction of libraries, since it was utterly impossible that, in the terrible catastrophe which had overtaken the city, the splendid collections of books given in the Notitia Urbis, namely the Palatine and Ulpian libraries, or the libraries belonging to princely houses, could have been preserved. And as in Rome, so throughout Italy, the war of annihilation between Goths and Byzantines swallowed up the priceless treasures of ancient literature, with the exception of such remnants as had happily been collected and saved in the rising monastaries of the Benedictines.

The public buildings lastly were taken into account in a paragraph. "We command," it says, "that the accustomed privileges and grants to the city of Rome be continued henceforward, be they for the restoration of public buildings, for the channel of the Tiber, for the market, for the harbor of Rome, or the restoration of the aqueducts, in such manner that the costs shall be provided only out of such revenues as have been set apart for the purpose."

Justinian now turned his attention to ecclesiastical affairs. These he hoped to establish on a permanent basis, and ecclesiastical matters constitued henceforward the question of gravest import in the relations between East and West, between Rome and Byzantium. The fall of the Gothic kingdom had redounded to the advantage of the Bishop of Rome; the Arian heresy was now completely overcome; the independent kingdom in Italy was removed; his own importance in the city was increased by Justinian's ordinances; and lastly, the ruin of the old Roman nobility left bishop and priesthood masters of the field in Rome. The decay of all political virtue and manliness, and the decline of learning were the chief causes that contributed to raise the priesthood to power; and we may observe, that only in periods of exhaustion of thought and demoralization of literature such as this, does the priesthood ever attain supremacy. The church stood in the midst of the ruin of the ancient state alone upright, alone vigorous, alone conscious of an end and aim; around her desolation reigned. She had to mourn but as a momentary loss that independence which she had enjoyed under the uncertain rule of the Arian stranger. She had been free under the Goths, but during the war she had already discovered the position which the emperor had decided to adopt towards her, and when the clash of weapons was stilled and Rome sank into a provincial town under the military yoke of Byzantium, the papacy had to face a doubtful and troublous future. On one side these troubles were of a theological nature, on account of the restless and sophistical spirit of the East, where Greek philosophy, not yet entirely extinguished, was indefatigable in contending against existing dogmas and in nourishing new theorems. Others had to do with her relations towards the state. The Byzantine emperors interfered in theological matters, not so much out of inclination for such controversies as because their interference gave them an opportunity of keeping the church subject to the state. In Justinian, whose only greatness consisted in having, through his jurists, completed the Roman Code, the policy of imperial despotism rose again to a fearful pitch; and after him succeeding centuries offered the remarkable spectacle of the struggle of the Church of the West, represented by Rome, against the pagan absolutism of the state, embodied in Byzantium.

Vigilius meanwhile had remained in Constantinople, engaged in a dogmatic contest with the emperor concerning the dispute of the Three Chapters. After many difficulties, and after enduring some hard usage, Vigilius, by the shameless recantation of his earlier opinions, acceded to the desire of the emperor, and accepted the decisions of the Fifth Council (the second held in Constantinople). Justinian now yielded to the entreaties of the Roman clergy, who through Narses had implored the release of their bishop, and allowed Vigilius, and the presbyters or cardinals who accompanied him, to return to Rome. The pope, however, was taken ill on the way, and died at Syracuse, June 555. The pontificate of a Roman, who had reached the sacred chair by means of intrigue and crime, is memorable in history as being contemporary with the disruption of ancient Rome. The city preserves no memorial of his reign, beyond a metrical inscription lamenting the sack of the churches and cemeteries by the Goths.

Some months later the archdeacon Pelagius, a Roman of noble birth, and the most influential man who had appeared among the Roman clergy since the terrible days of Totila, was elected to S. Peter's chair. He had returned a second time to Constantinople, having, by the desire of the emperor, in whose favor he stood, accompanied Vigilius thither.

Justinian, who, since the subjection of Vigilius to the dogmas of Byzantium, had become ruler of the Western church, now commanded the election of Pelagius, and Pelagius therefore hastened to return to Rome. A great part of the clergy and nobility, however (the *Liber Pontificalis* no longer mentions the Senate), hesitated to have any communion with the newly-elected pope, on account of the suspicion which rested upon him of having been accessory to the sudden death of Vigilius. To free himself from this suspicion, he ordered a solemn procession, and by the side of the patrician Narses, and accompanied by the chanting of hymns, walked from the church of S. Pancrazio to S. Peter's, where, ascending the pulpit, the Gospels in his hands and the cross of Christ laid upon his head, he took the oath of purgation and asserted his innocence before all the people.

Pelagius succeeded to the papacy and the care of the unfortunate and almost annihilated city at one of the most terrible periods in her history. The distress was so great that the pope turned to Sapaudus, Bishop of Arles, with the entreaty that he would send him money and clothes, writing that "poverty in the city has so increased, that not without pain and grief of heart can we now behold our nobly born and prosperous acquaintance of former days."

.   .   .   .

Tradition relates that [Narses] the victor of Rome and Italy, a prey to avarice, the vice of old age, spent the remainder of his declining years in the accumulation of wealth; it asserts that he amassed piles of gold, and buried treasures so vast in a fountain in some town in Italy, that after his death it took several days to bring them to light. His wealth, it was said, excited the envy of the Romans, but it is probable that, more than his wealth, the people found the military despotism of Byzantium, the burden of taxation, the rapacity of the Greek vampires, the invasion of their churches, and the ill-usage to which Latin nationality was subjected, difficult to bear, and looked back with longing regret to the times of Gothic rule. Incapable of shaking the position of Narses so long as Justinian lived, the Romans sought to overthrow the favorite as soon as Justin the Young succeeded to the throne (565). The fall of Narses is perfectly in accordance with the nature of the rule of favorites in Byzantium, more especially when the dread which his power in Italy had awakened is taken into consideration. The Romans accused him to Justin and to Justin's wife Sophia, writing with audacious candor: "It were better for us to serve the Goths than the Greeks where the eunuch Narses reigns and oppresses us with slavery. Our most pious prince knows nothing of his oppressions; but deliver us out of his hands, or we shall give ourselves and the city up to the barbarians." In 567, after having been rector of Italy for sixteen years, Narses received his recall from the Emperor Justin. It is said that he fled from Rome to Campania on hearing that Longinus had been sent to fill his place in Italy. He either did not venture to return to Constantinople, or he defied the command on being informed of the threat of the Empress Sophia that she "would make the eunuch spin wool with the women." Legend relates that Narses replied that he "would weave her such a web as would take all her life-time to unravel," and that forthwith he sent messengers from Naples summoning the Lombards from Pannonia to Italy, sending, as evidences of the wealth of the country, choice fruits as well as other valuable things.

The fear of the Romans, who dreaded his revenge, was aroused by the departure of the irate governor for Naples, and Pope John was immediately despatched to try to prevail on him to return. "What harm have I done to the Romans, Most Holy Father?" cried Narses. "I will go and throw myself at the feet of him who has sent me, and all Italy shall acknowledge how with all my might I have striven for the country." The pope soothed the aged governor and brought him back to Rome. John took up his abode in a house in the churchyard of SS. Tiburtius and Valerianus, and there remained to consecrate bishops, while Narses returned to the palace of Caesars, where, sunk in grief and dejection, he soon afterwards died. His body, enclosed in a leaden coffin, was taken with his treasures to Constantinople. The assertion that he died in his ninety-fifth year is clearly an exaggeration, since it is utterly incredible that a veteran of nearly eighty could have conquered Italy in the face of such difficulties, and since, moreover, the date of his death must be fixed in 567. Neither is it probable that the dismissed governor lived six years quietly in Rome, nor that the Romans, already harassed by the Lombards, could oppose the commands of the emperor and the new exarch, whilst they retained Narses and his treasures.

The statements of the Latin chroniclers that Narses had summoned the Lombards into Italy admits of grave doubt. Favorable circumstances assuredly invited Duke Alboin to the depopulated country, the climate and fertility of which were known to all barbarians. Further, the Lombard hordes had already served under Narses himself against the Goths, and had become acquainted not only with the weakness of Italy, but also with that of the Byzantine Empire. Were it, however, true that the Greek general himself had summoned the invaders, the fact that such an act of high treason was not without parallel is shown by the history of Bonifacius, who, in a similar case, invited the Vandals to Africa. Narses found himself at the end of his life rewarded with the hatred of the Romans and the ingratitude of Constantinople; he already stood in friendly relations with the Lombards, and the revengeful thought of bringing a fresh barbarian horde into Italy would not, in a Byzantine, have been counteracted by any feeling of patriotism. We might, however, have supposed that the pride of the conqueror of Italy, or the sense of religion ascribed to Narses, would have deterred him from such a step. It was undoubtedly the latter motive which prompted him to yield to the pope's entreaties and return to Rome. He nevertheless died at tragic variance with himself and with his past, after the Lombards, following the progress which invariably impelled barbarians from inland countries to press toward Mediterranean shores

and the center of civilization, had already forsaken their Pan-
nonian homes. If, at the time of the Gothic invasion, Italy had become depopulated, the country, in consequence of the prolonged
wars, was now reduced to a desert, and the Lombards encountered as little resistance in settling down and replacing the void
left in the population as did the Slavs when, at the end of the
sixth century, they invaded Greece and covered her provinces
with a fresh stratum of inhabitants.

Alboin, the leader of the horde, appeared in the beginning of
April 568 in north Italy. His numerous followers, and with them
greedy swarms of Gepidae, Saxons, Sueves and Bulgarians, descended on the rich plains of the Po, where, in the fresh vigor of
their powers, they defeated the army of the Greek emperor. During three years the barbarian king besieged Pavia, and there at
length established the capital of his new Lombard kingdom;
whilst strong Ravenna, where the first German kings, as successors of the last Roman emperors, had dwelt, still remained the
capital of Greek Italy and the seat of its regents, the exarchs.
Thus, immediately after the fall of the Goths, a second Teutonic
kingdom was founded in northern Italy. This kingdom endured
for several centuries, and even now the territory watered by the
Po bears the name of the invaders.

Before continuing the history of the city, we may close our
present volume with a glance at the position to which Rome had
attained under the new institution of the exarchate.

Longinus, the successor of Narses, had already assumed the
government of Italy in Ravenna before the appearance of the
Lombards, and, following the precedent set in Africa, where the
government of the province had been administered by an exarch,
had adopted that title. A complete change in the government of
the country had been ascribed to Longinus; it being asserted that
he gave an entirely new form to the government, removing the
consuls, correctors, and presidents of provinces. Our knowledge,
however, of the new order of things is very imperfect. After the
time of Constantine the country had been divided into seventeen
provinces, thus enumerated by the Notitia: Venetia, Aemilia, Liguria, Flaminia and Picenum Annonarium, Tuscia and Umbria,
Picenum Suburbicarium, Campania, Sicilia, Apulia and Calabria,

Lucania and Bruttium, the Cottian Alps, Rhetia Prima, Rhetia Secunda, Samnium, Valerium, Sardinia, Corsica.

The government of these provinces had been administered by consulars, correctors and praesides, while, at the same time, the seven northern remained under the jurisdiction of the vicar of Italy, the ten southern under that of the vicar of Rome, and all under the prefect of the Praetorium of Italy. The Gothic kings had not altered this disposition of provinces, nor, although with Longinus the titles of governors disappeared, whilst the provinces remained, was any modification of existing arrangements introduced. His administrative changes first acquired importance under the advance of the Lombards. These newcomers pushed their conquests here and there in Greek Italy, rent the union of provinces and the unity of Italy, and even gave to the possessions of the emperor the form of separate dukedoms or "ducates," such, for example, as Venetia, the exarchate in a narrower sense, and Rome and Naples became.

Having stepped into the place of the prefect of Italy, the exarch succeeded to the chief power in all civil and military affairs. Under Constantine the civil had been separated from the military power; the Goths had maintained the system of Constantine, and the exarch rigorously adhered to the example of his predecessors in the government. Judges or "judices" were appointed in the provinces. These judges were under the supervision of the bishops; and military commanders, named in the chief cities "duces" or "magistri militum," in the smaller "tribuni," were also appointed. Notwithstanding these appointments, it cannot be shown that the provincial centralization was overthrown by Longinus, or that the provinces henceforth were split in consequence into "ducates," that is to say, greater and smaller towns with their territories, which received such titles from their military chiefs (*duces*). We may, however, conclude that through the weakening of the central power mainly, though also in a somewhat less degree through the dismemberment of the provinces in consequence of the Lombard conquests, the cities became isolated and restricted to a political life within themselves, while their bishops by degrees acquired increased authority.

With regard to Rome, we find that the traditional chief civil authority remained unaltered under Longinus, the prefect of the city continuing to retain his office as before. The supposition that the exarch did away with the consuls and the Senate, which had subsisted in name until his time, is an utter fabrication, since the ancient imperial consuls had already disappeared, and the title ex-consul remained in Rome, as in Ravenna, throughout the whole of the sixth century common and even attainable by purchase. The Senate endured in name as late as 579, when an embassy of Roman senators is mentioned as going to solicit help from the Emperor Tiberius against the Lombards. It is generally believed that Rome was politically governed by a dux appointed by the exarch, and that from the dux was derived the ducatus Romanus. Neither can it be doubted that, as a rule, the exarch, and at times the emperor himself, appointed a supreme official who also possessed military authority in the city. The extent of the jurisdiction of this official is, however, unknown, but, from the universal use of the title in cities and districts, we conclude that he was known as dux in Rome also.

No dux of Rome is, however, mentioned during the whole of the seventh century, though duces of Sardinia, Naples, Rimini, Narni, Nepi and so forth, often appear; even in the *Liber Diurnus*—the celebrated book of formulae of the Roman chancery—where we might reasonably expect to hear of such an official, no mention is made of a dux of Rome. In 708, however, the *Liber Pontificalis* suddenly names a dux, and the ducatus Romanus. The same authority has, however, already spoken of "judices" or officials before this period; officials appointed by the exarch for the administration of the affairs of the city. In the life of Pope Conon (686–87) it is related that his archdeacon hoped to ascend the papal throne through the influence of the "judices" who had been sent by John, the new exarch, to Rome. It therefore follows that the exarch, and apparently yearly, appointed more than one official for Rome; moreover, that these imperial judices, amongst whom we may understand the dux or magister militum, must have conducted the administration of military and fiscal affairs. The date, however, at which the idea of a "ducatus Romanus" arose, is altogether uncertain.

34

II

Rome under Pope Gregory I

Book III begins with descriptions of the decay that followed the Ostrogothic wars; of the Lombard attacks on Rome; and of the career of Gregory I (590–604) before he became pope and at the beginning of his pontificate. In the following sections, Gregorovius considers the government of Rome in this period, when Byzantine influence in the city, though challenged, was still felt. His comments on the rise of papal government are especially important for a grasp of Roman history in later periods.—EDITOR.

ALTHOUGH the records of the government of the city at this time are very scanty, so much at least is certain, that the military, civil, and political power in the city was in the hands of the emperor's officials, while a certain supervision belonged to the pope, to whom recourse was made in case of appeal. Generally speaking, we find the pope restricted to the church and its jurisdiction; nevertheless, Gregory [I, 590–604], as possessing the faculties suited to the circumstances of the time, was brought into a position which made him the tacitly recognized head of Rome, and with perfect right he is looked upon as the founder of the temporal dominion of the papacy.

From book III, ch. 2, secs. 2, 3, and 4.

Gregory's influence far outweighed the power of the imperial officials, the Romans reverencing their master and preserver in a
pope who united in his person the episcopal dignity and the renown of illustrious descent. Since the fall of the Gothic kingdom had extinguished the last remains of public life in the city,
Rome had suffered a complete transformation. Neither consuls,
senate, nor games recalled the temporal dominion; the patrician
families had almost entirely disappeared. Gregory's letters seldom
speak of any of the wealthy houses of ancient descent, except of
such as had removed to Constantinople, while time-honored
names are discovered connected with estates which already belonged to the church. Religious interests had completely thrust
civic affairs into the background, and, as we have already seen,
the Roman people had adopted an entirely spiritual garb. There
were no longer any public festivals but those of the church. The
only events which occupied the minds of the indolent people
were of a spiritual nature. The church had already become a
great asylum for society. Under the influence of natural disasters,
hitherto unparalleled, and of the horrors of war, the belief in
the approaching end of the world had gained universal acceptance, and the crowd of men anxious to enter convents and the
ranks of the priesthood assumed overwhelming proportions. The
needy there found food and shelter; the ambitious, dignity and
rank, in an age when the titles of deacon, presbyter, and bishop
had become for the Romans what those of praetor, tribune, and
consul had formerly been esteemed. Even soldiers deserted their
colors for the tonsure, and the candidates for ecclesiastical offices
were in all classes so numerous, that Gregory strove to enforce
some restraint, while the Emperor Maurice, by an edict of 592,
forbade soldiers from entering the cloister and civil officials from
being nominated to ecclesiastical offices. Roman poverty did not
stretch out its hands in vain for the treasures of the church. The
times when the consul scattered gold among the people, when
the prefect provided for the public distributions of corn, meat,
oil, and lard from the coffers of the state, no longer existed, and
the cry of the people for *"panem et circenses"* [bread and circuses]
made itself but half-heard. They desired bread, and the pope

gave it abundantly. Even as a monk in his cell on the Clivus Scauri, Gregory had daily fed the poor; as pope he still ministered to their necessities. At the beginning of every month he distributed corn, clothes, and gold to the needy, and at each of the great festivals bestowed gifts on the church and on charitable institutions. Like Titus, he held the day lost on which he had not satisfied hunger and clothed nakedness, and once, hearing that a beggar had died in the streets, he shut himself up, filled with remorse, and did not venture to approach the altar, as priest, for several days.

The public distribution of corn had in ancient times been made from porticos, theaters, and the granaries of the state. The Romans now thronged to the porches of convents and basilicas to receive food and clothing from spiritual officials. The crowds of pilgrims from beyond the seas found the ancient house in Portus, erected for their use by the Senator Pammachius, the friend of S. Jerome, ready for their reception, and on reaching Rome, whether as pilgrims or as fugitives seeking protection from the Lombards, received food and lodging in the hospitals, or in quarters provided for the purpose. Christian benevolence exercised true charity in the relief of genuine distress.

The property which gradually accrued to the church in gifts and legacies from private individuals was conscientiously devoted by Gregory to charitable objects. And the ecclesiastical possessions were already so vast and numerous that the pope, if not as yet wielding authority over dukedoms, had at least become the richest landowner in Italy. Possessor of the estates which the church inherited in the peninsula, and exercising over them a definite though limited jurisdiction, he appeared in the light of a great temporal prince. The property of the Roman church, assigned to the Apostle Peter, was scattered over various countries. It consisted of vast patrimonies or domains in Sicily and Campania, over the whole of Southern Italy, in Dalmatia, Illyria, Gaul, Sardinia, Corsica, Liguria, and the Cottian Alps. And, as a king sends ministers into his provinces, the pope sent deacons and subdeacons (*rectores patrimonii*), officials who united the attributes of spiritual with those of temporal overseers, or government councillors. The accounts of these officials were severely scrutinized, for Gregory possessed too strict a sense of honor to permit the ecclesiastical treasury to be polluted by questionable gains.

The many letters which he addressed to these rectors of patrimonies give an insight into the condition of the Roman peasant, such as it remained for several centuries. The property of the Church was cultivated by *coloni*, men bound to the soil, who paid a tax in money or in kind. It was usually named *pensio*, and collected by *conductores* or farmers of revenue. These officials frequently extorted half the gains of the coloni, and while they arbitrarily raised the measure of corn, at times compelled the peasants to increase the "modius" from the legitimate 16 sextarii, or 24 Roman pounds, to 25 sextarii, and out of 20 bushels of grain to surrender one. Gregory taxed these oppressions, fixing the modius decisively at 18 sextarii, and decreeing that out of 35 bushels one only was to be given up. These regulations affected Sicily, still the granary of Rome, from which regularly twice in the year, in spring and autumn, a fleet of corn sailed to Portus to supply the storehouses of the city. Were supplies lost at sea, the loss fell upon the poor *coloni*, amongst whom the compensation was divided; and Gregory warned the rectors not to delay the voyage beyond the favorable season, otherwise the loss would be ascribed to them. The economical regulations were exemplary. A register was kept for each colonus, called *Libellus securitatis*. This register stated the price paid, and to it the *colonus* could appeal. Had a failure of harvest or other misfortune befallen him, he might reckon on the equity of the pope to accord him a new inventory of cows, sheep, and swine. S. Peter's estates in Sicily prospered, and many salutary improvements were instituted. The great pope proved himself an excellent landlord, and, when sitting his horse in a procession, might have boasted that his palfrey was provided by the same ancient Trinacria, the renowned horses of which had once been the theme of Pindar's song. We cherish some doubts, however, as to whether Pindar would have considered the descendant race of apostolic steeds worthy of an ode. "Thou hast sent me," Gregory once wrote to the subdeacon, Peter, "a miser-

able horse and five good asses. The horse I cannot ride, because
he is wretched, nor mount the asses, because they are asses."

S. Peter's property within Roman territory consisted of four
separate groups on both sides the Tiber. The Patrimonium Ap-
piae, which comprised the entire district between the Via Appia
and the sea, as far as the Via Latina; the Labicanense between
the Via Labicana and the Anio; the Tiburtinum between the
Via Tiburtina and the Tiber; lastly, the Patrimonium Tusciae, the
most extensive of the four, which comprised the tract on the right
bank of the Tiber. Besides these, the church had acquired houses,
gardens, and vineyards in the city itself, which together formed
a Patrimonium Urbanum. Each division of the great patrimonial
district was divided into tracts for husbandry, called *fundus*, or
massa. With the title *fundus* was designated a small piece of
ground, to which *casae* or *casales* for the *coloni* belonged. Several
fundi together constituted a *massa*, or, according to the current
expression of present times, a "*tenuta*," and several *massae*, again,
formed a patrimony.

The church had become the possessor of a great part of the
Ager Romanus [state lands in central Italy]. Goths, Greeks, and
Lombards had, for two hundred years, trodden down the fields
belonging to the city, and the traces of the enemy extended in
ruins around the walls. The ground, on which some olive planta-
tions alone remained, was cultivated but sparingly by basilicas,
abbeys and noble landed proprietors. On the Campagna deserted hamlets, such as the Vicus Alexandri and Subaugusta,
crumbled to ruins. Convents owning a little cultivated land, and
a great many catacomb churches, which have long since disappeared, stood here and there amid the ruined villas of Roman
nobles. The columns and blocks of marble belonging to the country houses of former days were carried off to adorn the neighboring churches, as the monuments of the capital were despoiled for
the construction of the city churches. The whole of the Roman
Campagna, the most solemn and impressive plain in the world,
was reduced, even in the fifth century, to a melancholy waste.

The Roman church thus ruled over widespread districts in
Latium, the Sabina and Tuscany, as also in the most distant prov-

inces of Italy, and had therefore become a temporal power long before the rise of the political ecclesiastical state, of which these patrimonies formed the actual foundations. While private property gradually disappeared, the wealth of her treasury remained unexhausted. Out of his resources the pope was able to defray the expense of apparently incredible undertakings: the maintenance of the churches and of the city, the ransom of captives of war; further, the indemnity demanded for peace by the Lombards. To the treasury of her bishop Rome owed not only her release from the enemy, but occasionally also her almost independent position towards Ravenna, while the church adopted the attitude of poverty towards the emperor, and received with submissive gratitude the gift of a few pounds which he now and then let fall like golden drops of pity on the rubbish heap of Rome.

Reduced by war, famine, and pestilence, united with Constantinople only through a few officials, and cut off from Ravenna by the Lombards, scarcely controlled by the exarchs, and almost entirely devoid of military protection, Rome found in Pope Gregory a national and self-elected head.

Gregory in point of fact exercised almost the power of a sovereign, the reins of temporal government passing of themselves into his hands. That this was the case not alone with regard to the city, but also with respect to other places, is seen by the fact that he sent a certain Duke Leontius to the Tuscan fortress of Nepi, and admonished the clergy, ordo, and people to yield obedience to the orders of his nominee; further, that he even sent a tribune to Naples to protect the city already harassed by the Lombards, and that he commanded the troops stationed in the city to obey his behests. He had previously commissioned Bishop Januarius of Cagliari, in Sardinia, to see that guards were everywhere on the alert, and since Rome demanded his more immediate care, we can scarcely be surprised that, like a temporal overseer, he occupied himself with military measures, writing to the leader of the troops that he did not esteem it right that the soldiers should be withdrawn from the city, and also that he communicated with the military commander in regard to undertakings against the enemy.

The disastrous condition into which Italy was sunk, and the urgent distress of Rome, made Gregory the mediator of peace, and it was owing to his energies that peace was at length restored. So conscious was he of the greatness of his power, that he informed the emperor, through his nuncio, that had he, the servant of the emperor, desired the overthrow of the Lombards, they would have no longer had king, duke, or count. Foreseeing the conversion of the barbarian enemy, or dreading their revenge on the Catholic churches and lands within their territory, he agreed to an amicable peace, and strove to maintain it throughout the year. The intrigues of the exarch, however, frustrated his intentions, until the negotiations of his own envoy, the Abbot Probus, at length succeeded in obtaining it in 599. . . .

III

Cultural Achievements of Pope Gregory I

THE foregoing pages, which suffice to confirm our opinion of Gregory and his contemporaries, illustrate a few of the beliefs and delusions prevailing among mankind at the period. The student, however, anxious to pursue the subject more fully, may read the *Dialogues* written by the pope himself; four volumes filled with miraculous histories, with which Gregory is supposed to regale the ears of Peter, his faithful deacon, and where a word occasionally let fall serves to maintain the form of a dialogue. Written in the fourth year of Gregory's pontificate, few books obtained a like measure of success. In copies and translations the *Dialogues* spread over East and West; a version appeared in Arabic at the end of the eighth century, and Alfred of England later rendered them into the Saxon tongue. The editors, members of the congregation of S. Maurus, ascribed the conversion of the Lombards to the influence of these works, and the historian of Italian literature in a later age maintains that the contents of the *Dialogues* are of a nature calculated to impress the childish spirit of a barbarous people. Be that as it may, in reading anecdotes such as these, the wish involuntarily arises that the great pope had not been responsible for their authorship, and that the belief in such superstitions

From book III, chap. 3, secs. 2 and 3.

had not been sanctioned by the authority of so illustrious a man. Their usefulness as a means to conversion is doubtful or transient; their harmfulness has been lasting. They, nevertheless, possess a significance which we cannot overlook. These histories were national, Gregory only relating such legends as were calculated to increase the fame of Italian saints of his own time, and which, as evidence that the Roman church was still in possession of miraculous powers, could be used as a weapon against the Arianism of the Lombards. The whole of the second book is dedicated to the acts of Benedict, and the *Dialogues* went forth from the hands of the pope as silent missionaries of the Roman church throughout the provinces.

In return for the many marvellous histories which the great pope has related, he has himself become the subject of legend. In the eighth century it was believed that one day, when passing the Forum of Trajan, he looked with admiration on this work of Roman greatness. His attention was more particularly attracted by a bronze group, which represented Trajan, setting forth to battle, in the act of descending from his horse to give audience to a suppliant widow. The widow bewails her son, who had been slain, and demands justice of the emperor. Trajan promises to judge her case as soon as he has returned from the war. "If thou fallest however," asks the poor widow, "who shall secure me justice?" and the answer that his successor would award it, failing to satisfy her, she prevails on Trajan to dismount and grant her justice on the spot. Gregory, seeing this incident represented in bronze, overcome by grief that so just a ruler should be condemned to eternal perdition, wept at the thought all the way to S. Peter's, where, falling into an ecstasy, he heard a voice from heaven telling him that his prayer for Trajan had been heard, that the soul of the pagan emperor had been released, but that he must not again attempt to intercede for an unbeliever. Legend further adds that Gregory reanimated the dust of the emperor in order to baptise his soul; and, the ceremony ended, the body fell to pieces while the soul ascended to heaven.

The audacious idea of a pagan emperor, who, by his edict to Pliny, had pronounced Christianity a *religio illicita* [illegal religion], and delivered it over to the persecution of the state, being placed by one of the holiest of popes among the blessed in heaven was found to be at variance with the dogmas of the church. This pretty fable, which arose in the time of Rome's decline, has been severely condemned by Cardinal Baronius, who carefully white-washes the sainted Gregory from the innocent charge, and demonstrates that the pope was guilty neither of any compassion for Trajan nor of having ever prayed for a pagan. The cardinal might with justice have expressed some doubt as to whether bronze statues remained in the Forum in the days of Gregory, but he is instead so carried away by zeal on this occasion, that he heaps sins mountains high on the soul of Trajan, in order to thrust it further into hell. We shall not, however, trouble ourselves, either with regard to Baronius or to Cardinal Bellarmin, who gravely, though dispassionately, also rejects the legend, which we have only repeated here as one of the most remarkable memories of the decadence of Rome. It shows us the Romans of the eighth century, as, with enfeebled memory, they looked on the column of Trajan, and told each other wondrous tales of the deeds of their noble emperor. Thus the legend arose, and spread like some climbing plant in the Forum itself.

Of the condition of the Forum of Trajan at this period we are entirely ignorant. In the time of Paul[us] Diaconus, by whom the legend is related, that is to say in the eighth century, it appears to have not yet fallen into utter ruin. According to two statements made by Gregory's contemporary, Venantius Fortunatus, Bishop of Poitiers, down to the Gothic period, and even later, the people were here accustomed to assemble to listen to Homer, Virgil, or some other poet read aloud.

The bishop says:—

> Vix modo tam nitido pomposa poemata cultu
> Audit Trajano Roma verenda foro.
> Quod si tale decus recitasses auri senatus,
> Stravissent plantis aurea fila tuis.
>
> [Nowadays Rome the venerable hardly ever
> hears stately poems of such splendid refinement
> in Trajan's Forum. But if you had recited such

a glorious thing in the hearing of the Senate,
they would have scattered golden fillets
at your feet.]

And again:—

Si sibi forte fuit bene notus Homerus Athenis,
Aut Maro Trajano lectus in urbe foro.

[If perchance Homer were well known to
the Athenians themselves, or Virgil read in the
City at Trajan's forum.]

Although these lines apply as fitly to remote as to more recent
times, they might have been quoted by the historian of the Roman
Senate in the Middle Ages as evidence of the continued survival
of the Council of the Fathers. . . . Down to the time of Gregory
the custom of reciting poetry in the Forum of Trajan still survived,
and [we] are consequently led to inquire into the state of learning
at the time.

During the rule of [the Ostrogothic rulers, father and daughter,] Theodoric [ca. 454–526] and Amalasuntha [ca. 500–535] . . .
schools in Rome [were] well cared for and [were] provided with
teachers paid by the state. The Gothic period is further graced by
the last names of eminence in Latin literature, by Boethius and
Cassiodorus, the Bishops Ennodius, Venantius Fortunatus, and
Jordanes. The writings of these distinguished men show that
poetry, history, philosophy, and eloquence still flourished. The
classic, poetic art of antiquity had not as yet been banished under
the influence of the church, and at the same time that the verses of
Virgil were declaimed in the Forum, the ex-comes and subdeacon
Arator might have been heard reading his poem, amid the applause of an appreciative audience, in the Basilica of S. Pietro ad
Vincula (544). The author in this poem renders the history of the
apostles into hexameters by no means barbarous, and in the inscription to Pope Vigilius, to whom it is dedicated, justifies himself
by saying that meter is not foreign to Holy Writ, as is shown by
the Psalms, and asserts his opinion that the Canticles, Jeremiah,
and Job had originally been written in meter. The muse of Virgil,
which visited a subdeacon in the sixth century, carries him away

in some timid recollections, in which paganism now and then transpires. He makes use of Olympus for the heaven of Christianity, and innocently appeals to the Almighty under the name of Tonans, the ancient god of thunder. Vigilius accepted these pagan conceits in 544 with as little reluctance as did Leo the Tenth, when, in the sixteenth century, Christendom had become wholly imbued by the forms and ideas of antiquity. Paganism again appears, with its ancient meters, in the writings of Gregory's contemporary, the celebrated Irish monk Columba, the founder and abbot of the monastery of Bobbio, who died in 615, and who in his works naïvely places Christ alongside of Pygmalion and Danæ, Hector and Achilles.

The overthrow of public institutions by the Byzantine wars, and the fall of the Gothic kingdom, however, involved the destruction at the same time of the humane sciences. We no longer hear of the schools of rhetoric, dialectics, and jurisprudence in Rome; that of medicine alone, zealously cherished by Theodoric, may still to some extent have existed. Roman physicians apparently enjoyed a higher reputation than those of Ravenna, since Gregory invited Marianus, bishop of the latter city, to come to Rome to be treated for some chest complaint from which he suffered.

The cost of education had to be defrayed from the scanty resources provided by private rather than public means. Education could not be entirely neglected, and no doubt teachers and pupils of the humane sciences must have always been forthcoming. If we accept the pompous utterances of John Diaconus, we are led to believe that Rome was, under Gregory's government, in truth "a temple of wisdom supported by the seven arts, like pillars." Nor among the pope's companions was there any whose speech or manner bore the traces of barbarism; on the contrary, each and all were versed in Latin literature. The study of the liberal arts again flourished; the learned had no longer to take thought of their lives; the pope chose as his associates men of the greatest learning rather than those of the highest rank. John Diaconus sketches, in short, in the barbarism of his own century (the ninth) a picture which would have better befitted the later court of Nicholas the Fifth (1447–55). The learned monk laments but one shortcoming; namely, that in Gregory's Curia no one was able to speak Greek. The pope himself admits that he did not understand the language, and the fact seems strange, when we remember that he had lived so many years as nuncio at Constantinople, where, although Latin remained the official language and that of the court, he must have heard Greek in daily use. Neither did Byzantium boast any scholar capable of explaining Latin documents, and we are thus enabled to understand how entirely the two cities had become estranged from one another, and how completely Rome was severed from the classic literature of the Greeks. True, John Diaconus ascribes to Gregory a thorough acquaintance with all liberal discipline, and speaks of the pope as being so versed in grammar, rhetoric, and dialectics from his childhood that, although in his time, as he expresses it, literary studies flourished in Rome, the pope, as a scholar, had no rival in the city. The chronicler, however, effaces the brilliancy of his own picture when he tells us in plain terms that Gregory prohibited the reading of pagan authors to the clergy; he even quotes the notorious passage in the pope's letter which proves Gregory's hostile attitude toward the humane sciences; where, writing to the Gallic bishop, Desiderius, he tells him he is ashamed to hear that Desiderius had instructed some persons in grammar; speaks of ancient literature as "foolishness," declares it "godless" to set any value upon it, and maintains that there cannot be room in the same mouth for the praise of Christ and that of Zeus. He elsewhere admits that it was not his object to avoid barbarism of style, and that he disdained considering syntax and construction, holding it unworthy to force the word of God into the rules of Donatus.

The first of these passages is sufficient to prove that Gregory showed himself hostile towards the humane sciences, but we have no justification for asserting that he was himself ignorant or uncultured. His learning was of a theological nature. If he were acquainted with the dialectics of the ancients, a supposition which none of his writings, silent as regards philosophy, encourage, he put away such knowledge from his mind. His works bear the stamp of his time, but his language frequently rises in flights of rhetoric, and his Latin is by no means barbarous. His position forced him to confine his influence exclusively to the Catholic life, and while, with marvellous mental energy, he found, amid the cares of office and constant ill-health, leisure for his theological writings, it were vain to require from either the man or his time the culture of profane literature, or even a recognition of literature as a factor in the education of mankind. The man to whom England owed her conversion beheld Italy still here and there under the spell of the graceful myths of paganism, but could feel no attachment to the poets of antiquity; and Gregory the bishop must be judged by another standard than Cassiodorus the statesman of classic culture, who incited the monks of his cloister to the study of grammar and dialectics. Gregory was himself the law-giver and director of the pompous ritual of Rome. His biographer extols him as having founded the institutions for singers at S. Peter's and the Lateran; and the school of Gregorian music became the teacher of the West. The earliest papal choir embodied the musical traditions of paganism, and at the same time that Gregory declared war against the poets of the ancient mythology, he tolerated their rhythms in the sacred service of the Mass.

In later and even modern times many accusations have been levied against Gregory; these charges, however, do not admit of proof. It has been said that he suppressed the study of mathematic science. This reproach, however, rests on no other foundation than a passage, wrongly interpreted, of an English writer of the end of the twelfth century. The accusation brought against him by the same author, of having burnt the Palatine library, is of graver moment, and it is at least remarkable that in the Middle Ages legend related that the zealous promoter of Catholicism had destroyed the ancient library of Apollo. But the fate of the celebrated library which Augustus had once formed in the portico of the famous temple dedicated to the sun-god is completely obscure. It is possible, either that the Greek emperors may have had its contents conveyed to Byzantium, or that they may have perished in the vicissitudes that had befallen the city; or even that they may have survived, a prey to worms and dust, down to Gregory's own time. In the overthrow of learning the Augustan and

48

Ulpian libraries had found an unnoticed end, and, by degrees, the *Acts of the Martyrs*, the writings of the Fathers, the decrees and letters of the popes, filled the shelves formerly dedicated to those treasures of Greek and Latin learning, the destruction of which is even more to be regretted than that of the masterpieces of ancient sculpture. The first foundation of the Lateran library is ascribed to Hilary, and Gregory also speaks of libraries in Rome and of the archives of the Roman Church, predecessors of the present secret archives in the Vatican.

Since, however, the public monuments of Rome were not the property of the pope, but of the emperor, and since it is utterly impossible to conceive that the emperor would have sanctioned the wanton destruction of the greatest library in the city, we cannot forego the attempt to clear Gregory's memory from the atrocity laid to his charge. And if there be any truth in the report that the pope swore especial vengeance on the works of Cicero and Livy, it may in some degree console us to know, that by a happy accident, Cardinal Mai was enabled to rescue the books of Cicero's *Republic* from the grave of the Roman Middle Ages.

The advocates of the great pope were placed in a still greater difficulty by another no less serious accusation, namely, that Gregory, in his zeal for religion, had destroyed the ancient monuments, not only with the view of uprooting the last remains of paganism, but also in order to prevent the eyes of the pilgrims who flocked to the churches and graves of the martyrs from being attracted to the beauteous works of pagan antiquity. Two ignorant chroniclers in the fourteenth century, a Dominican and an Augustine monk, relate with satisfaction how the pope struck off the heads of the ancient gods and mutilated their limbs. A biographer of the pope at the end of the fifteenth century further recounts how Sabinian, the successor of Gregory, during a famine stirred up the people against the memory of the late pope, reminding them that he had destroyed the monuments of antiquity throughout the entire city. It was even asserted that he had thrown the statues promiscuously into the Tiber. This accusation, however, which found acceptance not only among Protestants, but also among numerous Catholics, is incapable of proof. Gregory must naturally have been indifferent to the beautiful creative art of the ancients, but our sympathy leads us to adopt the views of such writers as point to his love for his native city, to the emperor's right over all public works, and to the number of monuments which survived his days, as arguments in his defense. Nevertheless, we recognize a certain amount of justice in the assertion made against him during the Middle Ages. The reproach of vandalism is one shared by many popes in common with the barbarians, and the destruction of many a beautiful statue is undoubtedly due to the pious zeal of one or other bishop.

The city sank hopelessly day by day into ever deeper ruin. Gregory, who looked with indifference on the gradual destruction of the temples, regarded the broken aqueducts, which must inevitably perish did not the city provide for their restoration, with grief and dismay. He wrote repeatedly to John the subdeacon, his nuncio in Ravenna, earnestly entreating him to intercede with the prefect of Italy for their restoration. He implored the latter to entrust the charge to the vice-comes Augustus, who, it appears, was endowed from Ravenna with the ancient title of count of the aqueducts. Nothing further, however, appears to have taken place. The aqueducts were consigned to ruin, and, with the exception perhaps of some slight attempt at restoration, no single aqueduct was put into working order.

Generally speaking, during the reign of Gregory it is only when dealing with churches or convents that the historic names of once familiar sites obtain a casual mention; the monuments of antiquity are already veiled in the shadows of an ever-deepening night.

We must in these chapters restrict ourselves to dealing with the influence which the great bishop exercised on the city, and leave it to ecclesiastical history to describe the importance of his reign on matters belonging to the church. Before his elevation to the papacy, the long struggle which established the structure of ecclesiastical doctrine had been already fought out, the fundamental dogmas of the Trinity and of the nature of Christ already fixed. The age of the Fathers had ended, and a new era had begun, in the course of which the East became separated from the West, and the absolute power of the Roman pope gained full development. His predecessor Leo [I, the Great], having already attained in principle the recognition of the supremacy of the apostolic chair, Gregory not only ushered in the new era, but laid the foundations of papal dominion. The oriental dioceses of Antioch and Alexandria, however, resolutely contested the Roman claim to supremacy. Constantinople was yet more indefatigable in her resistance; her patriarch, John Jejunator [i.e., the Faster], adopting on his side the title of ecumenical or universal bishop. Gregory, as might have been expected, resolutely opposed the assumption of the rival prelate, while with shrewd humility he, first among the popes, adopted that of "servant of the servants of God."

The tension between the papacy and the East, which increased with time into an irreparable breach, enabled the West to attain an independence, essentially due to the union of the Roman church with the Germans. The importance of the Greek church was at the same time lessened, her partriarchates, the oldest foundations of Christianity, being for the greater part swallowed up by Islam.

To Gregory also was due the extension of the boundaries of his patriarchate in the West. According to the limits established by Constantine, the Bishop of Rome possessed jurisdiction over the ten suburban provinces of Italy, subject to the "Vicarius Romæ." The metropolitans of Ravenna, however, in the Æmilian and Flaminian territories, the Bishop of Milan in Liguria, the Cottian Alps, and the two Rhætias, and the Bishop of Aquileja in Venetia and Italy, disputed the apostolic power of the Roman bishop within their respective territories. Gregory, however, opposed to these claims the supremacy of the successor of S. Peter, and constituted himself essentially Patriarch of the West. . . .

IV

The Imperial Coronation of Charlemagne

Profoundly troubled times followed Gregory I's pontificate. Plague repeatedly depopulated Rome. The city's walls crumbled into ruins. Much of what survived from ancient splendor fell as plunder into the hands of the Emperor Constans, who despoiled the city during a speciously friendly visit (663). The popes themselves broke up ancient monuments to get architectural elements for their new buildings, especially churches. Torn by internal divisions and hard-pressed by the new power of Islam, Byzantium found it impossible to retain firm control of Italy. Gradually, the popes freed themselves from the last ties of Byzantine overlordship. In the chaotic power vacuum left by Byzantium's withdrawal from Italy, they slowly built up a territorial domain, the patrimonium Petri *("patrimony of St. Peter"); and, in the eighth century, they received formal recognition of their temporal possessions and rights by official acts, the "donations" of the Frankish kings Pippin and Charlemagne, his son. The series of diplomatic negotiations, of which these donations were incidents, led eventually to the imperial coronation of Charlemagne in Rome (800).—*EDITOR.

From book IV, ch. 7, sec. 3.

CHARLES had promised the pope [Leo III, 795–816] to come to Rome himself to celebrate the Christmas festival of the year 800. He went in August to Mainz, and, explaining to his nobles the duties which called him to Italy and Rome, announced his approaching departure. Before leaving France he invited Alcuin to accompany him, but illness or love of his monastery (that of S. Martin of Tours) detained the scholar, and the king playfully reproached him with preferring the smoke-blackened huts of Tours to Rome's glittering palaces. The abbot of S. Martin, however, sent his muse to accompany his king, and the muse, inspired with visions of the future, announced that Rome, the capital of the world, the fount of the highest honors, the treasure-chamber of the saints, awaited Charles as ruler of the empire and as patron, and foretold that he was called thither to set up his tribunal, to establish peace, to restore the pope by his judicial sentence, and lastly, under God's will, to rule the universe.

Charles advanced with his army to Ravenna, there remained seven days, proceeded to Ancona, and, having despatched Pipin with a part of his troops against Grimoald, the recalcitrant duke of Benevento, continued on his way. The approach of the most powerful man of the time, behind whose shield Rome and the church stood protected, roused the city to the highest pitch of excitement, and while to some he appeared in the light of a dreaded avenger, and to others in that of a savior, all expected unusual events.

Ancient Nomentum, as early as the fourth century the seat of a bishop, still stood on the Nomentan Way at the fourteenth milestone from the city. Here Leo, with the clergy, militia, and populace, waited to accord a solemn reception to the king. It was the 23d November. Charles halted and dined with the pope, and after Leo, in an introductory conversation, had assured himself as to the prospect of events in Rome, the pope returned to the city, to receive his judge the following day. The king passed the night in Nomentum, and on the 24th advanced to the city. Instead of entering by the Nomentan Gate, he made a circuit of the walls and crossed the Milvian Bridge, in order first to reach S. Peter's. The pope awaited him on the steps of the Basilica, and led him into the cathedral.

Charles summoned a meeting of clergy, nobles, and citizens. This parliament, a synod in the form of a tribunal, assembled in S. Peter's on the 1st December. The king, clad in the toga and chlamis of the patricius, took his seat beside the pope. Archbishops, bishops, and clergy were ranged around, while the inferior clergy and the united Roman and Frankish nobles remained standing. Charles, addressing the assembly, announced that he had come to Rome to restore the disturbed discipline of the church, to punish the outrage committed on its head, and to pronounce judgment between the Romans the accusers, and the pope the accused. Before the tribunal of the patricius would be heard the complaints which the rebellious Romans had to bring against the pope, and sentence of guilty or not guilty would be pronounced. Charles's judicial authority was undisputed. In him the Frankish bishops recognized the universal head of the church; and the pope, who had submitted himself to the enquiry of his plenipotentiaries, was, like every other Roman, his subject, and as such appeared before the tribunal of his judges. There can be no doubt that Leo subjected himself to this tribunal. The Frankish chroniclers assert the fact in plain terms; the *Liber Pontificalis*, however, conceals the proceedings of the enquiry, and asserts that the bishops unanimously rose and declared: "We should never presume to judge the apostolic chair, which is the Head of the Church of God; since we ourselves are judged by it and by His Vicar; over it there is no judge. Our conduct is in accordance with the custom of ancient times. In conformity with the canon we submit to that which the chief priest considers right." The same authority further goes on to say that the pope replied: "I follow the example of my predecessors in the pontificate, and am ready to purge myself from the false accusations which malice has brought against me."

Leo might have appealed, among other examples, to the case of [Pope] Pelagius [I]. Accused by some of the Romans of complicity in the death of Vigilius, his predecessor, Pelagius, had publicly exculpated himself by an oath in S. Peter's; and the ceremony had taken place under the eyes of Narses, who at the time as patricius represented the majesty of the emperor. Leo followed the example of his predecessor, although not until after the observance of judicial procedure had been fulfilled, that is to say, until Charles had accorded a second hearing to his accusers. The plaintiffs brought forward their charges; they were, however, unable to substantiate them, and Charles gave his verdict in favor of the bishops, who, declining to pronounce sentence, left it to the pope to take the oath of purgation. The ceremony took place a few days after the opening of the parliament. In presence of the king, the bishops and optimates of the city assembled in S. Peter's, and in sight of the populace, who, in closely serried masses, filled the nave of the church, the pope mounted the steps of the same chancel that Pelagius had formerly ascended, and, the gospels in his hand, pronounced the formula as follows:

> It is known, beloved brethren, that evil-doers have risen up and have injured my life with their grievous accusations. Charles, the most gracious and illustrious king, has come to the city with priests and nobles to judge these men. Therefore I, Leo, Pontifex of the Holy Roman Church, judged by no man, nor forced by any, but of my own free will, purge myself in your presence, before God, who knows the conscience, before His angels, and before S. Peter, Prince of Apostles, in whose sight we stand. I maintain that I have neither committed the sins whereof I am accused, nor have ordered them to be committed, and I call God, before whose tribunal we shall one day appear, and before whose eyes we here stand, as witness of my innocence. This I do, not compelled by any law, nor because I desire to impose any custom or decree on my successors or my brother bishops, but in order the more surely to free your minds from unjust suspicion.

After Leo had confirmed this assurance by an oath, and the clergy had sung the Te Deum, the accused pope again sat spotless on the apostolic chair, and his opponents, or the nobles who had previously been condemned to death, Paschalis, Campulus, and their confederates, were surrendered to the executioner. The pope, however, decided to pardon them, justly fearing that the execution of [Pope] Adrian [I]'s relatives, and men so well known, would increase the hatred with which he was already regarded. Upon his intercession, Charles banished them to France, where prisoners under sentence of exile were now sent, instead of to Byzantium as in former days.

These proceedings were closed by one of the most eventful acts in the records of history; that of placing the crown of the Roman Empire on the head of the Frankish king. Three hundred and twenty-four years had rolled away since representatives of the Roman Senate had appeared before [Emperor] Zeno, to lay the insignia of empire in his hands, and explain that Rome and the West no longer had need of an emperor of their own. During this long period of changing fortune and ever increasing decay the Byzantine emperors had continued to govern Italy as a province. The religious sentiment of mankind clung firmly to the idea of the Roman Empire, and, even as late as the end of the eighth century, emancipated Italy and the West revered its shadow in the title of the Byzantine emperor. The institutions of antiquity, on which the throne of the Cæsars had rested, had vanished; the idea of the empire, however, still survived. It was the consecrated form in which the republic of mankind and the visible church had, for centuries, found its representation. The Germans, who had destroyed the Western Empire, now, after having been received into Roman civilization and the bosom of the church, effected its restoration. And the church, whose laws controlled the West, created anew from within herself the Roman Empire, as the political form of her cosmopolitan principle, and that spiritual unity within which the popes had embraced so many nations. Her supremacy over all churches of the West could, however, only attain complete recognition through the emperor and the empire. The restoration of the empire was rendered necessary by the formidable power of Islam, which not only harassed Byzantium, but, from the side of Sicily and Spain, also threatened Rome. The Greek emperors could rule the West together with the East so long as the Roman church was weak, so long as Italy lay sunk in lethargy, and the German West swarmed with lawless barbarians. It was no longer possible to do so when the church attained independence, Italy consciousness of her nationality, and Europe had become united in the powerful Frankish Empire, at the head of which stood a great monarch. Thus the idea of proclaiming Charles emperor arose, and thus was carried out the scheme with which the irate Italians had threatened [the Byzantine Emperor] Leo the Isaurian at the beginning of the Iconoclastic controversy. The West now demanded the occupation of the imperial throne. True, the Byzantine Empire had, in the course of time, acquired a legal sanction. Byzantium, however, was but the daughter of Rome. From Rome the imperium had proceeded; here the Cæsars had had their seat. The illustrious mother of the empire now resumed her rights, when, as in ancient times, she offered the imperial crown to the most powerful ruler of the West. Contemporary chroniclers, looking at the state of the world at the time, found that the imperial power, which, since the days of Constantine, had had its seat, first in part and then exclusively, with the Greeks at Byzantium, was no longer to be held by one man alone. Two years before the outrage on the pope, the dignity of the emperor had also been violated in the person of Constantine the Sixth. The Roman Republic was tyrannized over by Irene, an infamous woman, who had put out the eyes of her own son; and this being the case, the imperial throne was considered vacant. The crown of Constantine was therefore transferred to the Frankish monarch, already in possession of Rome, the capital of the realm, and of many other seats of ancient empire. A transaction so momentous, and rendered necessary by the ideas of the time and the demands of the West, but which, nevertheless, bore the semblance of a revolt against the rights of Byzantium, could scarcely have been the work of the moment, but more probably was the result of a sequence of historic causes and resolutions consequent upon them. Can we doubt that the imperial crown had long been the goal of Charles's ambition and the ideal of such of his friends as cherished Roman aspirations? He himself came to Rome evidently to take the crown, or, at least, to form some decisive resolution with regard to it, and during his sojourn in France the pope had declared himself ready to help in the accomplishment of this great revolution. The popes had but hesitatingly renounced allegiance to the legitimate imperial power of Byzantium, a power which, even after the Frankish princes had obtained supremacy in Italy, they had continued to recognize from impulses of tradition as well as policy. Necessity had forced them to throw themselves into the arms of France, and to bestow the dignity of patricius on the Frankish princes; the popes, however, had received as a reward the State of the Church, and this state could only be protected by Frankish intervention. The expulsion of the pope from Rome, where he had become ruler, at length decided the question. Leo the Third found himself obliged to allow the possession of the imperial power to pass into the hands of a Western dynasty, that of the staunchly Catholic line of Pipin, a line which had received consecration at the hands of his predecessor Stephen. The zeal for the faith displayed by Pipin and his successor promised protection for the Latin church, and the Frankish power the defence of Christendom against heathens and barbarians, while from Byzantium nothing could be expected but dogmatic heresies and the continuation of the despotic rule of Justinian. These parallel considerations had long since been weighed one against the other.

We may suppose that Charles's clerical friends were the most zealous supporters of the scheme, which perhaps was not received by the pope with a like degree of enthusiasm. Alcuin's letter proves that he, at least, had already been initiated into the idea; and the Frankish envoys, after a year spent in Rome, had doubtless come to an understanding with the Romans, on whose vote the election mainly depended. The Romans it was who, exercising the ancient suffrages of the Senate and people, had elected Charles their patricius, and who now, in virtue of the same rights, elected him emperor. And only as emperor of the Romans and of Rome did he become emperor of the entire state. A decree of the Roman nobility and people had undoubtedly preceded the coronation; and Charles's nomination as Roman emperor (in strict accordance with the plan of a papal election) was effected by the three traditional elective bodies.

The great revolution which extinguished the ancient rights of the Byzantines was not to appear the arbitrary deed of either king or pope, but the act of God Himself, and therefore the legal transaction of Christendom, as expressed by the voice of the Roman people, of the parliament of the united clergy, optimates, and citizens assembled in Rome, Germans as well as Latins. The Frankish chroniclers themselves say that Charles was made emperor by the election of the Roman people, quote the united parliament of the two nations, and enumerate the list of the members who took part in the parliament: the pope, the entire assembly of bishops, clergy, and abbots, the Frankish senate, the Roman optimates, and the rest of the Christian people.

The resolution of the Romans and Franks was announced to Charles in the form of a request. Are we to believe that, like Augustus in former days, he made a feint of reluctance to accept the supreme dignity, until it was forced upon him as an accomplished fact? Are we to receive as hypocritical the assurance of a man so pious and heroic, when he asserts that the imperial crown came upon him wholly as a surprise, and adds that he would not have entered S. Peter's had he known of Leo's intention? Had not Charles's son, Pipin, been purposely recalled from the war against Benevento, in order to witness the imperial coronation? An explanation of these conflicting statements has been sought in the statement of Eginhard, who maintains that Charles's hesitation was dictated by respect for Byzantium; that he had not yet assented to the scheme, and had sought by negotiations to gain the recognition of the Greeks to the election; that, therefore, the coronation really did take him by surprise, and, with regard to the time chosen, seemed inopportune. This view is supported by reasons of probability, which, however, solely concern the occasion chosen for the coronation, since to his elevation to the imperial throne Charles had already long given his consent. The ceremony had been fixed to take place on the occasion of his visit to Rome, and his friends looked forward with certainty to the event.

In order to put an end to all further hesitation, the act itself was performed without preparation and without pomp. Such was indeed the object of the pope, who, anxious to appear the leading figure in the transaction, intended, by means of the coronation and consecration, to acquire for the church a position of supreme authority; he, the supreme head of the church, now making emperor the man elected by the Romans and Franks. Nothing could have been more simple, nothing more unimposing, than this act of universally historic importance. As Charles, having knelt before the high altar of S. Peter's on Christmas Day, rose from his knees, Leo, moved as it were by divine inspiration, placed a golden diadem on his head, and, at the same moment, the assembled multitude, who awaited the signal and understood the significance of the act, made the church resound with the shout which had formerly hailed the elevation of a Cæsar: "Life and victory to Charles the most pious Augustus, crowned by God, great and peace-giving emperor of the Romans." Twice was the shout repeated, the multitude in this, the most eventful moment that Rome was to witness for centuries, being carried away in a transport of enthusiasm, while the pope, like another Samuel, anointed the new Cæsar of the West and his son Pipin. Leo invested Charles with the imperial mantle, and, kneeling befoɪe him, adored the head of the Roman Empire, crowned of God by his hand. The ceremony ended with the Mass, when Charles and Pipin offered the gifts already prepared for the various churches. On S. Peter's they bestowed a silver table with valuable vessels in gold; and on S. Paul's similar gifts. They presented a gold cross, set with precious stones, to the Lateran basilica, and gifts no less valuable to S. Maria Maggiore.

Charles thus renounced the title of patricius of the Romans, claiming henceforward that of emperor and Augustus. The new title could not increase the power of a prince who had long been ruler of the West. It expressed, however, the formal recognition of his absolute dominion, placing him before the world in the "God-given" dignity of a Cæsar; a dignity with which he had been invested in Rome, the chief sanctuary of the church and the ancient seat of universal monarchy. When, in later times, the German empire came into conflict with the papacy, doctors of canon law advanced the theory that the emperor received the crown solely by favor of the pope, and traced the investiture to Charles's coronation at the hands of Leo the Third. The emperors, on the other hand, appealed to the shout of the people: "Life and victory to the emperor of the Romans, crowned by God," and asserted that they derived the crown, the inalienable heritage of the Cæsars, from God alone. The Romans, on their side, maintained that Charles owed the crown entirely to the majesty of the Roman

Senate and people. The dispute as to the actual source of empire continued throughout the entire Middle Ages, and, while exercising no actual change in the world's history, revealed an indwelling need of mankind; the necessity, namely, of referring the world of facts back to a rudimentary right by which power becomes legalized. Pope Leo the Third as little possessed the right to bestow the crown of empire, which was not his, as Charles did to claim it. The pope, however, regarded himself as the representative of the empire and of Romanism; and undoubtedly, as the head of Latin nationality, and still more as the recognized spiritual overseer of the Christian republic, he possessed the power of accomplishing that revolution which, without the aid of the church, would have been impossible. Mankind at large regarded him as the sacred intercessor between the world and the Divinity; and it was only through his coronation and unction at the papal hands that the empire of Charles received divine sanction in the eyes of men. The elective right of the Romans, on the other hand, in whatever form it may appear, was uncontested, and in no later imperial election could it have been of so decisive legal significance. If the Romans, from whom the new Augustus derived his title, had, in the year 800, declared themselves opposed to Charles's election, the Frankish king would either never have become emperor, or else his imperial authority would, as a usurpation, have lacked the last semblance of legality. Charles could not therefore be regarded as emperor in the absence of the consent of either the pope or the Romans. With the Romans, however, the Franks and other German races represented in Rome by the scholæ of the foreigners, were now associated; and the elective right, which had originally belonged exclusively to the Senate and people of Rome, a right, moreover, never recognized by Charles, lost its significance now that the power of the State rested in the German nation, by which Frankish and German kings were alike elected.

Another question, fruitful of dispute, at the same time presented itself, namely, whether the Roman Empire had, as the champions of the papal investiture asserted, been made over from the Greeks to the Franks by means of the pope. Were it the case that Leo possessed neither the exclusive power nor the right as pope to bestow the crown of the empire on the Frankish king, it follows that he could not transmit it from the Greeks to the Franks. The very phrase, "translation of the empire," contains merely a half truth. When the design of making Charles emperor arose, the idea of the unity of the empire still existed so powerfully as a dogma, that the separation of the West from the East was never even dreamt of. After the fall of Constantine the Sixth, therefore, Charles occupied the throne considered vacant, not as rival emperor, but essentially as emperor and successor of Constantine and Justinian. It was even said that he contemplated marriage with Irene. The empire was to be transferred, but to a new dynasty, to the Frankish kings, not to the people of the Franks. It is more than probable that Charles, as well as Leo, believed in the possibility of preserving its indivisibility, like that of the church. But the hope proved a dream. The new empire remained Western, and never again attained that connection with the East possessed by the ancient state in the time of Honorius and his successors. The offended Greeks continued to regard it as a usurpation; they complained that the ancient ties between Rome and Byzantium had been severed by the ponderous sword of the Franks, and that Rome's more beautiful daughter, Constantinople, had been separated for ever from her aged mother. A deep chasm henceforward lay between East and West. Church, civil institutions, science and art, customs and ways of life, even recollections of the past were severed from one another. The Greek Empire became orientalized, and remained sunk in numb rigidity during six hundred sad, though honorable, years; while the Roman attained an unexpected degree of vigor in the development of national life in the West.

Thus the Roman Empire was revived. To the minds of men an ancient form seemed to be restored; but the restoration was merely apparent; for the life within was new. Not only was the political principle of this life essentially Teutonic; the empire itself, by a bold stroke, had been removed from the sphere of merely political causes and made dependent on the Divine Will, the fief of which, representing itself as a theocracy, it soon claimed to be. The church, the Kingdom of God on earth, appeared as the vital principle of which it was itself the civil form, the Catholic body. Without the church the empire was impossible. No longer Roman laws, but the institutions of the church, formed the structure and bonds that united the Western nations, and made them a Christian commonwealth. The civilization of antiquity, the religion, the moral law, the priesthood, the Roman language, the festivals, the calendar, everything in short that nations possessed as common property, they derived from the church. The Roman idea of a universal republic, as of the unity of mankind, found its only visible form in the church. The emperor was its head and patron, its promoter and governor, the secular vicar of Christ. To the nations and peoples who were united under his empire, and who, willingly or unwillingly, recognized his imperial authority, he stood in identically the same relation as the pope had stood in towards the national churches and metropolitans before he had succeeded in establishing the complete centralization of the church. The new Cæsar of the West, after the time of Charles the Great, possessed neither territorial power nor state authority; his imperial majesty rested rather on a dogma derived from the laws of nations than on any international right. It was a power of altogether ideal authority, and devoid of all practical basis.

The appearance of the theocratic principle in the West, distinct from the ancient Roman idea of the state, operated with such effect that, in the course of time, the church itself or the pope, the spiritual vicar of Christ, became the sole dominating power. The mystic way of looking at the actual world, which prevailed throughout the Middle Ages, and which now appears to us as a purely sophistic toying with symbols, conceived the universe as formed, like man, of the union of soul and body, and made the long contested dogma of the two natures in Christ, the human and divine, applicable also to the political conception of mankind. This theory redounded to the advantage of the pope, since the church was the soul, the state merely the body of Christendom; the pope the Vicar of Christ in all divine and eternal relations; the emperor vicar only in the state, in transient and earthly things; the former the life-giving sun; the latter merely the lesser light, the moon which irradiated the darkness of earth's night. The dualism existing between emperor and pope became a contest of principle, and the new Western power, which arose in the year 800, showed itself in the contrast which divided Latinism and Teutonism; a contrast which has influenced and still influences the whole history of Europe. These differences were, however, scarcely apparent, even in their germs, at the time of Charles the Great. Before his imperial majesty, as before that of the ancient emperors, paled the splendor of the bishop of Rome, who had knelt in adoration before him, and who, like every other bishop in the state, was his subject. After the long tumult caused by the migrations of races, Charles's coronation sealed the reconciliation of the Germans with Rome, the alliance between ancient and modern, the Latin and the German world. Germany and Italy henceforward remained the supporters of civilization. They continued reciprocally acting one upon the other during long centuries, while beside them and out of the union of the two races other prosperous nations arose, in which now the Latin, now the German, element preponderated. All the life of nations became henceforward bound together in a great concentric system of church and empire, and out of this system sprang the common civilization of the West. This dualism held humanity enthralled during so long a course of centuries, and by so strong a spell, that the political organization of antiquity can not be compared to it either in power or in duration.

Periods momentous in the history of the universe rarely inspire the wonder of contemporaries, and only succeed in obtaining full recognition from the minds of a later generation. Thus it happened with regard to the coronation of Charles the Great. From the standpoint of after ages scarcely any moment in the annals of the human race attains so high importance. It is a moment of historic creation when, out of the chaos consequent on the dissolution of antiquity and the deluge of wandering tribes, a firm continent arises, on which the history of Europe centers, moved less by mechanical laws of force than by an essentially spiritual power.

V

Rome and the New Empire

CHARLES derived the title of his empire from Rome, but the material which filled the ancient form had become essentially Teutonic; and in calling the new empire the Germanic-Roman we but give expression to the alliance of those opposing elements on which the development of Europe rested. One nationality continued the history of mankind as an unbroken inheritance; it handed the possessions of the ancient civilization, together with the ideas of Christianity, on to posterity;—the other received and resuscitated or developed both civilization and religion. Rome had drawn the German world to herself. The Roman church had subdued barbarism, had brought nations under a social system, and lastly, had united them to a common ecclesiastical-political principle, which had its seat in the Eternal City. On Byzantium now seemed to be laid the task of accomplishing the like work for the Slav nations; the task, however, remained unfulfilled, because the Byzantine Empire lacked the creative social principle possessed by the Roman church, and also because the Slav races, unfitted for the higher ideas of the state and of civilization, remained incapable of receiving the inheritance of Hellenic culture. The thought of a Slavic-Greek empire still lingers in Russia, not, however, as the national object of an imperfect development,

From book V, ch. 1, secs. 1 and 2.

but rather as the consciousness of a neglected historic opportunity which it is now no longer possible to revive.

While Byzantium was thus banished from the history of the West, Rome for the second time entered on a splendid position among the nations of the world. After the Rome of the Cæsars had destroyed the political autonomy of nations, new states had arisen through the various migrations of the peoples, and the church had proclaimed the moral equality of races, or their Christian citizenship. The ideal of a single and indivisible humanity, of the Christian republic, now appeared as the thought of a new age. The ancient capital of the restored empire, the apostolic center of the church, called herself the mother of Christian nations, and represented herself to the moral *Orbis Terrarum* [world-unity] as the *Civitas Dei* [City of God]. The first imperfect outline of a society of nations united by means of a moral idea had been advanced, but this "Holy Empire" had yet to take form; and the entire Middle Ages were, as even the present time is, nothing more than a continued struggle to give a living form to the sublime Christian ideal of the love and liberty which encompass the world.

The city likewise received a new significance within the narrower circle of her history. Her escape from the repeated attacks of the barbarians, and her final rescue from the hands of Lombards and Greeks, was a fact of historic importance. After Pipin and Charles had put an end to the final struggle of the Germans for Rome, they drew a line round the emancipated city and made the pope lord of all the territory within. The Frankish king, the new emperor, vowed as overlord to defend this ecclesiastical state dedicated to S. Peter against all foes, within and without, for no prince or people could exclusively possess Rome—the common property of mankind. In a higher sense than ancient Rome, the metropolis of Christendom represented a universal principle. She must, therefore, be free and accessible to all nations alike; the high priest within her should be subject to no king, but the supreme head of the empire and of the church—that is to say, to the emperor. It was this idea of Rome's neutrality as the ecclesiastical center of nations, up to which the waves of humanity, ceaselessly stirred by political and social storms, should never advance, that succeeded in preserving the little State of the Church for the pope until our own day, while Charles's great monarchy and a hundred kingdoms around fell to dust. Who can deny that the idea of a sacred metropolis, a temple of eternal peace in the midst of struggling humanity, a universal asylum of culture, of law, and of reconciliation is great and admirable? Had the institution of the papacy but remained devoid of ambition and worldly desire, had it escaped dogmatic stagnation, and advanced with the development of a widening life, with the social forces of the world and the discoveries of toil and culture, it would have constituted almost the highest cosmic form, in which mankind should have seen the expression of its unity and harmony. However, after the expiration of its first and most glorious period, the papacy became the essentially retarding principle in the drama of history. The greatest idea latent in the church never attained fulfilment; but that it had once existed in the papacy serves to make the papacy the most venerable of all institutions which history has beheld, and that the city of Rome was the classic receptacle of this idea suffices to secure for her the everlasting love of mankind.

Rome for the second time became the legitimate source of the empire. The great traditions of the Roman Empire as of the political order of the world, were there preserved; Charles called himself therefore emperor of the Romans since there was no other empire than that, the origin and conception of which were allied with Rome. On this account the Byzantine rulers also continue to call themselves Roman emperors. Rome, it is true, was politically a lifeless ruin, but the possession of the city by Charles was equal to the possession of a legal diploma, genuine and hallowed by antiquity. Nevertheless, the claim of Rome to be still the root of the empire would have been nothing more than an antiquarian recollection had the church not restored the conception of universality. By means of this idea Rome governed the ancient provinces of the Cæsars before Charles received the imperial crown, through which he again united these provinces in an Empire. The unity of the ancient empire was based essentially upon Roman law, but in the new the like unity was attained by the code of ecclesiastical law. Hierarchical claims replaced the political rights which the city no longer possessed, and the popes strove rapidly to remove the semblance of sovereignty which the Roman people had exercised on the occasion of Charles's election. They represented the German Cæsar as the vassal of the church, the empire as the emanation of the divine will ratified by the papal unction. Did the Romans of Charles's day but reflect on the dominion which their city exercised on the most distant countries by means of the system of the church, by the universal application of the Roman canon, by the introduction of the Latin tongue in schools, churches, synods, and secular transactions, and lastly, by the remains of classic learning and art, they must have acknowledged to themselves that, although widely different in nature, this dominion was scarcely inferior to the dominion of Trajan.

Meanwhile, Rome was only the ideal head of the empire, circumstances fortunately for mankind never allowing the city to become again its political center. Had it again attained this position, empire and papacy together would have formed an illimitable power, and Europe would have been swallowed in a hierarchical despotism more formidable than the ancient despotism of the Cæsars. Charles renounced the idea of making Rome the capital of his monarchy, and this renunciation was one of the most momentous actions in the record of history. The independent development of the Western nations, and finally that of the church, were thereby rendered possible. The forged donation of Constantine had truly anticipated the consequences in store for the papacy, if the head of the empire again made his residence in Rome. The most imminent danger threatened the Roman bishopric at the moment of the restoration of the imperium, but happily for the bishopric the peril was averted. The opposition which existed between German and Roman elements divided for ever imperial and papal power; and the antagonism between the two forces, which mutually curbed and limited one another, preserved the freedom of Europe. For, as the new emperor was the product of the conquering energy of the German race, and the pope a creation of Rome and the Latin race, it followed that these two national elements should further mould these two universal forces in themselves; that the north should develop the political, the south the spiritual institutions, Germany the empire, Rome the church. The West, according to Charles's design, was to have two centers, round which the great system of the Christian republic should revolve—the papal city and the imperial city, Rome and Aachen; while he, the emperor, was to remain sole head of the universal empire and the church.

Inward opposition, however, and the force of German individuality, which opposed the sentiment of liberty and the obstinacy of individual independence to the Roman principles of authority and system, soon shattered Charles's fabric, and the papacy rapidly fell from the pinnacle to which the pious monarch had raised it. The Germans struggled against Roman and Latin influences. In the city itself a violent conflict arose between civil aspirations and ecclesiastical immunities; and the history of the two memorable centuries contained in this volume reveals the most glaring opposition in the life of Rome until the tenth century closes with that period when the Saxons raise the papacy from the ruin into which it had fallen, and restore Charles's shattered system in a copy from which, however, the theocratic ideas have gradually disappeared before the imperialism of ancient Rome.

Charles spent the winter following his coronation in Rome, dwelling not in the ancient Palatium, which he left to its decay, but in one of the episcopal buildings (which he converted into a palace) beside S. Peter's. All the Carolingians who came to Rome made their abode in this quarter, and here the imperial legate also dwelt. The distance of Germany, and the resolve not to make his residence in Rome, prevented Charles from building any new imperial fortress. Had he built a palace of the kind, chroniclers would not have failed to mention and describe it, as they have described the palaces of Aachen and Ingelheim.

Charles the Great, sage and hero, died a few months later at Aachen, on January 28th, 814, at the age of seventy-one. The restorer of the Roman Empire was buried in the Church of S. Maria which he had built, and an ancient Roman sarcophagus, chiselled with the Rape of Prosperpine, apparently served as his coffin. If we compare one with another, the three periods of Roman history which will ever stand conspicuous as summits in the life of the people—the period of Cæsar and Augustus, when the Roman world monarchy was founded; that of Constantine, when Christianity rose to dominion; and finally, the age of Charles, when the system of Germanic-Roman civilization arose out of the ruin of the old empire—we shall find that the third does not yield in importance to either of the other two. Charles's age was fertile in new forms of life, and truly creative. It closed the period of barbarian migrations and reconciled the Germans with Rome. It did not allow antiquity—the buried treasure chamber of knowledge and culture—to be lost to impoverished humanity; but, laying prejudice aside, began to revivify it and adopt it as an essential and imperishable force in the process of intellectual development. The great tradition of the *Orbis Terrarum*, or of the unity of the world, formerly the political end and aim of the Roman Empire of the Cæsars, which arose contemporarily with Christianity, was revived in the age of Charles the Great. This age transformed the ancient imperium into the Western monarchy, which found its inmost bond of cohesion in the principle of the Christian religion. Charles was the Moses of the Middle Ages, who successfully led mankind through the deserts of barbarism and bestowed on them a new code of political, ecclesiastical, and civil constitutions. In his theocratic empire was exhibited the first attempt to establish the new federation of nations in the form of a Christian republic.

The emperor bequeathed a portion of his treasures to the twenty-one metropolitan churches of the empire. Five of these churches were in Italy: Rome, Ravenna, Milan, Aquileia, and Grado. Two silver tables—one square, and adorned with a relief of Constantinople; the other round, with a representation of Rome—formed part of the curiosities of the imperial palace. The former of these tables Charles presented to S. Peter's, the latter to Ravenna. Both monuments of early mediæval art have perished. The table presented to Rome remains unnoticed in the life of Leo the Third, although the *Liber Pontificalis* makes frequent mention of a large golden cross, another of the emperor's votive gifts. The table, however, with the relief of Rome, which, following the instructions of his father's will, the Emperor Lewis sent to the Arch-bishop Martin, reached Ravenna during the boyhood of Agnellus, and was seen by the historian.

Rome received a further bequest of valuable vessels, and thus Charles, who had endowed the church with so many privileges, such vast possessions, and so much gold and silver, was more liberal than any ruler of either earlier or later times. He was the true founder of the ecclesiastical state, and of the power of the popes, of whose later illimitable expansion, however, he never even dreamed. For, although the devout son of the church, which he recognized as the strongest bond of his empire and the divine principle of human civilization, he in no wise blindly surrendered himself to her service. He respected the immunity, which he him-self had established, of the metropolitan of Rome, but never for-got that he was ruler of the entire monarchy. His people re-garded him as the chief director of all ecclesiastical affairs; he founded bishoprics and convents; he issued canonical regulations; he instituted schools for the people, and by embodying the con-stitutions of the church in his code, gave these constitutions his supreme ratification. Both episcopate and synods stood at the same time under his determining influence.

The grateful church later invested him with the nimbus of saintship. Her struggles with the Hohenstaufens reminded her of the fact that the great monarch had been the pious founder of the ecclesiastical state, and the Crusades revived the memory of the Christian hero in the minds of men. Like Octavian or Cæsar, he had become mythical; and it was reserved for a pope from the south of France, Calixtus the Second, in 1122, to pronounce gen-uine Turpin's celebrated history of the life of Charles and Roland, of which the pope himself may possibly have been the author. The rapidity with which the figure of Charles was lost in myth is shown by a chronicler, who, writing his barbarous annals in the monastery of Soracte before the end of the tenth century, already related the story of the monarch's expedition to the Holy Sepul-chre. And as it is scarcely likely that the monk himself invented the fable, but more probably received it as an already accepted tradition, we may venture to place its origin yet half a century earlier. Meanwhile, as the Charles of history had never become nationalized in Rome, neither did the Charles of legend. A stranger like Theodoric the Great, although a Roman emperor, his figure was never associated with any place or building in the city, and he consequently faded from the memory of the Romans. It is worthy of remark that not a single word in the *Mirabilia* [a twelfth-century hagiographical guide to Rome, derived from earlier *itineraria* of pilgrims] recalls the memory of Charles the Great.

VI

The Rise of Papal Supremacy in the Ninth Century

THE personal weakness of Charles's successors, their despicable passions, their quarrels with regard to the monarchy, which was irrevocably disorganized by feudalism, had at this time greatly increased the authority of the pope. Nicholas the First united the sacred dignity with an intrepid spirit such as but few popes have possessed. Distinguished birth, physical beauty, education, as good as the times permitted, were combined in him; and since Gregory the Great no pope had been favored to such a degree by the good fortune which power attracts to itself. He succeeded in humiliating the royal as well as the episcopal power, and the enfeebled empire sank under Lewis, who had no male heir, and who, so to speak, buried it in a series of energetic but petty and endless wars in southern Italy, into a more and more empty name. Meanwhile, however, in the papacy there arose the idea of universal spiritual monarchy, which was later erected by Gregory the Seventh and perfected by Innocent the Third. The conception of Rome as the moral center of the world still lingered in imperishable tradition. The more the empire lost unity and power, and the less competent it became to form the political center of the Chris-

From book V, ch. 5, sec. 1.

tian commonwealth, the easier was it for the papacy to advance the claim which it put forth, that of being the soul and principle of the Christian republic, while the secular rulers now sank into mere changeable instruments.

From stress of circumstances, as also from a great historic impulse, the papacy had restored the Roman imperial power, and scarcely was the Empire created when the secret struggle of the spiritual against the political system began. Had the Roman emperor been able to govern as a Christian monarch like Constantine and Theodosius, had all autonomy in the provinces been suppressed, the pope might then have divided the dominion with the emperor, and, resigning to him the troublesome task of temporal government, have retained the spiritual supremacy. But within the monarchy of Charles the motive power of human nature had called into being a multitude of separate forces, all alike inimical to papacy and empire: nationalities, provincial churches, national dukes, national bishops, kings, right and liberties, privileges and immunities of every kind,—forces of natural disintegration and of German individuality which declared war to the systems. They weakened the empire, the unity of which was only mechanical and its basis of a material and changeable nature. The indivisible moral principle of the papacy, however, enabled it in spite of passing defeats, to subdue these hostile forces. Neither interrupted by time nor affected internally by political revolutions, it always conquered its opponents—royalty, episcopacy or the empire. The faith of mankind itself, the one irresistible power on earth, accepted it as the supernatural source of these institutions and as the immovable axis of the spiritual world.

In Nicholas [I] the consciousness of the monarchy of Rome found its personal expression. Although it may be asserted that the possession of the state of the church and of the city, which had been confirmed by the empire, was not essential for spiritual supremacy, it must be admitted that it strongly furthered the views of the papacy and invested them with an invaluable independence on an invaluable spot. The possession of a great kingdom in any other part of the world would never have given the papacy the foundation it possessed in the little territory which

74

had Rome for its capital. In the time of Nicholas the First the patrimonies of S. Peter were still the undisturbed property of the church, whose treasury was filled with wealth incalculable. Nicholas's predecessors had founded cities, had equipped armies and fleets, had formed an Italian league, had defended and saved Rome, and Nicholas himself ruled as king over the beautiful country which stretched from Ravenna to Terracina. It is said that Nicholas was the first among the popes to be crowned with the tiara which the unbounded arrogance of his successors afterwards surrounded with a triple crown. To the monarchic spirit of such a man the crown was nothing foreign, but Nicholas saw in it more than the symbol of the temporal state which the church acquired and soon lost. The spurious Donation of Constantine rendered good service to the claims of the popes, and the extent given to these claims by this audacious forgery shows at the same time how far-reaching were the aims of the papacy. More important, however, were the pseudo-Isidorian decretals, which incorporated in themselves that donation of territory. These memorable fabrications of several letters and decrees of bygone popes, interspersed in a collection of acts of councils, and foisted upon the celebrated Isidore of Seville, date from the middle of the ninth century. Nicholas was the first among the popes to make use of them as a code of papal rights. They furnished the church with privileges such as made it entirely independent of the state; they placed the royal power far below the papal, below even the episcopal. At the same time, however, they exalted the pope high above the episcopate as inaccessible to the decrees of the provincial synods, and represented him as the supreme judge of metropolitans and bishops whose office and power, removed from royal influence, should be subject to the papal command. In a word, they ascribed to the pope dictatorship in the ecclesiastical world. In these decretals Nicholas the First recognized the most serviceable weapons for the struggle against kings and provincial synods. Over both powers he triumphed; while the emperor, who foresaw the danger which threatened the political principle, was forced to play the part of spectator at the papal victory.

The death of this great pope (November 13th, 867) created a

profound impression. The world testified to the fear and admiration in which it had held him; those, however, who had been struck or threatened by his thunderbolts, cheerfully raised their heads, hoping for freedom and the abrogation of the papal decrees.

The choice of the Romans fell upon Adrian, the aged cardinal of S. Marcus, the son of Talarus, and a member of the same family as Stephen the Fourth and Sergius the Second. The envoys of the emperor present in Rome, offended because they had not been summoned to the election, were appeased by the explanation that the Romans had not infringed upon the rights of the crown, since although the constitution undoubtedly prescribed the imperial ratification of the elected candidate, it nowhere ordained that the election should take place under the eyes of the legates. They were tranquillized with this assurance; the emperor himself ratified the election, and Adrian the Second was consecrated pope on December 14th.

He celebrated his accession to the pontificate by an amnesty. He admitted some of the clergy excommunicated by his predecessor to his first mass, among them the notorious Cardinal Anastasius and also Teutgaud of Treves. He pardoned this repentant offender, and allotted him as dwelling a cell in the monastery of S. Andrew on the Clivus Scauri. Some of the prelates accused of high treason languished in exile. The emperor had also sent the bishops of Nepi and Velletri into banishment, an action which shows the completeness of his imperatorial power. Adrian begged for their restoration. Other Romans, laymen, had been sent to the galleys as guilty of high treason: the pope obtained their release. It appears that during the vacancy of the sacred chair many had fallen victims to accusations, false or otherwise, made to the imperial envoys. The interregnum at that time had already produced a state of anarchy, and had favored the tyranny of the powerful, of which a very surprising occurrence affords an illustration. Shortly before Adrian's consecration, Lambert, duke of Spoleto, had attacked the city. In league with the disaffected in Rome, where there dwelt many influential Lombards and Franks, some of them even bearing the ducal title, and perhaps still unaware of the ratification of the election, Lambert ventured on a measure which far outstepped the limits of his authority. This authority invested the dukes of Spoleto, in accordance with the constitution of the empire, with the right, on the death of the pope, of superintending the election of a successor; and generally speaking the duke of Spoleto appears at this time as viceroy in Roman affairs. Entering the undefended city, Lambert assumed the demeanor of a conqueror. He confiscated property belonging to the nobility and sold it or presented it to the Franks; he sacked churches and convents, and permitted his soldiers to ravish Roman maidens both in the city and neighborhood. He then retired. The pope wrote letters of complaint to the German emperor, and excommunicated all Franks and Lombards who had summoned Lambert or had taken part in the sack. This incident reveals the approaching dissolution of the Carolingian Empire. It ushers in the period of utter confusion in Italy, of the disputes of the dukes with regard to Rome, and of the war of factions in the city itself, which we shall soon have to describe.

Lewis was in southern Italy. He had issued a general summons to his Italian vassals to rise and attack the Saracens at Bari, and was on the point of beginning the campaign from Lucania. Here the complaints of the Romans reached him; he lacked the time, however, and perhaps the desire to punish Lambert by depriving him of the duchy, which he only did, and on quite other grounds, in 871.

Adrian the Second was severely tried in the early years of his pontificate by some terrible experiences. His enemies, adherents of the late pope, grudged him the tiara, and spread the report that from fear of public opinion he wished to annul the acts of his predecessor by which the papal power had risen to such a height. Adrian hastened to silence these reports; he tranquillized the Roman patriots by the assurance that he had never forsaken the path of Nicholas the First, and won their favor by ordering a public prayer for the late pope and by the solemn recognition of his decrees. Adrian further commanded the completion of the basilica which Nicholas had begun. While he thus pacified the friends of his predecessor, he irritated his enemies, who consequently gave him the ambiguous name of Nicolaite [meaning either "Nicholas's partisan" or "a married priest"].

Of this party, which was supported by the Franks, Cardinal Anastasius and his brother Eleutherius were prominent members. They belonged to the highest ranks of the nobility, and were sons of the wealthy Bishop Arsenius, who could not brook the fact that his son had been excommunicated by Leo the Fourth and his hopes of the tiara ruined by Nicholas the First. Adrian had a daughter born in lawful wedlock before he had entered holy orders. On his elevation to the papacy he betrothed the maiden to a noble Roman. Eleutherius, however, impelled either by love or by hatred, carried off the bride-elect and married her. The outraged pope, impotent to punish a powerful man who held himself entrenched within the walls of a strong palace, sent urgent letters to the emperor begging him to dispatch envoys to judge the criminal. At the same time the father of Eleutherius hastened to Benevento to win over the avaricious empress by gifts, but was there overtaken by death. The imperial missi came to Rome. Eleutherius, in a transport of rage, stabbed the daughter of the pope and her mother Stephania, who willingly or otherwise had accompanied her child. The imperialists, however, seized the murderer and beheaded him.

Moved by these events, the unfortunate Adrian summoned a synod. He renewed the excommunication against Anastasius, to whom, justly or unjustly, a share in his brother's crimes was attributed, threatening him with the anathema if he withdrew more than 40 miles from the city or usurped any ecclesiastical function. The Cardinal received the sentence on October 12th, 868, in the basilica of S. Prassede, and swore to submit to it. These events showed the height to which the defiance of the Roman nobility had attained. At the time still controlled by imperial authority, as soon as this authority was extinguished in the city, it was to assume the control over the papal chair.

VII

Urban Administration after the Revolution of 932

After Pope Adrian II's death (872), Rome fell on very evil days. The last Carolingian emperors proved incapable of preserving order in their homelands, much less in the distant city from which their empire took its name. Saracen attacks, brigandage in the countryside, feuds among the great families within Rome's walls produced complete political and economic disorder. The popes had gradually built up a principality for themselves since the eighth century, and Nicholas I and Adrian II governed this state at its height. The lands and rights of the patrimonium *Petri were largely dissipated in the early tenth century, as the papal office became a prize snatched at by the aristocratic Roman families in their private wars. Intrigues of two women, Theodora and her daughter Marozia, dominated the city. Conspiracy drove out Marozia's husband, Hugh of Provence, who held the title "King of Italy," and made her son by an earlier marriage, Alberic,* de facto *ruler of Rome. The papacy was in his gift. Gregorovius describes the revolution that brought Alberic to power.*—EDITOR.

THE changes in Rome were in no way prompted by the romantic

From book VI, ch. 2, sec. 2.

79

ideas which we shall see develop in the city at a later age. They
were essentially aristocratic, and Rome was an aristocratic republic. From the time that the popes had acquired the secular
government they had been continuously opposed by the Roman
nobility, with ever increasing success. The strong hand of the first
of the Carolingians had been able to keep the nobility in check;
the fall of the imperial power left them uncontrolled. At the end
of the ninth century they had become masters of the civic administration, and under Theodora, and still more under Marozia,
they had usurped the reins of power. The illegal influence of a
woman—an influence which had rested on the power of her
family and on her non-Roman husbands—was removed by the
revolution of 932. The same revolution had, however, raised
this woman's son to be head of the city, legalizing his power by
election and title. Depriving the pope of the secular dominion,
it bestowed it on his brother, and the revolution was at the same
time a family and a state revolution. In banishing Hugo, the Romans gave it to be understood that they no longer recognized any
foreigner, either king or emperor, as their overlord, and that they
intended to govern themselves by national institutions. Rome
made the remarkable attempt to attain political independence;
and the capital of the world suddenly entered the ranks of the
little Italian dukedoms, such as Venice, Naples, and Benevento.
The Romans wished to form, within the circuit of the various
donations which constituted the State of the Church, a free
secular state, and to limit the papal authority, as it had been limited in earlier times, entirely to spiritual matters.

The new title with which the city invested its new overlord
was neither that of consul or patricius of the Romans, titles
which, being generally in use, were commonly assigned him by
his contemporaries. The dignity of patricius at this time signified
the entire secular and judicial power in Rome. It was, however,
allied with the idea of viceroyship, such as that which the exarch
had once exercised, and therefore pointed to a supreme power
above the patriciate. The Romans would not recognize this
power, and therefore gave Alberic the title of *princeps atque omnium Romanorum senator* [prince and senator of all Romans],

and Alberic signed his acts according to the style of the period: "We, Alberic, by the grace of God, humble prince and senator of all the Romans." Of these associated dignities only the title of princeps was new to Rome. It was a political title, and denoted the declaration of independence made by the city and the Roman state, as also the elevation of Alberic to the dignity of prince. In the same way Arichis of Benevento had assumed the title of princeps when, after the fall of Pavia, he declared himself an independent prince. The kingship being separated from the papacy, this title signified the power of the temporal prince in opposition to the spiritual, in possession of which the pope remained. It was therefore placed in an emphatic position before the title of senator, and it appears that in diplomas and chronicles the title *senator* is occasionally absent. Neither is it found on the Roman coins of Alberic. The entirely civic dignity of a "senator of the Romans" had been borne by Theophylact; but it was probably now increased by the addition of "all," and Alberic was herewith acknowledged as head of the city and people.

No trace is to be discovered of the existence of the Roman Senate in the eighth century: nor even during the Carolingian period does it show any sign of life. We find the word "Senatus" all the more frequently used in a general sense, however, among historians of the ninth and tenth centuries, and also in documents. Since the Roman Empire had been restored, and the ancient titles of imperator and augustus, and even the specification of the emperors' post-consulates had been revived, reminiscences of antiquity were increasingly awakened; and if the Frankish optimates were glad to call themselves "Senatus," how much more eagerly must the Roman nobility have seized on the title. It therefore came so generally into use that we read it even in the acts of a council, where it is decreed that the pope shall be elected by the assembled clergy on the motion of the Senate and people. The views, however, of those writers, who inferred the continued existence of the Senate in the tenth century from the survival of the ancient name, are no longer tenable. The existence of a Senate implies the existence of actual senators, or individual members who called and signed themselves senators; but al-

though we find Romans subscribing themselves as consul and
dux in numberless documents, both before and after this period,
we have discovered none in which a Roman calls himself "sena-
ator." The title appears only in a collective sense, and is used of
the Senate in general, of the noble senators, *i.e.* of the great
men of the city. Theophylact [Theodora's husband] was the
first Roman who, since the extinction of the ancient Senate,
called himself senator of the Romans; and the addition of "all"
shows that there is no thought of a formally constituted Senate.
At the same time we do not believe that the title senator in
Alberic's case corresponds to "senior" or "signor," but that it was
used to express more definitely his municipal power. While the
Romans made over the consulate to Alberic for life, they expressed his enlarged authority within the new Roman republic
by conferring on him the title of "senator of all the Romans";
and we must not overlook the fact that in later times also Rome
had frequently no more than one senator. This title was, moreover, hereditary in Alberic's family and in none other. Even the
women bore it. His aunt, the younger Theodora, and her daughters, Marozia and Stephania, were called *senatrix*, and even
bore the full title *omnium Romanorum*. Thus, curiously enough,
women in Rome were called senatrix, while at the same time no
man bore the title senator save Alberic, and afterwards his descendant, Gregory of Tusculum.

The dominion of Alberic therefore rested mainly on the aristocracy; its most secure foundation was the power of his own family.
His father's services were not forgotten; his father [also named
Alberic], however, in his later days had become an enemy of
Rome, and had always been an intruder; and the young prince
was therefore never spoken as the son of Alberic, but always as
the son of Marozia. For Marozia was for some time the head of
the family which was afterwards named the Tusculan, and it was
essentially from her that Alberic inherited his power. The house
of Marozia (she herself disappears from history, and her end is
unknown) embraced through marriage-alliances many other families in the city and its territory. Alberic, powerful in Rome
through his wealth, his vassals and the possession of S. Angelo,

attracted the other nobles by the hope of the common advantage of independence. He endowed them with the highest offices in the administration, and perhaps also with property belonging to the church. The circle of those on whom the government devolved, or who possessed a right to take part in public affairs, could now be determined. All definite information regarding Alberic's institutions, however, fail us. We hear neither of a Senate on the Capitol, nor of new magistrates. Neither patricius nor prefect is named, for Alberic united the authority of both in his own person. Neither can we suppose the existence of any civic constitution in the sense of later times. Nobles and burghers had not yet appeared in the light of opposing factions, and it was only out of such an opposition that these constitutions arose. In a city without trade and without industries, a city filled and ruled by priests, there could scarcely be a burgher class. It possessed only clergy, nobles and populace. The cultivated and active middle class, upon which civic freedom and power depend, was absent in Rome. We have read attentively the documents of the period to try to discover some traces of the life of the Roman burgher. We have here and there found witnesses adduced with the epithet of their industries, such as *lanista, opifex, candicator, sutor, negotiator*. The thought never occurred to the wool-worker, the goldsmith, the blacksmith, the artisan or the merchant, that he also had a right to a share in the civic government. Only on the occasion of the papal election did the burghers raise their voices in acclamation. They assembled in the scholæ or artes, which continued to exist under their priors, to discuss matters touching their own interests. They were dependent on the nobles, whose clients, like the coloni or farmers, they often were, and who stood to them in the oppressive relationship of patrons and creditors. The new ruler of Rome must, however, have bestowed privileges upon them connected with their guilds. The lower class, lastly, though essentially dependent on the church and its liberality, was glad to change its ruler, and willingly obeyed a Roman prince, who was powerful, young, liberal, and of handsome and commanding presence. And since otherwise in the disturbed condition of affairs Alberic would never have been able to retain his authority so long, the iron hand of the young ruler repressed the tumults and protected the burghers against the oppression of the powerful.

In order to strengthen his position, he was obliged to direct his attention chiefly to the organization of the military power. The militia of Rome still existed as scholæ, as is shown by the formula retained in contracts, where the tenant is forbidden to transfer real estate to religious places or to the *numerus, seu bandus militum.* Alberic secured the adhesion of the city militia by taking it under his management and pay. He strengthened and organized it afresh, and perhaps to him was due a new division of the city into twelve regions, each of which comprised a militia regiment under a standard-bearer. As we shall presently see, the city militia gained increased importance after his time. He made use of this force to defend himself against the intrigues of the hostile clergy and the jealous nobles, as well as against Hugo's attempts. The Roman nobility, clergy and people took the oath of obedience, and henceforth this intrepid man appears as monarch of the city and of the territory belonging to it.

His diplomas were dated, according to custom, with the pontificate and year of the pope; the papal money, however, was stamped with his name, as it had formerly been with the name of the emperor. The extent of his power is no less recognizable in his judicial acts. It had been previously the custom to hold courts of justice in the Lateran or Vatican, in presence of the pope, the emperor, or the imperial missi. No sooner, however, had Alberic deprived the pope of the temporal power, than the tribunal of the princeps of Rome became the highest judicial court. The princeps continued to hold courts of justice at various places; but it is significant of the change of affairs that he also instituted a tribunal in his own palace. Although he owned the palace on the Aventine which had been his birthplace, he nevertheless dwelt in the Via Lata, beside the Church of the Apostles, and apparently on the spot now occupied by the Palazzo Colonna, whose owners (the present Colonna family) claim the princeps as their ancestor. We have already spoken of this quarter as the most aristocratic in the city. It was the quarter of the nobility, the most

84

animated part of Rome, and was surrounded by magnificent ruins, not only those of the Baths of Constantine, but also those of the forum of Trajan, and was adjoined by the Via Lata, which included the upper part of the present Corso.

A document which still exists records a placitum held by Alberic in his palace. On August 17, 942, Leo, Abbot of Subiaco, appeared before him in a dispute concerning the monastery. The following were the judges of Alberic's curia: Marinus, bishop of Polimartium and Bibliothecarius, the Primicerius Nicholas, the Secundicerius George, the Arcarius Andrew, the Saccellarius, the protoscrinarius of the apostolic chair, together with the most prominent nobles of the city; Benedict called Campanino (that is to say, count in the Campagna), probably a relative of Alberic, Kaloleo, the Dux Gregorius de Cannapara, the Vestararius Theophylact, the Superista John, Demetrius son of Meliosus, Balduin, Franco, Gregory of the Aventine, Benedict Miccino, Crescentius, Benedict de Flumine, Benedict de Leone de Ata, the Dux Adrian, Benedict, the son of Sergius, and others. Two distinct classes of judges are here evident. To the first class belonged, as previously, the ministers of the papal palace, prelates, who soon after the time of Alberic were called *judices ordinarii*. The princeps of the Romans then accepted the papal organization of justice unaltered. The second class was formed as before by the city nobility, who now, however, appeared as curiales or courtiers of the prince. These nobles were obliged to appear at these courts of justice as assessors, a duty which was often very irksome. Permanent assessors, such as the French *scabini* or the later *judices dativi*, did not as yet exist. The "optimates" were therefore actual judges who pronounced sentence, or were present in the capacity of *boni homines*.

VIII

Character of the Ottonian Empire

Sensing that his own death was near, Alberic had the Romans promise to elect his son, Octavian, as pope when the incumbent, Agapetus II, died. Octavian succeeded his father as "senator of all the Romans" in 954, and, on Agapetus's death, he became pope as John XII (955–64). Reversing Alberic's policies, John invited Otto I, the German king, to go to Rome as the pope's ally against local enemies. Otto entered Rome in 962, and, by coronation, revived the empire of Charlemagne.—EDITOR.

OTTO and Adelaide were crowned at S. Peter's with unexampled pomp. After an interval of thirty-seven years the empire was again revived, and, withdrawn from the Italian nation, was restored in the foreign race of the Saxon kings. One of Charles's greatest successors was crowned by a Roman, who curiously enough bore the name Octavianus. But the momentous transaction was devoid of all true dignity and consecration. Charles the Great had received the imperial crown at the hands of an honored and venerable man. Otto the Great was anointed by an undisciplined boy. Meanwhile the history of Germany and Italy was by means of this coronation diverted into a new path.

From book VI, ch. 3, sec. 1.

Character of the Ottonian Empire

The empire of Charles when called into existence had possessed a lofty justification in the imagination of mankind. The
great Frankish monarchy, in which nationalities still stood weak
beside each other, had been conceived under the form of the
new Christian republic. The emancipation of the city from the
dominion of Byzantium, the necessity of opposing a strong Christian power to the formidable dominion of Islam, and the needs
of the papacy, had contributed to the foundation of imperial
power. But this theocratic empire fell by the pressure of its inward development. The ferment in society, where old and new,
Roman and Teutonic elements, mixed together, divided the second empire. The feudal system transformed officials into local
hereditary princes; secular and religious power were united. A
permanent revolution in possession and right was generated in
the body corporate of the monarchy, and the subdivision of
estates amongst the heirs hastened its decay. Nationalities suddenly began to separate from one another; the center of Europe
fell into two hostile divisions, and after one hundred and fifty
years of existence, the empire was dissolved and reduced to the
chaotic state, which resembled the conditions that had prevailed
before it had arisen: the pressure of new barbarians, of Normans,
Hungarians, Slavs and Saracens; the devastations of provinces,
the overthrow of learning and art, the barbarism of manners,
the relapse of the church into the state in which it had been sunk
before the time of Charles; the enervation of the papacy, which
had lost its spiritual power, and the state created for it by Pipin
and Charles, and a choas of aristrocratic factions in Rome, more
dangerous than that which had existed in the time of Leo the
Third. The Italians, it is true, had attempted to make the Roman
imperium a national institution. Their attempt had, however,
failed, and the papacy itself sought its salvation in the restoration of the imperium through a foreign princely house which
stood far from Italy and Rome.

The Roman Empire was now restored by the German nation,
but mankind could no longer return to the ideas which had prevailed in the time of Charles. The tradition of the empire did
indeed still powerfully survive. Many voices were heard in Ger-

many lamenting its fall and desiring its restoration as a benefit to the world. The reverence of mankind for the institution, however, had been diminished by its unfortunate history of a century and a half. The unity and cohesion of Charles's monarchy endured no longer. France, Germany and Italy were already separate countries, each striving after independence in its political forms. While Otto the First now restored the empire, it became clear that the task was one which none but a great man could accomplish; that a weakling could not sustain the struggle against the feudal system, the papacy, and national tendencies. The empire was therefore restored only in an ideal and artificial, though also in a great political form. The conqueror of the Hungarians, the Slavs and the Danes, the protector of France and Burgundy, the lord of Italy, the heroic missionary of Christianity, to which he had opened a new and wider field, deserved to be a new Charles. His country was always called the land of the Franks, and his German tongue the Frankish. He now brought the Roman imperial power to the German nation, and this energetic people took to itself the honorable but thankless task of becoming the Atlas of universal history. The influence of Germany soon brought about the reform of the church and the restoration of learning, while in Italy itself it was the German elements which fostered the city republics. Germany and Italy indeed, the purest representatives of the antique and the German character, the fairest provinces in the kingdom of the human intellect, have been brought by a historic necessity into this lasting connection. When we consider it is essentially to the connection of Germany with Italy that mankind owes the foundations of universal European culture, we ought hardly to regret that the Roman Empire was imposed like a destiny upon Germany, causing her for centuries to shed her blood on the other side of the Alps.

IX

Culture in Tenth-century Rome

THE number of ancient buildings was still immense. The greater part of the triumphal arches, porticos, theaters, baths and temples existed as magnificent ruins, and at every step displayed to living generations the greatness of the past, the insignificance of the present. And it is solely by means of this antique character— a character which dominated the city throughout the entire Middle Ages—that many historic phenomena can be explained. Since the days of Totila no enemy had injured Rome; no emperor or pope, however, had protected the monuments. Charles the Great had already carried off columns and sculptures to Aachen, and the popes, who at first looked on the ancient monuments as the property of the city, had soon neither mind nor time nor power to trouble themselves about their existence. The Romans were left at liberty to plunder the city; priests purloined columns and marbles for their churches, nobles and clergy built towers upon the splendid buildings of antiquity; the burghers erected their forges, looms and spinning factories in bath and circus. When the fisherman of the Tiber offered his spoils for sale on the bridges, or the butcher displayed his meat, or the baker his loaves, in the theater of Marcellus, these wares were exposed on blocks of rarest marble, which had once perhaps served as seats in theater

From book VI, ch. 7, secs. 4, 1, and 2.

or circus for the rulers of the world, for Cæsar, Mark Antony or Augustus, and for many a consul and senator. The sarcophagi of heroes were employed as cisterns, washtubs, or troughs for swine, even as they are today. The table of the shoemaker or the tailor may with equal likelihood have been the cippus of some illustrious Roman, or a slab of alabaster at which some noble matron had performed her toilette in days long past. Although in the tenth century the city probably retained but few of her ancient statues in bronze, the number of marble statues must still have been considerable. In almost every street or square the eye must have rested on the prostrate or mutilated works of ancient art; and porticos, theaters, and baths had not even yet so hopelessly degenerated into dustheaps as to have become completely divested of all their sculptured ornament. Statues of emperors and illustrious Romans stood or lay uncovered on the ground; many ancient frescoes still remained on the walls. The feeling for works of art, however, was so utterly extinct that no author of the time accords them a single word. The Romans themselves regarded them simply as serviceable material. For centuries the city had resembled a vast limekiln into which the costliest marble was thrown and there reduced to mortar. It is not without reason that in diplomas of the tenth and eleventh centuries names such as Calcarius, the limeburner, are of frequent occurrence. These names were not used to denote the occupation of their owners, but as signifying that these men were the possessors of, or lived beside, limekilns. Thus, for centuries, Romans sacked and destroyed their ancient city, cutting and breaking it to pieces, burning and transforming it; yet there was always something remaining. . . .

WE dedicate the last chapter of this book to the survey of intellectual culture in the tenth century, and shall close it with a glance at the outward aspect of the city. At scarcely any other period could the barbarism of Rome have been equally great, and since the causes of this barbarism are clear, we can scarcely be surprised at the results. In the age of the Borgias and the Medicis, moral corruption was veiled by an outward show of

90

classic culture; the vices of the church were hidden behind the tapestries of Raphael; but in the tenth century all show of outward beauty was unknown. The portrait of John the Twelfth was as essentially different from that of his remote successor Alexander the Sixth, as was the tenth from the fifteenth century. In the age of Charles, the West, struggling to recover the possession of antique culture, was lighted by a gleam of learning and of art. Poetry, painting and architecture were cultivated. Ancient works were diligently studied and transcribed in legible characters. On the fall of the Carolingian Empire, Saracens, Normans and Hungarians invaded the West; the papacy became transformed into a Roman barony, and the Western world relapsed into barbarism.

The ignorance which prevailed among the clergy throughout the whole of Italy was more especially conspicuous in Rome. At Rheims the Gallic bishops declared that "there is no one at present in Rome who has studied the sciences, without a knowledge of which, as it is written, a man is incapable of being even a doorkeeper. The ignorance of other priests is in some degree pardonable when compared with that of the bishop of Rome. In the bishop of Rome, however, ignorance is not to be endured, since he has to judge in matters of faith, mode of life and discipline, the clergy, and in short the universal Catholic church." The papacy defended itself from this attack through Leo, the apostolic legate and abbot of S. Boniface, as follows:

The representatives of S. Peter and his disciples will neither have Plato, Virgil nor Terence as their masters, nor the rest of the philosophic cattle, who, like the birds in the air, soar in haughty flight, like the fish of the sea disappear in the deep, and like sheep graze on the earth step by step. And therefore you say that those who are not fed with such poetry should never even be invested with the rank of doorkeeper. I tell you, however, this assertion is a lie. Peter knew nothing of these things, and he was appointed doorkeeper of heaven, and the Lord himself said to him: "I will give thee the keys of the kingdom of heaven." His representatives and disciples are therefore instructed in apostolic and evangelical teaching. They are not, however, adorned with the parade of eloquence, but with the sense and understanding of the word. It is written that God chooses the simple of the world to put to shame the mighty, and from the beginning of the world God has not chosen philosophers and orators, but the illiterate and unlearned.

Such was the bold avowal of the papal Curia in the tenth century. The church openly confessed her ignorance of humane learning and even her contempt for philosophy; she denied S. Paul, the learned doctor of the world, but pointed out how the ignorant fisherman Peter possessed the keys of heaven. The educated bishops of Gaul and Germany finally laid down their spiritual arms before the rock of Peter.

Together with the convents, where for a time the Benedictines had cultivated learning, schools also fell to decay. Even the school for choristers at the Lateran, which from the time of Gregory the Great may be regarded as the religious university of the city, must have sunk to the lowest depth, if indeed it still existed. The libraries mouldered to decay, the monks were scattered or worked no longer. If any possessed of literary tastes still remained, they were prevented from writing by the dearth of paper. For since Egypt, the ancient home of the papyrus, had fallen into the power of the Arabs, the scarcity of writing material had been keenly felt in Italy, and to this cause Muratori in part ascribes the intellectual barbarism of the tenth century. The production of manuscripts was exorbitantly dear; consequently throughout Italy parchments already written on were utilized, the original contents having previously been erased in order that the parchment might serve a second time. To these palimpsests, unfortunately, we more frequently owe the loss than the preservation of the writers of antiquity. The ignorant monk destroyed the books of Livy, Cicero or Aristotle, and upon the leaves, from which he had erased the wisdom of antiquity, wrote antiphonaries or lives of the saints. The manuscripts of the past were thus transformed like its temples. The goddess who had inhabited a splendid pillared portico made way (paganism having been expunged) for a martyr; the sublime ideas of Plato were wiped from the parchment and their place was usurped by the canon of the Mass. Neither do we hear of libraries or copyists in Rome at a time when both in Germany and France infinite pains were expended on the collection of books.

The learning of the clergy was limited to the study of the Creed, the Gospel and of the Epistles, if indeed they could either read or explain them. Mathematics, astronomy and physics gave no evidence of life. Classic culture was reduced to the scanty idea of "grammar." An age, the writings of which were nothing but a continued abuse of grammar, and whose very language arose from the complete dissolution of all laws that governed the Latin tongue, truly demanded no learning of a high order. Grammar was, however, still taught in Rome, and from time to time we encounter the title "grammaticus," a title which had been borne by Leo the Eighth. The insecurity of the prevailing conditions, party strife and revolutions prevented the success of any literary institution in Rome, if the thought of any such institution were cherished. On the other hand, however, the survival of a Roman school of law is unquestionable, more especially in a period when the *lex Romana* obtained new luster and the Roman judges received the code of Justinian with solemn ceremonial, in order to judge Rome, Trastevere, and the universe in accordance with its institutions. Although the *Graphia* describes this and other formalities of Otto's court with minuteness, and speaks of various court officials, it mentions neither doctors of law, scholars, nor grammarians. It speaks, however, of the theater as of a pageant necessary to the court.

The passion for theatricals, formerly so predominant in Rome, began to revive during the Carolingian period in the guise of Christian festivals. Scenic plays, though condemned by the church as works of the devil, had everywhere survived. Terence was studied wherever classic antiquity was cherished, and Roswita of Gandersheim wrote her Latin dramas or moralities on purpose that they might supplant the pagan Terence in the hands of her nuns. The Vatican still preserves as a highly valued treasure a manuscript of Terence of the ninth century. Its miniature imitations of classic art represent scenes from the comedies of the poet; the name of its compiler (Hrodgarius) seems, however, to point to France as the country to which the manuscript owed its origin. It is a fact that plays were acted in northern Italy in the tenth century; and at a time when so many Greek expressions were in vogue, the actors were called Thymelici. And thus, in an age when the Greek tragedies themselves were forgotten, the Thymele of the stage of Sophocles lent its name to comedians. Atto of Vercelli complained of the sympathy shown by the clergy for theatrical representations. He counsels them to rise from table as soon as the Thymelici enter, and informs us that at ancient banquets the guests were always entertained with mimes; that plays were acted at marriage festivals, and further, that such entertainments were general, and that it was usual to give them in Easter week. Throughout Christendom the story of the Passion and other Biblical representations were represented at this season. Profane dramas also were acted on festival occasions. If such representations took place in northern Italy, we may assume that they were also given in Rome. It is doubtful, however, whether comedies of Terence or Plautus were there enacted, the immediate neighborhood of the saints probably preventing these masterpieces being represented even as a luxury of the court in the palace of Otto the Third. Of games in the amphitheater or of the chase of animals we hear nothing. Gladiators and venatores were merely remembered as antiquities. Mimes, singers, actors, and dancers, however, undoubtedly existed, and we may suppose that they appeared not in churches and palaces alone, but also occasionally acted in the Colosseum, or in the ruins of some theater, as they do in the arena at Verona, or in the Mausoleum of Augustus in Rome at the present day. The *Graphia* has dedicated two paragraphs to theatrical amusements; the only notice of the drama since the days of Cassiodorus. Poets, comedians, tragedians, scenery, orchestra, histriones, saltatores, and gladiators are enumerated, and the expression "thymelic" then actually current shows that the amusements here mentioned were something more than antiquarian recollections. It is not too much to assert that mythological scenes were represented at the courts of Hugo, Marozia, and Alberic, and if John the Twelfth drank to the health of Venus and Apollo in a boisterous freak, his imagination was at the time probably excited by some theatrical performances in the Lateran in which these pagan deities had been represented.

With regard to classic literature the Romans aways possessed
the advantage of retaining the heritage of their ancient speech,
and the further advantage of having a key to it in their vulgar
tongue. While acquaintance with the ancients, both in France
and Germany, remained exclusively the hard-won acquisition of
the learned, a possession in which the people claimed no share,
it cost Romans of the tenth century but little effort to understand
the language of their ancestors, even when the sense of the words
had become obscure. The writings and documents of the tenth
century clearly show that the vulgar tongue had made a great
stride towards the formation of the Italian language, and for the
first time we find the "lingua volgare" spoken of in Rome as a
distinct language side by side with Latin. The epitaph of Gregory
the Fifth extols him as having been able to instruct the people in
three languages—German, Latin, and the vulgar tongue. This
was spoken even by the learned, and John the Twelfth, as a Roman noble, was apparently unable to express himself fluently in
any language but the Italian. Although Latin remained the language of literature, religion, and jurisprudence, it disappeared
from common use, and the few authors of the time laboriously
struggled against the adoption of Italian, into which, owing to
its close resemblance to Latin, their pens frequently strayed.
Precisely on this account, acquaintance with ancient authors was
easy to the Italians. And although Horace, Virgil, and Statius
were no longer recited in the Forum of Trajan, they were still
explained by the grammarians in their schools, miserable though
these schools may have been.

After the revival of learning under the Carolingians, acquaintance with the ancient poets was esteemed a necessity of literary
education, and the schools founded by the Carolingian princes
in Italy cultivated a knowledge of classics. At the end of the tenth
century a curious case, which made a sensation in Ravenna, shows
the zeal with which the study of the ancients was occasionally cultivated. The Scholasticus Vilgard was so deeply enamored of
Virgil, Horace, and Juvenal, that these poets appeared to him in a
dream and promised him immortality. He openly avowed that
their teachings possessed the strength of articles of faith, and he

was consequently summoned as a pagan before the spiritual tribunal. These refined studies were diligently pursued in Germany. Otto the First, it is true, spoke scarcely any Latin; his son and grandson, however, were thoroughly versed in ancient literature, and his brother, the Archbishop Bruno, a Saxon Mæcenas, restored the palace schools of Charles, and even surrounded himself with Greek grammarians. Among Roman matrons Imiza, to whom Gerbert wrote various letters, appears as the sole instance of an educated woman of the time. Other Italian women of noble family were *literæ nesciæ*, ignorant of writing, while in Germany, Hedwig of Swabia read Virgil and Horace with the monk Ekhard, and maidens of noble birth were unwillingly forced to study the —to them unintelligible—classics in the convent schools of Gandersheim and Quedlinburg. Although they remained ignorant of the geography and history of their native country, they were made acquainted through Virgil with the most fabulous districts of Italy. The German nun, Roswita, wrote Latin epics and dramas, and Adelaide, as well as Theophano, might have challenged comparison with the Lombard princess, Adalberga. Rome thus derived no advantage from her familiarity with the classic languages, and in education Roman society remained behind that of either Germany or France. While Otto the Third proposed to restore the empire of the philosopher, Marcus Aurelius, the Romans believed that the equestrian statue of this emperor was that of a peasant who had taken a king unawares and made him a prisoner. And although fables may remain the peculiar possession of the uneducated, the muse of literature has nevertheless a perfect right to complain of the ignorance which prevailed in Rome, where, throughout the entire course of the tenth century, not one single name appears conspicuous for talent or literary attainments.

Meanwhile foreigners like Ratherius of Verona, an errant native of Liége, who owed his learning to the monastic school of Laubes, or natives like Atto of Vercelli, the panegyrist of Berengar, and Liutprand of Cremona, rose to fame in Lombardy. Each of these men shows a pedantic erudition, and their writings, both in poetry and prose, are adorned with fragments from the classics—fragments which look as completely out of place as the remains of friezes and columns inserted in the churches and palaces of the Middle Ages. The same characteristics are found in John Diaconus, the biographer of Gregory, and also in some Roman authors of the tenth century. They are also displayed in Otto the Third, by whom fragments of the Roman Empire, titles, vestments, ideas were eagerly adopted into the mediæval state, where they appeared as a complete patchwork of the classics. The robe worn by the age was coarse in material, but adorned by antique trimmings and figures. The passion for ennobling a barbarous time with recollections of the past was universal. From the days of Charles onwards, passages from Virgil or Statius had been recited with enthusiasm, and the art of making verse was so common in the time of the panegyrist of Berengar, that in the opening of his poem the author makes an apology, saying that in those days there was no demand for poetry, since verses were written in the country as well as in the towns. Meanwhile in Rome the sole evidences of poetry were found on gravestones, the doors of churches, or in tribunes, which were as formerly covered with couplets. Some of these verses were barbarous in the extreme, a few tolerable, as, for example, the epitaphs of the Crescentii. The striving after florid excess is everywhere evident; the turn of thought heavy and mystic as the time itself. The authors of these verses were probably laymen or grammarians rather than clerics.

The light of human culture, nevertheless, can never be entirely quenched. Not the fall of the Roman Empire, nor the ravages of wandering barbarians, nor the first pious fury of Christendom, were able utterly to extinguish the sacred fire of Greece. Learning seems occasionally to flow in secret channels below the surface of history, coming to light unexpectedly in an apparently erratic manner, and, like a spring, quickening a succession of minds into life. When the intellectual work of Charles's age seemed to have perished under a fresh inroad of barbarism, Germany and England suddenly became centers of a new intellectual movement, and the reform of monasticism issued from France.

Odo of Cluny was not merely a saint such as Romuald, he was a scholar who had studied philosophy, grammar, music, and poetry at Rheims. In reforming Roman monasticism he must have furthered the restoration of ecclesiastical learning, for, since education and schools were in the hands of the monks, they must have shared the reform which overtook the order. It is true that we know nothing of any papal decree concerning convent or parish schools at this date, such as the decrees promulgated by Ratherius and Atto in Lombardy; we may, however, assume that such were issued by the better popes in the days of Alberic. Learning slowly returned to the Roman monasteries, and we have already seen a monastery on the Aventine distinguished as a center round which pious monks gathered. These enthusiasts, with their title of "Simple" or "Silent," offered by their learning no contradiction to the audacious apology for ignorance which their Abbot Leo Simplex made on the score of Rome's divine rights. Their influence, nevertheless, contributed to the restoration of the more serious occupations on the part of the monks.

The terrible darkness in which Rome had lain had been already interrupted in the latter part of the tenth century. The succession of obscure popes had come to an end, and a German and a Frenchman had swept away the barbarism which had so long prevailed at the Lateran. Had the cultivated Gregory the Fifth been granted a longer and more tranquil reign, he would doubtless have directed his energies towards the reform of scientific learning. Sylvester the Second would have been still more zealous in the same task. Gerbert [of Aurillac, Pope Sylvester II] in Rome is like a solitary torch in the darkness of the night. The century of the grossest ignorance closed strangely enough with the appearance of a renowned genius; and the eleventh was opened by the same Sylvester as by a prophet, foreseeing, as he did, the Crusades which were to follow. Rome, it is true, can merely claim the honor of having served, during some unquiet years, as the scene of his studies, which here met with no response. If the Romans noticed their aged pope watching the stars from his observatory in a tower of the Lateran, or surrounded in his study by parchments and drawing geometrical figures, designing a sundial with his own hand, or studying astronomy on a globe covered with horse's skin, they probably believed him in league with the devil. A second Ptolemy seemed to wear the tiara, and the figure of Sylvester the Second marks a fresh period in the Middle Ages, that of the scholastics.

The knowledge of Greek philosophy—and the fact redounds to the honor of Rome—was acquired by the pope through the medium of one of the last of the ancient Romans—that is to say, through Bœthius. Bœthius's translations of and commentaries on the works of Aristotle and Plato, as also his versions of the mathematicians Archimedes, Euclid, and Nicomachus, served to keep alive the fame of the senator. In the tenth century Bœthius shone as a star of the first magnitude. He was studied as eagerly as Terence or Virgil. His *Consolation* [of *Philosophy*] can be recognized as the model of the writings of Liutprand, who, like him, mingled verses with prose. Alfred the Great translated the works of Bœthius into Anglo-Saxon, and commentaries upon them were later written by Thomas of Aquino. Gerbert himself united, like Bœthius, a multitude of gifts and attainments. He honored his teacher in a panegyric in verse, and it is curious to note that the writing of the poem was prompted by Otto the Third. The same emperor who brought the ashes of Bartholomew from Benevento, who laid the relics of Adalbert in the basilica at Rome, erected a marble statue to the philosopher Bœthius at Pavia, for which Gerbert [Pope Sylvester II] apparently wrote some verses.

Italian annalists produced some works even in the tenth century, and the books written by Liutprand in northern Italy are not devoid of life and spirit. Venice brought forth her earliest chronicle, the valuable work of the Deacon John, minister of Pier' Orseolo the Second. The continuation of the history of Paul Diaconus, known under the name of the *Chronicle of the Anonymous of Salerno*, was compiled in Campania. Even in Rome and its neighborhood some historic records were collected, and Benedict of the monastery of S. Andrew in Flumine below Soracte wrote a chronicle during the time of the Ottos. The ignorant monk determined to compile a universal history, the first part of which he pieced together from various sources, such as Anastasius, Bede, Paul Diaconus, and Eginhard, as well as some chroniclers of Germany and Italy. For times nearer his own, besides the continuation of the *Liber Pontificalis*, he made use of all the information that reached his ears; for he could have been an eyewitness of but comparatively few events. His information concerning contemporary occurrences is of doubtful value, and is frequently drawn from untrustworthy sources. Benedict's chronicle—a piece of barbarous patchwork—marks the lowest depth of decadence to which the tongue of Cicero could reach. Had the author but written Italian as he spoke it, the work would have formed a valuable monument of the *lingua volgare* of the time. He wished, however, to write Latin, and consequently produced an absurdity. His chronicle is not, therefore, of the same use to the philologist who is studying the rise of the Italian language, as other writings, more especially other documents of the same time. The Latin language in this chronicle, and perhaps also in that of Andrew of Bergamo, reminds us of the rude ecclesiastical ornamental sculptures of the tenth and eleventh centuries, in which the natural outlines are set at naught in every leaf and every figure.

Benedict made use of the tract of an imperialist contemporary entitled, *Of the Imperial power in the City of Rome*. This remarkable production glorifies the imperium of the Carolingians, describes the nature of the imperial power over Rome, and laments its decline through the coronation of Charles the Bald. The author falls into various errors when speaking of the condition of the city before the time of Charles the Great, and also awakens many doubts. The scrappy style of the production is barbarous; the language, however, is readable, and it is probable that the author was not a Roman, but a Lombard, writing either in the imperial monastery of Farfa, or in the convent on Soracte, before the restoration of the imperium by Otto the First. If written in Farfa, however, it was probably the solitary product of this utterly corrupt monastery in the tenth century, since it is only after the restoration of the order that we are able in the eleventh century to extol the exertions of the Abbot Hugo, and the great activity of Gregory of Catania in the cause of literature.

In Rome itself the invaluable *Liber Pontificalis*, which was interrupted at the life of Stephen the Fifth, was continued in the tenth century in the form of short tables, called catalogues. As there were no longer buildings or votive gifts to be described, these catalogues briefly give us the names, descent, and length of reigns of the popes, and add some meager accounts of isolated events. Nothing shows more clearly the barbarism of Rome in the tenth century than the continuation of the celebrated *Liber Pontificalis*, which now sinks back to the level of its first beginnings. . . .

X

Rome in the
Early Eleventh Century

THE eleventh century forms one of the most important epochs in the annals of the papacy. A greater contrast between the utter decay and the sudden revival of the same power is nowhere else encountered in history. The extinction of the house of Otto was succeeded by conditions which resembled the conditions that had followed the extinction of the Carolingian Empire. The papal power sank both morally and politically, while the city exerted itself to obtain its final emancipation from the papal yoke. Its efforts proved unsuccessful, since the papacy remained an indestructible principle hostile to civic development, a principle which could only be temporarily repressed but could never be removed, and which, through the aid of foreign powers, was always able to recover its ascendency. In Rome no burgher class existed sufficiently strong to form a firm foundation for a secular constitution. There still remained merely the powerful noble families, the captains or great feudal vassals of the church in city and country, who snatched the power from the pope, to quarrel for it among themselves. These men ruled Rome as patricians in the first half of the eleventh century; they appointed popes from amongst their relatives, and made the sacred chair a family possession, and

From book VII, ch. 1, sec. 1.

the papacy fell into a condition of such utter barbarism that the times of the most infamous emperors of antiquity seemed to have been renewed. Then followed, however, that memorable reaction which, with marvellous rapidity, raised the Roman church into a cosmopolitan power.

Civic affairs contributed very materially to work this result; the city itself providing the immediate causes for far-reaching movements. Its existing relations to the emperors and the popes, even the events which occurred within the narrow circuit of its walls, its opposition to the spiritual dominion, the difficulty in which the popes were placed through the civic nobility, the permanent condition of indigence, self-defense, and vigilance in which they were kept, all these causes contributed to produce more or less remote effects and widespread political results. We may assert that, without the constant opposition of the city of Rome to the spiritual government, the history of the papacy would not have followed the course which it took both before and after Gregory VII.

The conception of the Roman patriciate from the eleventh century onwards became of worldwide importance. It invested the German kings, who snatched it from the Roman nobility and allied it to their crown, with power over the city and the right of nomination to the sacred chair. It therefore became the foremost object of the struggle between the church—struggling to obtain her emancipation—and the state. The church had scarcely entered on the path of inward reform when she strove with all her power to throw off the yoke of the Patricius [i.e., the German king, as *patricius Romanorum*]. Neither creatures of the nobility, nor creatures of the king, were to be appointed to the papacy: the papal election must be free and the independent work of the clergy. The patriciate of the city thus called forth the celebrated statute of election of Nicholas II and the creation of the College of Cardinals, and the struggle of the popes against the patriciate at length developed into a struggle against the right of investiture in general.

The great conflict concerning investiture governed the history of the city in the latter half of the eleventh century. Rome continued to be its source and the scene of strife on which Hilde-brand [Pope Gregory VII] displayed his genius and his marvel-ous activity, not only in founding a new ecclesiastical state with feudal territories, but in forming the papacy, after its emancipa-tion from the patriciate, into an all-ruling power. Tedious civil wars and terrible misfortunes overtook unhappy Rome in conse-quence of the great struggle between the church and the empire, and we shall see these struggles prolonged into the twelfth cen-tury, until the city itself issues from these great convulsions dur-ing the period of the rising city republics of Italy, itself in the new form of a republic. . . .

XI

The Last Days of
Pope Gregory VII

Zeal for church reform took root in tenth-century Germany. The Ottonian rulers and their higher clergy encouraged the foundation of new monasteries and the rehabilitation of spiritual life in old ones. Their work had an important counterpart in the great monastery of Cluny, in Burgundy. In the eleventh century, reformers, with the strong assistance of the Emperor Henry III, intruded the reform movement into the papacy itself. Their work chiefly concerned questions of clerical discipline, such as simony and clerical celibacy, until Pope Gregory VII (1073–85), Hildebrand, contested the right of laymen to bestow temporal rights and lands on men who had been elected, but not consecrated, as bishops and abbots. The practice of lay investiture had grown up naturally in a society that expected higher clerics to perform the same military functions as secular princes, and to stand in much the same relationship to their kings. Gregory VII reasoned that it corrupted the true teaching of the church because it cast aside free election of bishops and abbots through the action of the Holy Spirit. He argued that it enabled laymen to grant spiritual offices to such persons as could extort them in return for past services, win them by promise of favors, or purchase them outright. His opposition to lay investiture brought on a long and bitter conflict with the German king Henry IV. In the following section, Gre-

gorovius describes Henry's retreat from Rome, the sack of the city by Gregory's Norman allies from southern Italy, and the final days of the great Pope's life.—EDITOR.

WHILE Henry was retiring, Guiscard's horse had already reached the Lateran gate. The Norman had come by forced marches along the Latin Way through the valley of the Sacco; he appeared before Rome on May 24, three days after the retreat of the emperor. First pitching his camp at Aqua Martia, he cautiously remained there for three days, uncertain whether Henry had only deceived him by his departure, in order suddenly to attack him in the rear. The Romans kept the city barricaded. Their manly resistance against Guiscard honorably fills a short chapter in their mediæval history. Their distress deserved genuine compassion; their emperor, to whom they had surrendered the city, had abandoned them, and after the sufferings of a three years' siege, the unhappy city found herself exposed to the avarice of the Normans and Saracens who had been summoned by the pope. Robert held negotiations with traitors and Gregorians within the walls, headed by the consul Cencius Frangipane. In the dawn of May 28, his knights scaled the gate of S. Lorenzo, and having entered, hastened to the Porta Flaminia and broke it open. The army, which there stood ready, thus made its way into the city. The Romans, it is true, threw themselves against the Normans, but the duke finally drove them through the flames of the Field of Mars over the bridge to the other side of the Tiber, released the pope from S. Angelo, and led him to the Lateran.

The capture of Rome, a glory which adorns but few heroes, shines in the history of this great soldier prince, to whom fortune was more constant than to Pompey or to Cæsar. He had defeated the army of the emperor of the East in Albania, had put to flight the emperor of the West, and he now replaced the greatest of popes on the throne of Christendom. Gregory VII, standing be-

From book VII, ch. 6, secs. 3, 4, and 5.

side his preserver Guiscard, presents a spectacle so remarkable as seldom to be met with in history. As the pope gratefully clasped the hero of Palermo and Durazzo in his arms, he may have remembered Leo IX, and, Guiscard himself may possibly have surveyed with astonishment the altered aspect of affairs, and, while he now saved a pope from the hands of his ruthless enemies, may have called to mind the battlefield of Civita, where he had knelt before another pope who was his prisoner.

The unhappy city, however, which was surrendered to his soldiers for plunder, became the scene of more than Vandal horrors. The Romans rose on the third day, and with furious indignation attacked the barbarous conquerors. The imperial party, which had reassembled, hoped by a desperate onslaught to rid themselves of their oppressors; the young Roger hurried from the camp with a thousand men at arms to the aid of his father, now reduced to the direst straits. The city fought valiantly but in vain; the despair of the people was stifled in blood and flames, for, in order to save himself, Robert had set fire to a portion of the city. When both flames and the tumult of battle had subsided, Rome lay a heap of smoking ashes before Gregory's eyes; burnt churches, streets in ruins, the dead bodies of Romans formed a thousand accusers against him. The pope must have averted his eyes, as the Romans, bound with cords, were led in troops into their camp by Saracens. Noble women, men calling themselves senators, children and youths were openly sold like cattle into slavery: others, and among them the imperial prefect, were carried as prisoners of state to Calabria.

Goths and Vandals, nevertheless, had been more fortunate than were the Normans, since Goths and Vandals had found Rome filled with inexhaustible wealth, while the plunder of the Moslems in the service of the duke could no longer have been comparable to that which their predecessors had ravished from S. Peter's two hundred and thirty years before. The city was now terribly impoverished, and even the churches were devoid of ornament. Mutilated statues stood in the ruinous streets or lay in the dust amid the relics of baths and temples. Hideous images

107

of saints remained here and there in the basilicas, which were already falling to decay, and attracted the spoiler by the gold which was possibly still affixed to them by votaries.

The brutal fury of the victors satisfied itself for some days in robbery and murder, until the Romans, a cord and a naked sword round their necks, threw themselves at the feet of the duke. The grim conqueror felt compassion, but he could not make good their losses. The sack of Rome remains a dark stain on Gregory's history, as also on that of Guiscard. It was Nemesis that compelled the pope, however hesitatingly and reluctantly, to gaze upon the flames of Rome. Was not Gregory VII in the burning city (and it burned on his account) as terrible a man of destiny as Napoleon calmly riding over bloody fields of battle? Leo the Great, who preserved the sacred city from Attila and obtained alleviation for her fate from the anger of Genseric, forms a glorious contrast to Gregory, not one of whose contemporaries has recorded that he made any attempt to save Rome from the sack, or ever shed a tear of compassion for her fall. What to this man of destiny was the destruction of half Rome in comparison with the idea for which he sacrificed the peace of the world?

Years afterwards a foreign bishop, Hildebert of Tours, who visited the city about the year 1106, lamented its ruin. . . .

Hildebert beheld the destruction of the city in the beginning of the twelfth century; its ancient and its new ruins and the still fresh traces of the enemy. The talented poet was shocked at the pagan emotions which Rome awoke within him, and sought to efface them by means of a second elegy, in which he placed words of consolation in the mouth of sorrowing Rome. "When I still," for so he caused the unfortunate sibyl to speak, "when I still took pleasure in idols, my army, my people, and my marble magnificence were my pride. The idols and the palaces are fallen, people and knights have sunk into servitude and Rome scarcely remembers Rome; but now, I have exchanged the eagle for the cross; Cæsar for Peter, and earth for heaven."

These exalted reflections could not, however, console the Romans for the ruins of their city, through which they wandered as beggars. Rome had become the poorer by many thousand inhabitants through war, flight, death, and imprisonment. For centuries she had suffered no such violent blow: twenty years of civil war, storms within and without, and lastly fire, had added their ravages to those inflicted by the first hostile destruction which she had actually suffered since the time that Totila had torn down her walls. We can enumerate a series of monuments which owed their destruction to this period.

Henry's attacks on S. Paul's had apparently effected the ruin of the ancient colonnade, which stretched from the gate to the basilica; and with the capture of the Borgo the Vatican portico was destroyed. The Leonina had perished by fire; S. Peter's itself must have been injured. Within the city Palatine and Capitol had been laid waste, and the fate of the Septizonium, at that time the finest portion of the imperial palaces, must have been shared by other fortified buildings. Nevertheless the destruction under Cadalus [actually, Wibert of Ravenna, the antipope Clement III] and Henry was inconsiderable when compared with the burning under the Normans. For Guiscard twice set the city in flames; first when he entered by the Flaminian Gate; and again when he was attacked by the Romans. The Field of Mars, possibly as far as the Bridge of Hadrian, was destroyed by fire; the remains of the porticos in this neighborhood and several other monuments perished; the mausoleum of Augustus escaped owing to the mode of its construction, and the column of Marcus Aurelius owing to its isolated position on an entirely open piazza. The hitherto thickly inhabited quarter of the Lateran was destroyed by fire as far as the Colosseum, and the Lateran Gate itself was henceforward known as the "burned." The ancient church of the Quattro Coronati was reduced to ashes; the Lateran and several churches must have suffered severely; the Colosseum, the triumphal arches, the remains of the Circus Maximus can hardly have escaped. All the chroniclers who have incidentally described the frightful catastrophe, unanimously affirm that it was responsible for the destruction of a great part of the city. A historian, living at the end of the fifteenth century, with justice pronounced the opinion, that Rome had originally been reduced to the lamentable condition which it presented at his time by the hatred of the Normans. The formerly thickly populated Cœlian (the region of the Colosseum), it is true, still remained inhabited. But it, too, gradually became deserted and the like fate befell the Aventine, renowned for its splendor until the time of Otto III. The traveler of the present day, who visits these two ancient hills and finds in their silent desertion nothing but ruins and the remains of early churches, may recall the fact that this desertion is due to the Norman destruction. This quarter of the city became gradually forsaken, and the inhabitants thronged more and more into the Field of Mars, where new Rome arose.

Owing, moreover, to internal causes, the destruction of the city made rapid progress at this period. The building of churches had formerly contributed to its ruin, and the transformation of ancient monuments into fortresses and towers now effected the like result. Foreign cities, too, even sent to Rome, as to a quarry, for stones and columns. The beautiful cathedral of Pisa—built in the eleventh century—the celebrated cathedral of Lucca, consecrated by Alexander II, were undoubtedly adorned with columns which had either been presented by Rome, or had been purchased from the city. When Desiderius [of Monte Cassino, later Pope Victor III] built his basilica, he bought columns and blocks of marble in Rome, which he caused to be shipped from Portus, and although, amid the booty which Robert [Guiscard] carried off to Salerno, pagan statues can scarcely have been forthcoming, it is probable that it contained valuable ornaments and columns which were afterwards employed in building the cathedral of S. Matthew in this southern city. It is possible that, like Genseric, Robert may also have removed actual works of art, for some remarks uttered by Hildebert in his first elegy allow us to conclude that, even after the Norman sack, statues of marble or bronze still survived in Rome.

The horrors committed by his liberators condemned Gregory VII henceforward to an eternal exile, which was his just punishment in the highest sense of earthly destiny. His career ended in the ruins of Rome. Although the Romans had promised submission, he must nevertheless have foreseen that, as soon as the Normans had withdrawn, he would fall a victim to their revenge. Robert took hostages, placed a garrison in S. Angelo, and in June departed with the pope into the Campagna, where he attacked Tivoli in vain, but destroyed other fortresses. From some of these heights on the Campagna, Gregory must have turned a last painful look on Rome, in order to take farewell of the theater of his struggles, of the Eternal City, which he left in ruins behind him. He might tell himself that he had not been defeated, but that neither had he conquered. With gloomy thoughts he must have mentally followed Henry to the Po on his triumphal progress homewards, Henry who had conquered the city, who had obtained the imperial crown, who had raised an antipope to the sacred chair, and had compelled Gregory himself to go forth, a fugitive, into exile, laden with the curse of Rome. While one of the enemies proceeded northwards, the other was obliged to turn with the troops of Roman prisoners to the south, condemned to gratitude towards a vassal who carried him off into a foreign land. The departure of the great pope from ruined Rome amid the swarms of Normans and Saracens, against whose fellow-believers he had formerly preached a crusade, his sorrowful journey to Monte Casino and Salerno, where he went to eat the bread of exile at the hand of his friend Desiderius, form a tragic end to the drama of his life, a drama in which eternal justice obtains as glorious a triumph as in Napoleon's lonely death on St. Helena.

Gregory died on May 25, 1085, occupied with schemes of returning to Rome at the head of an army. On his deathbed he sighed: "I have loved righteousness and hated iniquity, therefore I die in exile." The words reveal the fundamental basis of his character, which was great and manly. This grand spirit, a character almost without equal, does not, however, stand amid the glorious ranks of sages and reformers who are reverenced by all races without distinction as benefactors of mankind. To Gregory belongs a place among the rulers of the earth, men who have moved the world by a violent yet salutary influence. The religious element, however, raises him to a far higher sphere than that which belongs to secular monarchs. Beside Gregory Napoleon sinks to an utter poverty of ideas.

Gregory was the heir of the ancient aims of the papacy. But

his unexampled genius as ruler and statesman is his own, and no one, either in ancient Rome or in modern times, has ever attained to his revolutionary daring. This monk did not shrink from the thought of overthrowing the order of things existing in Europe, in order to raise the papal throne upon its ruins. His true greatness, however, lies behind his papacy. As pope he aimed too high, thinking in his brief moment of power to compass at once the work of centuries. He who desires the impossible must appear a visionary, and as that of a visionary Gregory's attempt to seize the dominion of the political world must be regarded.

Marvelous was the strength with which he won the freedom of the church, and founded the dominion of the hierarchy. The realm of priests, who bore in their hands no other weapons than a cross, a gospel, a blessing and a curse, is more remarkable than the united empire of Roman or Asiatic conquerors. As long as the world lasts this spiritual empire will remain a unique, unexampled phenomenon of moral power. Gregory VII was a hero of this priestly empire alone. His purpose, it is true, embraced mankind as a church, but the church only existed for him in the form of the papal monarchy. The idea of setting up a mortal as an infallible and God-like being, holding the keys of heaven and hell, and of submitting to him, at once the apostle of meekness and the vicar of God, the whole world, is so astonishing, that it will continue to awake the surprise of the latest generations of mankind. The idea was the outcome of an age of slavery, of barbarism and necessity, when suffering humanity desired to have the principle of good embodied in a personality before its eyes, a personality which to its comfort it could always see and reach. The transference to a human being of the power to bind and to loose in moral affairs is perhaps the most wondrous fact in the history of the world. It is, however, explained by the fact that in the Middle Ages the church represented the universal needs, the strongest passions, and, at the same time, the highest ideas of mankind. It was not until after the struggles which dated from Gregory VII that the laity, hitherto rude, vicious, and uncultured, began to show signs of intellectual life.

112

No wonder, therefore, that the greatness of the church assumed this audacious character in Gregory. History, however, has not ratified his unchristian ideal, for this ideal remained below the loftier conception of humanity. The teaching of the apostles endures; time has long overthrown the hierarchical principles of Gregory, or culture, becoming universal, has turned them to derision as the belated dreams of the obscurantist and the fanatic. We may reproach Gregory with having severed the church into two halves; into the profane laity, deprived for ever of all rights of election, and the sacred and self-elective priestly caste. The conception of the Christian republic was indeed falsified by the Gregorian principles, for the hierarchy usurped the place of the church. Into this hierarchy Gregory infused a spirit of Cæsarism. If this system, perfected on his lines, united in itself all political forms—democracy, aristocracy, and monarchy—it must, nevertheless, be granted that its machinery, directed by a single will, and the centralization of all dogmatic power in a caste, engendered all the evils of clerical despotism and tyranny; and we can understand that the work of Gregory VII necessarily entailed the German reformation.[1]

The best work that Gregory accomplished was a result undreamed of by himself, the awakening of intellect in the world, by means of a struggle which for the first time stirred all the moral depths of life. From this one man proceeded a movement, immeasurable in its extent, which spread through every circle of church and state. The gigantic struggle between these two forms, which together represent the social whole, their original barbarous feudal blending, their gradual separation, their permanent division, constitute the historic life of the Middle Ages. And even now we are occupied with the problem of how to render church and state completely independent powers, how to rescue them from their last hierarchical rigidity, to equalize them

1. In vol. IV, pt. 1, p. 300, Gregorovius observes: Henry [IV] placed his country under an eternal debt of gratitude, for had it not been for his heroic courage, Germany would have fallen into vassalage to the spiritual tyranny of Rome. Henry IV was a predecessor of the Hohenstaufens, and will ever live as a great and tragic champion in the history of the German nation.

in the principles of freedom and justice, to make them work together, and thus at last to build up a universal empire of culture
and peace. In the age of physical force and barbarism, mankind
was incapable of grasping the lofty ideas of Christianity. Was the
church of Gregory VII and of the Middle Ages the realization of
Christianity? Are these pure ideas, the expression of nature in
its eternal personal and social aspect, even now realized? The
extinction of the Frankish feudal state, and the decline of the
power of the Gregorian church, have rather begun to denote a
new phase in the history of the human race. Those still gigantic
ruins of the Middle Ages sink one after the other before our
eyes into the great stream of the harmony of life, which, after
countless struggles, still encompasses this hard and tedious world,
and bears us onward to a happiness, the anticipation of which
must gladden every noble spirit.

114

XII

Cultural Life in the Eleventh Century

WE close the history of the city in the eleventh century with a glance at the condition of intellectual culture during the period —a subject of which, however, we have but little to say.

During the tenth century we failed to discover a single Roman possessed of literary talent, nor in the eleventh is any such forthcoming. There is something appalling in this intellectual desert, even although explained by the history of so bloody a period. Since the middle of the eleventh century, the seeds of a newer cultivation had developed in the rest of Italy. The rising freedom of the cities spurred the citizens on to intellectual activity; the secular schools made the first attempt to obtain emancipation from the church; jurisprudence was cultivated; trade created and fostered information, and great events demanded that they should be described. Rome alone remained untouched by these influences—all energies were there consumed in the great struggle for reform; the popes, educated in Germany or Gaul, who headed the movement, exerted themselves to purify churches and convents from moral corruption, but had not leisure to educate a cultured clergy. The series of popes, in part infamous, which continued until the Synod of Sutri (the Romans themselves called them "idiots"), serves to mark the period of profoundest barbar-

From book VII, ch. 7, sec. 5.

ism, until Rome became animated once more by German and Gallic culture, as it had been animated in the time of Sylvester II and Gregory V. The reforming popes were foreigners, as were also the better of the cardinals by whom they were surrounded.

We know nothing of the condition of the Roman schools at this time. Documents show us that doctors of law, scholars and masters existed elsewhere, although not in Rome. Wipo summoned Henry III to emulate the example of the Italians and to send the sons of the German nobility to school, but it was scarcely in Rome that he had become acquainted with the praiseworthy custom. Nobles and citizens were less educated in Rome than in Bologna or Pisa, Pavia or Milan, although even in Rome grammar schools, where the knowledge of the ancients was taught, must always have remained in existence. For the study of grammar was at the time widespread in Italy, and great value was placed on an artificial and rhetorically coloured style.

In literature and profane science Rome remained behind the rest of Italy in the same degree as in the tenth century. The example of the rhymed chronicle of the monk Donizo of Canossa, who described the life of the great Countess Matilda in verse, it is true, barbaric; that of William of Apulia, in whom the heroic career of Robert Guiscard found, if not a Virgil, at any rate an intelligent narrator, roused no Roman monk to emulation; nor was the lyric poetry of Damiani, or that of Alfanus of Salerno, any more successful. Of inscriptions or epigrams there are also but few examples at this period. Church music, however, had received a fresh impetus since Guido of Arezzo, a Benedictine in the monastery of Pomposa near Ravenna, had invented notes and had thereby inaugurated the series of intellectual discoveries by which barbarism was wiped from the human race. The envy of his brethren of the cowl banished Guido from the cloister, and the first inventor in the history of Christian culture became also its first martyr, and even likened himself to that artist who was put to death by Tiberius for having discovered an indestructible kind of glass. Tedald, Bishop of Arezzo, gave him shelter, and shortly after the ignorant John XIX summoned him to Rome. The pope allowed Guido to explain his antiphonary, soon learnt to sing a strophe, and gave orders that the marvelous system should be taught in the school for choristers in the Lateran. We still read the letter in which Guido relates his triumph. The happy monk left Rome, promising, however, to return to teach his new invention. Rome, perhaps, made no effort to detain her illustrious guest, or else he fled, as he himself admits, from the fever-stricken desert. Among the reasons advanced by a cardinal in the time of Gregory VII to account for the ignorance of the Roman clergy, next to poverty, which prevented students from frequenting foreign schools, was the unhealthiness of Rome, which kept foreign teachers at a distance. The marshiness of several portions of the city must, indeed, have rendered it an actual catacomb. It was, moreover, poor, and filled with factions, and the papal court at this time gave no encouragement to learning. Neither Lanfranc of Pavia, the tutor of Alexander II, nor the more celebrated Anselm of Aosta, the pupil of Lanfranc, the father of scholastic theology, was attracted to Rome. From the monastery of Bec in Normandy, these stars of the first magnitude in the eleventh century illumined each in turn France and the entire West, and successively died as archbishops in Canterbury.

Not even of those popes who furthered reform is any decree in favor of schools recorded, and it was reserved for Gregory VII, in 1078, to revive the order that schools for the clergy should be erected beside all churches.

Concerning the libraries in Rome at this period we are in utter ignorance. Nevertheless it is probable that measures may have been taken for their support, the series of librarians remaining unbroken during the eleventh century, while during the twelfth three only are mentioned, and during the thirteenth not a single librarian is known to us by name. The decay of learning cooled the ardor for the completion of the Lateran library, and scarcely any monks remained in Roman monasteries who understood the art of writing codices. Damiani complains of the dearth of copyists, and that but few were capable of reading at sight that which he had written. Rome was still put to shame by the Italian monasteries which here and there cherished learning. . . .

117

II

THE STRUGGLE OF LORDSHIP
AGAINST REPUBLIC

I

Foundation of the Roman Commune

Gregorovius considered in some detail the last stages of the In-
vestiture Conflict, especially the tumultuous pontificate of Paschal
II (1099–1118) and the settlement agreed to by Pope Calixtus II
and Emperor Henry V (Concordat of Worms, 1122). After dis-
cussing the papacy's stance as a political power in early twelfth-
century Italy, he wrote about the insurrection of the Romans
against Pope Innocent II (1130–43) and their establishment of
the Roman Senate (1142–43). This led him to the social context
*in which the Roman commune was founded.—*Editor.

The installation of the senate was the result no less of the already
developed freedom of the Lombard cities, than of the peculiar
conditions of Rome. From the eleventh century these cities had
already acquired their autonomy under the shadow of the church,
which had previously held them in tutelage. The Ottos, and still
more the emperors of the Salic house, had by degrees made over
to the bishops the power of counts, and at the same time had
bestowed many privileges on the cities. The cities gradually
deprived the bishops of their jurisdiction, and became communes
with their own magistrates. The citizens of strongly fortified
towns made use of the struggle between church and state, which

From book VIII, ch. 4, sec. 1.

121

not only weakened the bishoprics but also dissolved the union with the empire, to rise to the surface between the two enfeebled powers as a third and youthful force. In the beginning of the twelfth century the greater number of communes in Lombardy, Tuscany, the Romagna, and the Marches were governed by consuls annually elected, into whose hands the power formerly wielded by the count, as well as the larger part of the public revenues, had fallen.

The sight of free republics irritated the Romans. At a time when so many other cities had renounced episcopal authority, their city still remained under the sovereignty of a bishop. They must now shake off this sovereignty. But their bishop was the pope. And the pope's territorial supremacy had not arisen recently, like that of the bishops, from privilegia of exemption, but dated at least from the Frankish constitution. Civil wars, schism, and long exile had weakened the papal supremacy like the imperial power; nevertheless, in spite of recurring periods of impotence in temporal matters, the bishop of Rome could always advance powerful defenders for his dominium temporale. Such were his sacred papacy, the expeditions of the emperors to Rome, the Normans, the revenues of Christendom. Thus Lombard cities became free and Rome did not, although earlier than they she had struggled for her freedom under Alberic and the Crescentii.

We have spoken of the internal hindrances to the autonomy of the city. Milan, Pisa, Florence, Genoa attained liberty and wealth by means of a patriotic nobility and by the energy of a great citizen class who obliged the nobles to seek a post of honor beside them on the council board. In Rome there were but two lay classes—the nobility and the populace. The nobility shared honor and power with the clergy, and the populace, owing to the unproductive nature of the city, remained condemned to take no part in political life. In the twelfth century no defensive association existed between the free citizens of Rome, such as existed in other cities. Documents show us Roman nobles freighting vessels or making commercial contracts, but the Roman merchant class does not yet come prominently forward; shopkeepers and moneychangers are alone spoken of in the acts of this period, and are distinguished by the trivial epithet of "Magnificus." The scholæ and guilds undoubtedly continued under their ancient forms, but they remained under the patronage of the great.

The only political defensive association of the Roman citizens was the militia, with its guild companies and their captains. The burgher class capable of bearing arms, who were possessed of independent property and full citizenship, were divided according to regions, of which twelve were contained in the city, while Trastevere was still traditionally designated as the fourteenth region. We can only suppose these companies to have been possessed of a vote in public affairs, as when they took part in the election of the prefect, assented by acclamation to the election of the pope, and were summoned occasionally by the ruling nobility and even by the pope to the Capitol to confirm resolutions as the populus Romanus. In a poor city a citizen could not acquire respect by his property, but only by means of arms, and in such a warlike period even the Roman militia was a force. Through this association under a banner (*bandus*), the citizen class acquired a political right and the power of resistance against the feudal rule of the nobility. Moreover, out of the mass of the free citizens some families already emerged, who rivaled the nobility both in long descent and wealth; these formed an upper burgher class, and by degrees passed into the aristocracy or became new senatorial families. Since the Roman nobility never, as in Venice, became a close corporation, it is as a rule impossible to separate illustrious burgher houses from the patrician families. For old houses fell to decay and new houses arose, and, like the Pierleoni, suddenly entered the ranks of captains and princes. This remains the case in Rome to the present day, where tenure made and still makes the duke and baron.

There were consequently in Rome an older and a more recent nobility of many families, who, with their clients, formed, as it were, clans. These patricians no longer showed their guests the wax masks of their illustrious ancestors in their dwelling rooms. They, nevertheless, claimed descent from the Anicii and Maximi, from Julius Cæsar and Octavian; and it may have been that a few of them were actually the degenerate descendants of ancient Roman families, resembling the marble slabs of the destroyed palaces of antiquity, from which the towers of these barbarous consuls had been pieced together. The following are the best known of the patrician families of Rome in the twelfth century: the Tusculans and Colonna, the Crescentii, the Frangipani, Pierleoni, Normanni, Sassi, Latroni and Corsi, the Maximi; the houses of Sant' Eustachio, among them the Franchi and Saraceni; the Astaldi, Senebaldi, Duranti, the Scotti, Ursini; the Buccapecora, Curtabraca, Bulgamini, Boboni, Berardi, Bonfilioli, Boneschi, Berizo, houses long risen from the burgher class. In Trastevere the Papa, Papazurri and Muti, Barunzii, and Romani, the Tebaldi and Stefani, Tiniosi, Franculini, Brazuti, and others. Already the names of many families reveal their descent from Lombards, Franks, or Saxons who had followed the emperors to Italy. Time and a common law had gradually effaced the differences of race, but the imperial party in Rome was chiefly composed of this nobility, which was German and immigrant, while the national and later republican party, headed in earlier times by the Crescentii, retained the consciousness of its Roman blood. The ancient title of dux was no longer in use, although the nobles still called themselves "consuls," and precisely in the twelfth century was this ancient Roman title borne with distinction. It was now used to denote the judiciary and ruling magistracy essentially; although in no way in imitation of Lombard consuls, since with the suffix *Romanorum* it had always been common in Rome before it became adopted in Italian cities. The nobility bestowed it on their most powerful members, the heads of the aristocratic republic. The title "Capitaneus" common in northern Italy was also used in Rome for the nobles who had received investiture from the pope. The captains were the great landed nobility, the comites and vice-comites in the Campagna, whose oath of vassalage pledged them to the military service of the pope. The civic nobility also entered the ranks of the captains, when the pope gave them castles in fief. The pope had, moreover, excluded the provincial nobility, formerly so powerful, from civic affairs; the counts of Nepi and Galeria, the crescentii in the Sabina, the counts of the Campagna of the family of Amatus had fallen into decadence, or remained banished to their provincial towns, while newer consular families, such as the Frangipani and the Pierleoni, who

124

had risen to the surface in the war of factions, seized the reins of power.

Besides the captains there was lastly the class of smaller feudal tenantry (the *milites*), vassals of the nobles or of the churches. In Rome, and more especially in the towns of the Campagna, where the greater part of the freehold had come into the possession of the church, they formed a knightly nobility, which may be compared to the vavasors in Lombardy and the Romagna.

Thus the nobility, who, like the patricians in ancient Rome, had formed themselves into clans, possessed the reins of government in the city as early as the eleventh century, and more especially since the quarrel for investitures. Cornelii and Claudii would have gazed in surprise on these men, who, dwelling in castellated triumphal arches and porticos, called themselves consuls of the Romans, and met together as a Senate amid the ruins of the Capitol. For the nobility assembled on the Capitol before the new Senate was appointed by the people, and the *Consules Romanorum*, chosen from their midst, were the presidents of an oligarchy which, without fixed constitution, and in a tumultuous manner, ruled and misruled the city. The despotism of these nobles was finally overthrown by the people, and in this overthrow lies the significance of the revolution of 1143. While in Lombardy the consuls had risen simultaneously with the communes, in Rome the commune, which had just been formed, overthrew the consular rule of the nobility, and erected the communal council in its place, according it the Roman name of the Senate (*Sacer Senatus*).

Moreover, the revolution had originated with the nobility themselves after their quarrel with the pope respecting Tivoli, and the burgher class raised its head for the first time during this revolt. Sudden though the rise may have been, it had long been prepared; for the scholæ of the militia, which had acquired strength in the wars of the eleventh century, already formed political corporations, coveted a share in the government, and meditated the erection of a democratic republic. The tyranny of factions rendered feudal dominion, which favored the papacy, insupportable to the populace. A party among the nobles regarded the pope as a territorial lord, and even the actual head of Rome, to whom belonged the investiture of the imperium. This was the genuine feudal aristocracy of the popes, their political support in Rome, and the earthly splendor of their court. The popes conferred on these vassals estates and taxes, and invested them with prefectures, curial dignities, judgeships, or consulates in city or province. They dexterously divided the advantages, however, or kept their *protégés* severed by jealousy. They more gladly endured the faithlessness of these consuls than the chance that they should look for support to the burghers, whose public spirit they feared to awake. For the fate of the popes would in this case have been the fate of all other bishops, who with the rise of the communes lost their civic power.

A spark finally sufficed to kindle the burgher revolution, which was perhaps associated by secret, and to us unknown, ties with northern Italy. In 1143 Rome made the attempt to form an association of the different classes, such as had been formed in Milan, Pisa, Genoa, and other cities. The lesser nobility, from jealousy towards the "consuls," united with the burghers, the new commune seized the Capitol, declared themselves the actual Senate and made war against, or banished all such nobles as refused to join them. The captains immediately rose, also the members of the imperial party, and the company of the pope, and Rome was divided between two hostile camps, the ancient consular party of the aristocrats and the new senatorial commune of the people on the Capitol.

The establishment of a free burgher class deserves to distinguish a new era in the history of Rome, and the tranquil spectator of history gazes with astonishment on the ruins of the now legendary Capitol, occupied by a rude and ignorant people who called their leaders senators. These men knew nothing of Cicero or Hortensius, of Cato or Cæsar, but like the ancient plebians made war on a haughty race of patricians, of wholly or partly barbarous descent. They deprived the high priest of Rome of the temporal crown, demanded that the emperor of German race should recognize them as invested with the majesty of the Roman people, and on the ruins of ancient temples still asserted that Golden Rome was mistress of the world.

II

Power of the Commune under Pope Eugenius III (1145-53)

For a time, Arnold of Brescia was the soul of the Roman commune. He observed an austere mode of life and his firm condemnation of corruption among the clergy had been intellectually sharpened by his study in Paris. Arnold first came to prominence in the 1130s when he aroused the people of Brescia to cast out their bishop. Forced to go into exile in France, he reprimanded Saint Bernard for pride and envy. Through Bernard's influence, he was driven to retreat in Zürich, and thence he went to Rome (1145). Arnold made common cause with the commune, vigorously preaching against Pope Eugenius III and the Curia, which he called "a house of commerce and a den of thieves." Gregorovius now turns to the milieu in which Arnold moved.—EDITOR.

THE cardinals forthwith assembled in the church of S. Cesario on the Via Appia, and unanimously fixed their choice on Bernard, the abbot of S. Anastasius *ad Aquas Salvias*. And hence through his pupil the ideas of the saint of Clairvaux obtained possession of the papal chair. Bernard of Pisa had no genius; his own master even felt dismayed that, at a time so critical, a simple monk should have been placed on the throne of Christendom. The electors, however, must have discovered in him sufficient intelligence

From book VIII, ch. 4, secs. 4 and 5.

and energy of purpose. His friends asserted that the succoring grace of God endowed the artless monk with intellect, grace, and eloquence. The sainted teacher [Bernard of Clairvaux] eventually dedicated to his timid pupil, whose apostolic feet he now kissed in self-abnegation, his golden book *De Consideratione*, which still remains the most useful manual for such popes as desire to administer their office with humility and prudence.

The new pope was able to take possession of the Lateran unhindered, but the senators barred his way to S. Peter's, where his consecration ought to have taken place. They demanded his renunciation of the civil power, and the recognition of the republic. Rome stood in arms. The pope fled on February 17, the third day after his election, to the Sabine fortress of Monticelli, and was followed by the dismayed cardinals. They proceeded to Farfa, where Eugenius III was consecrated, on February 18, 1145.

He took up his abode at Viterbo at Easter and there remained eight months. During the struggles between Henry IV and the papacy, Viterbo had attained municipal power, and at the end of the eleventh century had acquired a municipal constitution with consuls at its head. It nevertheless remained subject to the popes, who henceforth frequently found refuge within its walls. Rome meanwhile remained the scene of wildest uproar. The palaces and towers of such nobles as belonged to the papal party, and of the cardinals, were sacked and destroyed; the populace abandoned themselves to violent excesses. Even pilgrims were seized, and S. Peter's was again fortified with engines of war. The popular government now abolished the city prefecture. The office represented the imperial power in Rome, and its abolition must therefore be taken as signifying that the Romans, embittered by [the Emperor] Conrad's disdain, threatened to sever themselves from the imperium. The Patricius should alone represent the majesty of the Roman Senate and people, and all nobles who refused to recognize the Patricius were banished.

Meanwhile Eugenius III assembled the vassals of the church in Viterbo; the greater number of the counts of the Campagna were hostile to the city, with which they were not allied by any tie. In some cities counts had been established since antiquity;

128

other cities were governed by papal delegates bearing the Roman titles of præsides and rectors. Rome determined to subjugate both counts and provincial cities, as Milan and other republics had subjugated their neighbors. The papal cities resolved to be again entirely free, although few were strong enough to emulate the example of Rome. Among these, however, was Corento, the ancient Tarquinium, a busy mart, which in 1144 already owned a municipality with consuls. The provincial nobility also sought to attain independence, while the Roman Senate strove to compel them to receive their feudal investiture on the Capitol instead of in the Lateran, and either to live in the city under the laws of the republic, or to recognize these laws. Eugenius was soon able to unite several vassals of the church, who had done homage to him at Narni, with the Tivolese, Rome's bitterest enemies, and to send them against the city, where the papal party was at war with the Senate. It is possible that the excommunication with which he threatened the Patricius Jordan may have had some effect, and the wearied populace finally demanded the return of the pope, whom they determined to recognize. The pope prudently agreed to a treaty, perhaps saying to himself that it was better to place the Roman republic under the authority of holy church, than that the emperor should place it under the authority of the empire. The Romans consequently removed the Patricius, again appointed a prefect, and recognized the supremacy of the pope, who acknowledged the existence of the commune under his investiture. After the conclusion of the treaty with the Roman people, shortly before Christmas 1145, Eugenius III was able to leave Sutri, and make his entry into the Lateran. His return resembled a triumph.

The city commune had thus wrung its recognition from the pope, and the pope on his part had preserved the principle of his government, since from him the Senate received investiture. In this curious phantom of ancient times the name alone was Roman, the character was new. In the list of twenty-five senators given us in the oldest document preserved of the *Acta Senatus* of the Middle Ages, scarcely any names are mentioned but those of people of the burgher class, names hitherto unknown to history, and among them is even one of a painter by profession. The majority of its members being of the burgher class gave the Senate a plebeian stamp, although many nobles had already joined the commune. A fresh election took place every year in September or November, probably in the presence of papal plenipotentiaries. The original number of members is unknown and was afterwards variable, but since soon after 1144 the number of fifty-six senators was accepted as the standard, it appears that, as in ancient times, so again now, Rome was divided into fourteen regions, from each of which four senators were elected, and that the Senate was thus drawn from the fourteen companies of the city. The full Senate formed the great council or consistorium and a committee of consiliatores or procuratores of the republic was placed at its head. Consiliatores are also found in Genoa and Pisa, in the capacity of assistant councillors to the consuls. In Rome, however, while the Senate possessed the legislative power, they held the executive power as the supreme governing council. They were elected from amongst the senators, and they frequently changed office during the year. Consiliatores and consistorium thus form the major and minor council, and all full citizens and electors of the Senate compose the popular parliament which assembled on the Capitol to assent to the decrees and to listen to the vindications of the magistrates retiring from office. It is difficult to say what were the revenues of the Senate, and what royalties it appropriated. It must already have deprived the pope of the right of coinage; hence, after an interval of several centuries, silver pieces again passed through the hands of the Romans, on which the ancient legend, "*Senatus populusque Romanus*," was engraved, but which now bore in addition the portrait of an apostle with the inscription, "Prince of the Romans."

Civil justice also devolved on the Senate; the court of justice of the Capitol (*Curia Senatus*), composed of senators and men learned in law, frequently received Palatine judges and Dativi as proctors within its limits, so that in several placita senatorial and papal tribunals are found side by side. The Senate also endeavoured to bring even civil cases of a spiritual nature, where both accusers and accused were priests, before her tribunal—the

Forum Senatorium. The popes, however, resisted the attempt. For the papal Curia still survived alongside of the senatorial, and in ecclesiastical disputes the papal placita are always independent of the senatorial decrees. From these decrees the litigants frequently appealed to the pope, as, on the other hand, persons judged by the papal tribunal frequently appealed to the Senate. Such are the principal features of the constitution which the Romans now created for themselves. It does honor to their civic energy; since, although recognizing in principle the supremacy of the pope, they retained their political autonomy, and Rome henceforward became properly a self-governing republic, which made war and peace independently of the pope.

Meanwhile the treaty with Eugenius III did not calm the profound disturbance in the city and territory. Nobles and clergy looked with anger on the Senate, which strove to extend its authority over the entire Campagna. Tivoli gave rise to fresh tumults. The Romans demanded its destruction, and the harassed pope permitted its walls to be pulled down a measure, however, which failed to satisfy the Romans. Eugenius III fled from his tormentors at the end of January 1146 to Trastevere, or S. Angelo, which the Pierleoni still retained. Weary of life like Gelasius, he bemoaned his troubles and sighed, in the words of S. Bernard, that, instead of the sheep of Peter, the shepherd tended wolves, dragons, and scorpions in Rome. He went to Sutri in March, to Viterbo in May, and stayed there until the end of the year; thence he proceeded to Pisa, and in March 1147 through Lombardy to France, where King Lewis was preparing for the second Crusades.

Eugenius had fled but had not been driven away by force of arms, for even after his two-years' absence the Romans continued to recognize the foundations of the treaty and to regard the Senate as having been invested in its office by the pontiff. Meanwhile they now felt themselves entirely free; Tivoli was immediately attacked and punished by the execution of several of its citizens. Rome seemed to have reverted to ancient times, as in her Senate, so in the wars, which she waged now as then against Latin and Tuscan towns, which again formed an alliance against her. In order to indemnify themselves, the great nobility also attacked many patrimonies of the church. Each seized what he could. The State of the Church was split into petty baronial despotisms, which were hostile alike to the papacy and to the Senate, and which weakened or hindered the autonomy of Rome. The rule of these noble tyrants was especially strong in Latium, a poor district where there were no wealthy communes to form a counterpoise such as existed in Tuscany or Umbria. The energy of the Roman people was thus dissipated in struggles with towns and captains, while Rome itself, where Jordan Pierleone now appeared as standard-bearer of the civic power, was torn by internal civic wars, and stood in violent revolution.

It was at this time that Arnold of Brescia, who had remained hidden in exile, reappeared as a demagogue in Rome. The celebrated schismatic had returned to Italy on the death of Innocent II, and, having promised silence and submission, was released by Eugenius III in Viterbo from the ban which had previously been laid upon him. His penance was to be performed at the holy places in Rome. Thither, therefore, Arnold went, perhaps at the same time that Eugenius returned to the city from Viterbo, and at first lived in concealment. After the pope's flight to France, however, he came forward publicly, and, heedless of the oath which he had taken to the Curia, loudly preached his old doctrines to the Romans.

The revolution in Rome took great hold upon him. Friends, whom he had either found in the city or recently made, encouraged him to dedicate his talents to the cause of the people. He acquiesced, filled with the enthusiastic hope of thus accomplishing his ecclesiastical and social ideal in the overthrow of the *dominium temporale* [temporal lordship]. Nothing could have been more gratifying to Arnold than the establishment of the Roman commune. Should the attempt to deprive the pope of the civil power succeed, it would entail the fall of all the remaining ecclesiastical states, and Christian society would again approach the democratic conditions of the early unpolitical church. Arnold's chief work must consequently be to aid in the formation in Rome of a republic founded on civic liberty.

The religious sect which he had founded in Brescia was revived in Rome. His doctrine of apostolic poverty and purity of morals won him many friends: women more especially became his enthusiastic followers. His adherents were known as Lombards or Arnoldists. The Roman Senate eagerly imbibed the doctrines of the fiery popular orator on their political side. A man clad in the monastic habit, emaciated by fasting, stood like a specter on the ruins of the Capitol and addressed the *patres conscripti* on the same spot where senators, voluptuous rulers over thousands of slaves, had addressed their ancestors. Arnold's glowing declamations, to which the Fathers of the church and Virgil, the law of Justinian and the Gospel, alike contributed, were delivered in the corrupt Latin, the *"lingua rustica,"* or peasant's tongue, to which Varro or Cicero would have listened in horror, but which, as the tongue of Dante, was destined a century later to create a new literature.

Arnold spoke frequently in public parliaments. He described the pride, the avarice, the hypocrisy and the vices of the cardinals, he called their college a table of money changers and a den of robbers. He loudly announced that the pope was not a successor of the apostles as a shepherd of souls, but an incendiary and a murderer, a tyrant over churches and a corrupter of innocence, who fed his body and his treasure chests on the property of others. Neither obedience nor reverence was due to him. Nor was any toleration to be shown to such as desired to reduce Rome, the seat of the empire, the source of freedom, the mistress of the world, to subjection.

We may imagine how these speeches, uttered by a reformer of strictly moral life, inflamed the minds of the Romans, already filled with hatred against the priestly rule. Arnold was the man of the hour; the republic on the Capitol took him formally into its service: it also made use of him as councillor in matters relating to the civic constitution: for it has come to pass that in every age in Italy ecclesiastical reformers have stepped into the domain of politics and become demagogues. The practical insight of the Lombard may have been darkened by the ruins of Rome, and become too deeply steeped in ancient traditions.

The revival of the study of the law of Justinian combined with the monuments and traditions of antiquity to hold the Romans within an enchanted domain. While other democracies developed in accordance with natural laws, the Romans strove to restore the ancient forms of their republic, and lost themselves in enthusiastic dreams of the worldwide supremacy which was their due. Arnold himself counselled the people to rebuild the Capitol and to revive the ancient order of senators, even that of the knights. We must not, however, regard the institution of knighthood simply as a fantastic whim; other cities also created knights, and Arnold probably wished to combine the petty nobility (who were friendly to the populace), and to install them as an armed force in opposition to the aristocracy of consuls and captains.

As the lower ranks of the nobility entered the commune, so the inferior clergy laid hold of the idea of the equality of the priesthood. War was made on all sides against the Gregorian hierarchy, which was contrasted with the long-overthrown likeness of primitive Christianity. The clergy of the smaller churches revolted against the caste of cardinals, who already, like the great nobility (to whose ranks they for the most part belonged), owned castellated palaces in the city and were accustomed to live like princes.

Eugenius meanwhile had returned to Italy from France in June 1148. He excommunicated Arnold at a synod held at Cremona in July. Apprehensive of a movement among the clergy in Rome, he addressed them a letter from Brescia, menacing them all with punishment did they give ear to the sectary.

While Arnold inflamed the populace with enthusiasm for democracy, his old adversary Bernard was active to quench the brand. The practical application of his own Christian principles, concerning the illegality of the political rule of the bishops, the saint himself still owed to the world, and it was with difficulty that he could think of Rome otherwise than in the possession of the pope, even if the form of government remained a matter of indifference. After Eugenius' second flight he wrote to the Romans; he implored the indulgence of the "exalted and illustrious people," that he, an insignificant person, should venture to address them, but he explained, as every bishop of the present day explains, that the violence offered to the pope concerned the entire Catholic world.

> Your fathers rendered the universe subject to the city, but you would make the city the byword of the world. You have banished the papacy, now beware what will become of Rome; a headless trunk, a face without eyes. Scattered sheep! Return to your shepherd. Illustrious city of heroes, reconcile thyself with thy true princes Peter and Paul.

The saint spoke with indignation but with diplomatic reverence for the name of Rome, but he secretly hated the Romans. He elsewhere draws a picture of them, and calls this exalted people proud, covetous, vain and mutinous, unmanly and false.

> Their speech is arrogant but their actions are mean. They promise everything and perform nothing. They are at the same time honeyed flatterers and bitter slanderers, in short, worthless traitors.

Eugenius was not to owe to the saint, whose pupil he had been, what Innocent II had once owed him. Neither in Conrad did he find a Lothar. Both parties summoned the king to Rome; both made use of the same phrase, that Cæsar should take what belonged to Cæsar; but their sense and intention differed in each case. Conrad III, owing to his disastrous Crusade, to which he had been driven by the exhortations and false prophecies of the holy abbot, was kept far from Italy, but returning by Aquileja in the beginning of 1149 he determined on the journey to Rome. Roger's alliance with Guelf, the rebellious duke of Bavaria, urgently demanded the journey, while Roger, mindful of Lothar's victory, employed every means to keep him at a distance. Conrad had formed an alliance with the Greek Emperor Emmanuel, and the Pisans were again to lend him their fleet. On the other hand, the pope required the help of the Sicilians against the Romans, and feared that Conrad would agree to the treaty which they repeatedly offered him.

At the end of the year 1148 Eugenius went to Viterbo, a town with which the Romans were already at war. In the beginning of 1149 he ventured into the neighborhood of Rome. Count Ptolemy received him in Tusculum, where he was also greeted by Lewis of France on his return from the Crusade. The king saw with astonishment the helpless position of the pope in the gloomy fortress; he nevertheless went on to Rome, to visit the various holy places as a pilgrim, and the republicans of the city received him with all due honor. Eugenius, who had brought the necessary money with him from France, collected the vassals of the church and reinforcements of mercenaries in Tusculum, placed Cardinal Guido of Puella at the head of these troops, and in his distress formed an alliance with King Roger, who lent him soldiers. Rome was now reduced to the uttermost extremity, but the republicans valiantly repulsed the attacks of the enemy.

The Senate at this time wrote repeatedly to King Conrad, inviting him to come and rule over empire and city. The citizens, Sixtus, Nicholas, and Guido, now councillors of the republic, announced that they had banished the Frangipani and Pierleoni, and urged Conrad to take the Roman commune under his protection. But as they received no answer, and the difficulty increased, the Senate addressed him another letter in 1149. Its memorable contents show that the chasm which separated the Romans of the twelfth century from the temporal power was just as deep, and was explained with as much certainty, as at the present day, when their remote and unarmed descendants still assemble amid the timeworn ruins of the Forum and Capitol, to protest against the civil power of the pope, and to stick by night placards ending with the cry, "Viva il Pontefice—non Re," at the corners of the streets.[1]

Six hundred seventy-three years had rolled by since the degraded senators had explained to Zeno in Byzantium that Rome no longer required a Western emperor; that she was satis-

1. A proclamation during the Carnival of 1862 says: Romans! He who cares for his own dignity, who is conscious of the greatness of the destiny which Providence has preserved to Italy and her capital, finds sufficient satisfaction in the Forum and all such places as recall her ancient grandeur. There the true citizen of Rome, in the recollection of the glory of his ancestors, beholds the foundation of our speedy renascence after so many centuries of disgrace. *Viva il Pontefice non Re!* Rome, February 20, 1862.

fied that Odoacer should rule over Italy as Byzantine Patricius. Six hundred fourteen years had passed since the Senate had addressed its last letter to Justinian, imploring him not to withdraw his favor from Rome and the Gothic King Theodat. Now there appeared before the throne of the German king Romans who, coming from the neglected ruins of the Capitol, again called themselves senators, who announced that they had restored the ancient Roman Senate, and invited the king of Germany to be the successor of Constantine and Justinian.

To the illustrious ruler of the city and of the world, Conrad, by the Grace of God, King of the Romans, always Augustus, from the Senate and the people of Rome; health and a properous and glorious rule over the Roman empire. We have already informed your royal nobility by frequent letters of that which has happened through our means, have told you that we remained faithful to you, and that your crown may increase in splendor is our daily wish. We are, however, surprised that you have not vouchsafed us any answer. Our unanimous endeavor is that we may again restore the empire of the Romans, which God has entrusted to your guidance, to the might that it possessed under Constantine and Justinian, who, empowered by the Roman Senate and people, governed the world. We have, therefore, by the help of God, restored the Senate, and defeated many enemies of your imperial rule, in order that what belonged to Cæsar should be yours. We have laid a solid foundation. We are security for justice and peace to all such as shall desire them. We have conquered the fortresses of the civic nobility, who, supported by Sicily and Pope Eugenius, hoped to defy you, and have either held these towns for you or have destroyed them. We are, therefore, harried on every side by the pope, the Frangipani, the sons of Pierleone (with the exception of Jordan our standard-bearer), by Ptolemy, and by many others. They desire to prevent our crowning you emperor. Meanwhile we suffer much hardship out of love to you, since there is nothing too hard for those who love, and you will give us the recompense due from a father, and merited punishment to the enemies of the empire. Shut your ears to the slanderers of the Senate; they will rejoice at our discord, in order to ruin you and us. Remember how much harm the papal court and these our former fellow citizens have caused your predecessors, and how, with Sicilian aid, they have sought to do still further harm to the city. Nevertheless, with Christ's help we hold out manfully for you, and we have already driven several of the empire's worst enemies out of the city. Hasten to our aid with imperial power; the city is at your command. You can dwell in Rome, the capital of the world, and, more absolute than almost any of your predecessors, after every priestly obstacle is removed, can rule over the whole of Italy and the German empire. We entreat you do not delay. Deign to assure your willing servants of your well-being by letters and messengers. We are now actively occupied in restoring the Milvian Bridge, which to the misfortune of the emperors has long been destroyed, and we hope soon to complete it with strong masonry. Your army will therefore be able to cross it, and to surround S. Angelo, where the Pierleoni, according to arrangement with Sicily and the pope, mediate your ruin.

> *Rex valeat, quidquid cupit obtineat super hostes,*
> *Imperium teneat, Romæ sedeat, regat orbem,*
> *Princeps terrarum, ceu fecit Justinianus.*
> *Cæsaris accipiat Cæsar quæ sunt, sua Præsul,*
> *Ut Christus jussit, Petro solvente tributum.*

> [Let the king prevail; let him gain whatever
> he desires over the enemies. Let him hold the
> empire. Let him sit at Rome. Let him rule
> the earth, prince of lands, as did Justinian. Let
> Cæsar receive what are Cæsar's, and the pope
> what are his own, as Christ commanded,
> with Peter paying tribute.]

Finally we entreat you to accord our envoys a good reception and to put confidence in them, since we cannot write all that we would. They are noblemen; the senator Guido, James, son of Sixtus, the procurator, and Nicholas their companion.

The magic influence exercised by the traditions of the ancient Roman empire is a curious phenomenon in the history of the Middle Ages. A single great recollection became a political power; the Roman emperors on the throne of Germany; the Roman popes on the chair of Peter, the Roman senators on the ruins of the Capitol, all dreamed of their legitimate right to the sovereignty of the world. We are not informed as to how the Roman envoys were received at the German court or how they were dismissed. Conrad III now saw two claimants quarrel for the right of bestowing the imperial crown, and he preferred to receive this crown from the hands of a Roman pope, rather than from those of a Roman senator. The pope had undoubtedly entered into an alliance with his enemy Roger, and the Romans therefore already hoped that Conrad would lend them a willing ear. Conrad himself must have recognized that since the days of Henry III no other king had been offered so favorable an opportunity of restoring the imperial power in Rome, and (by the destruction of the *dominium temporale*) of depriving the papacy of the fruit of Gregory VII's victories. He received letters from the Romans telling him that prudence commanded him to become the mediator between the pope and Rome, and to place the new republic under the protection of the empire. Did he comply with their behests, the papal election would in future depend on him.

Conrad, detained in Germany, where he was at war with the Guelf party, and devoid of any true insight into the condition of Rome, paid no heed to the wishes of the senators, although he probably rejoiced in the weakening of the papal power. The influence of many friends of Roman freedom was counteracted at his court by the clergy, more especially by the abbot Wibald of Stablo and Corvey. This influential man had been won over to the side of Eugenius, and he guided the opinions of the king. It thus came to pass that the sorely harassed Romans were again obliged to receive the pope into the city at the end of the year 1149. A new peace was formed between the Senate and the pope, which was of as short duration as the former. For as early as June 1150, Eugenius returned to Latium, where he took up his abode in fortified Segni, now in Ferentino. During three years the papal court wandered through the Campagna, close to Rome and yet in exile. Eugenius now feared that Conrad would recognize the Roman commune, and that the league between the city, Pisa, and the Greek emperor would overthrow the temporal throne of the papacy. Nevertheless, Wibald comforted him with the assurance that he had nothing to fear.

The Romans renewed their proposals and offered Conrad the imperial crown, necessity having forced them to recognize the historic right of German kings. Conrad, whose hands had been left free by the defeat of Guelf in 1150, now wished to go to Rome to settle affairs in the city. His journey was resolved on at two imperial diets in 1151, and he at last condescended to reply to the

Romans. He was silent concerning the Senate, but his letter, addressed to the city prefect, the consuls, the captains, and the Roman people, politely announced that he would accept their invitation and come to tranquillize the cities of Italy, to reward the faithful, and to punish the rebels. His envoys were addressed no less to the Romans than to the pope, who, filled with pious hope, received them at Segni, in January 1152. An understanding was arrived at. Eugenius III abandoned the cause of Roger and now even invited the princes of Germany to aid the emperor with all their power in his journey to Rome.

Accident, however, spared the history of the Hohenstaufens a sad page, in which the first of the line would have shown himself an inglorious enemy of the Roman republic, in the service of the pope. The manly prince died in the midst of his preparations on February 15, 1152, the first German king since Otto I who had not worn the imperial crown—a fact which in no way diminished his power. The thousands of lives which each Roman coronation usually cost the fatherland, had this time been sacrificed in the deserts of Syria. And Italian patriots should therefore for once extol a German king, that, in spite of the urgent entreaties of Italy (they usually forget these invitations), he did not descend the Alps like some destructive Attila. They might congratulate their country that during fifteen years it remained untraversed by any progress to Rome and enjoyed enviable conditions, but that they are themselves unfortunately obliged to admit that Italy has never been so disunited, or torn asunder by such furious civil wars, as during these fifteen years of purely domestic history.

On Conrad's death his nephew Frederick, the immortal hero Barbarossa, who was destined to be the glory of Germany and the terror of Italy, ascended the German throne on May 5. Eugenius, as well as the Romans, hastened to secure the friendship of the new ruler; the republic, however, looked with jealousy on the royal envoys, whom the pope alone received. A letter expresses the ill humor of the Romans and their opinions concerning the judicial relations of the emperor to the city. "I rejoice," so wrote a follower of Arnold to Frederick, "that you have been elected king by your people, but I regret that you follow the coun-

140

sel of your priests, through whose teachings things divine and human have become confused, and that you did not consult the sacred city, the mistress of the world, the creator of all emperors." The writer deplores that Frederick, like his predecessors, had determined to receive the imperial crown from the hands of false and heretical monks, whom he calls Julianists. He proves to him, from the precepts of S. Peter and from Jerome, that the clergy had nothing to do with secular rights. He derided the Donation of Constantine as an absurd fable, which old wives laughed to scorn, he showed how the imperium and every magisterial office was an emanation from the majesty of the Roman people, to whom therefore alone belonged the right of creating him emperor. The writer finally required him to send envoys and lawyers to Rome, in order to place the empire on a legal foundation in accordance with the law of Justinian, and to prevent a revolution. The human mind had happily made rapid strides in the path of progress.

The Romans of the present day who dispute the temporal authority of the pope, derive their arguments from the majesty of the Italian nation, of which Rome is the capital, and to whose natural right the merely historical right of the popes must yield. Like their forefathers, they support their reasoning with the argument that the papacy is only a spiritual office, and corroborate it by the authority of the Bible and the Fathers of the church. But in the time of Arnold the theory of the unity of the nation was unknown, and the patriots took their stand on the ground of antiquity. The majesty of the Roman people was for them the source of all power, the Roman empire an indestructible conception, and the emperor the magistrate of the republic, elected and installed by the people. When they laughed at the fable of the transference of the imperial power to the popes through Constantine, and the papal right of investiture mystically transmitted from Christ or Peter, they gave expression to the reasonable principle that no kingdom existed simply by the grace of God, but that the authority of the crown emanated from the people alone. The Romans of the twelfth century placed the imperium on the—to them—legitimate foundation of Roman law. They hit the humor of an ambitious monarch when they told him that, according to this law, the emperor was the supreme law-giving power in the world; but they required him to regard his power as committed to him by the Roman Senate and people. They mingled the Cæsarian despotism of Justinian with the fundamental laws of democracy.

Frederick I had therefore to choose between the pope and the Roman commune as the sources of his imperium; he acquiesced in all the arguments of the Romans against the supreme right of investiture which the pope claimed; he laughed at the assumptions of the Senate, which seemed to him absurd; and like all his predecessors he also resolved to let himself be crowned by the pope "through the grace of God." The first steps of his reign were prudent and conservative. Without taking cognizance of the new Roman republic, he continued Conrad's negotiations, and, owing to the instrumentality of the cardinal-legates Gregory and Bernard in Constance, a treaty highly favorable to his interests was concluded with the pope in the spring of 1153. Frederick undertook to make peace neither with Rome nor with Sicily without the pope, but to use his influence in making the city as submissive to the sacred chair as it had been a hundred years earlier. He promised to maintain the *dominium temporale* of the pope, and to aid him in the recovery of all that he had lost. Eugenius promised in return to crown him emperor and to lend every species of protection to his throne.

The negotiations between Frederick and the pope had meanwhile given rise to a violent revolt in Rome. The democrats and Arnoldists demanded the abolition of the conditions agreed upon with Eugenius and the appointment of a hundred senators with two consuls to be annually elected. Eugenius informed Frederick of these occurrences and represented them as tumults of the populace, who now themselves wished to elect an emperor. The Romans undoubtedly threatened to repudiate the German empire and to set up a national emperor of their own. Only a letter of Eugenius, however, throws a passing light upon this remarkable occurrence.

Nevertheless the pope was able to leave Segni in the autumn

of 1152, and at the end of the year to enter the city, where the overthrow of the democrats had inclined all the moderates to come to terms. Senate and people received him with honor after, as is to be supposed, he had recognized the commune. We may also infer that the banished nobility were permitted to return; these nobles, however, as consuls of the Romans and courtiers of the pope, continued in opposition to the Senate. Eugenius III was able to end his days peaceably in Rome, and with the help of the people even to reduce rebellious barons in the Campagna to subjection. Quiet subtlety succeeded in achieving what weapons had not been able to accomplish. "Eugenius laid the entire population under such great obligations to him, by his benefits and gifts, that he ruled the city almost as he willed, and had he not been removed by death, he would, with the aid of the people, have deprived the senators of their newly acquired dignities." We need not accept this statement unhesitatingly, since Eugenius in no wise succeeded in subjugating the Roman republic, and since Arnold, his most hated opponent, remained with his followers unpunished in the city.

Eugenius died at Tivoli on July 8, 1153, and was buried in S. Peter's with solemn ceremonial. The unassuming but astute pupil of S. Bernard had always continued to wear the coarse habit of Clairvaux beneath the purple; the stoic virtues of monasticism accompanied him through his stormy career, and invested him with that power of passive resistance which has always remained the most effectual weapon of the popes.

143

III

The Coronation of Frederick Barbarossa and the Death of Arnold of Brescia

THE cardinal Conrad, a Roman belonging to the Suburra, mounted the papal throne as Anastasius IV on July 12, 1153. His election was unanimous, and was not disputed by the Senate, for although the senators were present at the ceremony of election, they did not yet interfere in spiritual affairs. The popes, however, now found themselves opposed by a new power, which refused recognition to them unless they on their side recognized it. The aged Anastasius does not seem to have made any encroachments on the Roman constitution. He lived peaceably in the city, and died there on December 3, 1154.

The papal chair was now filled by a man of unusual energy, Nicholas Breakspear, an Englishman by birth. Thirst for knowledge had driven the son of a poor priest of S. Alban's to France, where, after varied fortunes, he became prior of S. Rufus near Arles. His culture, his eloquence, and his handsome presence attracted the attention of Eugenius III when Breakspear came to Rome on business connected with his convent. The pope made him cardinal of Albano, and sent him as legate to Norway, where he ordered the affairs of the church with great circumspection. Nicholas, just returned from this mission, was unanimously elected, and ascended the sacred chair as Adrian IV on Decem-

From book VIII, ch. 5, secs. 1 and 2.

ber 5, 1154. The English have only once seen the chair of Peter filled by one of their countrymen, and this, their only pope, ashamed to solicit alms at home, had gone when a boy to foreign lands. Years passed, and the beggar of S. Alban's wrote to the English king that Ireland and other islands belonged by right to him as pope.

Adrian IV at once confronted the Roman commune with an imperious aspect; the Senate refused to recognize him, he refused to recognize the Senate. He determined to overthrow the constitution on the Capitol, and hoped to accomplish his object by means of Frederick's arms. The king had already entered Italy in October, and had ratified the treaty of Constance. Adrian demanded the expulsion of Arnold, which his predecessors had repeatedly desired, but had never been able to attain. The most dangerous of all heretics, protected by the Senate and idolized by the populace, was able to preach his doctrines for years in the very face of the popes. With the overthrow of this one demagogue, Adrian hoped to bury the republic, and the Romans, who had little to expect from Frederick, turned in secret to William I, who had succeeded his celebrated father Roger on the throne of Sicily in February 1154, and had immediately quarrelled with the pope. It is possible that he may have been invited to invade the State of the Church before the German king came to Rome.

Adrian IV could not even take possession of the Lateran, but was obliged to make his dwelling in the fortified basilica of S. Peter. The proposal which Italy makes to the pope of the present day, namely, that he should rest satisfied with the Leonina, where, like a great abbot, he might live in monastic freedom, was carried into effect by the Romans at this period, since Adrian IV was practically restricted within the limits of the Leonina. Meanwhile the growing hatred of the priests, whose resistance frustrated the civic aspirations of the Romans, soon gave rise to a catastrophe; a cardinal was stabbed on the Via Sacra, and Adrian represented the deed as an offence against the majesty of the church, and laid the interdict on Rome. Not even when personally maltreated by the Romans had any pope ever before employed this—the most terrible of all weapons—against the city.

The resolute Englishman did not hesitate to wield it. In order to compel the people to banish Arnold, he laid Rome under a curse. We must realize the relation of the interdict—a species of moral starvation—to the belief of the age, in order to understand its force. With the imposition of the interdict, all religious cere-monies ceased, no mass was read, no sacrament was celebrated, beyond those of baptism and the communion to the dying, and these only under terrifying forms. The dead were not buried in consecrated ground, and marriages only received the benediction in the churchyard. Never had human ingenuity devised so blood-less, yet so terrible, an instrument of force; nor in a superstitious age could any have proved more efficacious in reducing great princes to submission, a word pronounced by a priest having power to stir their despairing subjects to revolt. The interdict, which prior to the twelfth century had been but rarely called into use, was henceforward employed by the popes to threaten cities and countries; but the cruel measure of punishing the guilty few, at the cost of suffering to the countless innocent, revenged itself on the church, by diminishing the affection in which she was held, and by encouraging heresies. The efficacy of the interdict was finally blunted by its frequent use and by the growth of education.

For a short time the Romans bore the interdict with defiant contempt; but the pious and weak, the women and priests, over-came the defiance when the fourth day of Holy Week had passed without a mass. On Wednesday the people rose in uproar, and the senators were compelled to throw themselves at the feet of the pope and implore mercy. He consented to remove the inter-dict on condition that Arnold was banished. The unfortunate reformer suffered the fate of all prophets; the people whom he had so long held spellbound surrendered him. After having dedi-cated his talents for nine years to civic freedom, he fled from Rome. Wandering from adherent to adherent, from fortress to fortress, the outlaw hoped to reach one of the republics of central Italy, beyond the reach of the papal arm. On Wednesday in Holy Week (March 23) Adrian removed the interdict; the moral darkness vanished from Rome, and for the first time the pope was conducted in festal procession to the Lateran.

Meanwhile William I [of Sicily] afflicted the church with war; he laid siege to Benevento, and burnt Ceprano and other fortesses in Latium; but as the German king approached and Rome remained quiet, he retreated from Frosinone and Aquino, after having committed fearful devastation. Frederick I was already in Tuscany, where he summoned Pisa to equip her fleet for the war, which, in alliance with the pope, the Apulian exiles, and the emperor Emmanuel, he now contemplated against the Normans. The terror of his warlike deeds in Lombardy preceded him; he approached by the Via Toscana, more formidable than Henry V, while the pope remained uncertain whether to expect a friend or foe. The fate of Paschalis II [whom Henry V had seized and forced to take what many thought a heretical position on lay investiture] had made an indelible impression on the Curia, and no treaty could diminish the tension which existed between the two powers. When German kings advanced against Rome, the defenseless popes trembled, as before enemies who came to murder them, while the kings themselves weighed the possibility of meeting their death by poison or the dagger. Below the silken pallia hung the whetted swords which the Romans unfailingly seized to attack the national enemy. If the coronation took place, the popes found themselves in the position of Daniel in the lion's den. But they adroitly cast a moral spell over the grim Roman kings, and once more breathed freely when these formidable advocates of the church departed, having obtained the crown, left parchments behind them, and fought the accustomed coronation battle.

At the beginning of June Adrian went to Viterbo, accompanied by the prefect Peter, by Oddo Frangipane, and by other nobles of his court. Frederick's rapid march filled him with dismay; he consequently sent three cardinals, who met the king at San Quirico in Tuscany. In order to test his disposition, the pope demanded the surrender of the heretic Arnold. The fugitive had shortly before fallen into the power of Cardinal Oddo at Bricalo, but had been restored to liberty by the Viscounts of Campaniano, who brought him in safety to their fortress, and there honored him "as a prophet." Anxious to remove every hindrance to his coronation, Frederick did not hesitate to show his goodwill. He sent troops to the fortress, had one of the counts arrested, and compelled the surrender of Arnold. The friend of Abelard was handed over to the papal legates to be judged in Rome at a fitting opportunity.

Negotiations for the coronation were carried on with anxious circumspection; the suspicious Adrian had retired to Civita Castellana, but Frederick reassured him by again swearing to fulfil the treaty of Constance. The German army encamped at Campo Grasso near Sutri, where the pope was to come from Nepi, and the meeting between the two potentates was to take place. As Adrian rode to the royal tent on July 9, a most curious scene took place within sight of the army. In order to avoid the humiliation of holding the papal stirrup, the proud young monarch had not come to meet the pope. The popes had long claimed this service, and many princes had rendered it. In remembrance of Christ's humility, the pontiffs, it is true, had called themselves the "servants of the servants of God." At the same time, however, they required the emperors to serve them as grooms. It is amusing to notice the panic terror which the omission of this ceremony caused among the cardinals; they turned their horses, fled back to Civita Castellana, and left their pope in the lurch. He dismounted in confusion and threw himself on a seat. Only now did the young hero come to greet him. Frederick cast himself at Adrian's feet, but the offended pope refused him the kiss of peace. A stirrup became the subject of long and serious negotiations between the two highest dignitaries of Christendom, until the princes who had previously accompanied Lothar to Rome persuaded the king to yield in the childish controversy. The following day the mighty emperor performed the part of groom to the vicar of Christ, walked at the distance of a stone's throw beside the palfrey of the former beggar of S. Alban's, and vigorously adjusted his stirrup.

Frederick had not yet heard the voice of the second power

which possessed a legal right over the imperial election—the voice of the Roman people. Their mutual relations remained doubtful, and it was uncertain whether Rome would open or shut her gates. No emperor had been crowned since the Senate had been constituted on the Capitol. The envoys of the young republic of the Romans presented themselves before Frederick on the southern side of Sutri. Their demands, their address, the answer of the Hohenstaufen, even in the literary setting of Otto of Freising, are valuable evidences of the time.

"We ambassadors of the city," thus spoke the envoys from the Capitol, "not insignificant men of Rome, are sent by the Roman Senate and people to thy Excellency. Benevolently hear what the illustrious mistress of the world, whose sovereign thou, with God's help, wilt soon be, offers thee. Dost thou come in peace, I rejoice. Thou desirest the empire of the world, and I gladly rise to hasten forward with the crown. Why shouldest thou not approach thy people in peace and mercy, thy people, who, striving to throw off the unworthy yoke of the priests, have awaited thy coming so long and anxiously. May the splendor of ancient times, the freedom of the illustrious city, return. May Rome under such an Emperor again seize the reins of supremacy over the rebellious world, and may her ruler with the name also unite the glory of Augustus. Thou knowest that, through the wisdom of her Senate and the bravery of her knighthood, Rome has stretched forth her arm with might from sea to sea, to the ends of the world—yea, even to the isles beyond the confines of the earth. Neither the waves of the ocean nor the inaccessible Alps could protect nations: Roman valour has overcome all. But unfortunately (thus her own guilt has avenged itself) that glorious princely nobility of our olden times (I speak of the Senate), has vanished from us, has degenerated into unwarlike indolence, and with the decline of wisdom, power has also decayed. Then I arose; to restore thy glory and that of the divine republic, I revived Senate and knightly order, that by the counsels of the former and the weapons of the latter the ancient majesty might return to the Roman empire and to thee. Shall not this rejoice thy Highness? Does not a work so glorious and so advantageous to thy dignity seem

149

deserving of recompense? Then listen, O Prince, with kindly patience to what I have to say concerning thy duty and mine, but chiefly thine rather than mine. For 'from Zeus is the beginning!' Thou wast my guest; I have now made thee a citizen. What was mine by right I have given thee. Thou art, therefore, pledged first of all to uphold my good customs and to swear to the laws, ratified by thy predecessors, so that they may not be injured by the fury of the barbarian. Thou shalt pay 5000 pounds to my officials, whose duty it is to proclaim thee on the Capitol; thou shalt avert every injury from the republic at the cost of thy blood, and thou shalt confirm this by oath and documents." Frederick indignantly interrupted the pompous orators at this point. They stopped in dismay, while the man who had been the moving spirit among them awaited in chains hard by in a tent the fate which had been hastened by such a discourse.

As the young prince listened to the bombastic harangue of men, who, issuing from the ruins of decayed Rome, adopted a tone such as the ancient Senate had never ventured to use in presence of the Cæsars, he may probably have thought that madmen stood before him. No contrast could have been harsher than that in which an emperor of the Germans, a Frederick I, found himself in relation to the Romans. The Hohenstaufen monarch, filled with a sense of his own power, did not understand the new spirit of liberty which had inflamed the cities of Italy. Rome, however, still commanded such reverence that he condescended to reply to the senators.

"I have heard much," he answered, "of the valor, still more of the sagacity of the Romans. I am therefore surprised that your speech should be inflated by such foolish arrogance and be so destitute of all reason. Thou holdest up before me the nobility of thy ancient city, thou exaltest the past of thy republic to the stars. I grant it, and with thy historian I say 'virtue once dwelt in this republic.' Rome has experienced the change of things under the moon; or has perchance this city alone been able to escape the law of all earthly things? It is known throughout the world how the flower of thy nobility has been transplanted from this our city to Byzantium, and how for a long time the degenerate Greek has drained thy precious life-blood. Then came the Frank, whose noble deeds belied not his name, and deprived thee of even the last remains of nobility and independence. Wilt thou know where the ancient glory of thy Rome, the dignified severity of the Senate, the valiant chastity of knighthood, the tactics of the camp and invincible military courage have gone? All are now found among us Germans; all have been transmitted to us with the empire. With us are thy consuls, with us thy Senate; thy legions are here. Thou owest thy preservation to the wisdom of the Franks and the sword of their chivalry. History can tell whether our illustrious forefathers, Charles and Otto, received the city by the grace of anyone, or whether they wrested it by the sword, with the remainder of Italy, from the Greeks and Lombards and then incorporated it with the Frankish kingdom. This is witnessed by thy tyrants, Desiderius and Berengar; they died old and grey in Frankish chains, and our country still preserves their ashes. But thou sayest the new emperors are summoned by thee. It is true. But why? Thou wast oppressed by enemies, and by thine own strength couldst not deliver thyself from the effeminate Greek. Thou didst then entreat the aid of the Frank; misery summoned fortune, impotence power, anguish self-conscious strength. Thus summoned, I came. Thy ruler was my vassal, thou thyself art still my subject, I am the rightful owner. Who dares to snatch his club from Hercules? Perhaps the Sicilian on whom thou placest thy hopes? Let the past teach him, for the arm of the German is not yet disabled. Thou demandest from me a threefold oath. Listen. Either thy demand is just, or otherwise. Is it unjust? Thou oughtest not to make it, nor I to consent. Is it just? I acknowledge an obligation assumed of my own free will. It is therefore unnecessary to confirm it by an oath. How should I violate the law with thee, when I have to preserve it for the most insignificant? Wherefore should I not defend the seat of my empire whose boundaries I am determined to restore? That is shown by Denmark, which has just been subjugated, and other countries also would prove it, had not my Roman journey interefered. Finally thou demandest a sworn promise to pay money. Is Rome not ashamed to traffic with her emperor as with

151

a usurer? Are we to be compelled to give whatever is asked of us instead of being a dispenser of favor? The fulfilment of due services is expected from lesser men, but the great repay as a favor only that which has been merited. Why should I withhold from thy citizens the customs inherited from my illustrious fore-fathers? No. My entrance shall be a festival for the city; but to those who unjustly demand what is unjust, I will justly refuse all."

Frederick's answer, in the rhetorical form in which his histo-rian has given it, was the expression of the German national pride arrived at the zenith of its three centuries of universal suprem-acy. Had it simply had reference to the senators of Rome it would have been overstrained; it was, however, rather the manifesto of the Hohenstaufen coronation program. The Hercules struck down the claims of the pretenders with his club. He even fell upon the pope, who claimed to be the sole and true maker of emperors. No one now ventured to depict the complaisant Lothar [III] in the Lateran, kneeling to receive the crown from the pope [Innocent II], or dared to place below the picture the audacious inscription:—

> The king to keep the law hath sworn, and at the gate of Rome
>   doth stand,
> Then swears allegiance to the pope, the crown receiving from his
>   hand.

The folly of the Romans in addressing so powerful a ruler in this pompous manner corresponded to their lofty ideas concern-ing the majesty of the Eternal City, which, by the institution of a Senate, they hoped to invest with a new life. But had any man of enlightenment superior to the level of his age been found within the imperial tent, he would have laughed at Frederick, who shared with the senators the fantastic ideas of the legitimate authority of the Roman emperors over the world.

The Roman envoys rode back in anger. Frederick might now expect the republic to close the gates of the city and to defend it against him. The pope advised him to occupy the Leonina with picked men, who would be admitted by the papal adher-ents. He also advised that Cardinal Octavian, a man of German sympathies, should join this force, in order that so ambitious a rival might be removed from the emperor's tent. A thousand horsemen were sent, who occupied the Leonina without opposition in the dawn of June 18.

The same day Frederick, who had received no greeting from the Romans, moved in order of battle from Monte Mario to the Leonina, where he was awaited by the pope, who had preceded him. The coronation took place in S. Peter's, the basilica being occupied by troops. The shouts of triumph of the Germans resounded like thunder in the lofty cathedral, as the young Cæsar took the sword, scepter and crown of empire. Rome, however, did not acknowledge him as emperor; the city gates remained barred and the people deliberated on the Capitol, where the palace of the Senate had been rebuilt a short time before. Nothing better illustrates the shadowy nature of the mediæval empire in Rome itself than this coronation performed in the papal suburb, while it was expected that the Romans, from whom the emperors derived their title, would rush across the bridges of the Tiber brandishing their arms. An impassable chasm of education, of requirements, of race separated the emperors of German origin from the Romans. If they hated the foreigner Adrian IV as their territorial ruler, they could nevertheless reverence him as pope, but Frederick must at this time have been utterly insupportable to them. He had not sworn to the laws of the city, to which all emperors were accustomed to swear; he had neither heard the votes of the Romans nor listened to the usual acclamations; nor had he repaid them by gifts. The Romans had every reason to feel offended. Their demand that the emperor should recognize their constitution was reasonable, and it was imprudent to refuse it. A time came when the emperor repented this refusal, and when he tendered the oath to the despised citizens. After the popes had ceased to be candidates for the elective votes of the Romans, the people also found themselves deprived of all share in the election of these emperors. At a time, however, when the civic and political conceptions of law were penetrated through and through with traditions of antiquity, the Romans could not be induced to confess that the Eternal City was anything but the place where pope and emperor received their highest consecration. While other cities shone conspicuous by their wealth and power, Rome's only glory was that she was Rome. Gregory VII had assigned the task of representing the world monarchy to the papacy, and the Romans on their side dreamed that this supremacy was to be attained by the majesty of the people and by the imperial office by them established.

Their inherited claims and their struggles against the popes, who strove to extinguish the political idea of the city, have impressed for centuries a tragic character on their history, a history unparalleled in the annals of mankind. In this struggle, which has continued down to our times, and under the influence of which the present history is written—in this struggle against one and the same destiny, the only allies of the Romans were the walls of Aurelian, the Tiber, the malaria, and the shades and monuments of their great ancestors. Only now, when the city of Rome has no other ambition than the desire of descending to the ordinary rank of capital of a country, has she found a helper and ally in the Italian nation.

The emperor having obtained his crown, retired to his camp on the Neronian Field, while the pope remained in the Vatican. But early in the afternoon the angry Romans rushed across the bridges into the Leonine city. Wherever they encountered the enemy singly, they cut them down; they plundered clergy, cardinals, and adherents of the imperial party; they finally attacked Frederick's camp, whence they perhaps hoped to rescue their prophet Arnold. The emperor and the army rose from the coronation banquet; it was reported that pope and cardinals were in the hands of the populace. Henry the Lion entered through the breach in the walls which had formerly been made by Henry IV, forced his way to the Leonina, and attacked the Romans in the rear. It cost the valiant army some trouble, however, to overcome them. Their courageous conduct showed that the constitution of the republic was not altogether a fantastic whim. A varying struggle, which lasted until night, took place at the bridge of S. Angelo, and with the Trasteverines at the ancient

154

Fishpond, until the citizens were overcome by superior numbers. "Our soldiers were seen," thus wrote an ancient German chronicler, "mowing down the Romans, as if they would say, 'Here, O Rome, take German iron for Arabian gold; thus does Germany buy the empire.'" Nearly one thousand Romans were slain or drowned in the river; several [thousand] were wounded, about two hundred were taken prisoners; the remainder saved themselves by flight into the strongly fortified city, while S. Angelo, in the possession of the Pierleoni, remained neutral.

In the morning the pope appeared in the imperial camp to implore the release of the prisoners, who had been given into the custody of the prefect Peter. So incomplete, however, had been the bloody victory that even the great emperor, who regarded himself as the lawful ruler of the world, was obliged to depart without even having entered the city. The Romans at this period showed themselves entirely worthy of their freedom; they manfully bade defiance to the emperor from behind their walls; they refused to sell him the necessaries of life, and were ready to continue the struggle. Frederick consequently broke up his camp on June 19. He took the pope and all the cardinals with him as fugitives and retreated toward Soracte; all along his line of march through the Roman district he ordered the towers which the Roman nobles had erected on their estates to be pulled down.

It is probable that Arnold's execution took place at this time, and in this same neighborhood of Soracte. The end of the celebrated demagogue is as obscure as the end of Crescentius, his contemporaries passing it hastily by as if in awe. After his surrender he was handed over to the city prefect, who with his powerful family owned large estates in the county of Viterbo. They had long made war on the Roman commune, had suffered severe injuries at its hands, and consequently cherished feelings of bitter indignation against Arnold. After he had been condemned by a spiritual tribunal the prefect sentenced him (and undoubtedly with the emperor's sanction) to death as a heretic and rebel. The unfortunate man courageously refused to recant; he asserted that his teaching was just and salutary, and that he was ready to die for his principles. He only asked for a brief respite that he might confess his sins to Christ; he knelt with uplifted hands, prayed to heaven and commended his soul to God. The executioner himself was moved to pity. Such is the account given by a recently discovered poem, written by a Brescian of imperial sympathies. This author, in common with other contemporaries, says that Arnold was hanged and then burned, in order that none of his remains might fall into possession of the Romans—a fact which proves to what degree he was idolized by the people. According to others, his ashes were thrown into the Tiber. The scene of his execution is nowhere designated with certainty.

The smoke from Arnold's funeral pyre darkens the youthful but already blood-stained majesty of the emperor, to whose immediate needs he fell a sacrifice. But avengers already existed in the burghers of the Lombard cities, who were later to compel Frederick to recognize the glorious work of freedom which had been so powerfully influenced by Arnold's spirit. The hand of the mighty has often unconsciously shattered the instruments of great movements, movements which have overwhelmed the mighty themselves. Frederick did not see Arnold of Brescia in the light in which he now appears to us, and the emperor had perhaps heard but little of the reformer. Of what importance to him was the life of a single heretic? And even were he acquainted with the facts of Arnold's life, he had been at war with the cities of northern Italy and with Rome, and could never, therefore, have been favorably disposed to the Lombard—the political innovator. He thus destroyed a glorious force, which might later have been of the greatest service to himself. Frederick showed but little foresight in Rome. Instead of magnanimously restricting the Roman democracy within reasonable limits, as he might easily have done, and then removing it from the papal influence and placing it under the authority of the empire, he repelled it with blind contempt, made enemies of several other cities, and at length saw all his extravagant schemes fall to ruin.

Arnold of Brescia heads the series of celebrated martyrs for freedom who died upon the funeral pyre, but whose ardent genius rose like a phœnix from the flames to live through centuries. We might even call him a prophet, so clearly did he see into the spirit of his time, so far did he advance towards the goal, which, not until 700 years after him, Rome and Italy are hoping to reach. The already mature consciousness of his age was incarnate in the gifted person of the reformer, and the first political heretic of the Middle Ages was the logical consequence of the quarrel for investitures. The struggle of the two powers and the transformation of the cities were the great practical phenomena which served him as a historical basis. An inner necessity drew him to the spot where the root of all the evil lay. If Arnold had not gone to Rome, had not ended his life here, he would have been an incomplete figure of his age. But Rome, oppressed at the same time by the weight of her ancient greatness, and by the two supreme powers in the world, could not permanently maintain her civic freedom. The constitution, to which Arnold may perhaps as a lawgiver have largely contributed, nevertheless long survived him; the school of the Arnoldists or politicians never died out. Arnold is the historic precedent for all the forces, theoretical or practical, which have revolted against the secular character of the clergy; this so much the more because his aims were not sullied by any sordid motives. For even his most violent opponents admitted that he was only influenced by enthusiastic conviction. Arnold surpasses all his successors in the struggle for Roman liberty, not only in the greatness of his time, but also in the loftiness of his aims. Savonarola, with whom he has been compared, is frequently rendered offensive to every manly judgment by the monastic character of his intellect and by his claims to supernatural powers. But neither miracles or oracles are attributed to the friend of Abelard. He seems to have been sane, manly, and clear; whether it is that he really was so, or that history has withheld many circumstances of his life. His teaching was of such enduring vitality, that it is still in harmony with the spirit of our time, and Arnold of Brescia would now be the most popular man in Italy. For so obstinate is the ban of the Middle Ages under which Rome and Italy are still held, that the soul of a heretic in the twelfth century has not yet found rest, but must still haunt Rome.

157

Frederick crossed the Tiber at Magliano, and proceeded by Farfa, as Henry V had done before him, to the Lucanian Bridge. Here the festival of SS. Peter and Paul was celebrated with great splendor under tents, and the pope absolved the German troops of all blame for the blood which had been shed in Rome. The cities of the Campagna hastened to discharge the oppressive *foderum* to the emperor, other cities to do him homage, or to place themselves under his protection, and Tivoli, which out of hatred to Rome had ranged itself under the papal banner, now even hoped to throw off the authority of the pope. Envoys of the commune (which was now undoubtedly headed by consuls) gave the keys of the town to the emperor as overlord. In revenge against the Romans, Frederick would have strengthened a town which was at enmity with the Senate, but Adrian advanced the rights of the church, and the emperor released the Tivolese from the oath of subjection which they had just taken, and gave them back their town. The restitution of Tivoli was the pitiful compromise enacted by the pope, to whom Frederick could not fulfil his promise to make him sovereign of Rome.

He advanced to Tusculum, and remained with Adrian in the Alban Mountain until the middle of July. He made an effort to attack Rome, but his expedition was of no avail: nor could he entertain William I's challenge to fight him in Apulia, his great German vassals justly refusing to sanction the proposal. Neither could he at this season enter on any undertaking against the Romans. The malaria now appeared among his discontented troops; he was obliged to turn and, not without some painful self-reproach, to abandon the pope to his fate. He gave the prisoners into Adrian's hands; took leave of him in Tivoli, and set forth on his northern progress by way of Farfa. With barbarous indignation he reduced the ancient and celebrated city of Spoleto to ashes on his route. And like Demetrius in ancient times the great Hohenstaufen might with justice have been called "destroyer of cities."

IV

Pope, Commune, and Emperor at the End of the Twelfth Century

*Hostile relations with the commune forced Pope Alexander III to spend all but about three years of his twenty-two year pontificate (1159–81) outside of Rome. Gregorovius describes Alexander's political relations with the great powers in Italy, and then analyzes the modus vivendi worked out by pope, commune, and emperor after Alexander's death.—*EDITOR.

THE fact that three of [Pope] Alexander [III]'s successors were forced to live in exile is sufficient to show the relations that subsisted between the popes and the city. The figure of Frederick's great opponent towers like the figure of a hero over the commonplace forms of these three popes, who died after having inhaled a few breaths of misfortune. The ebb succeeded the flow—an ever-recurring law in the history of the papacy.

Lucius III, Ubaldo Allucingoli, of Lucca, hitherto cardinal-bishop of Ostia and Velletri, was not even elected in Rome, but was raised to the papacy by the College of Cardinals assembled at Velletri, and was ordained on September 6, 1181. After an agreement with the Romans he came to the city in November,

From book VIII, ch. 6, secs. 3 and 4.

and was allowed to remain some months. The spirit of Arnold still survived in Rome, and each pope was obliged to win toleration for himself, or else to live in exile. Since Lucius refused to concede the privileges accorded by earlier popes, it would seem that he was already at enmity with the Romans. Tusculum remained a permanent source of strife. The fortress was the object of a hatred bordering on frenzy to the Romans, as Fiesole was to the Florentines, until Florence destroyed her neighbor in 1125. The Tusculans had vainly sought protection under the banner of the pope; with great efforts they rebuilt their walls and made a desperate resistance to the repeated attacks of the enemy. When the Romans attacked Tusculum with increased force on June 28, 1183, Lucius III, who remained shut up in Segni, summoned [Archbishop] Christian of Mainz from Tuscany; Christian came, and the recollection of the battle of Monte Porzio sufficed to drive the Romans back twice. The warlike archbishop advanced to the walls of the city, but the August fever, which had formerly killed his celebrated companion Rainald, also proved fatal to himself. At first the fierce enemy of the sacred chair, afterwards its defender, the brave hero bore the papal blessing to his grave; he died in Tusculum, the scene of his actions, and was buried there. Christian, who was one of the greatest princes of his age, was also a living satire on every pious effort made to divest the bishops of the offensive character of worldliness, since he, the archbishop of Mainz (for as such he was recognized after the peace of Venice), remained a jovial knight until his death, kept a harem of beautiful girls, and, clad in glittering armor, rode a splendid horse, swinging the battle axe with which he shattered the helmet and head of many an enemy.

His death was a severe blow to the pope, who now summoned the princes to his aid, but only received words and some money in answer. The Romans turned with increased courage against all such places as remained faithful to the pope. They devastated the territory of Tusculum in April 1184, and carried their ravages far into Latium. Their hatred of the clergy was fierce and barbarous; on one occasion they seized a company of priests in the Campagna, put out the eyes of all but one, placed miters, inscribed with the names of cardinals, on their heads, and, setting them on asses, ordered the one priest whom they had spared to conduct the sad procession to the pope. Lucius III fled to the emperor at Verona, whither Frederick, having concluded a peace with the cities on April 30, 1183, had arrived from Constance. The emperor's meeting with the pope gave rise to many disputes concerning the investitures and Matilda's bequest. Lucius also refused to bestow the imperial crown on Frederick's son King Henry, by which a Carolingian custom would have been revived. The request was discussed with great vehemence in Verona; and the emperor parted from the pope in anger. He had, however, previously appointed Count Berthold of Kunsberg as commandant of Campania in Christian's place, with orders that he was to defend Tusculum against the Romans. The Romans were even excommunicated by Lucius at the council of Verona. For the rebels against the *dominium temporale* were classed with the heretical sects of the time, who were ever becoming more powerful,—the Waldenses, Cathari, Humiliates, the Poor of Lyons, and others,—as Arnoldists, and were solemnly cursed. Lucius III died at Verona on November 25, 1185. The melancholy but ingenious lines placed on his grave admirably depict his fate and that of other popes of the age:—

> *Lucius, Luca tibi dedit ortum, Pontificatum*
> *Ostia, Papatum Roma, Verona mori.*
> *Immo Verona dedit verum tibi vivere, Roma*
> *Exilium, curas Ostia, Luca mori.*

[Lucius, Lucca gave you birth; Ostia, the pontificate; Rome, the papacy; Verona, death. Or rather, Verona gave you true life; Rome, exile; Ostia, cares; Lucca, death.]

His successor, as melancholy a figure as himself, remained in exile in Verona. This was Humbert Crivelli, archbishop of Milan, a violent and unyielding spirit, and a strong opponent of Frederick. He was consecrated as Urban III on December 3, 1185. The tension which existed between him and the emperor now developed into open enmity, an enmity largely based on Frederick's refusal to surrender the disputed estates of Matilda. The brilliant success which German statesmanship had attained in Sicily proved a further ground of anxiety to the Curia. After a brief prime, Roger's dynasty neared its end; William II was childless; he consequently gave his sanction to the marriage of Constance, the daughter of Roger, his aunt and heiress, to Henry [VI], son of Frederick. Without any regard to the pope, the feudal lord of Sicily, and in defiance of his opposition, the ominous union was celebrated at Milan, where Frederick formally created his son Cæsar. The pope refused Henry the imperial crown, and (since he remained archbishop of Milan) the crown of Lombardy also. The emperor consequently had the ceremony performed by the patriarch of Aquileia. Sicily, the anxiously guarded fief of the sacred chair, which had so often served as a protection against the German kings, must necessarily fall to this very German empire on William's death. The loss of Sicily was therefore the heaviest defeat which Roman policy could suffer, and for the time the most glorious victory on the side of the German court, which had now attained, through diplomatic arrangements, the object for which so many emperors had hitherto fought in vain. The acquisition of Sicily was to make amends for the loss of Lombardy, and a Hohenstaufen dynasty was founded both in Sicily and in Matilda's territory [Tuscany]. But these immense gains soon became the curse not only of Italy but of Germany, which had bitterly to expiate the unpatriotic policy of the Hohenstaufens.

At his father's command Henry entered the state of the church as an enemy; the Romans gladly joined him; the districts of Latium which still adhered to the sacred chair were ravaged, and the pope was deprived of every hope of return. Urban III meanwhile died in Ferrara, on October 20, 1187. Jerusalem had but just fallen (on October 2), and the news struck like a thunderbolt the heart of a pope who bore the name of the fortunate predecessor during whose pontificate the Holy City had obtained her freedom. The fall of Jerusalem shook the whole of Europe with such force as to thrust into the background the most important matters in the West, and the energies of pope and emperor, of kings and bishops, were again directed towards the East.

Albert of Mora, a Beneventan, and chancellor of the church,

was immediately (October 25, 1187) consecrated at Ferrara as Gregory VIII. He was old and of amiable disposition, and desired nothing beyond peace with the empire and a crusade to Jerusalem. The papacy was exhausted by its struggles under Alexander III. Meantime the empire had become stronger; the peace of Venice and that of Constance had put an end to the war with the cities, and the alliance with Sicily had suddenly increased the imperial power. While popes banished from Rome sighed in exile, not a single enemy appeared against Frederick throughout the whole of Italy. Urban III himself would not have ventured to launch the anathema against the emperor, and the gentle-natured Gregory VIII hastened to make peace with King Henry. He promised to advance no opposition to his claims on Sicily, and moreover to recognize the rights of the empire in Italy. Henry VI, therefore, suspended hostilities and sent Count Anselm with Leo de Monumento, consul of the Romans, to treat with the pope. The two envoys accompanied Gregory to Pisa, where he went to effect a reconciliation between this republic and Genoa, and to rouse it to take part in the Crusade. He was here overtaken by death on December 17, 1187.

The cardinals, with the assistance of the Consul Leo, immediately elected the bishop of Palestrina as pope, and Paolino Scolari, who belonged to the Regione della Pigna, was consecrated as Clement III in the cathedral of Pisa, on December 20, 1187. A Roman by birth, he succeeded in effecting the peace with the Capitol for which Gregory VIII had prepared the way. After successful negotiations, he returned to Rome, accompanied by the Consul Leo, in February 1188, and was received with every honor. During the forty-four years' existence of the Roman Senate the popes had been almost incessantly victims of the civic revolution. We have seen how sorrowfully Innocent II and Celestine II ended their days, how Lucius II had been killed by the blow of a stone, how Eugenius, Alexander, Lucius, Urban III, and Gregory VIII had spent their lives in exile. Clement III at length brought the papacy back to Rome, but was forced to make a formal peace with the city as with an independent power. This was the result not only of the Lombard victories but also of the energetic resistance of the Romans to emperor and to pope. The establishment of the Roman democracy forms an important act of the period, for although lacking the fortune and the foundation of the Lombard and Tuscan cities, it nevertheless proves the Romans to have been possessed of praiseworthy energy and prudence.

Generally speaking, Rome assumed the same attitude towards the pope as that which the Lombard cities had acquired towards the emperor, or fell back on the treaties of the times of Eugenius III and Alexander III. The charter which the Roman Senate compiled and swore to on May 31, 1188, in the forty-fourth year of its existence, has fortunately been preserved to us. According to the articles of this peace, decreed in vigorous language by the authority of the sacred Senate, the pope was recognized as overlord. He invested the Senate on the Capitol, which was obliged to take the oath of fidelity to him. He again acquired the right of coining money, a third part of which fell to the Senate. All revenues which had formerly been papal returned to the pope, the Senate merely retaining the Lucanian bridge on account of its feud with Tivoli. The restitution of all that by right belonged to the sacred chair was to be settled by document. The pope further indemnified the Romans for their losses in the war; he undertook to give the judges and notaries, the senators and the officials of the Senate, the customary presents of money. He promised one hundred pounds annually for the restoration of the city walls. It was also decreed that since the Roman militia was to be paid by the pope, the pope might summon it to the defense of the patrimony. No article defined whether the republic had the right of making peace and war with its enemies without regard to the pope; this liberty, nevertheless, was taken for granted, since Rome was free. And although titles and honors of temporal authority were respectfully awarded him, the pope found himself in his city in much the same position as did other bishops in other free cities. A formal agreement was concluded concerning the now papal towns of Tusculum and Tibur, the hatred of the Romans towards them being the actual reason for their treaty with the pope. Clement III unscrupulously sacrificed the unfor-

tunate Tusculum, which had sought shelter under the wings of
the church, as the price of his peaceful return to Rome. He not
only gave the Romans permission to make war on the fortress,
but even promised them the aid of his vassals, and pledged himself to excommunicate the Tusculans should they fail to surrender
to the Romans before January 1. The unfortunate city was to be
destroyed, its property and people were to remain in the hands
of the pope.

A special treaty with the captains established their relations
with the Roman commune. We have no precise knowledge of its
articles, but the great nobility were undoubtedly compelled to
acknowledge the Senate, to take their part in the commune as
cives, and thus to contribute to the formation of the commune as
a whole.

The pope was to choose ten men out of every street (*contrada*)
of every region in Rome, five of whom were to swear to the peace;
the united Senate swore to the treaty itself. We gather here that
the Senate was composed of fifty-six members, some of whom
formed the ruling committee of consiliarii.

The city itself, which was redivided after the institution of the
free Roman commune in 1144, now consisted of twelve regions.
These divisions had no ordinal numbers, but merely local names,
and were as follows: Montium et Biberatice; Trivii et Vie Late;
Columpne et S. Marie in Aquiro; Campi Martis et S. Laurentii in
Lucina; Pontis et Scorteclariorum; S. Eustachii et Vinea Teude-
marii; Arenule et Caccabariorum; Parionis et S. Laurentii in
Damaso; Pinee et S. Marci; S. Angeli in Foro Piscium; Ripe et
Marmorate; Campitelli et S. Adriani. The Leonina remained, as
an entirely papal district, outside the regions; not so, however,
the Trastevere and the island in the Tiber, which, formerly two
regions, were afterwards counted as one—the thirteenth.

The constitution of 1188 showed a marked advance on the
part of the Roman commune. The imperial authority of Carolingian times was as completely set aside as the patrician power of
Frankish times. The rights of the emperor in particular were left
utterly unheeded. The ties between Rome and the empire were
severed when the popes acquired the freedom of election. Fred-

erick I himself had disdained the votes of the Romans on his own election and finally in the treaty of Anagni, and with the renunciation of the prefecture he also renounced the exercise of the imperial power in the city. Rome had advanced beyond her ancient conditions; the pope possessed neither governing nor legislative power; his secular position, on the contrary, was limited to the possession of regalia and church property and to feudal relations. He was powerful because he still remained the greatest landowner, dispensed the greatest fiefs, and could command numerous "men." His authority as a territorial ruler consisted, however, merely in the investiture which he conferred on the freely elected magistrates of the republic, or in the alliance of papal with civic justice in cases of a twofold nature. The removal of the papal power by the unaided energy of the Roman commune is consequently one of the most honorable deeds in the history of mediæval city, which could now again lay claim to the esteem of mankind in civic matters.

In 1189 Clement III succeeded in obtaining from Henry [VI] (who acted as his father's representative) the restitution of all the property belonging to the State of the Church of which Lucius had been deprived. The pope now concentrated all his attention on the great Crusade, in which at first the emperor Frederick, and afterwards Philip Augustus, king of France, and Richard of England, took part. Roman nobles now also went to the East—a Pierleone and even the Prefect Theobald, both of whom fought by the side of Conrad of Montferrat against Saladin at Acre. None of the crusading armies came near Rome. And although Richard Cœur-de-Lion, who sailed from Marseilles in the beginning of August 1190, landed at Ostia, he dismissed the cardinal (who in the name of the pope came with a polite invitation that he would honor the capital of Christendom by a visit) with a refusal. In a previous century no king would have declined the like invitation; on the contrary, a monarch would have considered himself fortunate in entering the gates of the sacred city, habited as a pilgrim, to visit the graves of the apostles. But times were changed. Richard, the successor of pious Anglo-Saxon kings, who in ancient days reached the summit of bliss when they took the cowl in Rome, contemptuously informed the cardinal that nothing was to be found at the papal court but avarice and corruption. He passed the city by, marching along the wooded and marshy coast to Terracina, and thence sailed to Messina, where he entered into negotiations with the Sicilians. On December 16, 1189, William II, husband of Richard's sister Johanna, had died, and the national party in the island had given the crown to Count Tancred, a natural son of Roger of Apulia, the eldest son of King Roger. Henry VI, husband of Constance, prepared to overthrow by force of arms the "usurper," who had received investiture from the pope. He was, however, prevented by troubles in Germany in the first instance, and by the death of his father in the second. The aged Frederick, who had formerly wished that fate, instead of sending him to Italy, had sent him to Asia like Alexander the Great, met his death in a Syrian river on June 10, 1190.

The immortal hero Barbarossa, the true imperial colossus of the Middle Ages, lives in German history as an object of national pride, in popular tradition as the symbol of the return of glory to the German empire. But in Italy, although the character of the age may afford some mitigation of his conduct, his ravages and the ruin of noble cities furnish plentiful grounds for hatred. The obstinate struggle of the empire against the cities, or the quarrel for civic investitures, was no less important and salutary than the contest for the spiritual investitures waged by the Henries. Had it not been for Frederick's despotic plans and wars, the freedom of the cities would not have attained such rapid development, nor would these cities have won such speedy recognition of their political rights. Barbarossa, contrary to his intentions, rendered at least this service to Italy, which resisted him so valiantly. The long and fatal connection between Germany and Italy through the empire will be denounced by such men as judge universal history by the narrow measure of the prosperity of the fatherland; outside this limited horizon the lament is vain and foolish. This only may we say, that, after the peace of Venice, Italy and Germany were already fully ripe for separation. By the Sicilian marriage, however, Frederick unfortunately reunited a tie that was already virtually severed, and the unity and power of Germany were thus uselessly sacrificed to the domestic policy of the imperial dynasty and were condemned afresh to tedious wars beyond the Alps.

The youthful Henry VI coveted the imperial crown; his envoys hastened to the pope and even to the Senate, whose vote again commanded respect, and the legal standing of which the king promised to recognize. Clement III, troubled by the threats of Henry, who was irritated with the pope for having given Sicily in fief to Tancred, fixed the coronation for the following Easter, but himself died at the end of March 1191.

The cardinals immediately elected the aged Hyacinth, son of Peter Bobo, a Roman of the Orsini family, as pope under the name of Celestine III. Henry was already approaching with a large army, and Easter was at hand. The new pope delayed his ordination in order to defer the coronation, concerning which negotiations were still pending. It was possible that the hostile attitude of the Senate might also prove a cause of delay, and Henry VI used his most urgent entreaties in order that he might forthwith move against Sicily. The Romans availed themselves of these accidental circumstances to recover possession of Tusculum. The afflicted town had for three years made a desperate resistance against the united attacks of the pope and the Senate; in their extremest need they had turned to Henry, begging for protection, and had accepted the German garrison which he readily gave them. The Roman envoys, however, declared that they would oppose his coronation unless he gave Tusculum into their hands; that on the contrary, if he yielded, they would obtain his immediate coronation from the pope. Henry consented to this shameful breach of faith, but threw the responsibility on the pope, who allowed himself to be bound by dishonorable conditions. The coronation over, Tusculum was to be given by Henry to the pope, by the pope to the Romans.

Not until Henry drew near with a great military force did Clement allow himself to be ordained in S. Peter's on April 14, in order that he might, although unwillingly, perform the coronation the following day. The king entered the Leonina from the

Field of Nero. Celestine crowned him and his wife Constance in S. Peter's on April 15, and the next day the Germans pitched their camp on the slopes of Tusculum. The unhappy town soon suffered a tragic fall. It was given back to the pope and by him surrendered to its destroyers, and the Romans fell on their defenseless victim. Not a single stone was left upon another in the whole of Tusculum, while, contrary to faith and treaty, the inhabitants were strangled or banished into misery. Such was the wanton caricature of the celebrated destructions of Lodi, Milan, and Crema—a characteristic feature of this period of the emancipation and destruction of cities. Owing to the twofold treachery of emperor and pope, one of the oldest cities of Latium was destroyed for ever on April 17, 1191. In ancient times it had in the Catos bestowed renowned patriots on its much more youthful neighbor; in the Middle Ages it had given it tyrants in the shape of rude consuls and patricians, the Tusculan counts, and popes, who, although for the most part bad, were some of them men of intellect and energy. The name of Tusculum is associated with the darkest period of mediæval Rome, and we cannot survey the melancholy ruins on the sunny heights without recalling memories of Marozia, the Alberics and Theophylacts. The powerful family of the counts of Tusculum disappeared or perhaps survived in branches in Rome and the Campagna, of which the Colonna is the most celebrated. These nobles also obtained possession of the ancient ancestral palace of the Tusculans beside S. Apostoli in Rome, where the counts had so frequently held their tribunals as consuls of the Romans.

The property of the ruined city fell, according to treaty, to the pope; the remainder of the inhabitants went to swell the population of the surrounding district.

The new emperor marched from Rome to Apulia to dethrone King Tancred, and the weak Celestine offered no opposition to his intention beyond useless prayers. The union of Sicily with the empire, which ran counter to all the traditional principles of the popes, was a source of trouble, but Celestine was powerless to prevent it. After rapid victories and heavy losses in Apulia, Henry VI was obliged to return to Germany in 1191, and the pope, rejoicing in his departure, ventured the less to infringe the treaty concluded with the Romans. Celestine III was the only pope who for many years spent the whole of his pontificate in Rome. All exterior conditions favored the continued existence of the republic, but interior circumstances prevented its vigorous development. Christian Rome was capable of transient ebullitions in favor of freedom and greatness, but was deprived of genuine manly civic virtues through the papacy. The priest-ridden city no longer produced a citizen of the heroic stamp of antiquity. The unfortunate people, who were condemned to indolence, and whose year numbered more festivals than working days, lacked property because they lacked civic activity, and for this reason lacked also conscious dignity and force. The causes of the condition of the Romans are evident, and it was impossible that any people in the world could have permanently resisted their influence. The city guilds, if any survived, were too inconsiderable to afford any support to the Roman middle class, which was poor and weak. It could not vanquish the patricians and captains, who, either allied with the pope, or independent, now weakend, now shattered the republic. Had the nobility been of the same mould as the nobility of Genoa and Venice, a permanent patrician government might have been formed in opposition to the popes, but the Roman nobles, engaged neither in commercial nor in agricultural pursuits, were for the most part illustrious beggars or vassals of the popes, of the bishops or the pious foundations in Rome. The church had gradually reduced all these nobles to a state of vassalage, and had prevented, as far as she was able, the accumulation or settlement of family property. The property of the wealthy was consequently insecure and passed from hand to hand. In reading the contracts of the time our surprise is awakened by the frequency with which fiefs and fortresses were bartered and exchanged. Only a few families, such as the Colonna and Orsini, succeeded in founding actual hereditary lordships in the Campagna.

When, after the peaces of Venice, of Constance and of Rome, the nobles perceived that the commune was acquiring stability, they renounced their previous system of obstruction. The former consuls entered the commune to make it aristocratic; members of the nobility filled the Senate, where it was easy for them to obtain election. After 1143, the majority of the Senate was entirely plebeian; nobles entered it by degrees, and after the time of Clement III and Celestine III it numbered more patricians of ancient lineage than burghers or knights. The competition for the Senate was so great that the normal number of members (fifty-six) was soon overstepped.

In consequence of these altered conditions a revolution took place in 1191; the populace revolted against the aristocracy, overthrew the constitution, and placed, as in ancient times, a single man at the head of the government. This may have been done in imitation of other cities, which towards the end of the century had entrusted the authority to a sole ruler, instead of to the hitherto ruling consuls. The Romans no longer called the head of their republic patricius, nor as in other Italian towns podestà, but senator or summus senator. This dignity they bestowed on Benedict Carushomo, a man undoubtedly of middle-class origin, who had seized the power during a revolt. The government of many had shown itself weak; the rule of the one immediately proved strong, for the senator Benedict deprived the pope of all revenues both inside and outside the city, and appointed his judges in the provincial districts also. The pope would not at first recognize Benedict, but he afterwards yielded and consented to the change in the constitution.

Rome perhaps owes to this senator the first municipal statute which it issued and which was ratified by the entire people. A few isolated notices concerning Benedict's activity have come down to us. And it might perhaps have gratified the energetic senator to know that his memory is still preserved in a monumental inscription in Rome. His office lasted about two years; he was then overthrown in a revolt and was long kept a prisoner on the Capitol. Giovanni Capoccio was now created sole senator. This Roman belonged to one of the families of the smaller nobility, who owned towers beside S. Martino and Silvestro, some of which still remain erect. He also governed with energy. On his retirement he was succeeded in office by Giovanni Pierleone.

A fresh revolution took place, however, about 1197; the old constitution of fifty-six senators and the executive committee of consiliatores was restored. And since the Senate was at this time essentially composed of captains, the change must have been due to the feudal nobility themselves.

In the struggle of factions in the commune and in the mania for novelty, peculiar to all democracies, lay the pope's only hope; he therefore prudently left the Romans to themselves. The papacy was severely threatened, Henry VI having subjugated Sicily after King Tancred's death in 1194. The perfidy with which this unscrupulous prince exterminated the last descendants of the Norman dynasty and the Norman nobility roused the national feeling of Italy. The Lombards, menaced by a new imperial despotism, saw the freedom which they had so heroically acquired threatened with ruin. Henry, as formerly his father, bestowed the public offices in Italy on Germans; he made his brother Philip Duke of Tuscany and invested him with the estates of Matilda. Conrad of Uerslingen had already received Spoleto in fief, and the General Markwald the Romagna and the Marches. Henry's power encompassed the State of the Church like a ring of iron. He occupied the patrimonium as far as the very gates of Rome. With more than youthful intrepidity, with foolish exaggeration, the son of Barbarossa conceived the ideal of the empire; he dreamed of the restoration of imperial universal supremacy, of the enslavement of Italy, of the destruction of the Gregorian papacy. He wished to recover the imperial rights in Rome which his father had renounced, and, endowed as he was with a spirit so energetic, he would undoubtedly have succeeded had he been granted a longer life. The city prefect maintained a lasting opposition to the pope, whose official he refused to be. His position hitherto, owing to the imperial investiture, had been too independent and respected for him calmly to bear the prospect of its loss. We consequently find the prefects at this time constantly in Henry's retinue, which they purposely hastened to join. Henry VI also drew the Frangipani to his side. The Frangipani, at this time the most powerful vassals of the church, opposed a permament defiance to the popes, who were obliged to leave them in

172

possession of the seaport of Terracina. Here they ruled as despots and frequently soothed the rebellious commune by treaties.

In November 1196 the emperor set forth on his last expedition to Sicily, accompanied by the prefect Peter, by Markwald and Conrad of Spoleto, and marched through Roman territory to Tivoli, Palestrina, and Ferentino. He did not touch Rome, but from Tivoli held negotiations with the pope concerning the coronation of his little son Frederick, which he anxiously desired. Rome was suffering from a famine, and the pope begged Henry to relieve it by supplies of corn. The ill-treated Sicilians rose against the tyranny of the emperor, whose own wife joined the rebels. Henry quenched the insurrection with an inhumanity unparalleled save in the history of Asiatic sultans; but after having reduced the flourishing kingdom to a desert, he was himself removed by death. Henry VI, in whom some of the great qualities of a ruler were united with unscrupulous want of honor, avarice, and the barbarism of a despot, died at the age of thirty-two at Messina, on September 28, 1197. He was followed to the grave by Celestine III on January 8, 1198. The heir of the dread power of the empire was a helpless child, under the guardianship of a bigoted Sicilian mother; the heir of the impotent pope, however, was one of the greatest characters in the annals of the papacy.

The good fortune of the church was unbounded.[1]

---

1. The gigantic work of the *Annals* of Baronius ends with the death of Celestine III. I shall begin vol. v. with Innocent III. It has been granted me to write every line of this history in the deep silence of Rome, and I deem myself happy in having been able to pursue the work during this memorable present, which has given a new direction to the fortunes of the illustrious city. [This volume was begun on November 8, 1860, and was finished on April 27, 1862. Victor Emmanuel entered Naples on November 7, 1860. Gæta capitulated February 13, 1861, and Francis II and his queen took refuge in Rome. Victor Emmanuel was proclaimed king of Italy, March 14, 1861. Cavour died June 6, 1861.–TRANSLATOR.]

173

V

Entente between the Commune and Pope Innocent III (1198-1216)

AFTER the chivalric and religious enthusiasm of the twelfth century, the succeeding century shows mankind arrived at a fuller maturity, engaged in fierce struggles for the acquisition of a civic constitution, and already enjoying a life ennobled by work, by knowledge, and by art. The thirteenth century is the culmination of the Middle Ages, on which the church stands conspicuous in the fulness of her power, while with the Hohenstaufens the ancient German empire passes out of history in order to leave the field clear for independent national states. The empire, with a last superhuman effort, continued under Frederick II the struggle for its legitimate existence against two tendencies of the age, to the united force of which it was obliged to succumb. It fought against the universal dominion of the papacy, and, as in the second half of the twelfth century, the papacy formed an alliance with the Italian democracies, which, by means of the principle of Latin municipalism, overthrew the foreign institution of German feudalism. The thirteenth century is the age of a great struggle for freedom against an obsolescent but legitimate constitution; of the revolution of the middle class against the feudal aristocracy; of democracy against the imperial monarchy; of the church against the empire; of heresy against the papacy. It is a period,

From book IX, ch. 1, secs. 1, 2, and 4.

174

above all, invested with a special luster by the republican freedom of Italy. Within strongly walled and no less strongly governed cities, which enclosed a surprising amount of genius,
property, and energy, the mother country of European culture
rose to her first still imperfect consciousness of her own nationality. This period of the Middle Ages was the period of the cities.
As in ancient times, man was again above all a citizen. The city,
with its families and clans, with its organized guilds, realized
for the second time in history the conception of the state. If we
overlook the idea expressed by this remarkable municipal spirit,
the return of Italy—the true motherland of cities—to a communal
system of politics, immediately after her escape from the decayed
framework of the empire, may appear as a retrograde movement.
That idea was the victory over feudalism, the recovery by learning and labor of the good things of life, the creation of a national
culture which was the work of civic society. The energies of the
laity, developed by a tedious process, demanded a system in
which they should be combined and protected. This protection
was furnished by the free cities, the most glorious product of the
Middle Ages, the ever active seminaries of a new culture. Italy
flourished again independently in her democracies, and again
sank into deepest misery when these free cities fell to decay.

The restriction of the state to the city, of the nation to the
citizens of the communes, is nevertheless an inadequate condition of things, and one in which the higher elements remain unexpressed. Cities formed leagues as in ancient days, but it was
impossible to extend these leagues into an Italian confederation.
The empire, which was still predominant, and the papacy, which
possessed its own city, prevented any confederation of this kind;
and the church, which recognized the impossibility of carrying out the Guelf idea of a papal theocracy of Italy, by the foundation of a French monarchy in the south, rendered every prospect of union vain. Alike incapable of creating a political nation
the cities fell in a condition of narrow isolation. The force of
faction which kept their political life weak, and which bore witness to the need of some symbol for a universal political cult,
availed itself of the opposition between the church and the em-

pire, and created the world historic factions of the Guelfs and the Ghibellines. The obstruction of national unity caused the vital sap which (otherwise than in ancient Italy and Greece) was not drained by colonization to stagnate in narrow channels; and after the great struggle between church and empire was ended, the cities, seething with energy, broke out into class and civic warfare, the results of which were necessarily, in the first place, the rule of the mob, afterwards the reign of civic tyrants, and finally the rise of petty principalities.

In like manner the city of Rome also manifested the municipal tendency. Consistently enough, she put aside the last connecting link with the empire at the same time that the communes, in alliance with the papacy (which had now become a national institution), defeated the feudal empire in Italy. It was the popes who severed these links, who extinguished the ancient conception of the *Respublica Romana* as the source of the imperium, who robbed Rome of the support of the empire, and brought the city into a position of dependence on the church. The city fought incessantly, and with the greater energy against the pope, who claimed imperial rights over her; she attained her civic autonomy, and at brilliant intervals even acquired complete independence as a republic. Incapable of making good her claim to be regarded as the *Urbs Orbis* [the City of the World], incapable of becoming the head of a universal confederation of Italian cities, she restricted her ambition to the aim of ruling the territory of the Roman duchy from the Capitol. We see her in the thirteenth century confined, like Milan or Florence, within limits thoroughly adapted to a municipality. Not till the following century did she aspire to a fantastic ideal. It is curious to see the Romans, untroubled by the affairs of the world, seriously occupied with their republic at home. While the empire became reduced to a shadow, while the church attained her great object, that of becoming the constitution of the world, the gaze of the Romans remained fixed on the hoary Capitol; the people barred their gates in the face of the popes as well as of the emperor, and thought of nothing but how to bestow the best constitution on their community. The municipal history of Rome in

176

the thirteenth century contains some honorable pages, which extort our admiration for the Roman populace, who in the midst of difficult conditions periodically asserted their independence. For although in the thirteenth century the papacy had reached the summit of its supremacy, it remained entirely impotent in Rome.

At the beginning and end of the great century depicted in our fifth volume, Innocent III and Boniface VIII stand as the two pillars which mark the confines of the most important period of the history of mediæval culture. They mark at the same time the culmination and the downfall of the papacy.

On January 8, 1198, Cardinal Lothar was unanimously elected pope in the Septizonium, and was proclaimed as Innocent III. He was the son of Count Thrasmund of Segni, a member of one of the ancient ruling families of Latium, which owned property at Anagni and Ferentino. His family was probably one of those which, in the tenth century, had borne the office of count in the Campagna, as the Crescentii had borne it in the Sabina; nevertheless it was not until after the time of Innocent III that the title of count became permanently the name of the family, henceforward known as de Comitibus or dei Conti. Lothar's ancestors were Germans who had migrated to Latium, as is shown by the names of Lothar, Richard, Thrasmund, and Adenulf, which survived in the family. The Conti had not acquired any prominence in the history of the city, but Claricia, the mother of Innocent III, was a Roman member of the family of Romanus de Scotta.

Lothar, who was young and wealthy, had studied in Paris and Bologna, had acquired great scholastic learning and an extensive knowledge of jurisprudence, and as a priest had served with distinction among the adherents of Alexander III, until Clement III made him cardinal-deacon of S. Sergius and Bacchus on the Capitol. At the age of thirty-seven he ascended the sacred chair. He was handsome, although of short stature, and was endowed with great eloquence and an all-subduing will.

Scarcely was the election accomplished when Innocent was assailed with cries for gold from the Roman populace. Instead of offering gifts of homage, the Romans demanded them from their popes. The oath of fealty was constantly purchased, and the municipality further required the payment of 5000 pounds from every newly elected pope. Before Innocent had actually ascended the throne, it was in danger of being overturned. As he yielded to the impatient cries of the Romans, he resolved to extract a permanent advantage out of an abuse. He was not parsimonious as Lucius III to his own misfortune had been; he gave liberally, and thus gained over the majority of the populace; papal largesses, however, on so vast a scale were a disgrace, and might be fairly called the price of his accession.

Lothar was consecrated in S. Peter's on February 22, 1198. Accompanied by the prefect of the city, the senator, the nobility, the provincial barons, the consuls and rectors of the cities, who appeared to do him homage, he immediately made his solemn progress to the Lateran.

.   .   .   .

From his throne Innocent III cast a glance over the dominions he governed, and beheld nothing but ruins; he surveyed the task on which he was about to enter, and saw the world reduced to conditions such as invited the rule of the strong man. The temporal power of S. Peter had been completely destroyed under Innocent's weak predecessor. The more distant provinces of the ancient State of the Church had fallen into the possession of German counts, generals of Henry VI, to whom they had been given in reward; the districts in the neighborhood of Rome, into the power of the nobility or of the Senate. Innocent's first task must consequently be to restore the dominion of the papacy in its immediate surroundings. That he succeeded in this and in still greater undertakings with unexpected rapidity, was due to the consternation into which the imperial party had been thrown by the death of Henry VI and the sudden state of orphanage in which the empire was left. Beside the coffin of its oppressor the papacy suddenly rose from the depths of impotence to become the national power in Italy.

The republic on the Capitol having lost its support, Innocent succeeded in restoring papal authority in the city by a first audacious stroke. Two magistrates still remained in the way of the rule of the sacred chair; the prefect as representative of the rights of the Roman empire and the senator as representative of the rights of the Roman people. Henry VI had again reduced the prefecture of the city to an imperial office, and Peter, the city prefect, to his vassal. Finding himself deprived of protection, the prefect offered, as the price of his recognition, to yield subjection to the pope. On February 22, 1198, Peter tendered the oath of vassalage to Innocent III and received the purple mantle of the prefect as a symbol of investiture from his hands. The functions of his office are but vaguely indicated in the formula of oath which has been preserved. The prefect did homage to the church as a papal vassal, who is merely entrusted with the temporary management of an estate; he swears to maintain the rights of the church, to provide for the safety of the streets, to exercise justice, to preserve the fortresses for the pope, to refrain from arbitrarily building new ones; he promises not to divert to himself the allegiance of any vassals in the patrimony of the church, to renounce his administration whenever the pope may command. The territory subject to the prefect is not, however, specified. In ancient Rome this territory had extended to the hundredth milestone, and thence the Romans in the Middle Ages traced their right to govern the entire district of the city by means of communal judges. Even in the fifteenth century [Pope] Martin V granted a document to a secretary of the city, in which utterance is given to the following principle:

> After the imperium had been handed over to a prince, the city of Rome was transformed into a prefecture; she has always retained her independent authority as such, and since this authority reaches to the hundredth milestone, it follows that the city territory extends the same distance and that the entire district comprised within these limits is subject to the jurisdiction of Rome; the city there possesses the rights of the republic, the *merum* and *mixtum imperium* [pure *and* mixed sovereignty], the royalties, rivers, roads, harbors, customs, coinage, and the like.

The Roman municipality claimed the administration of the entire district from Radicofani to Ceprano, from the Sabine Mountains to the sea, but it does not appear whether the prefect exercised jurisdiction within this territory or not. The power of the

179

once dreaded criminal judge had been destroyed by the democracy on the Capitol; the senator had thrust the prefect from his office, the head of the municipality had supplanted the imperial provost. The nature of this office at the beginning of the thirteenth century and after the extinction of all imperial fiscal rights is utterly obscure. He still held a police tribunal in the city as also outside it. But his influence resided no longer in his office, but in his landed possessions. The city prefect had, for instance, become ruler of large estates in Tuscany, where he had acquired the adherence of many captains of Matilda's party. As early as the end of the twelfth century a territory near Viterbo appears as the scene of his ambitious exertions, and in the thirteenth the prefecture is seen to have become hereditary in the ruling family of Vico, a place which has now disappeared, but whose name is borne by a little lake. It must have long been endowed with the revenues of Tuscan estates as a formal fief of the prefecture; the noble house of Vico then, however, transformed this official fief, as well as the prefecture itself, into a hereditary possession; a possession which had been greatly extended by purchase and robbery. Innocent III in vain sought to obstruct this hereditary transmission, by giving a merely temporary tenure to the prefect Peter, a member of the family.

In the year 1198 expired the last remains of the imperial power in Rome, which had been represented under the Carolingians by the missus, later by the prefect. The office had so completely fallen into abeyance that the pope was at a loss how to deal with the antiquated figure of the prefect. Innocent III in 1199 had already conceded him, as papal missus, the authority of a justice of the peace in the cities of Tuscany and Umbria, also in Spoleto; and it was in these territories that the lords of Vico later rose to increased power. For the main point was, that the prefect of the city henceforward attained a prominent dynastic position as Capitaneus in Tuscany. He retained his judiciary authority in Rome and the civic territory, and we may regard him as governor of the city. He continued to appoint judges and notaries; he possessed police authority; he provided for the security of the streets, and supervised the prices of grain and the market. The pope, who in him respected the oldest magistrate of Rome, often attempted by his means to cast the senator into the shade. He gave him a representative dignity full of pomp and splendor, the *præfectus urbis* being always found in the immediate neighborhood of the pope in all coronation processions. On the fourth Sunday in Lent he was regularly invested with the golden rose, which he was then accustomed, mounted on horseback, to wear with solemn pomp through the streets.

With equal good fortune Innocent III on the same day acquired supremacy over the Roman municipality. The republic on the Capitol, which had again become aristocratic, still lacked the foundations of an organization resting on the strength of the people. Its executive power wavered between an oligarchic and a monarchic form, between too many rulers and a single podestà. Thus fifty-six senators had been elected in 1197, but at the time of Innocent III's consecration there was but one senator. The municipal head of Rome incessantly disputed the pretensions of Saint Peter; Benedict Carushomo and his successors had made themselves independent of the sacred chair, had appointed rectors in the Roman country towns, and had even sent communal judges into the Sabina and Maritima; for the Romans asserted that these provinces were by right demesnes of the city. The municipality demanded the jurisdiction of the city district, under which it understood all the territory of the former Roman duchy. As other Italian cities had annexed the ancient countries, so Rome determined to become the ruler of her own duchy. At the time that Innocent III ascended the throne Scottus Paparone, a noble Roman of ancient family, probably related to the pope on his mother's side, was senator. Innocent persuaded him to abdicate; by means of bribes he induced the populace to renounce the important right of freely electing a Senate, which the pope declared to be a papal privilege. He now appointed an elector (Medianus), who appointed the new senator; whereupon the justitiarii, hitherto appointed by the Capitol, were replaced throughout the civic territory by papal judges. The Senate consequently fell into the power of the pope in 1198.

We still possess the formula of oath tendered by the senator:

I, senator of the city, will henceforth in the future be faithful to thee, my Lord Pope Innocent. Neither by word or deed will I contribute to thy loss of life or limb, or be privy to thy imprisonment. That which thou personally entrustest to me, either by letter or messenger, will I confide to no one to thy hurt. Any injury meditated towards thee, of which I have any knowledge, I will prevent. Should that not be possible I will warn thee by letter and trustworthy messengers. According to my power and knowledge will I aid thee to uphold the Roman papacy and the regalia of S. Peter, which thou ownest, or to recover that which thou dost not own, and I will defend that which thou hast regained against all the world: S. Peter's, the city of Rome, the Leonina, Trastevere, the island, the fortress of Crescentius, S. Maria Rotunda, the Senate, the coinage, the honors and dignities of the city, the harbor of Ostia, the domain of Tusculum, and above all both the privileges within and without the city. To the cardinals, to their court and to thine, will I guarantee perfect security when they go to church, while they remain there, and on their return. I swear faithfully to observe all I have promised, so help me God and these holy gospels.

From this formula it is evident that even at this time the city of Rome (*urbs romana*), which consisted of twelve regions, was separated not only from the papal Leonina but also from Trastevere and the island. The Trasteverines were regarded entirely as foreigners, since no inhabitant of the quarter could be elected a Roman senator.

It were a mistake to believe that the pope henceforward acquired a direct and royal power over Rome. Monarchical rule, in the sense of present times, was so entirely foreign to the Middle Ages, that it never occurred to Innocent III to doubt the independence of the Roman municipality. All popes of this period recognized the city of Rome not only as a civic but also as a political and autonomous power. They sought to influence this power; they assured its supremacy in principle; they frequently appointed or ratified the appointment of the senators, but they made no disposition either over the will nor over the power of the people. Their dominion was solely a title of authority, nothing more. For the Romans continued to deliberate on the Capitol in free parliament, had their own finances, their own army, and continued to decide on war and peace without questioning the pope. They made war on cities, even on those in the State of the Church, or concluded treaties with them. For these cities also were for the most part free communes while other places in the Roman district paid, according to treaty, feudal taxes to the Capitoline treasury and received their podestàs from the senator. The vigorous character of the Roman nobility at this period and the respect which the commune enjoyed are shown by the fact that, in the first half of the thirteenth century, we find so many Romans podestàs of foreign cities. These cities, standing for the most part in defensive alliance with Rome, frequently besought the Romans in solemn embassy to give them a noble Roman as regent. The series of such podestàs, who signed themselves in all acts as *consules Romanorum,* is opened as early as the year 1191 by Stephen Carzullus, and in 1199 by John Capocci, both at Perugia; also in 1199 at Orvieto by Peter Parentius as Podestà of Orvieto, where he was slain by the heretics of the Ghibelline party and is still honored by an altar in the beautiful cathedral.

.   .   .   .

Innocent hoped that he had now tranquillized Rome; opposition, however, to the papal rule, quarrels concerning the constitution, and feuds between the nobility kept the city in continued strife. From amongst the patrician families some houses rose with the thirteenth century to new power, while the earlier ruling families of the Pierleoni and Frangipani receded into the background. The popes themselves also became the founders of houses which were bound to them by family ties and which aimed at the tyranny of the cities. But neither the Colonna (already an ancient race) nor the Anibaldi were among the families of whom we speak; the Conti, Savelli, and Orsini, however, owed their greatness to the popes.

Celestine III had endowed his nephews of the house of Bobo with property belonging to the church, and had thus founded the fortune of a family who were kinsmen of the Orsini. The race of Ursus, soon to become celebrated, is conspicuous in the Roman Middle Ages through several popes, through a long series of cardinals, of statesmen, and of military leaders. Among all the Roman families the Orsini alone could vie on terms of equal birth with the Ghibelline Colonnas. Their origin is, however, obscure. The records of the family in the Roman archives (which are devoid of critical value) trace it to Spoleto, but the statements of these documents are mere fictions. Some authorities represent the cradle of the race to have been situated on the Rhine. But the names Ursus and Ursinus are ancient Roman, nor can it be shown that the powerful Roman house owed its foundation to Saxons who migrated to Italy under the Ottos. A fortunate man, probably a warrior endowed with rude energy, called Ursus, the Bear, became the founder of a race which, in numbers and tenacity, put royal dynasties to shame. The date and the person of this ancestor are veiled in obscurity. Only so much is certain, that the name Ursus is found in the time of the Ottos.

At the beginning of the thirteenth century "the sons of Ursus," already numerous and powerful, inhabited towered palaces built upon ancient monuments in the region Parione. They dwelt in hereditary feud with the race of Romanus de Scotta and of John Ocdolinae, relatives of the Conti, and in the autumn of 1202, during Innocent's absence in Velletri, drove these families from their homes. The pope on his return demanded peace, and the senator Pandulf banished the hostile factions, one to S. Peter's, the other to S. Paul's. A murder committed in revenge immediately set the city in uproar. Theobald, an Orsini, was slain on the road to S. Paul's, and immediately the entire family of Ursus forced their way into the city, and crying for revenge, carried the body of the murdered man through the streets, and destroyed the houses of the enemy. The fierce hatred borne to the relatives of the pope extended to the pope himself. He was accused, and with justice, of nepotism, for he had been at pains to provide his ambitious brother, Richard, with a princely estate in Latium and had successfully accomplished his object.

Richard lived in Rome, where, with means furnished by the pope, he built the gigantic tower of the Conti, released Count Odo of the house of Poli from his numerous creditors, but appropriated according to treaty Odo's estates, ancient fiefs of the church. Odo had promised that his son should marry Richard's daughter; he now retracted his promise and demanded the resto-

ration of his property. But having no valid ground for his demand, he incited the people against the Conti. The relatives of
the Poli, nobles, who owing to bad management of their property
and tedious lawsuits were in reduced circumstances, frequently
paraded the streets as suppliants, half naked and carrying crosses.
They uproariously forced their way into S. Peter's on Easter day;
they even interrupted the papal procession, and finally they offered their estates, which were mortgaged to Richard, to the
Roman people on the Capitol. The fair possessions of the house
of Poli included nine fortresses on the frontiers of the Sabina
and Latium. The Romans immediately stretched forth their
hands; the pope, however, hastened to represent his claims upon
these fiefs of the church to the senate; he invested his brother with
the estates in question as security, and soon afterwards the entire
fiefs of the Poli were transferred in perpetuity to the Conti.

The senator Pandulf, who was devoted to the pope, had opposed the proposals of the Poli for legal reasons, and had merely
drawn upon himself the hatred of the populace. The Capitol was
attacked; the senators within escaped but with difficulty; with
difficulty also the pope's brother, Richard, whose tower was attacked by the people and declared the property of the city. Innocent himself escaped to Palestrina in the beginning of May 1203.
In the very days that the Latin crusaders conquered Byzantium,
the great pope found himself driven to bay by the petty feuds
of the Roman barons, exposed to the fury of the populace, and
forced to flight. The contrast between his sense of power as pope
and the actual straits in which he found himself in Rome caused
him profound depression. In the autumn, when the thrilling news
of the fall of Constantinople had already reached him, he was
taken so seriously ill at Anagni that the news of his death was
announced.

Meanwhile November was drawing near, when the new Senate was to be elected. The discontented people desired fifty-six
senators, and the pope, with whom negotiations were held
through envoys, ordered—as he was entitled to do—the cardinals, by whom he was represented, to appoint twelve electors.
The populace shut up these cardinals as in a conclave, within the

tower of one of their leaders, John de Stacio, who had erected his house in the ruins of the Circus Flaminius. The cardinals were forced to swear that they would elect at least two candidates from the faction hostile to the pope. Pandulf the retiring senator nevertheless surrendered the Capitol to Innocent's adherents, and the newly elected Senate divided on the ground of the trial with Richard into two hostile parties. The popular party pronounced the Poli estates civic property; their opponents rejected this decree. Rome was torn asunder by furious war, until the populace, oppressed by the nobility, urgently invited the pope to return. He first refused, then came in May 1204, with the courageous resolve to quell the disturbances and to order the Senate (the re-election of which was to take place at the end of six months), according to his will. Innocent, received in Rome with every honor, immediately tranquillized the disturbances by prudent measures: he appointed as elector a man respected by all parties, his former opponent, now perhaps his friend, John Pierleone. Pierleone elected as senator Gregory Petri Leonis Rainerii, a near relative of his own, a noble distinguished by integrity but not by energy. The democratic party, however, would not hear of peace, nor would they concede the elective right to the pope. They assembled in the Circus Flaminius, pronounced the treaty of 1198 null and void, and elected an opposition Senate under the title "good men of the commune."

Rome was thus split into a papal and a democratic faction. Pandulf of the Suburra, Richard Conti, Peter Anibaldi, the family of the Alexii, and Gilido Carbonis were the leaders of the former; John Capocci, Baroncellus, Jacopo Frangipane, Gregory and John Rainerii, who had again joined the popular side, headed the opposition. The bitter civil war was a struggle concerning the constitution and was based on a principle of serious importance. The adherents of the ancient communal constitution refused to surrender the election of the Senate to the pope, and with this right gradually to relinguish every other. The Poli lawsuit, moreover, entered into the question, the growing power of the house of Conti affording just grounds for suspicion. John Capocci, the most energetic enemy of the pope, again placed himself at the head of the populace, while the ex-senator Pandulf commanded the papal following, and Richard provided the money. Fighting was carried on in the streets throughout the entire region from the Colosseum to the Lateran and the Quirinal, on the slopes of which stood the towers of the three captains, Richard, Pandulf and Capocci.

The manner and nature of these civil wars are highly characteristic of this rude and vigorous time. As soon as the factions arose they built towers and opposition towers of bricks or wood with furious activity, thence to hurl stones on one another with the savage rage of uncouth Lapithæ. These fortresses sprang up in the course of a night, were built and fashioned amid brawls and tumult, were overthrown today and rebuilt on the morrow. They were erected on the remains of temples, baths, and aqueducts, and were provided with projectiles, while the narrow streets were barricaded with iron chains, and the churches were fortified. Pandulf, besieged by Capocci in his palace (which stood in the Baths of Æmilius Paulus, on the site of the present Via Magnanapoli), planted a wooden tower on an ancient monument and hence attacked the adjacent fortress of the enemy with equal energy. The Alexii built a colossal tower on the Quirinal; Gilido Carbonis even erected three towers, and Peter Anibaldi built one in the neighborhood of the Colosseum. The amphitheatre belonged to the Frangipani, who still remained in possession of the dignity of Lateran Counts Palatine, but who, while ruling over several fiefs on the Campagna, no longer retained in the city the authority which they had once possessed. Innocent III, it is true, had rendered the five sons of Oddo Frangipane, Jacopo, Oddo, Manuel, Cencius and Adeodatus, a service in the year 1204, by forcing the commune of Terracina to surrender them the fortress of Traversa; he had, however, taken Terracina itself under his protection against the desire of these barons and had in consequence offended them. They no sooner discovered that Anibaldi, a relative of the pope, wished to invade the precinct of their fortress, than they attacked him and, hurling down projectiles from the battlements of the Colosseum, sought to hinder the progress of his tower.

The hostile parties brought kinsfolk, vassals, and tenantry to their aid, and war was fiercely waged day and night with projectiles, with sword and fire. Rome resounded with the clash of arms and the thud of falling stones, while the pope remained shut up in the Lateran, the quarter where his friends the Anibaldi dwelt, but where not even in the remotest chamber of the palace did he escape the din of war. The brave Capocci took Pandulf's fortress by assault on August 10, and pushed as far as the Lateran, where they destroyed the fortified remains of the Aqueduct of Nero. But the pope's gold fought with greater efficacy against the democrats, and the wearied people desired peace. Innocent proposed the following treaty: four umpires were to decide the quarrel between the opposition Senate and Richard Conti, and were also to decide on the election of the Senate; the pope would yield to their decision for the year. These terms offended the popular party, who foresaw their own defeat. The bell of the Capitol summoned a parliament, and John Capocci rose and said:

> The city of Rome is not accustomed to yield to the church in her conflicts, is not used to conquer by judicial sentences but by power. Today, however, I see that she will be defeated; contrary to the decision of the people and to the oath of the senators she surrenders the domains to the church, and confirms the Senate to the pope. If, in spite of our numbers and power, we bow to the pope, who will again dare to resist him? Never did I hear of a peace so disgraceful to the city, and I will refuse in every way to vote for it.

The opposition of the demagogue induced John Pierleone Rainerii also to record his veto. The parliament dispersed in uproar and recourse was again had to arms. The pope triumphed; the four umpires adjudged him the right of electing the Senate, and the Roman commune with this decision lost an essential part of its political power.

Innocent with great sagacity had attained his object, and with equal sagacity now made but moderate use of his victory. Unable to find a single man who was welcome as senator to both parties, he agreed to the election of fifty-six senators, foreseeing, however, the unfortunate consequences in store for them. This plural government was permanently set aside six months later, when the new senator, apparently the energetic Pandulf of the Suburra, restored quiet to the city. The firmness of the pope achieved great success. After the strenuous efforts of five years he subjugated the Capitol. Thus the Roman people forfeited in succession their three great rights: the papal election, the imperial election, and the election of the Senate.

Peace between the city of Rome and Innocent was finally concluded in 1205. The pope changed the form of the civic government; the executive power lying henceforward in the hand of a single senator or podestà, who, directly or indirectly, was appointed by the pope. A period of greater tranquillity for the popes, although frequently interrupted by conflicts, began in Rome with this constitution.

VI

Achievement of Innocent III

THE quarrel for the German throne was definitely settled at the immense council which Innocent assembled in the Lateran on November 11, 1215. Otto's advocates and Frederick's envoys received the decision that the former was deposed, the latter recognized. More than 1500 prelates from every land of Christendom, besides princes and ambassadors from kings and republics, knelt at the feet of the mightiest of the popes, who sat as ruler of Europe on the throne of the world. This splendid council, the last solemn act of Innocent III, was the expression of the new power which Innocent had infused into the church, and the unity in which he had preserved her. The close of the life of this extraordinary man was also its zenith. On the point of going to Tuscany to effect a reconciliation between Pisa and Genoa, and to win these maritime powers to the side of the church, he died at Perugia on June 16, 1216, without having lived too long for his glory.

Innocent III, the true Augustus of the papacy, although not a creative genius like Gregory I and Gregory VII, was one of the most important figures of the Middle Ages, a man of earnest, sterling, austere intellect, a consummate ruler, a statesman of penetrating judgment, a high priest filled with true religious fervor, and at the same time with unbounded ambition and appalling force of will; a bold idealist on the papal throne, yet an entirely

From book IX, ch. 3, sec. 1.

practical monarch, and a cool-headed lawyer. The spectacle of
a man, who, if only for a moment, ruled the world according to
his will in tranquil majesty is sublime and marvellous. By astutely
turning the circumstances of its history to the best account, by
adroitly applying canon laws and fictions, and by guiding the religious fervor of the masses, he imparted such a tremendous power
to the papacy that it carried states, churches, and civic society
irresistibly onward in its mighty current. His conquests, achieved
solely by the force of sacerdotal ideas, were, like those of Hildebrand, marvelous in regard to the shortness of his reign; Rome,
the State of the Church, Sicily, Italy, became subject to him, or
turned to him as to their protector; the empire, driven back beyond the Alps, bowed beneath the papal sentence. Germany,
France, and England, Norway, Aragon, Leon, Hungary, distant
Armenia, the kingdoms in East and West had recognized the
tribunal of the pope. The trial of the Dane Ingeborg [Queen of
France], who had been repudiated, offered Innocent the opportunity of making the powerful monarch, Philip Augustus, subject to ecclesiastical law, and a dispute about investiture left him
feudal lord of England. His masterly action against the English
king, to whose crown right he did violence, his presumption in
making free England over to a foreign prince, Philip Augustus,
the game which he played with impunity with this very monarch,
his successes and victories are things which, in truth, border on
the marvellous. The wretched John laid down his crown in servile
fear, and received it back as a tributary vassal of the sacred chair
at the hands of Pandulf, a simple legate, but endowed with Roman pride and Roman courage of a thoroughly antique stamp.
The celebrated scene at Dover entirely recalls the times of ancient Rome, when distant kings renounced or assumed their
diadems at the bidding of proconsuls. It shines in the history of
the papacy, like the scene at Canossa, the pendant of which it
was. It deeply humiliated England, but no people rose so quickly
and so gloriously out of their humiliation as this manly nation,
who wrung the Magna Charta—the foundation of all political
and civic freedom in Europe—from their cowardly tyrant.

Innocent's good fortune was unbounded. All the forces of the world converged on the moment when this pope appeared, to become powerful owing to their means. He saw realized the audacious dream of Hildebrand—the subjugation of the Greek church to the laws of Rome—since, after the conquest of Constantinople by the Latin crusaders, the Roman rite was introduced into the Byzantine church. No pope had even again so loftly and yet so real a consciousness of his power as Innocent III, the creator and destroyer of emperors and kings. No pope so nearly attained Gregory VII's audacious aim, that of making Europe a fief of Rome, the church the constitution of the world. Kings headed the long list of his vassals; princes, counts, bishops, cities, and nobles followed in succession, all bearing feudal patents from a pope. He encompassed the church with terror; the fear which the despotic command of Rome spread among mankind in the time of Nero and Trajan, was not greater than the servile reverence of the world before the mild exhortation, or the threatening thunderbolt of the Roman Innocent III, the majestic priest, who could address trembling kings in the language of the Old Testament: "As the rod lay beside the tables of the law in the Ark of the Lord, so lie the terrible power of destruction and the gentleness of mercy in the breast of the pope." Under Innocent the sacred chair became the throne of dogmatic and canonical authority, the political tribunal of the peoples of Europe. During his reign West and East recognized that the center of gravity of all moral and political order lay in the church, the moral universe, and in its pope. This was the most favorable constellation which the church ever entered in the course of history. In Innocent III the papacy attained a giddy and untenable height.

VII

The Commune:
Revolt, Heresy, and Defeat

*Conflict with the Emperor Frederick II dominated papal politics from the accession of Pope Gregory IX (1227–41) until Frederick's death (1250). In 1228, a proimperial faction drove Gregory IX from Rome, and the next year, Frederick forced the papal armies out of Apulia. In the following sections, Gregorovius discusses the settlement which allowed Gregory to return to Rome and the events which led to a momentary papal victory over the commune.—*Editor.

Gregory IX spent the winter in Perugia, without any prospect of returning to Rome, beyond that offered by a reconciliation with the emperor. Before, however, this had been effected, unhoped for circumstances conducted him back to the Lateran. "The cataracts of the heavens" opened and discharged themselves over the "godless" city. The Tiber rose on February 1, 1230; the Leonina and the Field of Mars were flooded; the Bridge of the Senators (*Ponte Rotto*) was swept away, and the inundation was followed by famine and pestilence. Chroniclers describe this pestilence as one of the most terrible that Rome ever endured. The Romans who, forgetful of their pope during his long exile, had robbed the

From book IX, ch. 4, secs. 2, 3, and 4.

193

clergy and had harbored heretics, now remembered with superstitious dread that the Holy Father was their territorial ruler.
Envoys hastened to Perugia; Peter Frangipane, chancellor of the
city, and the aged and valiant exsenator Pandulf of the Suburra
threw themselves at the feet of the pope, implored mercy for the
people who had been led astray, and begged him to return to the
orphaned city. Gregory, arriving on February 24, received with
exultant cries by the Romans, and led to the Lateran, may have
bestowed a glance of contempt upon a people who for more
than a century had been accustomed to drive away their popes,
in order to receive them back with songs of rejoicing. When these
popes returned from their exile to the "city of blood," it was only
by means of gold that they purchased a brief interval of rest. The
biographer of Gregory IX conscientiously enumerates the many
thousands of pounds that this pope distributed among the Romans whenever they consented to his return.

Gregory found Rome steeped in profound misery, filled with
"the weed" of heresy, a number even of the clergy being here-
tically inclined. He therefore resolved to issue a severe decree
as soon as peace was concluded with the emperor. After tedious
negotiations with Hermann, grandmaster of the Teutonic Order,
and under conditions so favorable for the pope that it was easily
perceived how little Frederick had undervalued the power of his
adversary, peace was arranged at S. Germano on July 23, 1230.
The State of the Church was restored, even some towns of Campania (among them Gaeta) were retained by the pope for a year
as hostages; the freedom of election and the exception of the
clergy were, moreover, not to be interfered with in Sicily.

After the emperor had been released from the ban in the chapel
of S. Justa near Ceprano, on August 28, he was escorted by the
cardinals to the pope at Anagni. There, on September 1, the two
adversaries greeted one another with courtesy. During the first
three days of September they dissembled their hatred, and dined
and conversed together in the family palace of the Conti. But notwithstanding their professions of friendship, they parted with the
conviction that there was not room in Italy for two men such as
themselves.

Returning to Rome in November, Gregory sought to gain over the Romans by a series of benefits. He caused the Bridge of the Senators to be restored, the cloacæ to be cleansed; he procured supplies of grain, distributed money among the people, and built a hospital for the poor in the Lateran. These measures gained him the favor of the masses and facilitated his blow against the heretics, from whom he desired to purify the city. Innocent III's war of extermination against the heretics, his orders for their eradication from all cities, appear to have only increased their numbers. Thousands girt their loins with the cord of S. Francis, but many more fell away from the faith. Heretics were numerous in the State of the Church, in Viterbo, in Perugia, in Orvieto. Lombardy was filled with them, the Guelf city of Milan was the seat of their principal church. Pyres blazed in vain. During the exile of the pope the heretics had collected in Rome itself. Political views easily made common cause with religious views, and among the Roman heretics the Ghibelline sect of the Arnoldists was assuredly more numerous than that of the Poor of Lyons. Furthermore dogmatic heresy was not distinguished from political heresy; for the church regarded the attacks upon the freedom and property of the clergy, such as the edicts of the civil magistracy, who strove to impose taxes upon them and to render them subject to the civil tribunal, as rank heresy.

It was the first time that a trial for heresy on a large scale was held in Rome, and that pyres blazed publicly. The inquisitors erected their tribunal in front of the doors of S. Maria Maggiore; the cardinals, the senator, and the judges took their places on the tribune, and the populace, open-mouthed, surrounded this terrible theater, in which unfortunate creatures of both sexes and of every class received their sentence. Many priests, convicted of heresy, were, after a repentant confession, unfrocked and condemned to penance in their convents. Other heretics were burnt on piles of faggots, probably on the piazza of the church itself. This hideous spectacle, a reflection of the Albigensian war, following on the inundation of the Tiber and the pestilence, must have wakened profound agitation in Rome. If a chronicler of the fourteenth century speaks truth, the Romans even beheld the

195

unexampled and appalling sight of a senator executed for heresy. But the statement is a fiction. On his return Gregory must have appointed a new senator, and this was Anibaldo Anibaldi, a Roman of senatorial family, which precisely at this time rose to prominence, and which founded a powerful and richly dowered house in Latium. The celebrated name of Hannibal reappears in the Middle Ages in a noble family, which for centuries gave birth to senators, generals, and cardinals, but never to a pope. The Anibaldi were related to the Conti and the house of Ceccano, were like them of German origin, and were settled on the Campagna and in the Latin Mountains, where the Field of Hannibal above Rocca di Papa still recalls the once influential family. If in 1231 this Senator Anibaldo issued the edict against heresy, which is still preserved, the measure had assuredly been made one of the conditions of the pope's return. It was thereby established that, on his entrance into office, every senator should pronounce the ban against the heretics in the city and their adherents, should seize all heretics pointed out by the Inquisition, and should execute them within eight days after sentence had been pronounced. The property of heretics was to be divided between the informers and the senator, and was to be devoted to the repairs of the city walls. The houses which had sheltered them were to be pulled down. Persons who had concealed heretics were sentenced to fines in money or to corporal punishment, and to the loss of all civic rights. Every senator was to swear to this edict, and was not to be regarded as installed in his office until he had taken the oath. Should he act contrary to his oath, he was sentenced to the payment of two hundred marks and was pronounced incapable of holding any public office. The punishment incurred was to be inflicted by the college of judges called after the church of S. Martina on the Capitol.

The edict whetted the zeal of the informer by the prospect of acquiring property; and we may judge how busy avarice and private enmity were in the discovery of heretics. The pope drew the civic commune into the interests of the Inquisition and obliged the senator to lend it the secular arm. He was the legal executor of the sentence against heretics, as other podestàs were also in other cities. If this transference to him of the former penal judicature of the prefect increased his civil power, it nevertheless degraded him into acting as the servant of the spiritual tribunal; the solemn oath which he took to punish heretics was binding on himself, and over his own head hovered the terrible sentence of the Inquisition, which could accuse him of infraction of the duties of his office and consequently of heresy. The most important attribute of the senatorial office was consequently the execution of sentence upon heretics, and it is significant of the spirit of the age, that the duty of persecuting heretics was accepted as the first fundamental article in the statutes of Rome and of other cities in the State of the Church.

For the rest the senatorial decree only brought the edict issued on the imperial coronation into force in Rome, where it had hitherto probably been resisted. For the Inquisition now became another instrument in the hands of the pope for the subjugation of the people. Henceforward there were inquisitors in Rome, men who in the beginning were appointed from the Franciscan order. When condemning heretics the inquisitor stood on the steps of the Capitol and read the sentence in presence of the senator, of his judges and of several deputies or witnesses from among the clergy of the city. He then left the execution of the sentence to the senator under threat of excommunication in case of delay or neglect.

We shrink back appalled from a time of which Gregory IX's edicts were the expression, an age which made the detection of heresy the first duty of the citizen, and when public or private conversation on the articles of religion was regarded as a crime punishable with excommunication. In these rude times of new tortures and a new fanaticism, when religious fervor found amends for the fall of Jerusalem and a waning zeal for the Crusade in the persecution of heretics, and when, after the reign of Innocent III, religious intolerance reduced Christianity to the standard of the fanatical laws of Judaism, princes and heads of republics themselves emulated the clergy. Kings laden with crimes now rarely bestowed property on the church; they found it more convenient for the salvation of their souls to burn heretics, whose property they confiscated. To the minds of some monarchs the glare of the blazing faggots seemed like the aureole of piety, while others, through fear or calculation, endeavored to prove their orthodoxy by the most cruel persecution of heretics. Even Frederick II, whose culture and liberal opinions raised him so far above the level of his century that he was afterwards called a predecessor of Luther, issued in 1220 or 1232 laws so severe that they differed in no degree from the papal edicts. "The heretics"—thus he decreed—"wish to sever the undivided coat of our Lord; we command that they be delivered to death by fire in the eyes of the people." He issued these decrees on every occasion when he made peace with the pope, or whenever he required his aid; and such politically motivated persecutions as these redound more to his disgrace than any blind or sincere religious fanaticism would have done. His laws against heresy form the harshest contrast to the wise legislation—a legislation far in advance of his age—which he gave to his kingdom of Sicily in the August of the same year (1231).

The great trial of heretics made so little impression on the Romans, that no later than June 1 (1231) they forced Gregory IX to return to Rieti, where he remained until the summer of 1232. For disturbances caused by the war with Viterbo broke out in the city. Viterbo was the Veii of the Middle Ages to the Romans; they hated the town with a hatred bordering on frenzy; they determined to conquer it entirely and to make it a domain of Rome. With the consent of the pope, the Viterbese placed themselves under the protection of the emperor, who sent Reinald of Aquaviva to their aid. The Romans immediately revenged themselves by imposing taxes on the churches, and with unabated fury continued their warlike expeditions against Viterbo, even during the year 1232, when John of Poli was senator. Although related to Gregory IX, the son of Richard Conti had espoused Frederick's side, and it is scarcely probable that he had been elected with the pope's consent. He called himself at this time count of Alba, having been invested with this Marsian territory by Frederick.

The attempt made by the Romans to render Latium subject to the Capitol deserves more attention. A new spirit animated the Roman people. As in ancient times, in the days of Camillus and Coriolanus, they undertook conquering expeditions against Tuscany and Latium. The Roman insignia, the ancient initials S.P.Q.R. on a red and gold banner, and the Roman national army, formed of the citizens and the vassals of the Campagna under the command of senators, were seen once more in the field. In the summer of 1232 the Romans advanced to Montefortino in Volscian territory; the pope, who had gone to Anagni in August, was even menaced from beneath the walls of his ancestral city. Gregory sent three cardinals with large sums of money to the enemy's camp, but they still continued their hostile interference with his enterprises in the Campagna. For Gregory IX was as active as Innocent III in increasing the patrimonies of the church. He took communes under his protection, and demanded the oath of fealty from their podestàs. He paid the debts of free communes, made them in return vassals of the church and acquired the right of planting fortresses within the circuit of their walls. He relieved barons who were in debt, and thus obtained possession of their fortresses, which they willingly received back as fiefs, in order that they might not fall into possession of the city of Rome. The like happened in Latium, where he bought two fortresses, Serrone and Paliano, which belonged in part to the Colonna, and then fortified them as papal strongholds. The Roman civic commune, which claimed jurisdiction in the Campagna, forbade the pope to continue these proceedings; they even threatened to destroy Anagni, but Gregory continued the building of these fortresses even during the winter, and made Serrone, Paliano, and Fumone castellanies of the church.

The Romans finally returned to the city, while Gregory remained at Anagni. He sought the intercession of the emperor, in order to arrange a peace with Viterbo, and to effect his own reconciliation with the Romans. Frederick could not render any effective aid, since the revolution in Messina demanded his presence in Sicily. The Romans, however, obeyed his exhortations, and the Senator John of Poli came to Anagni in March 1233 to invite the pope to return. Timid cardinals tried to dissuade him from venturing into "the city of the roaring beasts," but Gregory came and was received with respect on March 21. The populace offered a reconciliation in exchange for money, and he made his peace with the city without the knowledge of the emperor, who had intervened in the affairs of Viterbo and Rome, and who afterwards reproached him on this account, as with a breach of faith. A treaty was also made with Viterbo in April; the city of Rome obtained the recognition of her supremacy; and she also remained in possession of Vitorchiano. This fortress was henceforth regarded as a domain of the city, received the honorable title of "the faithful," and the right of filling the office of the Capitoline beadles, who were henceforward called "Fideli."

A demon, says the biographer of Gregory IX was happily banished from Rome, but seven others entered. No later than 1234 the Romans rose in an actual struggle of despair against the civil power of the pope. They would perhaps have been happier, but scarcely more deserving of respect, had they abandoned their undoubted claims. At this period, however, when every city was a state, the relation of Rome to the pope could not be apprehended in the same way as in later centuries. The Romans were constantly struggling to obtain the freedom of episcopal power which other cities had long since acquired. They saw these cities flourishing in two great leagues and ruling over what had formerly been counties. If Viterbo gloried in a great number of fortresses, which paid their tribute and received their laws in her town hall, we can understand that Rome could not endure her own civic impotence. The perpetual war with Viterbo was merely the symbol of the efforts of the Romans to subjugate Tuscany. Their relations to the empire had now completely changed. Since the imperial rights in Rome had been ceded to the popes, and since the popes had acquired the right to bestow the Roman crown, the point of dispute was whether or not imperial election still belonged to the Roman republic. This privilege, which even in Barbarossa's time the Romans had demanded, weapon in hand, was carried in the current of the new papal power. The Romans only made war with the papacy as with the supreme territorial power; their principal object was to erect within the limits of the ancient duchy a powerful free state such as Milan, Florence, or Pisa, whose example encouraged while it shamed them. In the treaties of the emperor which ratified Innocent's State of the Church, this duchy appears for the first time as united under the formula, "all the country from Radicofani to Ceprano," and, as the ancient foundation of the new State of the Church, opens the list of the papal provinces. The church could not trace the possession of this territory, where it had owned provinces from of old, from Frankish diplomas, but from actual facts which are lost in the obscurity of history. Within her administration she embraced three provinces, the patrimony of S. Peter's (Roman Tuscany), the Sabina, the Campagna, and the Maritima, although she was not actually mistress of all the cities within this district. Only a few of them acknowledged her feudal supremacy and, after having transferred the "plenum dominium" to the pope, received magistrates at his hands; others only recognized his authority as protector.

The city of Rome now pronounced all these ecclesiastical provinces to be within the district of the city. She made good her claims on every occasion when energetic men stood at the head of her commune and were opposed by feeble popes. She then sent her judges to the provincial towns, imposed ground rents upon them, seized the monopoly of salt, obliged them to yield military service and to send their representatives to the public games. The claims of the Capitol were disputed not only by the pope but also by the free cities, such as Tivoli, Velletri, Terracina, and Anagni in the Campagna, and by the hereditary landed nobility, who knew quite as well as the pope how to buy the dominion of the cities. The barons bought this dominion from the communes themselves, or became milites of the pope or of the ecclesiastical corporations for a yearly rent, which was often insignificant. At this period consequently the entire country from Radicofani to Ceprano was split into several little and frequently hostile states, and within the limits of a short journey a traveller could traverse a district governed here by the papal Camera, here by the city of Rome, here by a free republic, a baron or a Roman

201

convent, while in many cases it happened that all these various rulers were endowed with sovereign rights.

In 1234 the city of Rome, at an unfavorable time, made the attempt to throw off papal dominion and to form a free state within her boundaries. Had she succeeded, she would have extended her territory, nearly to the limits of what she had possessed shortly before the Punic war. It is singular that in this most serious revolt the Romans should have revived an ancient custom, in erecting boundary stones (*termini*), furnished with the inscription *S.P.Q.R.*, which denoted the civic jurisdiction.

They demanded from the pope the right of electing the Senate, the right of coining money, of imposing various taxes, and the established tribute of 5000 pounds. They abolished the jurisdiction and the immunity of the clergy, as did many, even tiny, republics at this time. They required that the pope should never pronounce sentence of excommunication on a Roman citizen, aleging that the illustrious city possessed the privilege of exemption from ecclesiastical punishments. Although the Romans may have taken no offense at the excommunication of their emperors, nevertheless in their civic pride they considered the papal censure as entirely inapplicable to themselves, as the scourging of a Roman citizen had been considered in antiquity.

Lucas Savelli, a man of great power, nephew of Honorius III and ancestor of a celebrated family, no sooner became senator (in 1234) than he issued an edict pronouncing Tuscany and the Campagna the property of the Roman people. He sent judges of the Senate into both territories to receive the oath of homage, yielded either voluntarily or under compulsion, from the people. Roman soldiers occupied Montalto in the Maritima, where a huge fortress was erected as the symbol of Roman supremacy. Corneto itself was obliged to do homage to the Senate. The pope with all the cardinals fled once more to Rieti at the end of May. What would have been the fate of the papacy, had the city succeeded in becoming a civic power such as Milan or Pisa? To prevent her attaining this position was the task of the church, and among all the cares of the pope the subjugation of the Capitol was not the least. The flight of Gregory, the excommunication which he thundered against the senator and the communal council, roused the Romans to such fury that they sacked the Lateran palace and the houses of the cardinals. They raised an army and vindictively marched against Viterbo. The pope meanwhile was not left without allies; many barons and cities of Latium, such as Anagni, Segni, and especially Velletri, remained faithful to him, and, jealous for their own liberty, opposed a strenuous resistance to the Romans. Gregory fortified Radicofani and Montefiascone in Tuscany, while Viterbo, reduced to despair, was his surest support.

The popes invariably summoned foreign aid to quell their rebellious country, and never has Christendom refused them money or soldiers. Gregory IX implored the Catholic world to lend him weapons against the defiant city. He wrote to the vassal kings of Portugal and Aragon, to the count of Roussillon, to the duke of Austria, to the bishops of Germany, Spain, and France. Even the emperor was prepared to help. The revolt of his son Henry in Germany and his treacherous alliance with the Lombards would have proved fatal to Frederick had Gregory favoured Henry's cause. Frederick consequently hastened unasked with his second son Conrad to Rieti, to offer his troops to the pope against the Roman populace. The weaker was sacrificed for the sake of the stronger. Gregory and Frederick had need of one another; necessity made them unwilling allies and placed the city of Rome at war at the same time with both emperor and pope.

The papal troops were led by the cardinal legate Rainer Capocci, a Viterbese, a man of restless activity and military talent, whom the pope had appointed rector of the patrimony in Tuscany. Rainer heads the not insignificant series of cardinals, who as generals acquired glory for the church. After having effected a junction with Frederick's troops, he marched to Viterbo, to strengthen the town and to drive the Romans out of Castel Rispampano. This fortress was stoutly defended by the Romans, while the impatient priests reproached the emperor, that instead of raising his eagle in serious war against the Romans, he had been flying his falcons in the Tuscan Campagna. They shouted of treason when he returned to his kingdom in September. He had, however, left troops under the command of Conrad of Hohenlohe, count of Romaniola, with the cardinal in Viterbo. Many German knights remained in the service of the pope. Crusaders lent their talents and their swords to the church against Rome; even Englishmen and Frenchmen, believers and adventurers, placed themselves under the banner of the cardinal. Raymond of Toulouse hoped, by fighting against the Romans, to discharge the vow which had been imposed upon him of making a Crusade, and the wealthy Bishop Peter of Winchester, exiled from the English court, offered his welcome services.

On the emperor's departure the Romans valiantly advanced to the attack of Viterbo. Seldom had they been inspired by such military ardor, or been under arms in such numbers. An assault of the Germans and the citizens of Viterbo developed into a bloody battle which was lost by the Romans. Many men of noble family, and not a few Germans, remained on the field. Since the ill-fated day of Monte Porzio, the Romans had not suffered any such severe loss in open battle; and now, as then, they saved themselves behind their walls. The victors followed them, and the result of the battle was the recovery of the Sabina and of Tuscany by the pope. The thankless priests were now forced to acknowledge that so decisive a victory was solely due to Frederick's aid.

The Romans, it is true, continued the war, pronounced Cardinal Rainer under the ban, and proclaimed the pope banished from Rome for life, unless he gave compensation for their losses. They even once more attained some success in the field; but their strength was consumed; their finances, in spite of the taxes levied on the churches, were exhausted. When, in the spring of 1235, Lucas Savelli retired from office and Angelo Malabranca succeeded him as senator, three cardinal legates prevailed on Rome to make peace. The city did not attain the object of her heroic struggle, but, about the middle of May, 1235, again recognized the supremacy of the pope.

The document containing the treaty of peace, which reveals

the form and nature of the Roman republic in an attractive manner, runs in substance as follows:

We, Angelo Malabranca, by God's grace grand senator of the illustrious city, empowered by the exalted Senate, and in virtue of the mandate and acclamation of the renowned Roman people, who are assembled to the sound of bells and trumpets on the Capitol, and acting on the proposal of the venerable Cardinals Romanus, bishop of Portus and S. Rufina, John Colonna of S. Prassede, and Stephen of S. Maria in Trastevere, with reference to the quarrel between the Holy Roman Church, the Holy Father, and the Senate and people of Rome, promise in the name of the Senate and people: That according to the mandate of the pope we will give satisfaction for the tower and the hostages of Montalto, for the oath of homage demanded from the Senator Lucas Savelli and the boundary stones erected in the states of the church. Also for the judges who demanded this homage in the Sabina and in Tuscany, and who occupied the estates of the church; for the sentence of outlawry passed on Cardinal Rainer of S. Maria in Cosmedin and on the notary Bartholomew; for the sack of the sacred palace of the Lateran and the houses of some cardinals; for the indemnity for damages exacted from the bishoprics of Ostia, Tusculum, Præneste and other estates of the church; and for the statute which decreed that the pope should not return to the city, nor that we should make peace with him until he had repaid the loan of five thousand pounds lent him, and registered by deed at Rocca di Papa, and had made good to the Romans all their losses. Empowered by a faculty granted by the Senate and people, we pronounce these sentences of outlawry and these decrees null and void.

And to remove every cause of dispute between us, the church and the pope (whom we honor as pious sons out of reverence to Christ, of whom he is the representative on earth, and to the prince of the apostles, whose successor he is), and especially because it is demanded by the fame of this noble and illustrious city, we command as follows: That no ecclesiastical person within or without Rome, neither the households of the pope nor those of the cardinals, shall be brought before the secular tribunal, or shall be constrained by the destruction of their houses or otherwise molested. That, however, which is said with regard to the households of the pope and the cardinals shall not hold good with reference to the Roman citizens of lay condition who have houses and servants in the city, although they be or call themselves members of the household. No priest, no member of an order, or layman whatsoever, while going to the apostolic seat or to S. Peter's, or remaining there, or returning thence, shall be brought before the secular judge; on the contrary, he must be protected by the senator and the Senate. No tax shall be levied on churches, clergy, or members of orders. We give perpetual peace to the emperor and his vassals, to the people of Anagni, Segni, Velletri, Viterbo, the Campagna, Maritima, and Sabina, to Count William (of Tuscany), to all other counts of the patrimony, and to all friends of the church. We command, and, by this present decree, ratify, that henceforward no senator, be it one or several, shall act contrary to this our charter. He who acts contrary thereto shall incur the severest anger and hatred of the Senate, and shall moreover be liable to pay one hundred pounds of gold towards the restoration of the city walls, after payment of which fine this privilegium shall none the less continue in full force.

This peace thus ended one of the fiercest wars that the republic of Rome ever waged against the papal power. The republic did not lose its civic autonomy, but was thrust back into the limits assigned it by Innocent III. It was found impossible to render the clergy subject to civil law, or the civic district to the jurisdiction of the Capitol. Owing to the aid of the emperor, the temporal dominion of the church was held erect, and unhappy Rome remained as before, a sacrifice to the greatness of the papacy.

VIII

Frederick II and Innocent IV: Opposition to the Doctrine of Papal Monarchy

Papal enmity toward Frederick II reached the point of impla-cable hatred under Pope Innocent IV (1243–54). Fleeing before imperial forces, Innocent went to France. He convened the Coun-cil of Lyons (1245) and secured its decrees of excommunication and deposition against the emperor. In response, Frederick is-sued a manifesto to his princes denouncing the sentences against him as evidence that Innocent and the clergy supporting the pope had abandoned the precepts of Christ and the primitive church.—
EDITOR.

THEY beg among you, you Christians, in order that heretics may revel among them, and you pull down the houses of your friends in order to build cities to the enemy. Do not believe, however, that the sentence of the pope can bend my lofty spirit. My con-science is clean; God is with me. I call him to witness: it has al-ways been my desire to lead back the priests of every class, especially those in high position, to the apostolic life, to the hu-mility of our Lord, and to the system of the pure primitive church. For at that time the clergy were accustomed to look upward to

From book IX, ch. 6, sec. 2.

the angels, were distinguished by miracles, by healing the sick, by restoring the dead, and by reducing princes and kings to submission, not by power of arms, but by a holy life. But these priests who serve the world, who are intoxicated with sensuality, despise God, because their religion has been drowned in the deluge of wealth. To deprive such men of their pernicious possessions, to remove the burden of their condemnation, is in truth a work of love, and to this end we and all other powers should diligently lay our hand, in order that the clergy should be deprived of all superfluity and, content with modest possessions, should conform to the service of God.

The grave accusations of the emperor were answered by the pope with the most extravagant theories in support of his authority to judge emperors and kings. For this was the essence of the papal scheme—to establish once for all, as an incontrovertible right, the doctrine of the church, which earlier events had already shown to be practicable, namely, that the pope had received authority from Christ to judge kings. Innocent IV consequently maintained that the pope was legate-general of Christ, who had entrusted him with full powers to act as judge over the earth; that Constantine had ceded the illegitimate tyranny of the empire to the church, that he had then only received the legal authority back in fief, that both swords belonged to the church, which consigned the temporal to be used in her service to the emperor on his coronation. He asserted that, according to ancient usage, the emperor should render the oath of subjection to the pope, from whom, as his overlord, he received title and crown. "The emperor," he wrote, "reviles the church because the miraculous powers of primitive times are no longer conspicuous, because, according to the prophecies of David, her seed is mighty on the earth, and her priests distinguished by honors and wealth. We ourselves prefer poverty in the spirit, which it is difficult to preserve in the superabundance of wealth; but we protest that not the use, but the abuse, of wealth is sinful." This letter is the most important document of the views of the mediæval priesthood concerning the papal office. Innocent IV therewith openly did away with the balance of spiritual and secular authority, and point blank demanded the union of the two powers for the sacred chair. Had the kings of Europe now made Frederick's cause their own, they would not later have had to fight for centuries against principles so exorbitant and so fatal to all liberty.

The spiritual life of the West at this period was divided between monasticism and chivalry, between feudal despotism and servitude, between credulous fanaticism and heretical freethought, between the active labor of the citizen and silent intellectual research; innumerable tendencies, rights, privileges, states within the state, broke it up, as it were, into various castes. Monarchy, which united and created nationalities, had not developed beyond its first beginnings. In the confused web of hostile party aims, national impulses, civic individualities and feudal lordships, the church stood as a firm, many-sided, but infinitely simple system, embracing all Christian peoples in her uniform hierarchy, her dogmas and canon laws, with Rome for her center and the pope for her uncontested head. The church, the imperium of souls, assumed the place of the empire. Kings and countries were tributary to the pope. His tribunal, as also his customs house, stood in every province, and the collective episcopacy recognized his supremacy. The very princes to whom Frederick II had appealed against the attacks of the priesthood on the civil power, were appealed to by the pope to place themselves under the banner of the church, which defended the liberty of kings and nations against the tyrannical aims of the Hohenstaufens; and the world consoled itself for the abuse of the papal power with the thought, that she at least found therein a tribunal to which emperors and kings were responsible. The world acknowledged this juridical authority in the pope; it merely sympathized with Frederick's complaints concerning the avarice of the clergy, which drained its wealth. These complaints were not new. All contemporaries, bishops, princes, historians, poets are full of them. The Roman Curia required money for its increased wants, and the pope required it to carry on his wars. Christian countries were consequently laid under contributions to provide funds for the church. The English would have revolted against the pope, had they found any support in their feeble king.

Frederick's summons evoked a still louder echo in France, where several barons formed a league of defense against the attacks of the clergy on their secular rights. The foremost nobles, among them the duke of Burgundy and the court of Bretagne, declared in the articles of the league that the realm of France "had not been constituted by written right, nor by the usurpations of the clergy, but by military power; that they, the nobles of the country, took back the jurisdiction of which they had been deprived, and that the clergy, grown rich through avarice, should return to the poverty of the primitive church."

Frederick's voice consequently found an echo in Europe; the spirit of independence stirred in secular society in revolt against the preponderating power of the clergy, who had fallen away from evangelical teachings. But these movements remained isolated. To deprive the pope of the supreme jurisdiction over princes, and to lead the church back to her nonpolitical origin by the secularization of her property, were the reforms which the great emperor desired, but to which he was unable to give more than verbal expression. He did not overstep the principles, which had already been more seriously discussed and more strongly expressed in the time of Arnold of Brescia, or during the war of investitures, than during his own time. Frederick fought until his death against the papacy, which his guardian, Innocent III, had recreated; but all his attacks were invariably concerned with the political power which had been usurped, never with the ecclesiastical authority of the pontiff. No Carolingian, Saxon, or Frankish emperor would have granted the pope so much as Frederick II was obliged to grant, after the principles of Gregory VII had been approved by the world, after he himself had abandoned the concordat of investiture of Calixtus, had recognized the deposition of Otto IV by the pope, and made use of this deposition as a step to his own throne. Facts were against him, and deprived his theory—namely, that popes possessed no jurisdiction over kings—of all effect. In his struggle with the papacy he remained weak and unsupported, because he acted in the name of an already abstract and therefore unpractical idea, in the name of the empire or of the secular authority in

general, not of an actual state and of a nation offended in its own
rights. No advantage bound kings to the empire; they followed
their separate interests, and, like bishops, still feared excommunication and deposition. In vain the quick-sighted emperor told
them that his cause was also theirs. That a pious man—a man,
however, who showed a resolute front to the church—occupied
the throne of France, that a faint-hearted prince sat on the
throne of England, were facts of inestimable advantage to the
pope. Henry III [of England], who violated the Magna Charta,
needed the help of the pope against his barons; nor did he support his brother-in-law [Frederick II] against the very Roman
hierarchy which had made his own kingdom into a fief of the
church. [In 1254, Pope Alexander IV sold Henry title to the
throne of Sicily on behalf of Henry's son, Edmund.] Lewis of
France, on whom Frederick had conferred the office of arbitrator,
rested satisfied with futile negotiations and avoided entangling
his flourishing French dominions, now developing into a monarchy, in the affairs of the empire. Germany, tired of the Italian
wars, which it determined no longer to regard as of imperial
interest, at first courageously resisted the artifices of Rome; then
it split into parties, put forward rival kings and began to desert
the great emperor, while he involved himself in the labyrinth of
Italian politics, and wasted the energies of his mind in a country which was too small for his genius. The voice of evangelical
heretics, valueless at the time, alone was raised in his defense.

Reconciliation became impossible when, after the sentence of
Lyons, the church passed from a passive state to one of vehement
attack. The pope firmly protested that he would never make
peace with, would never tolerate Frederick or his sons, "the brood
of vipers," on the throne. That which Innocent III had previously
contemplated, Innocent IV resolved to accomplish at any price;
to depose the Hohenstaufens for ever, to raise in their stead an
emperor, who, as a papal creature, would renounce all claims
on the State of the Church and Italy.

He prosecuted the war with every reprehensible means that
the selfishness of secular princes was accustomed to employ:
by the fanatical persecution of Frederick's adherents in every

country, as far as the power of the church reached; by encouraging revolt, by suborning the subjects of the emperor to acts of treason, by the wily intrigues of legates and agents, who, in search for a rival king, incited bishops and princes to rebellion, and even attempted to seduce Conrad, the emperor's own son, from his allegiance. Swarms of mendicant monks roused the popular mind to fanaticism, and the people calmly saw their wealth flow into the coffers of Rome, while remission of sins, on account of the holy Crusade, was dealt out to all who took up arms against their lord. The vow of the Crusade was exchanged for the duty of making war on the emperor. Gregory IX had already openly branded him as a heretic; the reproach of being an enemy to the Christian faith formed a powerful weapon in the hands of the priests. His Saracen surroundings, his clear-sighted intellect afforded occasion to the most venomous charges of malignity. The Crusade was preached against Frederick, as against an infidel, in every country, and a German prince, Henry Raspe, Landgrave of Thuringia, who set himself up as rival king in the spring of 1246, did not blush to summon the Milanese to arms against Frederick, as the "enemy of the Crucified." The emperor fully recognized that, in his continued war against the papacy, he would meet the same end as his predecessors in the empire. He longed for reconciliation with the church, even under humiliating conditions; he laid his profession of the Catholic faith in the hands of some bishops. They brought it in writing to the pope. The pope rejected it, resolved on the overthrow of Frederick and his family, and himself compelled the emperor to continue the war.

IX

Rome under Brancaleone

Aᴛ the time of the return of Innocent IV [to Rome, 1253], a citizen of Bologna, by his energy and greatness of mind, suddenly brought the senatorial office in Rome into high esteem, and imparted a transient splendor to the city. His rule and the constitution of the Roman republic, more especially during his time, deserve attentive consideration.

From the thirteenth century onwards the Italian free cities were accustomed to elect their podestàs from among the nobility of other communes with whom they stood in friendly relations. A stranger summoned to a six months' rule offered securer prospect of an impartial government, and less likelihood of the foundation of a tyranny, than the election of a powerful fellowtownsman would have done. Such an exchange of talents and energies between the democracies, who lent each other their most celebrated citizens as rectors, was the finest proof of republican fraternity and of common national ties. It greatly redounds to the honor of the Italians. And since as a rule only men of importance were summoned to the office of podestà, the invitation was in itself the most genuine testimony to distinguished talent. The student who would become acquainted with the genuine flower of the aristocracy in the great century of the republics of Italy, with her noblest knights, generals, lawgivers, and judges,

From book IX, ch. 7, secs. 1 and 4.

must read the lists of podestàs in individual democracies. These lists give at the same time a summary of the most distinguished families who stood at the head of the historic life of the communes in the thirteenth and fourteenth centuries. At a time when the rest of Europe failed to produce any eminent citizens, these registers awaken our astonishment by their wealth of statesmen and soldiers, such as Hellas and Rome knew in the prime of their republican days. The cities show that at this period they had obtained complete emancipation of their political intellect from the church, and display a brilliant picture of national citizenship, before the demon of party strife and the unchecked rule of the plebeians destroyed its brief splendor.

The Romans were accustomed to behold solemn deputations from various cities, even Pisa and Florence, appear on the Capitol, to implore a Roman noble to be their podestà. They themselves, however, had never hitherto gone to seek their senator at the hands of any foreign town. If they were reduced to this step in 1252, while Innocent IV dwelt at Perugia, they must have been driven thereto by the corrupt condition of their commune, and it was assuredly not the jealous nobility, but the populace maltreated by this nobility, who, in consequence of a revolt, formed a resolution to confide the authority of the hitherto divided Senate to a single upright and sagacious man as senator and captain, and to seek for such a man outside Rome.

The Romans turned to Bologna, a city which, owing to its school of law, enjoyed at this time a European fame; its wealth was vast, and since Fossalta its strength of arms redoubtable; a king lay imprisoned within its walls. The Bolognese council recommended to the Romans Brancaleone degli Andalò, count of Casalecchio, a man of ancient family, rich, respected, of severe republican spirit and an experienced jurisconsult. Brancaleone belonged by nature to the strong characters of Hohenstaufen times, was of the same mould as Salinguerra, Palavicini, Boso da Doara, Jacopo of Carrara, Azzo of Este, and Ezzelino. He was endowed with the same energy as these men of iron, but with neither their love of intrigue nor their terrible selfishness. And having fought for Frederick II even after the emperor's excom-

214

munication in the Lombard wars, he was acquainted with these party leaders.

· · · · · · · · · · · · · · · · · · ·

Brancaleone fell from power in 1256, and took up residence in Florence. The Romans recalled him as senator in 1257 for a term of three years. He set out with great severity to establish military and civil order in Rome. In this effort, he concluded an alliance with Manfred, an illegitimate son of Frederick II and Frederick's successor as king of Sicily. This placed Brancaleone in direct opposition to the faction of pope and nobility, and Alexander IV promptly excommunicated him. All the same, Brancaleone destroyed the fortifications of the nobles in Rome. After his death (1258), his uncle Castellano degli Andalò became senator, but the papal faction soon overthrew him (1259).— EDITOR.

Castellano had laid down his arms; he languished in prison, and, as formerly his nephew, was only saved from death by the Roman hostages, who were detained in custody by his friends in Bologna. The Romans, fearing for the fate of these boys, turned to the pope, entreating him to protect them. Alexander consequently demanded that the commune of Bologna would take the hostages under their own keeping. The commune refused. The pope consequently caused the bishop of Viterbo to lay Bologna under the interdict.

Castellano was finally saved by a remarkable movement in the cities of Italy, which followed on the fall of Ezzelino [da Romano, the great lieutenant of Frederick II] and his house. This tyrant of the Middle Ages, whose name has become a byword, had gradually extended his rule over the most important communes of Lombardy. No inducements held out by the popes had availed to make Frederick's son-in-law false to his principles, or persuaded him to enter the service of the church, which, at this price, would have pardoned every sin. After a heroic resistance he fell at last into the power of his united enemies at Cassano on

September 27, 1259. Historians depict the last struggles of this extraordinary man, in whom the spirit of the age transformed the germs of the highest virtues into diabolical crimes, so that he has become immortalized as the Nero of his time. They describe the rejoicings of mankind, who crowded to enjoy the sight of the imprisoned tyrant, and they liken the terrible captive to an owl sitting silent in the midst of a swarm of noisy little birds. Ezzelino, laden with the threefold curse, filled with silent contempt for the world, the papacy and the destiny which had been foretold him by astrologers, died on October 7, 1259, in the castle of Soncino, where he was honorably buried. Terrible was the fate of his brother Alberic, who had a second time deserted the church. After a desperate defense in the tower of S. Zeno, he had been obliged to surrender with his seven sons, two daughters, and his wife. His entire family was strangled before his eyes, and he himself was dragged to death by horses.

The terrible fall of the house of Romano, following on other appalling events, combined to fill the cup of horror to overflowing. Incessant wars and scourges had visited the cities. "My soul shudders," writes a contemporary chronicler, "to describe the sufferings of the time, for it is now twenty years since the blood of Italy has flowed like a stream, on account of the discord between church and empire." Mankind was suddenly thrilled by an electric shock which drove it to repentance; countless multitudes rose with lamentations in the cities, and, scourging themselves until they bled, advanced in processions of hundreds, thousands, nay, even tens of thousands. City after city was drawn into this current of despair, and mountains and valleys soon re-echoed to the touching cry: "Peace! peace! Lord, give us peace!" Many historians of the time speak of the strange occurrence with astonishment; all say that this moral tempest first rose in Perugia and then spread to Rome. It laid hold of people of all ages and conditions. Even children of five years scourged themselves. Monks and priests grasped the crucifix and preached repentance. Aged hermits issued from their solitary caves in the wilderness, appeared for the first time in the streets, and taught the same lesson. Men threw aside their clothes down to the girdle, covered their heads in a cowl and seized the scourge. They formed processions, and in files of two and two, carrying tapers at night, walked barefoot through the frosts of winter. They surrounded the churches with terror-striking songs; threw themselves weeping before the altars; and chanting hymns of the passion of Christ, scourged themselves with frantic energy. At one moment they cast themselves on the ground; at another raised their bare arms to heaven. Looking upon them the beholder must have been made of stone, to refrain from following their example. Dissensions ceased; usurers and thieves surrendered themselves to justice; sinners confessed; the prisons were opened; assassins made search for their enemies, and, placing a naked sword in their hand, implored them to kill them: these enemies, throwing aside the weapon in horror, fell weeping at the feet of their offenders. When these appalling bands of pilgrims approached another town, they rushed on it like a hurricane, and the infection of the flagellant brotherhood thus spread from city to city. It reached Rome from Perugia late in the autumn of 1260. Even the stern Romans fell into ecstasies. Their prisons were opened, and Castellano of Andalò was thus able to escape to his native city of Bologna.

The appearance of the flagellants is one of the most striking phenomena of the Middle Ages. A long and serious social confusion, the consequence of the war between the empire and the priesthood, had found expression in the pious frenzy of the Crusades and the longing of mankind for redemption; the same longing was repeated in the flagellant movement of 1260. Suffering humanity collected in the depth of its consciousness the impressions of the events with which it had been stirred—heresy, the Inquisition, and the stake; the fanaticism of the mendicant orders, the Tartars, the fierce struggle of the two universal powers, the devastating civil war in every city, the tyranny of an Ezzelino, famine, pestilence, and leprosy; such were the scourges which chastised the world at this period. The processions of these flagellants, who seemed like so many wandering demons, was the popular expression of a universal misery; the despairing protest and the self-inflicted chastisement of contemporary society, which was seized by a moral contagion as powerful as that which had laid hold of it in the time of the Crusades. In this dark form of penance mankind took leave of the historic period of the struggle between the church and the empire. Towards its close a genius appeared as its result. This was Dante, who, alone of all this mediæval world, created a unique monument. His immortal poem resembles the marvellous pile of some Gothic cathedral, which displays on its pinnacles all the most prominent figures of the time, emperors and popes, heretics and saints, tyrants and republicans, the old and the new, sages and creators, slaves and freemen, all grouped around the penitent genius of humanity, who seeks for liberty.

X

Rome in the Time of Charles of Anjou

*After Frederick II's death, the Hohenstaufen Empire fell apart. The emperor's heirs were unable to defend their rights. Germany dissolved into a welter of civil war, from which Rudolf of Hapsburg ultimately drew out the imperial title. Allied with the papacy against the last Hohenstaufen, the cruel and rapacious Charles of Anjou seized southern Italy and Sicily. His rule, together with that of Pope Martin IV, was shattered by the Sicilian Vespers.—*EDITOR.

CHARLES was now able to indulge in the scheme, which he had long since conceived, of subjugating the entire peninsula to his scepter, and even of conquering the Greek empire. But seated on the throne of Frederick II he remained only a hated despot. The conqueror was endowed with no sagacity as a ruler, no largeness of view as a lawgiver; to the lands which he ruled he left nothing but the curse of a long feudal despotism. The plans of his ambition were shattered, as were those of the Hohenstaufens, by the policy of the popes, by Italian party spirit, and by the feel-

From book X, ch. 4, secs. 1 and 4.

ing of Latin nationality which finally rose against the dominion of the Gallic stranger.

. . . .

A great event, however, suddenly destroyed the new grandeur of the king and the laborious work of the French popes. After the short dream of dearly bought security, the Roman Curia awoke to a new anxiety, the source of which was Sicily. The ill-used island rose against Charles of Anjou on March 31, 1282. The celebrated Sicilian Vespers constitute the sentence for all time pronounced by nations against foreign rule and tyranny; they were also the first successful restoration of the popular rights in the face of dynastic claims and cabinet intrigues. The Sicilians murdered all the French on the island, abjured Charles's yoke, and appealed to the protection of the church. The terrified Martin rejected their demands, and the heroic nation now gave the first victorious example of an entire country throwing aside the feudal links which bound it to the church. As early as the end of August Peter King of Aragon landed at Trapani, entered Palermo amid the rejoicings of the multitude, and took the royal crown of Sicily from the people. Manfred's son-in-law, the husband of Constance, came as the heir and representative of the Hohenstaufen rights, and the Swabian family thus for the third time appeared in history, now transformed into a royal house of Spain. Charles had hastened from Orvieto to his kingdom, only to suffer a disgraceful defeat. The successful revolution immediately found an echo in the republics of Italy, and the Ghibellines, inspired with fresh courage, seized their arms; even the cities of the State of the Church, so repeatedly injured in their rights, arose. Perugia renounced the popes. The carnage in Palermo had been repeated at Forli on May 1, 1282, when 2000 Frenchmen, under the command of John de Appia, enticed thither by a stratagem of Montefeltre's, were massacred.

Meanwhile in Rome Charles's bitter enemies, the Orsini, were striving to recover their lost power. Banished by Richard Anibaldi and the French prosenator, Philip de Lavena, they threw themselves into Palestrina and here offered resistance. The desire for freedom stirred among the Romans when they saw that Charles's power was tottering and that the Guelf party was shaken throughout Italy. They would no longer obey the king, their senator, nor the pope, who had retired to the fortress of Montefiascone, while they themselves undertook a military expedition against Corneto. Vain were Martin's entreaties; even a famine in the autumn of 1283, which he strove to alleviate, increased the excitement. Aragonese agents scattered gold and seduced greyhaired Ghibellines from their hiding-places. Conrad of Antioch, the sole witness of the terrible day of Tagliacozzo, who had escaped execution and imprisonment, again appeared, collected followers at Saracinesco, and passing beyond Cellæ along the Valerian Way, only too familiar to him, tried to enter the territory of the Abruzzi, where the fall of his house had been accomplished. He determined to recover his county of Alba; his attempt, however, failed, since the papal rector of the Campagna and Stephen Colonna of Genazzano dispersed his troops. But the old Ghibelline entered the Abruzzi in the following year and occupied several fortresses, and the pope was forced to send John de Appia against him. Revolts took place simultaneously in Latium.

In the meantime the Orsini acquired the upper hand in Rome. The Capitol was taken by assault on January 22, 1284, the French garrison was slain, the Prosenator Goffred de Dragona was thrown into prison, Charles's senatorial power was pronounced extinct, and a popular government was appointed. Such were the consequences in Rome of the Sicilian Vespers. A nobleman related to the Orsini, Giovanni Cinthii Malabranca, brother of the celebrated Cardinal Latinus, was appointed captain of the city and defensor or tribune of the republic. Martin IV in Orvieto, learning of the revolution, lamented the infringement of his rights, but yielded under protest. He confirmed Giovanni Cinthii as captain of the city, although only in the capacity of a prefect for the relief of the poor for six months; he recognized the priors elected by the guild of artisans and consented to the election by the Romans of a prosenator, who was to reign on the Capitol beside the captain. The administration of the civic revenues was entrusted to a single magistrate, the Camerarius Urbis. His astute compliance tranquillized the revolt; Richard Anbaldi, who had formerly ill-treated the Orsini in the conclave at Viterbo, now made submission, and at the pope's command went barefoot, a cord round his neck, from his home to the palace of Cardinal Matthew to sue for pardon. A public reconciliation of the factions took place. It was recognized that Charles's government was set aside, and the populace willingly received two papal representatives endowed with senatorial power, Anibaldus, son of Peter Anibaldi, and the energetic Pandulf Savelli. And Rome thus returned to the national system established by Nicholas III.

The following year, 1285, witnessed the death of both Charles and [Pope] Martin IV. The king, crushed and severely punished by the loss of Sicily, died at Foggia on January 7. He left the land, which he had conquered amid streams of blood, plunged in the same tempestuous condition in which it had been when he entered it. His ambitious plans were shattered; the heir and avenger of the Hohenstaufens had successfully penetrated into his country; he foresaw his own throne vacant on his death, since Charles II, his son and heir, was a prisoner in the power of Peter of Aragon [son-in-law of Manfred, Frederick II's illegitimate son and successor in Sicily]. A short time after the king, Martin IV also died in Perugia, which had again made submission to the church on March 28, 1285. Although, owing to the aid of the same Guido de Montfort who had murdered the English prince (and whom he had absolved in order to set up a rival to the Ghibelline Guido of Montefeltre), and owing also to the support of the king of France, he had been successful in reducing the Romagna and many cities to obedience, he nevertheless left Italy in flames behind him. The Ghibellines, whom he had countless times excommunicated, were not subdued; and Peter of Aragon regarded with contempt the anathemas which forbade him to wear the crown of Sicily. After countries and nations had long been sold, bestowed as presents, and trafficked with by popes and princes, the will of the people had arisen as the power which summons kings to authority. The same pope who, as papal legate, had inaugurated Charles's usurpation, was forced by a magnificent destiny to be the victim of this rebellion against the principles of dynastic authority. The antiquated weapons of excommunication were of no avail against the just sentence which fell on the two partners in iniquity, on Charles of Anjou and Martin IV.

XI

The Fourteenth Century: Papal Decadence

*The alliance that Charles of Anjou concluded with Popes Gregory X and Martin IV had tragic effects for the papacy. Deeply involved through it in Roman affairs, France sided, for its own purposes, with the Colonna faction against Pope Boniface VIII. French forces cornered the aged pope in Anagni and so abused him that he died soon after (1303). Control both of the city of Rome and of church affairs at the highest level had fallen from the popes' hands, and the papal residence itself was moved from Rome to Avignon, in a county finally owned by the papacy (1348) but well within the French sphere of influence. Thus began the "Babylonian Captivity" of the popes (1309–76).—*Editor.

THE history of the fourteenth century describes the decay of the feudal and hierarchical institutions of the Middle Ages. These two universal forms, the church and the empire—creations of the Latin idea of human society as a universal monarchy—now appear in entirely altered relations, languishing and threatened with ruin. The ancient German-Roman empire had already perished with the Hohenstaufens, had fallen into vassalage to the

From book XI, ch. 1.

church, and had been banished from Italy. But scarcely had this occurred, when the ancient hierarchical church suffered a like fate. The popes forsook Italy in the beginning of the fourteenth century. Frenchmen as they were, they entered the service of France and were robbed of their universal dominion.

The exile to Avignon was followed first by the schism, then by a general council, lastly by the Reformation.

When the gigantic struggle of the Middle Ages between the spiritual and secular powers was fought out, no mission of universal importance to the European world remained to the popes. The absolute dominion which they had acquired in the thirteenth century, they turned with suicidal policy against themselves and the church. They corrupted the church by countless abuses. Even in their impotence at Avignon under the protection of France, the popes, who acquired their great international position solely through opposition to the empire, again evoked the ancient war. But their challenge was answered by the reforming spirit of the West. Bold thinkers now disputed not only, like the Hohenstaufens, the secular, but also the spiritual jurisdiction of the pope. Heresy appeared in the evangelical forms of Wycliffe and Huss. Faith was severed from knowledge. It seemed as though the nations, matured by the indefatigable work of thought, would fall from the decayed framework of the Catholic church, even as they had burst the bonds of the Catholic empire. The doctrines of the Ghibellines revived in their philosophic view of the world the idea of the empire and of the imperial monarchy. Germany pronounced its empire independent of the Roman papacy, and the genius of Germany gave indications of its approaching severance from Rome in State and Church.

In the fourteenth century the Ghibelline idea, feudal and imperialist, purified from its origin and given philosophic form, triumphed over the Guelf, in so far as the Guelf principle, identified with Latin citizenship, was at the same time the principle of the Roman church. The Guelfs had fought for civic and national freedom in the first place, for the Catholic church in the second, and had prevented the union of the spiritual and temporal power in the emperor. The Ghibellines now disputed the union of the two powers in the pope. After Dante their political philosophy acquired the power of critical science. Like an increasing torrent the Ghibelline spirit flowed onward with growing strength and ended in the German Reformation, while the Guelf, limited more and more by local conditions, receded into Catholicism.

The struggle of the two parties filled the history of Italy for a considerable space, but in such distorted form that its moral value is no longer recognizable. The mother-country of western culture seemed in momentary danger of becoming extinct, like Hellas or Byzantium. The great institutions of the Middle Ages had arisen upon her soil. But what object now remained for the Italians when the ancient church and the ancient empire fell to decay and when popes and emperors forsook the country? Nothing, it appeared, but the war of destruction of the two factions, the remains of the church and empire. Without national constitution, a tumultuous chaos of struggling cities and tyrants, nobles and people, the dismembered land beheld the fall of the mediæval system with the same dismay as she had witnessed the fall of the first empire, and now as then foresaw the rule of the foreigner as the inevitable consequence. Italy, the utterly exhausted field of the struggle between church and empire, invoked in her abandonment the return of emperor and pope to restore peace and heal the wounds that had been inflicted upon her by party hatred. Neither pope nor emperor found the necessary balsams; but the genius of the Italians discovered the means of reconciling the combatants through a higher intellectual medium. In the renascence of classic culture, the factions of Guelf and Ghibelline, of church and state, were merged as distinctions unimportant to the world at large.

The revival of the ancient culture was the greatest national work of the Italians. It saved them from the fate of Greece, and for the third time gave them intellectual supremacy over Europe. But to their misfortune, they were unable, along with the literary and artistic revival, to create a national constitution, and consequently for the second time Italy failed to escape foreign rule.

The new classic culture made its seat in Florence, the first modern state, and from the fourteenth century onwards the true representative of the Italian national spirit. Florence took the place of Milan, the city of foremost national rank in the twelfth century, and of Bologna, the seat of Italian learning in the thirteenth. It even cast Rome into the shade. In the fourteenth century Rome was scarcely more than an honored name and title, a document smothered in dust, on which was inscribed claims to universal supremacy. The tragic abandonment of the city during the Avignonese period made her once more the object of the piety of mankind, and her sufferings were so great as almost to have become mythical to the imagination of later generations. The capital of the Christian world, from which the cosmopolitan ideas of the church and the empire and the entire culture of the West had disappeared, saw herself in danger of sinking into oblivion like a temple from which the service of the gods and the priesthood had vanished. It was actually during the period of the exile in Avignon that, we may say in her despair, the forsaken city demanded the return of her eternal and universal importance, and rose to the conception of the boldest claims which she ever cherished during the Middle Ages. From the Capitol she desired to revive the ancient ideal of empire, to unite nations once again in a universal monarchy, and at the same time to give a political and national constitution to divided Italy. The idea was neither Ghibelline nor Guelf; it was the Roman municipal idea. We shall see how this classic dream rose from the ruins of the city and then sank back into them for ever.

But one success the Romans achieved during the absence of their popes; they acquired a more independent form of municipal government and upheld their democratic state. As in Florence and the greater number of Italian free cities, so in Rome also the power of the old aristocracy was broken; the nobles were excluded from the republic, and consequently the burgher class with its guilds reigned supreme. Nevertheless the fall of the aristocracy entailed a severe loss in military power, and in the arts of statecraft and agriculture upon the cities. The liberties of the burgher class soon perished under the power of the demagogue. Tyrants became hereditary princes; and the universal decay of feudal institutions contributed to render Italy so defenseless, that the country suffered a second invasion of barbarians, in the form of homeless errant soldiery, such as it had witnessed in the collapse of the ancient Roman empire. Florence, powerful by the industry of her citizens, by her intellectual life, and above all endowed with political genius, was long able to preserve her liberty before the appearance of her princely inheritor. But for Rome this heir had been ready for centuries. He reaped the fruits of the destruction of the noble families. When the pope returned from Avignon, he found the democratic state of the popular tribune, of the Thirteen, and the Gonfalonieri exhausted and dying. And when the Roman Martin V, having quelled the schism, returned to Rome and permanently reestablished the sacred chair, he found the city, but lately the prey of bold leaders of mercenaries, ripe for papal rule. The classic dreams of the sovereign majesty of the Roman people and Senate made way for the practical necessity of order and general prosperity, and after some spasmodic protests and reminiscences, the municipal independence of the Capitol yielded to the commands of its papal masters.

The long vacancy of the sacred chair which occurred on the death of Benedict XI, the importance of the city, and lastly the removal of the papacy, had plunged Rome into utter anarchy. The four chief families fought for supreme power, while the Campagna was filled with the vindictive warfare waged by the Gaetani. In order to protect themselves from noble tyrants, the citizens appointed a popular government of thirteen men, making the Bolognese John de Ygnano captain. At the same time Paganino, a member of the ruling Guelf house of the Torri at Milan, was elected senator. In company with the popular council of the Anziani and the captain he governed Rome for a whole year. But the civic nobility were soon enabled to regain possession of the Senate. For scarcely had Clement V become pope when, at King Philip's command, on February 2, 1306, he reinstated the Colonna in all their former rights. He restored the purple to both cardinals and allowed Stephen to rebuild the ruined Palestrina. The Gaetani and all other adherents of Boniface VIII were thus driven from Rome, while the Colonna waxed more than ever powerful. They made a temporary reconciliation with the Orsini, and the two noble houses jointly occupied the Senate.

[Pope] Clement V now without difficulty obtained from the Senate the right enjoyed by his predecessors viz., the senatorial authority for life, with the additional privilege of allowing himself to be represented by deputy. The Capitoline republic thus returned to its former system. The transference of the civic authority in this form to the popes was advantageous to Rome, since the system placed some check on the nobility, reduced the danger of a tyranny, and created at least a permanent principle making for civic order. The political condition of Rome in the Middle Ages, when the commune formed an independent republic which excluded the priesthood from offices of state, but gave personal supremacy to each pope, was the most intelligible and also—for the Roman people—the worthiest solution of the abiding contest between the secular and the spiritual law. This system of government, which had been introduced by Nicholas III after the year 1278, long endured, until, to the misfortune of the city, it expired with the independent republic.

The Romans still hoped to see their pope and bishop reappear in his lawful abode, the Lateran. No one as yet seriously believed in the long duration of the papal exile. But the Gascon Clement V, the slave of France, never appeared in Rome. The king constantly threatened him with the prosecution of the trial against Boniface VIII, and in order to save the papacy from this humiliation, Clement surrendered to Philip's will. He abandoned the city of the apostles to his vicars, and left to his legates the task of tranquilizing Italy, where Ferrara was occupied by the Venetians, where Ancona and other cities of the Marches rose in revolt and elected Poncellus Orsini as their captain. To the indescribable dismay of the Romans, in 1308 Clement resolved on the formal removal of the Curia to Avignon. This city belonged to the king of Naples as count of Provence, and at the same time to the empire. The pope, in making his abode there, placed himself under the protection of a prince who was a vassal of the church. In the same neighborhood the pope also owned the county of Venaissin, which Raymond of Toulouse had been obliged to cede to the Roman church in 1228. The choice of a dwelling on the banks of the Rhone was consequently the best outside Italy that the pope could make, especially since the proximity of Marseilles afforded him ready communication with the peninsula.

The removal of the Curia, the uncertainty of the future, and the strife of factions, produced the most gloomy conditions in the city. On the night of May 6, 1308, by an unfortunate accident, the Lateran basilica was destroyed by fire. The beautiful ancient colonnades and the numerous monuments which rendered the church a museum of Roman history perished in the flames. The ruin of the mother church of Christendom seemed, as in the time of Stephen VI, to forbode a terrible judgment. Processions bewailing the event made their way through the dismayed city; weapons rested, enemies became reconciled; men hastened in pious zeal to remove the ruins and contribute money. The pope appointed a congregation of cardinals to provide for the restoration of the church. The work was prosecuted with energy, but was only completed under his successor.

The excitement of the moment past, superstitious dread of the threats of heaven never leaves any moral trace. The Romans soon forgot their pious vows; Colonna and Orsini continued in deadly enmity their ancestral wars. The absence of the pope left the nobility more unbridled than ever; these hereditary houses now regarded themselves as masters of Rome, left without her master. Their mercenaries encamped on every road; travellers and pilgrims were robbed; places of worship remained empty. The entire circumstances of the city were reduced to a meaner level. No prince, nobleman, or envoy of a foreign power any longer made his appearance. Seldom did a cardinal arrive as temporary legate, happy to escape as soon as possible from the sinister city. Vicars replaced the cardinals absent from their titular churches, while the pope himself was represented in the Vatican, as by a shadow, by some bishop of the neighborhood—Nepi, Viterbo, or Orvieto.

Clement V, implored by his representative in spiritual affairs to relieve the distress in Rome, sent a Minorite brother as peacemaker in January 1310. The monk found the senators Forte-braccio Orsini and John Anibaldi utterly unequal to their task, and the popular Council of the Thirteen at strife both with them and the nobility. These Anziani, the elected representatives of the regions, maintained a democratic commonweal (*populus*) be-side the aristocracy, and this rested essentially on the guilds with their consuls, principally on those of the agriculturists and merchants. The representatives of the citizens now requested the pope to restore peace to the city by means of an energetic and concentrated government. Clement, unacquainted with the conditions of Rome, left the choice of their government for an entire year to the citizens. He removed the senators from office; concerning the nobility and their privileges he vouchsafed not a single word. The right of the Roman people to self-government was consequently recognized by the first Avignonese pope. The French popes in the main favored the democracy in Rome. They were foreign to, and distant from, the city, which gradually lost importance in their eyes. They had no ties with the Roman feudal families; on the contrary, they strove to keep the nobility, who had hitherto been influential in the Curia, as far off as possible. They filled the cardinals' college with Frenchmen. We shall soon see the use that the Romans made of the elective right which Clement V had accorded them.

Meanwhile the change on the throne in Germany had given rise to important events. After the death of Albert of Habsburg at the hands of his own nephew, Philip le Bel endeavored to acquire the empire for his ambitious and powerful family, and to seat, if not himself, at least his brother Charles of Valois, on the imperial throne. The king held negotiations with the pope in Poitiers. The transference of the imperial authority to the dynasty of France, within the confines of whose kingdom the papacy had already been forced to take up its abode, would have made Philip ruler of Europe, and this Clement dared not allow. He strove to circumvent these designs, and sincerely rejoiced when the German electors shattered the schemes of France. The electors decided in favor of Henry of Luxemburg, a noble but powerless man, on whom the alliances of his house, education, and even ties of knightly vassalage to King Philip, had imprinted a half French character. The count was elected in Frankfort in November 1308, was crowned at Aachen on January 6, 1309, and as Henry VII ascended the German throne, which he mainly owed to the exertions of his brother Baldwin, archbishop of Tréves.

Without difficulty Henry obtained recognition from the pope, to whom, following the example of the Habsburgs, he at once conceded the right of ratification. He sent envoys from Constance to Avignon, who were actually to lay before Clement the decree of election, swear, in the king's name, devotion to the church, promise assistance in the Crusade planned by Clement, and beg for the imperial coronation. On July 26 the pope, with the condescension of a gracious ruler, recognized Henry's election as king of the Romans. He agreed to the imperial coronation, but explained that, owing to the intended council, he could not yet perform the ceremony, and proposed a delay of two years, dating from February 2, 1309. The claims of Innocent III, Gregory IV, and Innocent IV were thus recognized as rights without opposition by the empire; no German elector and no German king appeared any longer to doubt the pope's authority to examine and confirm the person of the emperor-elect; in short, to bestow the imperial crown as a fief of the church.

Henry held a diet of the court at Speyer. It was here determined that the journey to Rome should be made in the autumn of 1310. Haste such as this formed a contrast to the indifference shown by Rudolf and Albert towards the imperial crown, which had not adorned the head of any ruler since Frederick II. Henry VII, however, possessed no hereditary power, consequently neither prestige nor influence in Germany, where, on the contrary, he foresaw difficulties with Habsburg-Austria, with Bohemia and Bavaria. He imagined that the imperial crown would invest him with glory and power; he hoped to reunite Italy with Germany and restore the ancient empire of the Hohenstaufens. The ideal of the ancient Roman world monarchy awoke again in the enthusiastic brain of a German king, who had not been taught by history that the attempt to restore the ancient empire, or even the political and feudal alliance of the two countries, could ever again have any practical success. Nevertheless, it was Italy herself that gave inspiration and aim to Henry's ideas. The Ghibellines of Italy urgently summoned him, and the most distinguished Italians met him with an enthusiasm for the imperial monarchy which would have deluded the most prudent of statesmen.

In the beginning of the fourteenth century the condition of Italy had become unendurable to the Italians. The cities from the Alps to the Neapolitan frontier were torn asunder between Guelfs and Ghibellines. Everywhere anarchy, civil war, and exile prevailed; the independent republics were in constant revolt, involved in perpetual party feuds, or at war with cities and dynasties; the ancient federations of cities were dissolved; only isolated and temporary alliances took their place; the feudal lords of the previous centuries ruled as tyrants over the cities, purchasing the title of vicar sometimes from the pope, sometimes from the empire. The country, in short, presented a medley of national forces, which to depict is a task beyond the power of the historian. Visconti and Torri, Scala and Este, the Polentani, the Scotti, Montefeltre, Torrelli, the Manfredi, Malaspina, Guidoni, the Carrara, the Ordelaffi, Cavalcabò, the lords of Savoy, of Saluzzo and Montferrat, the Orsini and Colonna, and a hundred other nobles stood in arms, each following the dictates of ambition or intriguing force. Over this political chaos hovered the two ancient demons of the Guelf and Ghibelline parties. Advantage, or hereditary right, or the accident of the moment determined the choice of the party watchword, and it frequently happened that the name of the faction itself was based on no political principle. The program of the Ghibelline statesmen at this time, however, was the simpler and more clearly marked; their party, which owed its origin to the feudalism of the empire, strove to restore order in Italy under the authority of the legitimate emperor of German nationality. The Ghibelline idea was that of historic right. On the other hand, the idea of national independence cherished by the Guelfs was not set forth in any political system; the Catholic idea of a universal Italian confederation under the supremacy of the pope remained unexpressed, and beyond antagonism to German influence, their efforts had no common political aim. At the same time, the pope, their natural head, was far from Italy. His removal to France, to which the Guelfs had leaned ever since the fall of the Hohenstaufens, made the ties with France the more lasting; nevertheless, they found their most powerful protector in Italy and in the king of Naples, in whose town of Avignon the pope dwelt. The alliance with France, the absence of the papacy, the impotence of the empire, and the confusion which prevailed among the factions in Italy must have encouraged the designs for the extension of power in the peninsula cherished by the prince who occupied the Neapolitan throne.

Charles II of Naples had died on May 5, 1309, and Robert, his second son, obtained the crown, setting aside the claims of Charles Robert of Hungary, son of Charles Martel, eldest son of Charles II. The pope, whose favor he had acquired at Avignon, bestowed the investiture on Robert in August 1309. Clement thus secured his adherence, and the pope, recognizing in the king a desired support of the church in Italy, entrusted him with the defense of his temporal rights in the peninsula, and Robert remained the most grateful ally and most faithful advocate of the sacred chair. On his arrival in Italy from Avignon in the beginning of the year 1310, the Guelfs regarded him as a friend and protector; a fact which furnished additional grounds to the Ghibellines, who were without a leader, for desiring Henry's journey to Italy. The most illustrious men of their party cherished the ardent hope of a political messiah, and to this hope Dante gave expression in the mysterious form of the *Veltro*. The poet, wandering in exile, was the prophet of the Ghibelline ideal. His appeals, and even many passages of his poem, are valuable as political documents concerning the spirit of this memorable time. In contradiction to the history of the expeditions to Rome, which the Italians had execrated for centuries as incursions of the barbarians, Dante saw in the lawful kings of the Romans of German race the God-given saviors of Italy, whose sacred duty it was to restore the empire south of the Alps. Nothing more clearly shows the profound despair of the dismembered country than the fact, that its noblest citizens desired the return of the German emperor with a military force. The Italians censured the desire as the exaggeration of Ghibelline party passion. The poet-philosopher Dante, however, dreamed of a universal ideal, to which no party aims could reach, and to which the ancestry of the emperor was a matter of indifference. He was deluded by the Habsburgs, who never left Germany; he addressed angry reproaches to the shade of Rudolf, who had been oblivious of his duty, and to Dante Albert's murder seemed the judgment of heaven which admonished his successor to fulfil the neglected obligation. The poet's lines in the celebrated passage of the *Purgatorio* which describes the meeting between Virgil and Sordello—dithyrambs of patriotic sorrow rivalling the prophetic sublimity of an Isaiah—retained their force for all succeeding centuries, written, as it were, over Italy in characters of fire. He summons Henry to orphaned Rome:

> "Come and behold thy Rome, who calls on thee,
> Desolate widow, day and night with moans,
> 'My Cæsar, why dost thou desert my side?' "
> —Cary's Translation.

The contemplation of centuries had made the ideal of the Roman empire a dogma, for which the unity of the ecclesiastical constitution offered the strongest basis. To the imagination of mankind empire and church appeared as two distinct but interdependent forms, within which the Christian world, as a whole, was comprised. The idea of the empire consequently survived the fall of the Hohenstaufens and the long period when no German emperor was any longer seen. Neither the bitter struggle between empire and priesthood, nor the ever-growing national impulse among peoples gradually becoming independent, was able to extinguish this Roman universal ideal, which may justly be called the ideal of Christian antiquity. It was less on the convictions of the politician than on those of the philosopher that Dante based his hopes of the restoration to his country of unity, peace, and the glory of past times, through the greatness of the emperor.

Nevertheless, this universal monarch, even when created and crowned, was inferior in power to any king, and could scarcely prove formidable to a tyrant of north Italy. Dante's book, *De Monarchia*, the first political writing of importance since Plato, Aristotle, and Cicero, was not originally called forth by the journey of the Luxemburg prince, but, whenever written, it expresses those Ghibelline teachings which accorded such an enthusiastic welcome to Henry VII in Italy.

Dante's work cannot be called the program of a party, since it could only have been intelligible to highly cultivated intellects. Neither is it the work of a statesman, but of a philosophical thinker, steeped in the abstractions of the school, and not constructing his system from given conditions, but basing it on dogmatic hypotheses, and explaining it from general conceptions. Dante does not treat of the state but of the ideal of the universal republic. With scholastic method he develops three principles: that the universal monarchy—that is to say, the empire—is necessary to the well-being of human society; that the monarchical power—the one indivisible imperium—legally belongs to the Roman people, and through them to the emperor; lastly, that the authority of the emperor is derived immediately from God, and not, according to the opinion of the priests, from the pope, the vicar of Christ or God. This thoughtful work is the genuine expression of the convictions of the Middle Ages, and only as such is it intelligible to us. It rests especially on the dogma of the unbroken continuity of the imperium. It is only relatively speaking that we can say that Dante demanded the restoration of the empire, since according to his theory, the extinction of the empire was as utterly inconceivable as the extinction of human society. Whether the name of the emperor was Augustus, Trajan, or Constantine, whether Charles, Frederick, or Henry, whether he was of German or of Latin race, affected neither the character nor the lastingness of the Roman monarchy, which, older than the church, had gathered the church within its fold. The oneness of the universe was also the fixed principle for the political world of the Ghibellines. For them the only conceivable best system of the world was the rule of a sole emperor, and this view was supported not only by the historic facts of the Roman empire, but also by the Christian idea. If the church, the State of God, was one alone, must not the empire, its civic form, be one also? If there were only one shepherd and one flock, then must not the emperor be the universal shepherd of nations in secular affairs as the pope was in spiritual? Christ himself, who rejected all temporal jurisdiction, had been subject to the civil law, and had said, "Render unto Caesar the things that are Caesar's"; thereby declaring that the emperor was the universal head and lawgiver on earth.

The monarchy or imperial power, therefore, became glorified and idealized by the Ghibellines in proportion as the papacy had encroached on the domain of civil law, and, owing to its secularization, had sacrificed its priestly character. In their conflict with the emperors the popes had tried as far as possible to humble the conception of imperial majesty; they had finally attributed the origin of the empire solely to human weakness or to brute force, limited its province only to material and transient things, and regarded as its highest aim only the subservient one of preserving the liberties, rights, and possessions of the church, and of maintaining her orthodoxy by purging her from heresy. The Ghibellines warmly disputed this theory; they asserted that the empire was a divine institution, and was synonymous with the highest temporal good, with freedom, justice, and peace, that is to say, with human civilization. The danger that the emperors might usurp the spiritual power had been averted by the energy and genius of the popes; men, however, feared another bondage, for the church threatened to seize the empire, the pope the temporal power. It was the watchful Ghibellines who warned Europe of the danger, and Dante's *De Monarchia* was the tocsin sounded in the time of greatest peril. Therein the imperial power opposed the papal, as equally unlimited in secular things, and with equal exaggeration. Dante, in fact, professed imperialist theories no less absolute than those of the Justinianist jurisconsults of the Hohenstaufens. He maintained with philosophic earnestness that all princes, peoples, and countries, that land and sea were the lawful property of the single Caesar, indeed that every living being was subject to the Roman emperor. The Ghibelline doctrines were pushed thus far in opposition to the defiant tenets of Boniface VIII, who had claimed on behalf of the popes a similar absolute power as a divine right. The Dantesque idea of the empire was, however, by no means a program of despotism. The universal emperor was not to be the tyrant of the world, who would destroy lawful liberty and wipe out the diversity of ranks, communities, and races with their constitutions, but rather a justice of the peace, raised far above all party passion by the possession of all things, the chief minister or president of the human republic, in short, the incarnation of the idea of the good. We may say that this high ideal of the perfect temporal monarch was only the counterpart of the ideal of the pope, translated into the secular sphere. Too exalted alike for his times and for ours, it presupposes, if it is to be more than a poet's dream, the golden age of a universal republic, in which nations are only so many families enjoying unbroken peace, under the loving guidance of a freely elected father, who, according to Dante's theory, makes his dwelling in eternal Rome. The Ghibelline philosophy was consequently far removed from the idea of unlimited monarchy, such as was developed from harsh Protestantism. Nevertheless, the perfect ideal of the all-ruling and peace-giving emperor might conceal the germs of other Neros, Domitians, or Caracallas, and the conditions of the actual world might produce the crop of despotism. The philosophers and statesmen of antiquity would not have understood Dante's exalted utopia, and Constantine would have gazed with astonishment on the form (glorified by the halo of religion) which the ideas of the empire had assumed in the Christian imagination of mediaeval thinkers. The celebrated apotheosis, with which Dante deifies the holy empire in the picture of the golden eagle floating in Paradise, presupposes a cult of the political ideal of such religious fervor as only the early Fathers, Augustine, Jerome and Cyprian, cherished for the ideal of the church. There lies at the bottom of this enthusiasm for the Roman empire a deep love of historic humanity, the life of which in all its earthly relations is conceived as a revelation of the divine spirit with no lower claims than those of the church.

In spite of all abstractions, the progress of human thought in the beginning of the fourteenth century consequently lay on the side of the Ghibellines, who soon built a philosophic and legal foundation on which the reformation of the church and state was enabled to rise.

XII

Emperor Lewis IV and Rome

*In his Italian campaigns, Henry VII (1309–13) attempted to re-
vive the Italian power base which the empire had lost after Frederick II's death. Though he failed, his effort set a precedent followed by his successor, Lewis IV of Bavaria (1314–47). Lewis's
rule had special importance in the recurrent conflict between
empire and papacy. Frederick of Austria contested the validity
of Lewis's election as emperor and pressed his own claims. In
Avignon, Pope John XXII (1316–34) refused to acknowledge
either Lewis or Frederick as emperor until he had personally
judged the case, on the principle that popes had full powers to
decide a disputed imperial election. Lewis rejected the pope's
claims and incurred excommunication (1324). By the Declaration of Rense (1338), the German princes declared that, not papal
corroboration, but election by the princes conferred the imperial
title and authority. The coronations of Lewis as king of Italy
(1327) and as emperor (1328), described by Gregorovius in the
following excerpts, forecast this radical quietus on the conflict of
empire and papacy that had begun in the time of Pope Gregory
VII.—Editor.*

THE pacification of Germany soon made it possible for Lewis to
come to Italy, whither the Ghibellines invited him with increasing urgency, and desire impelled him to take the crown of em-

From book XI, ch. 3, secs. 3 and 4.

pire in Rome in defiance of the pope. In March 1325, by the treaty of Trausnitz, he became reconciled to his imprisoned rival [Frederick the Fair of Austria]. The pope sought in vain to prevent this work of peace in Germany. Necessity and prudence induced the former competitors for the crown to conclude the second and permanent treaty at Munich on September 5, and the pope, who urged France, Hungary, Poland, and Bohemia to make war on the Bavarians, happily did not succeed in dividing Germany and hurling Lewis from his lawful throne, beside which the Austrian with sullen resignation had been obliged to take his place as coregent and titular king.

In Italy, on the contrary, the league of the pope, Robert, the Florentines and the remaining Guelfs of Tuscany seemed more successful. Their alliance aimed above all at the overthrow of the dreaded Castruccio Castracane. This celebrated tyrant, of the Lucchese house of Interminelli, was endowed with more brilliant qualities, and favored with better fortune, than Ugo della Faggiola. From the prison into which Ugo had thrown him, he had passed in 1316 to the lordship of Lucca, where Frederick the Fair first made him imperial vicar, and where after 1324 he obtained recognition from Lewis. He had become leader of the Ghibellines, subjugated Pistoja, formed an alliance with the Visconti, and by incessant war reduced Florence to the verge of ruin. The harassed Florentines offered the signory of their city for ten years to Robert's son, Charles of Calabria. This prince first sent Walter of Brienne, titular Duke of Athens, as his vicar, and then himself entered Florence with a magnificent escort of knights and troops on July 30, 1326. He also assumed the signory of Siena, while John Gaetano Orsini, the only Italian on whom on his elevation John XXII had conferred the purple, was active as legate of the church and as peacemaker in Florence. On February 5, 1327, Bologna surrendered to Cardinal Beltram del Poggetto, nephew of John XXII; Modena soon did likewise. These successes of the Guelfs, but more particularly the appearance of the duke of Calabria in Tuscany, placed the Ghibellines in difficulties. Their envoys implored Lewis to come to Rome, and like Henry VII he yielded.

In February 1327 he assembled a truly illustrious parliament in

Trent. The brothers Visconti, Galeazzo, Marco and Lucchino, Can Grande della Scala, Passerino de Bonacolsis, Raynald and Obizo of Este, the Bishop Guido Tarlati of Arezzo, the envoys of Castruccio, the envoys of Frederick of Sicily, the plenipotentiaries of the Ghibelline cities of Italy, appeared before him. They promised to pay the king one hundred and fifty thousand gold florins as soon as he should arrive in Milan, and they urged him to come and take the Iron Crown without delay. Contrary to his original intention, Lewis swore to depart for Italy. His avowed aim was to wrest from the hands of foreign usurpers "the rights of the empire and the dominion of the world, which the Germans had acquired through streams of noble blood." The parliament in Trent partook of the character of a council, since renegade bishops, Minorites, and theologians were present. A formal process was instituted against the pope, who was pronounced a heretic. The reforming spirit of the time thus accompanied Lewis the Bavarian as an ally on his first appearance in Italy.

As the king, escorted by all the Italian nobles, descended from Trent into Lombardy on March 14, 1327, he came summoned like Henry VII, not, however, expected as the messiah of peace, but as a warrior prince and head of the Ghibellines, as the avowed enemy of the pope, and laden with the papal excommunication. These facts made him independent of all scrupulous considerations, and enabled him to advance rapidly to a definite goal. He passed his allies in review and found them sufficiently numerous. Only Genoa and Pisa, on which Henry of Luxemburg had leant for support, were now Guelf, and Rome was still doubtful. But that city was murmuring at the continued absence of the pope, and the Ghibellines were able to assure Lewis that it would declare in his favor. John XXII was not able to prevent the king's march to Rome, although he hurled fresh excommunications across his path.

The Lombard cities did homage to the king of the Romans, who had appeared with only 600 knights. He proceeded by Bergamo and Como to Milan, where he was received with splendor by Galeazzo on May 16, and where the Bishop Guido Tarlati, excommunicated by the pope, crowned him and his wife Margaret on Whitsunday, 1327. Numerous ambassadors from the Ghibelline cities and envoys of the Romans were present and invited Lewis to be crowned emperor. Fortune openly declared in his favor. His army was strengthened by reinforcements from Germany. Unlike the Luxemburger [Henry VII], who had shown himself impartial to weakness, he terrified tyrants by his severity. Instigated by their enemies, and suspicious of Galeazzo, he threw into prison at Monza the Visconti, who had opened Lombardy to him, and gave Milan a republican government. He thus drew upon himself the reproach of ingratitude, although Galeazzo by his tyranny had made himself utterly hated in Milan. Lewis avoided the errors of Henry VII; without waiting to lay siege to cities, without paying any heed to Beltram, the cardinal-legate in Parma, and Beltram's undertakings against Mantua, he advanced rapidly through Lombardy in August, crossed the Apennines and gained the neighborhood of Lucca, where Castruccio Castracane reinforced the imperial army with his experienced troops. Siege was immediately laid to Pisa. This city had hitherto been invariably Ghibelline but had been forced to renounce its principles by the revolution which had banished Ugo della Faggiola.

Meanwhile important events had taken place in Rome. At the end of the year 1326 the Romans had urgently entreated the pope to return, and had been answered by a refusal. As soon as Lewis entered Lombardy a fresh embassy was sent to Avignon, to explain to the pope that his absence would necessarily entail disastrous consequences. Messenger after messenger arrived at John's court. The city became disturbed. The ruins of streets, churches, and palaces still bore witness to the troubles of Henry VII's time, and a fresh imperial visit seemed to threaten like disasters. In order to avert them many urged that welcome should be extended to Lewis. Matthew Orsini, the Roman provincial of the Dominicans, brought, as envoy of the Romans, fresh and more urgent entreaties for the pope's return. John listened with ill humor and perplexity. Should he leave the security of Avignon and enter turbulent Rome in order to allow himself to be besieged in S. Peter's by a German king who thirsted for revenge? The envoys returned with empty words, but the impatience of the Romans did not await their answer. The people, so long deceived by the Avignonese popes, incited by Lewis's agents and won by Castruccio's gold, rose in April or May 1327. They banished Robert's adherents, seized S. Angelo, issued a decree, ordering the city to be closed against the king of Naples, and instituted a democratic government. On June 10 the pope wrote to the consuls of the guilds and to the twenty-six popular representatives; he lamented the innovations and implored the Romans to offer resistance to the enemy and to await a better time for his own return. The two syndics, Poncello Orsini and Stephen Colonna, knights of the Roman people, had excited popular suspicion, since, in contempt of the Romans, they had received the belt of knighthood from King Robert. On their return from Naples, they were not admitted to the city but were banished. On the other hand, Jacopo Colonna, called Sciarra, Jacopo Savelli, and Tibaldo of S. Eustachio stood high in the popular favor. Sciarra was appointed captain of the people and leader of the militia, and a communal council of fifty-two popolani was installed on the Capitol.

This revolution paved Lewis's way to Rome, where he was already proclaimed emperor. At the same time, on June 6 a parliament resolved to send a fresh embassy to Avignon, to explain to the pope that, unless he came without delay, the Roman people would be forced to receive Lewis. The envoys had instructions not to wait more than three days for an answer; the embassy consequently was little more than a form. It was received by the pope on July 7, and dismissed with the message that he would send an answer to Rome through his nuncios. On July 27 he wrote to the Roman people, that he regretted the brevity of the time and the insecurity of the roads and of Rome which prevented his coming; he bitterly lamented the revolution, the banishment of the nobles, the people's readiness to receive Lewis; and he exhorted the Romans to remain faithful to King Robert. At the same time he sent two nuncios to the city, commanded his vicar Angelo de Tineosis, bishop of Viterbo, to institute a public action against the Bavarian, and commissioned Gian-Gaetano Orsini, cardinal-legate in Tuscany, to hasten to Rome, or at

244

least to its neighborhood, and use his influence in his favor. He recommended the prelate to the popular government, as well as to the exiled nobles Poncello and Stephen, Pandulf of Anguillara and Anibaldo, who had retired to their fortresses in the country. He also wrote to Prince John of Gravina, who was again to undertake in Rome the task which he had successfully executed in Henry VII's time. He was already at Aquila with a body of troops; Norcia, Rieti, the Roman Campagna, the passes which led into the Neapolitan kingdom were all occupied.

John, who had been appointed vicar by King Robert, desired to enter Rome and was refused. He fell back on Viterbo. This free city for the first time had fallen under the power of native tyrants and was ruled by the Ghibelline family of Gatti. It refused admission to the prince; he laid waste its territory. At the same time Genoese vessels anchored in the mouth of the Tiber and seized Ostia on August 5. The Romans immediately sallied out to do battle and suffered a severe defeat; the Genoese burnt Ostia and retired. The defeat irritated the Romans against Robert, whom they now entirely renounced. The two senators appointed by the commune, Sciarra and Jacopo Savelli, the Chancellor Francesco Malabranca, and Tibaldo of S. Eustachio, organized the companies of the militia under twenty-five captains, appointed guards and barred the gates. For the legate, the Orsini and Stephen Colonna, who were in Narni with the Prince, were meditating an attack on Rome. The cardinal having vainly demanded admission on August 30, these enemies appeared on the night of September 27, entered the Vatican through a breach in the wall, and erected barricades. The alarm bell rang on the Capitol and the militia hastened to their meeting places. The threatened gates were protected by the militia of six regions, while Sciarra Colonna led other mercenaries into the Borgo of the Vatican. Morning was just breaking. The Romans courageously attacked the barricades and expelled the intruders. Leaving the Borgo in flames behind them, the cardinal and the prince fled from the city by the Porta Viridaria. Many knights lay dead; the celebrated Berthold Orsini, captain of the church and of the Guelf party, was carried away prisoner, and only protected from the popular fury by the magnanimity of Sciarra, his hereditary enemy. The chivalrous Colonna rode in solemn triumphal procession to the Capitol, and in memory of the victory endowed the church of the "Angel Fish-seller," in the portico of Octavia, with a golden chalice and a pallium. The victory of the Romans was crowned by the failure of an attack on the gate of S. Sebastian on September 29, when the Orsini and Neapolitans were defeated with losses by the militia. A paltry memorial, which has been more fortunate in surviving the course of centuries than the greater monuments of history, still recalls these distant times.

Sciarra Colonna now invited King Lewis to Rome, and since nothing any longer barred his path, the monarch was able to obey the summons. Pisa surrendered on October 8, paid a heavy indemnity, and received Castruccio, whom Lewis created duke of Lucca and Pistoja, and appointed rector and imperial vicar. Powerful Florence, defended by Charles of Calabria, would probably have been besieged in vain; Lewis consequently resolved to advance further. He set out for Rome on December 15. He celebrated Christmas at Castiglione della Pescaja, advanced unchecked across the Ombrone at Grosseto and proceeded through Santa Fiora, Corneto and Toscanello to Viterbo, where on January 2 he was received with open arms by Silvestro de Gatti, the city tyrant. Here he was joined, though unwillingly, by Castruccio, who feared that during his absence his Tuscan cities might slip from his grasp. Lewis halted in Viterbo, to await news of the decision arrived at in Rome.

His approach gave rise to violent disturbances in the city. Some members of the Council of Fifty-two were Guelfs in secret; others desired the signory without conditions for Lewis; others demanded that a treaty should be concluded before he was allowed to enter. An embassy to the king was agreed on. Sciarra, Tibaldo, and Jacopo Savelli, however, who had long come to an understanding with him and Castruccio, advised the king not to pay any attention to the embassy from the Capitol, but to approach without more ado. When the envoys now appeared and laid the conditions of the Roman people before him, Lewis left Castruccio to answer; the duke of Lucca made reply by ordering the trumpets to sound the signal to march. He himself hastened in advance to Rome, while the envoys were politely detained in the camp, and the roads were guarded by sentinels. On Tuesday, January 5, 1328, Lewis departed. When he encamped on January 7 with 5000 cavalry and numerous infantry on the Fields of Nero, he saw no signs of resistance; on the contrary, the citizens and several nobles, headed by Sciarra, accorded him a triumphant reception and led him to S. Peter's, where he made his dwelling in the papal palace. The king of the Romans entered the Vatican, which Henry VII had not been able to reach, with a band of heretics and reformers, who intoned the Te Deum in the cathedral of the apostle. He received no greeting from the Roman clergy; the cardinal-legate had imposed the interdict on the city. The greater number of the priests, all the Dominicans, even the majority of the Franciscans of Aracoeli, had vanished from Rome. Several churches stood empty. Many sacred relics, such as the handkerchief of Veronica, which had been conveyed to the Pantheon, were hidden. Nevertheless Lewis had, on his side, a sufficient number of clergy, even some bishops, who celebrated divine service in spite of the ban; the Minorites and other clergy were also ready to defy the pope's order. Thus the events of the times of the fourth and fifth Henries were repeated in 1328. All adherents of the pope trembled before Lewis's entrance as before an invasion of heretics; but the Ghibellines received him with shouts of joy in the city which the pope obstinately refused to inhabit.

The king soon made his dwelling in the palace of S. Maria Maggiore; he was free to roam the city at will, a privilege which had long been denied to any king of the Romans. He summoned a parliament on the Capitol on January 11. In opposition to the aims of the church and from necessity, he appeared before the people as a candidate for the imperial crown. Unlike his predecessors on their visits to Rome, he was fettered by no vows to the pope, and the fact gave him perfect freedom of action. The times were essentially changed; the ancient, exalted imperium was becoming democratic. Lewis and his wife took their seats on two

247

thrones before the assembly; the schismatic bishop of Aleria in Corsica returned thanks for the honorable reception accorded to the king, and in his name requested the imperial crown at the hands of the people. He was greeted with tumultuous applause; the assembly cried "Long live Caesar," and the signory of Rome was conferred for an entire year on Lewis as senator and captain of the people. The same parliament awarded him the imperial crown by a plebiscite and fixed the imperial coronation for the following Sunday, for which function four syndics were to be appointed as representatives of the people. For, as the Romans explained, Charles the Great had obtained the crown only after the Roman people had bestowed the imperium upon him. Although the ancient elective right of the republic had been set aside by the popes by the ratification, coronation, and anointing of the candidate chosen by the German electors, it had never been forgotten. After the restoration of the Senate in 1143, the Roman people had asserted their rights by acclaiming the king of the Romans, by inviting him to his coronation, occasionally by refusing him recognition. They had invariably disputed the ecclesiastical view of the translation of the empire, and had asserted that the emperor received the imperium through the authority of the Senate and people. The consciousness of this right became stronger after the popes removed to Avignon and no longer officiated at the coronation. Their absence gave the republic a new relation to the empire. It was more independent than for a long time previous. Tivoli, Velletri, Cori, Civita Vecchia, Viterbo, Corneto, several other towns in Tuscany and the Sabina did homage to the Capitol. Powerful republics and princes, even the king of Germany, sued for the favor of the Roman people, while the office of senator, which even the pope assumed and which added luster to the title of king of Naples, was regarded throughout Italy as the highest of republican dignities. Dante's book on the monarchy contributed incalculably to exalt the conception of the majesty and inalienable rights of the Roman people. And had not even Henry VII, in his quarrel with the cardinals concerning the place of coronation, appealed to the will of the people? His successor Lewis came accompanied by no plenipotentiary of the pope; came even under the papal ban. He could, therefore, only assume the crown contrary to the will of the Romans, or take it from their hands. Without reflection he resolved, in defiance of the pope, to recognize the people as the source of the imperium, and this act, which was at variance with the policy of the Hohenstaufens, became an event in the history of the city and powerfully influenced the immediate future. Lewis was driven to the step no less by the Ghibelline nobility than by his learned publicists, Marsilius and John of Jandunum. For in their treaties they had shown that the coronation at the papal hands was of no more value to the lawfully elected emperor, than the blessing, customarily bestowed by the bishop of Rheims, was to the king of France. They further asserted that it was only through the abuse of a ceremony, that the popes had appropriated a right that did not belong to them. They therefore demanded the coronation by the people as an effective proof that would put an end to the claims of the pope, and Lewis with courageous resolution left the decision concerning the empire to the Romans.

His democratic coronation was a sumptuous spectacle, such as Rome had never seen before. On the morning of January 17, 1328, clad in white satin and mounted on a white horse, he proceeded with his wife in an interminable procession from S. Maria Maggiore to S. Peter's. The cavalcade was headed by fifty-two standard-bearers on horseback, and troops of foreign knights. Before the king a judge carried the book containing the laws of the empire, and the prefect Manfred of Vico bore the unsheathed sword. His horse was led by the syndics for the coronation, Sciarra Colonna, Jacopo Savelli, Pietro de Montenigro of the Anibaldi, and the chancellor of the city, all clad in robes glistening with gold. They were followed by the fifty-two men, the corporations of Rome, the schismatic clergy, the barons and the envoys from the cities. The historian Villani, who has described the coronation procession, only cursorily remarks on some of the traditional ceremonies in S. Peter's; nevertheless the usual rites were doubtless exactly observed, and Lewis was also clad as canon of the cathedral. The customary form of prayer was recited by the clergy. According to the ritual the count-palatine of the Lateran should support the emperor while receiving sacred unction, and should take the crown in his hands; but since the count-palatine was absent, Lewis knighted the Duke Castruccio, and appointed him count-palatine of the Lateran as well as Gonfalonier of the Roman empire. The unction was bestowed by Bishop Albert of Venice (who had joined Lewis in Pisa), and by Bishop Gerard of Aleria; after which, in the name of the people, the crown was placed on the king's head by a Roman noble. This was the celebrated Sciarra Colonna, now the foremost man in Rome. Amid singular vicissitudes he had been conspicuous in the history of the city during a whole generation as party leader, senator, captain of the people, podestà and general in several cities. Who was not acquainted with this now ageing Roman of the days of Boniface VIII? Twenty-five years before he had stood in the burning palace of Anagni, his sword pointed at the pope's breast. He now held the crown of empire in S. Peter's, to place it on the head of a German king, who, for the first time in history, received the sacred diadem from the hands of a delegate of the people. During the consummation of the ceremony many conscientious knights in Lewis's retinue, and even Lewis himself, must have been assailed by doubts. The emperor, however, soon announced with decision that he had lawfully received the sacred diadem and the scepter through the Roman people. "In this manner," says the astonished contemporary Villani, "was Lewis the Bavarian crowned emperor by the people of Rome, to the great disgrace and offense of the pope and the holy church. What presumption in the accursed Bavarian! Nowhere in history do we find that an emperor, however hostile to the pope he may have been before, or may afterwards have become, ever allowed himself to be crowned by anyone but the pope or his legates, with the single exception of this Bavarian; and the fact excited great astonishment."

In order to prove his orthodoxy Lewis, immediately after the coronation, caused three edicts to be read aloud concerning the Catholic faith, the reverence due to the clergy, and the protection of widows and orphans. The procession reformed after Mass, and proceeded not to the Lateran, but, as befitted an emperor elected by the people, to the Capitol. The Romans accompanied, with shouts of joy, the first emperor whom they had elected and crowned. Not until evening did the procession reach the Capitol, where a banquet was prepared in the palace and on the piazza for nobles and populace. The imperial pair spent the night in the palace of the senators. The following morning Lewis appointed the Duke Castruccio senator, and then advanced with great pomp to the Lateran, where he made his abode.

Had the emperor immediately marched against Naples with the numerous army that he then possessed, he would, in Villani's opinion, have conquered the country without difficulty. But the strong measures which he was urged by his companions to take against the pope, caused him to waste precious time, and an unfortunate accident robbed him of his most energetic general. For on January 28 Pistoja fell into the hands of Philip of Sanguineto, who commanded for Charles of Calabria in Florence, and the news quickly drove Castruccio back to Lucca. He was the most important man at the imperial court, was loaded with honors, was Lewis's general and adviser, the soul of his enterprises, and more feared in Naples than Lewis's entire army. Castruccio left Rome on February 1, with 500 horse and 1000 archers, murmuring against the emperor for having caused him to leave Tuscany. His absence diminished Lewis's power and crippled his designs. He now appointed Sciarra Colonna and Jacopo Savelli senators.

After the duke's departure the emperor sent a troop of cavalry against the Guelf city of Orvieto. By means of the rack he extorted 3000 gold florins from the tyrant of Viterbo, who had welcomed him with open arms, and then threw him into S. Angelo. Penury, the inevitable accompaniment and scourge of every expedition to Rome, drove Lewis to violent measures. The Romans complained that for the sake of money he admitted to the city men who had been banished for murder, and that his soldiers seized food in the markets without payment, for the distress was great. On March 4 things came to an open revolt; a fierce struggle took place at the island bridge; barricades were set up. Filled with suspicion, Lewis strengthened the garrison of S. Angelo, recalled his troops from Orvieto and stationed them in the Borgo. Executions increased the discontent. Neither were traitors lacking. The Chancellor, Angelo Malabranca, even brought Neapolitan soldiers to Astura, whereupon the imperialists destroyed his palaces in the city and took Astura itself by assault. The worst was that Lewis, like Henry VII, found himself obliged to impose a forced tribute; the Jews were required to raise 10,000 gold florins, the clergy a like amount, the laity to provide another 10,000. The measure irritated the entire populace.

Meanwhile John XXII brought a number of suits against the emperor, whose unparalleled audacity had been crowned by such unexampled success. He pronounced null his coronation by the people, as also his appointment as senator; he laid on him the anathema and preached a crusade against him. He brought the Romans to trial, and required them to submit to the church within a given date, and to drive the Bavarian from the city. The hatred in the two camps reached a height unknown since the days of Gregory IX. Since Lewis's arrival a formal religious persecution had begun in Rome. In conformity with the doctrines of the monarchists, Marsilius of Padua had been appointed by the emperor spiritual vicar in the city, instead of the bishop of Viterbo; he had placed the Roman clergy under syndics, not only in order to compel the priests to celebrate divine service in the churches, but also to pave the way for the election of an antipope. The priests who refused to read Mass were tortured; a prior of Augustinians was even exposed in the den of lions on the Capitol. Marsilius and John of Jandunum posted accusations against the pope on the doors of the churches. The Minorites preached that John XXII was a heretic, and it was not difficult to prove the charge in the eyes of the people. It was reported in Rome that Robert's [I, the Wise, of Anjou, king of Naples] *protégé* had obtained the tiara by means of simony, that by his quarrelsome nature he had involved Italy in war, that his erroneous doctrines had occasioned a schism in the church, that he remained in Avignon in defiance of duty and right, and that he had determined to transfer the empire to France. It was necessary to put forward a pope who would restore peace to the church, and the sacred chair to the city of Rome. Lewis himself left these matters to the will of the Senate and people; and as he had recognized their right to the imperial coronation, so he gave them equal liberty to pronounce sentence on the pope.

In order to prepare the way for this great stroke, he assembled a parliament on the piazza of S. Peter's on April 14. He caused three edicts to be read aloud: All such as were found guilty of heresy or of *lèse-majesté* were, without further citation, to be brought before the tribunal. No notarial instrument from which the designation of the era of the Emperor Lewis was absent, was valid. All who had rendered aid to the rebels against the emperor were to be punished with the utmost severity. Assemblies of clergy and laity meanwhile examined into the orthodoxy of John XXII, and found the pope a heretic. Resolutions were drawn up, which were brought to the emperor by the syndics of both classes, with the urgent request that, in virtue of his authority as supreme judge, he would proceed against this heretic. Lewis consequently assembled a second parliament on April 18. Platforms were erected on scaffolds over the steps of S. Peter's, and, surrounded by his nobles, his clergy, his schoolmen, and the magistrates of the Capitol, the emperor seated himself on his throne, the crown on his head, the orb and scepter in his hands. Never had anything resembling this imperial-democratic spectacle been seen in Rome. Heralds enforced silence on the seething crowd. A Franciscan monk ascended the platform, and in a loud voice demanded three times, as in a tournament, "Is there any one here who will defend the priest Jacques of Cahors, who calls himself Pope John XXII?" All was silence. A German abbot then addressed a Latin speech to the people, and read aloud the imperial sentence, which pronounced Jacques of Cahors a heretic and antichrist and deprived him of all his dignities. This document, the emperor's reply to the decree of the pope which pronounced his own deposition, was the work of Marsilius [of Padua] and Ubertino of Casale. Lewis, an illiterate soldier, understood nothing of the theological questions of the church. But he utilized the quarrels of the monks in order to discover a ground for accusing John of heresy and for deposing him. For all the remaining complaints (and there were some with no lack of foundation, such as the assumption of the two powers, the denial of Lewis's legal election, the offense committed against the imperial majesty, the accumulation of untold treasure by the sack of churches and the sale of spiritual offices, the most culpable nepotism, the confusion due to war in Italy, the interdict against Rome, the residence in Avignon)—all these could not furnish ground for the deposition. Lewis gave expression to the feeling of the monks when he explained that he had been besought by the syndics of the clergy and people to proceed against Jacques of Cahors as against a heretic, and following the example of Otto I and other emperors, to give Rome a lawful pope. He consequently represented himself as merely the executor of this sentence, and, in virtue of the imperial edict, without further citation, pronounced John XXII deposed, as guilty of heresy and *lèse-majesté*. This proceeding was the practical outcome of the axioms of the monarchists and reformers, who had laid down the principle that the pope could be tried and punished, that his judges were the council and the emperor, as defender of the church and as holder of the judicial power, and that a pope who had deviated from the lawful faith could no longer have the power of the keys, and consequently could be deposed not merely by spiritual judges, but even by laymen. Earlier emperors had also appointed and deposed popes, but under the forms of law and on the ground of formal decrees of council. Lewis himself some years earlier had appealed to a general council against John XXII. But could the Capitoline parliament and a number of schismatic priests constitute a tribunal to judge the pope? The Roman clergy, the canons of the great basilicas and many other clerics were not represented, because they had long since left Rome. The sentence of deposition consequently awoke doubt or indignation among all intelligent people, and rejoicings only among the immoderate party and the seekers after novelty. The populace dragged a straw figure through the streets of Rome and burnt the heretic John XXII in effigy at the stake. Meanwhile it was not the dogma of the poverty of Christ, but another, against which the pope had sinned in the eyes of the Romans. He remained in Avignon and despised Rome, the holy city, which, according to the Ghibelline theory, enclosed the chosen people of God, and in the midst of which the priesthood and the imperium ought eternally to have their seat.

The bold action of a Colonna showed the emperor that he would encounter resistance in Rome itself, and that the Guelf party among the nobility was in nowise crushed. Jacopo, a canon of the Lateran, accompanied by four men in masks, appeared on April 22, in front of S. Marcello, produced John XXII's bull of excommunication and read the document, which no one had hitherto ventured to make public, to an assembly of more than a thousand men. He protested against Lewis's sentence and the decrees of the syndics, pronounced them null, offered to defend his assertion against any one with the sword, affixed the bull to the doors of the church, mounted his horse and rode unhindered through the city and back to Palestrina. The young Colonna was a son of Stephen, born during the latter's exile in France. Like so many sons of the nobility he had been provided with a stall in the chapter of the Lateran and was at the time chaplain to the pope. His father, formerly so zealous in Henry's service, had not presented himself before Lewis. While his brother Sciarra was the foremost man at the emperor's court, Stephen remained at his recently built castle of Palestrina. His prudent reserve secured a brilliant future to himself and his house; he remained in the most friendly relations with King Robert and with John XXII, especially as most of his sons had chosen a clerical career.

On April 23 the emperor summoned the leaders of the people to the Vatican. The assembly passed the resolution that, henceforward, every pope must make his abode in Rome, must never absent himself from the city for more than three months in the summer, or remove further than a two days' journey, and never without the permission of the Romans. Should he violate these conditions, should he fail to return after having been summoned three times by the clergy and people, he was to forfeit his office. It was a foolish decree, which degraded the head of the church

to the position of a podestà. So great was the irritation of the
emperor that he even passed sentence of death on John XXII as
a heretic, and as guilty of high treason.

The logical sequence of these measures was the elevation of a
new pope. The schismatic Minorities demanded in addition the
election of one of their fraternity, a disciple of poverty such as
Celestine V; and for the second time the prophetic kingdom of
S. Francis was to be recognized in such an ideal. The tiara was
offered to a member of the order, but he shrank back in terror,
and fled. Another showed himself less scrupulous. This was
Peter Rainalucci from Corbara, near Aquila, the former scene
of the history of the saint of Murrone. He was a Minorite
in the monastery of Aracoeli, and was reputed a man of
blameless life, but his after career shows that he was unqualified for the difficult role of antipope. The simple monk was
elected to the papacy at an assembly of priests and laymen. On
May 12 the Romans assembled on the Piazza of S. Peter's, where
the scaffolding erected for the scenes enacted earlier still remained above the steps of the cathedral. The emperor made the
pope-elect take his place under the baldacchino, and Fra Nicholas of Fabriano pronounced a discourse on the text, "And when
Peter was come to himself, he said, Now I know of a surety that
the Lord hath sent his angel, and hath delivered me out of the
hand of Herod and from all the expectation of the people of the
Jews." The bishop of Venice three times demanded from the
tribune whether they would accept Brother Peter of Corbara
as pope. The crowd assented, although they had hoped for a
Roman. The bishop read the imperial decree of ratification; the
emperor rose, proclaimed Nicholas V, placed the fisherman's
ring on his finger, clothed him with the mantle, and made him
sit on his right hand. And thus an emperor, whom they themselves had crowned, and a pope, whom they themselves had
made, sat in sight of the astonished Romans. The people entered
the cathedral, where a solemn service was celebrated. The bishop
of Venice anointed the antipope, and with his own hand the
emperor set the crown on his head. A banquet closed the tumultuous ceremony.

Frederick II, who, according to the avowal of the church, had been her most formidable enemy, must now have appeared as a man of moderation when compared with Lewis the Bavarian; for Lewis ventured on a measure which no great emperor had ever attempted before; he harassed the church with a schism such as she had not experienced for a hundred and fifty years. With incredible audacity he gave a democratic aspect to the quarrel between empire and papacy. He denied all the canonical articles which the Habsburgs had admitted concerning the supremacy of the pope. As the popes in earlier days had formed alliances with the democracy in order to make war on the emperors, so Lewis appealed (and for Rome the fact is one of the most important in her history) to the democratic principle of the majesty of the Roman people. He took the crown from the hands of the people; he also restored them the right of the papal election. After having pronounced all the cardinals heretics, he caused the pope to be elected by clergy and laity "according to the ancient custom," and ratified and crowned him of his imperial authority. In his letter of admonition to the cardinals at Avignon on the death of Clement V, Dante expressly recognized that they alone possessed the right of electing the pope, and not a single voice was then raised in Rome, which the popes had abandoned, to remind the people that the election had formerly lain in their hands. It was not until the revolution under Lewis that this recollection was awakened, and that too only by violence.

The important revolution was the consequence of the sojourn of the popes at Avignon, the effect of the quarrel which John XXII so foolishly invoked with the empire, and of the reforming principles of the monarchy, with which was associated the Franscian schism. The high-handed doings of John and Lewis, their tedious actions at law, the extensive researches into the imperial and papal authority, formed the close of this mediaeval struggle, which now passed over into more intellectual regions. The age of the reformation began; the ecclesiastical severance between Germany and Italy was perceptible in the distance, and became inevitable as soon as the political severance was accomplished.

Both powers, the world historic institutions of the Middle Ages which were pitted against one another for the last time, were, nevertheless, merely the shadows of their own past. The papacy after the fall of Boniface VIII, after its defeat at the hands of the French monarchy, after its flight to a corner of Provence, had sacrificed its universal majesty for ever. After the fall of the Hohenstaufens, after the surrender of the empire by the Habsburgs, and Henry VII's ill-starred expedition, the imperium also had vanished, and Lewis the Bavarian, who degraded it into an investiture by the Capitol, robbed the crown of Charles the Great of the last glow of its ancient splendor in the eyes of all who believed in the old imperial hierarchy. It is very remarkable that soon after the time when Dante glorified the Roman empire in its highest idealization, this very empire, under Lewis and his successors, actually sank to its lowest depth of desecration.

XIII

Empire, Papacy,
and Republic

THE city felt the absence of the pope an ever increasing misfortune. Against the dark background of the sufferings of a famished and tortured population, such as no chronicler has adequately described, we may observe the pompous processions of senators and magistrates, or the rude games on Monte Testaccio, but shall discover no trace of any life worthy of respect in the metropolis of Christianity. In poverty and obscurity she withered away, decayed and crushed, a rubbish heap of history, while the pope, forgetful of her claims, accumulated gold and treasures in distant Avignon. The profound sadness, which is characteristic of Rome in the Middle Ages, is deepened at this period, when the sight of the ruins of antiquity, of deserted and tottering churches, heralded the overthrow of the grandeur of the Christian world. Human passions never had a theater so overwhelmingly tragic as that offered by Rome at this time. Nevertheless, the savage feuds of the nobles, and the ambition of the barons, quarrelling for the shreds of the senatorial mantle or about a shadow or a name, raged day and night above its dust and ruins. The hostile houses of Colonna and Orsini severed Rome as the Guelfs and Ghibellines severed other cities. They numbered equally strong adherents, owned castles and fortresses throughout the Roman

From book XI, ch. 4, sec. 3.

territory and allies or protectors in distant places, even in Umbria and Tuscany. One party consequently could not overpower the other.

In 1332 the feuds became so violent that the pope sent two nuncios to Rome, Philip de Cambarlhac, his vector in Viterbo, and John Orsini, who still remained cardinal-legate of Tuscany and the Patrimony. From the attitude of John XXII it seemed as if he intended to come to Italy. In order to render the Bolognese subject to his nephew, he gave it to be understood that he wished to establish the papal chair in their city. Beltram, in fact, erected a fortress here, and the citizens, hoping for the arrival of the pope, to whom they forthwith made over the signory, did not hinder its construction. At the same time John soothed the Romans by the prospect of his speedy return, and instructed his nuncios to have the Vatican palace put in order. The shades of deserted Rome disturbed the repose of the pope in the palace at Avignon, for the conviction that Rome was the sole lawful head of the Christian world was indestructibly rooted in the human race. The Romans wrote despairing letters to the pope and once more entrusted him with the full civic authority. Since he again appointed Robert of Naples as his representative, it follows that the term of the king's senatorship must have expired in the year 1333. Robert made the Neapolitan Simone de Sangro his vicar. John XXII, however, did not appear in Rome. King Philip without difficulty still detained him, and it is hard to believe that the pope was serious in his intention. The Avignonese popes tormented the French kings from time to time with the prospect of returning to Rome, and the threat of leaving France was their sole weapon against monarchs whose serviceable prisoners they remained. A new and fierce war between the Colonna and Orsini, moreover, showed the pope how uninviting was the state of Rome. On May 6, 1333, the heads of the Orsini, Berthold and a count of Anguillara, marched with a strong escort across the Campagna to meet the enemy. The young Stephen Colonna encountered them at S. Cesario, and the two Orsini were left dead upon the field. The family immediately flew to arms, but in spite of inferior numbers the Colonnas gained the victory. The Orsini achieved nothing in the city; they merely strangled an innocent child of Agapito Colonna, who happened to have been brought to church by servants. The Cardinal-legate John Orsini, the uncle of the slain, was also drawn into the vindictive fray. Desire for revenge and family affection had completely stifled the voice of religion in this prelate. He summoned the vassals of the church to arms, united with the Orsini, destroyed the Colonna fortress of Giove, and thirsting for revenge entered the city, where he attacked Stephen Colonna in his own quarter. This forced the pope to take part against his legate. He ordered the cardinal to lay down his arms and restrict himself to his spiritual duties in Tuscany.

John XXII had more to lament than the ungovernable disturbances in Rome. Almost the entire state of the church was in open rebellion. The cities of the Romagna, irritated by the despotism of their rectors and castellans, threw off the yoke of the church. During the Avignonese period the popes almost exclusively sent Gascons and Frenchmen, mainly their relatives, as regents into the provinces belonging to the church. Unacquainted with the Italian character, and without any love for the country or people, as a rule utterly unqualified for their important posts, these rectors, like the proconsuls of ancient Rome, utilized their term of office merely to extort wealth and enforce their power. During his long government in Bologna, the pope's nephew, Beltram de Poggetto, had made himself almost independent. The Italians hated this high-handed foreigner, who was believed to be a natural son of the pope. Petrarch, who abhorred John XXII on account of his incessant wars in Italy, said that he had sent Beltram to Italy not as a priest but as a robber, with legions like a second Hannibal. Bologna at length rose on March 17, 1334, with the cry, "People, people, death to the legate and to the men of Languedoc!" All who spoke French were slain. The palaces of the Curia were attacked, and the legate besieged in his newly built fortress. Beltram owed his escape to the prudent intervention of the Florentines, who escorted the fugitive cardinal through the rebellious country. The fortress in Bologna was demolished to the last stone; the whole of the Romagna hoisted the standard of freedom, and the formerly powerful legate appeared as a fugitive before the papal throne.

The terrible condition of Italy at this time gave birth to phenomena similar to those which had been witnessed after the fall of Ezzelino. The flagellants appeared on both sides of the Alps. At Christmas 1333 the Dominican Fra Venturino of Bergamo preached repentance in Lombardy. He drew thousands after him. These penitents were called "the doves," from the sign of a white dove with an olive branch, which they wore on their breasts. Venturino had given them a habit like that of the Dominicans; they carried the pilgrim's staff in the right hand, the rosary in their left. Enthusiasts and adventurers, innocent and guilty, readily followed his banner, especially since the discipline of scourging was not too severe. The monk led his bands to Florence, where they were entertained for three days, and where many Florentines joined their ranks. They continued their pilgrimage by Perugia to Rome, to pray and institute peace at the abandoned graves of the apostles. Fra Venturino entered the city during the Lent of 1334, with an errant army of more than 10,000 men, who adopted the gentle epithet of "doves," but who traversed the land more like a swarm of locusts. Among them were Bergamaschi, Brescians, Milanese, Mantuans, Florentines, Viterbese, who, divided into companies of twenty-five, marched behind a cross singing litanies, and shouting the cry, "Peace and Mercy!" Aged men remembered having seen the predecessors of these penitents in Rome, when the castellan of Andalò owed his release from prison to their means. A chronicler has described this phenomenon of the flagellants and the attitude of their Roman contemporaries. The brethren of the dove were men who brought no money to Rome, but who claimed board and lodging. They were, however, willingly received, and Fra Venturino obtained shelter in the Dominican monastery of S. Sixtus on the Via Appia. His followers were well-disciplined; he preached to them by day; they sang laudes in the evening. After they had consecrated a banner in the Minerva, which depicted the Madonna between two angels playing the violin, the monk announced a popular meeting on the Capitol, where he would

preach repentance. The Romans listened in profound silence to
the discourse of the Bergamasco, but criticized his mistakes in
Latin. He extolled Rome as the city of the saints, whose dust
ought only to be trodden with the naked foot; he said that their
dead were holy, but their living godless; at which the Romans
laughed. They shouted their approval when he announced that
the pope ought to make his abode in Rome, but when he asked
them to give to religious objects the money which they had destined for the godless carnival diversions on the Navona, they
pronounced him a fool. The prophet remained alone on the Capitol. Attempts were made to seize him; he shook the dust of Rome
from off his feet, and exclaimed that he had never seen a more
corrupt people on the earth. He went to the pope at Avignon,
where he was accused of heresy. For the church had already forbidden the fanatic processions of the flagellants and forbade them
now. These mystics turned from the prescribed holy places and
sought salvation in the enthusiasm of their inward feelings; their
teachings were colored with heresy, and their extravagant character assumed the form of an independent sect, which was at
enmity with the existing church. Fra Venturino, severely censured at Avignon, because he had preached that the true head
of the church could only be found in Rome, was, it is true, absolved from the charge of heresy, but was sentenced to detention
in a remote spot. Such was the result of the attempt of the
preacher of repentance to turn corrupt Rome from her sins.

Meanwhile John XXII died on December 4, 1334, at Avignon,
ninety years of age. He had spent his long reign in un-Christian
strife and hatred, without any other love than that of money.
In his ambition he had filled the world with war, and the aged
figure, seated on the papal throne, presents a revolting aspect. His
litigious disposition, his immoderate and at the same time limited
mind, had forced the German empire into a dangerous war with
the papacy, and had occasioned a schism in the church. In spite
of his dealings with the world, his days and nights were occupied
in scholastic researches into trivial subjects, for he was an indefatigable pedant in study. In his last days he awoke a storm in
the church by the discovery of a new doctrine concerning the

vision of departed souls, of which he was pleased to assert that they could not enjoy a perfect sight of God before the day of judgment. This idle dogma about the heavenly state provoked such opposition on earth that John XXII was in danger of becoming a heretic, and was threatened with a summons before a council in France. A synod at Vincennes pronounced the pope's views heretical. He must have recanted shortly before his death, for he in no wise considered himself infallible. The profound commotion which his quarrel with the Franciscans finally engendered largely contributed to vivify and spread throughout Europe the germs of the Reformation, which had long been stirring in Christian society. In this respect his reign was more important for the history of the world than those of many celebrated popes. By their want of moderation Boniface VIII and John XXII did more to shake the Catholic hierarchy than any heresy had previously done. One evoked the secular, the other the ecclesiastical spirit of antagonism to the Roman dogma. For the rest, John, by his actions, gave practical ratification to his theory, that Christ and his apostles had owned property; for although himself an old man of simple habits, this Midas of Avignon was one of the wealthiest of popes. Eighteen million florins in gold, and seven millions in valuables, were found in his treasury, wealth which avarice and greed had extorted from the people by the reprehensible means of the newly introduced imposition of first fruits, and by reservations of all the spiritual offices in Christendom.

After election on December 20, 1334, and consecration on January 8, 1335, the cardinal of S. Prisca ascended the sacred chair in Avignon. Jacques Fournier, son of a miller in Saverdun in Languedoc, was a Cistercian monk and a doctor of theology. He had been successively bishop of Pamiers and Mirepoix, and had been made cardinal by John XXII. He was a learned man of strictest monastic inclination, hard and rude, but upright, and in many respects the direct opposite of his predecessor, whose abuses in the church he strove, with praiseworthy zeal, to remedy. He, too, hated the Minorities, and swore death to the heretics; but he was free from avarice and nepotism, from worldly ambition, and from all desire for war or strife. Although despising earthly pomp, he was severely tenacious of the temporal rights of the papacy.

Scarcely had Benedict XII become pope when he hastened to tranquilize Italy, which his predecessor had left in the flames of revolution, and to pacify Rome, where the war of factions had produced a state of utter misery. A new pope, a fresh embassy of the Romans, a fresh cry of despair from the aged and now unattractive spouse, who was still unwearied of inviting her faithless husband to return to her embrace. Immediately after Benedict's elevation, the Romans had solemnly invited him to the city, and he had sensibly recognized the justice of their wishes. He was sincerely inclined to grant their entreaties; but scarcely had his intention become known, when it was thwarted by the French king, and Benedict sighed that the sacred chair must remain in French bondage.

No means sufficed to reconcile the hatred of the hostile factions in Rome. Family fought against family, the populace against the nobility, the plebeians among themselves. A truce was occasionally agreed upon, then all sides rushed again to arms. Vain were the exhortations of Benedict XII. The factions entrenched themselves in Rome, where they barred one entrance after another. Stephen Colonna held four bridges, the remainder were occupied by Jacopo Savelli and his followers; on September 3, 1335, the Orsini destroyed Ponte Molle. The war extended as far as Tivoli, where Stephen Colonna constituted himself signor. On January 13, 1336, a truce was arranged by the intervention of Bertrand, archbishop of Embrun, whom the Romans had expressly appointed syndic and defensor of the republic. Napoleon and his sons, Jordan and the Count Palatine Berthold and his brothers, John of Anguillara, Angelo Malabranca chancellor of the city, Jacopo Savelli and the remaining relatives of the house of Orsini on one side; on the other, Stephen Colonna, his sons Stefanuccio and Henry, with the remaining scions of the house, met in the convent of Aracoeli. And here, curbing their mutual hatred, but their eyes scintillating anger and murder, the fierce adversaries held out their hands, and swore to a two years' peace.

At the end of the same year (1336) Petrarch was sojourning on the estates of his friend, Count Ursus of Anguillara, at Capranica near Sutri. He surveyed with horror the disastrous condition of the beautiful country, which swarmed with hostile bands and robbers; the shepherd stood in arms in the thicket guarding his sheep; the husbandman followed the plough, bearing sword and lance, and everything breathed only war and hatred. When he wished to journey from Capranica to Rome, the Colonna sent an escort of one hundred horse to guide him safely through the hostile ranks of the Orsini. Can we wonder that Benedict XII turned a deaf ear to the fervent prayers of the Romans for his return?

The civic power of King Robert had expired with his accession; a popular representative committee of thirteen men, captains of the regions, had been appointed, alternately with rectors, nominated by the two contending parties. So great was the confusion that Robert had to appoint vicars even at the beginning of the year 1337. The whole state of things was provisional and insecure; a constant vacillation between popular and aristocratic government prevailed. The pope had not yet been entrusted with the dominium; this precious gift was withheld until, finally, in July 1337, the afflicted people decreed to bestow the signory on Benedict in person. The Romans appointed him senator and captain, syndic and defensor of the republic for life. They hoped thereby to prevail on him to return, for so highly did they value the inestimable privilege of their freedom, and the lordship of the ruins of Rome, that they seriously believed therewith to entice the pope to their city. For the rest it is clear that the Roman republic remained perfectly independent of the popes, and that in their capacity of signors of the city the pontiffs could claim no other relation to it than that of protector and highest official for life, a position such as that with which other free cities endowed princes or tyrants in temporarily entrusting them with the signory. Benedict gratefully accepted the offered authority. He did not transfer it to King Robert, but first nominated the rectors of the Patrimony and of the Campagna to administer the Senate, and then installed two knights from Gubbio, Jacopo Canti de Gabrielis and Boso Novello Rafaelli, an old Ghibelline and a friend of Dante, as senators for a year. The act proves that he determined to maintain an independent attitude towards the Guelfs, and especially towards King Robert. The family feud, meanwhile, broke out with fresh fury. Jacopo Savelli, with engines of war, attacked the church of S. Angelo, of which John Colonna was cardinal, and destroyed his palace. In August 1337 the pope consequently ordered that peace should be renewed for three years. Some religious men also effected a reconciliation between nobles and people, and this work of peace, in the midst of the inextinguishable hatred of parties, seemed to be the effect of some divine miracle. Benedict XII was delighted at the tranquilization of Rome, but not trusting its stability, he ordered the surrounding cities to refrain from sending troops and to take no part in its factions. On October 2, 1338, he appointed Matthew Orsini and Peter, son of Agapitus Colonna, senators for a year. They issued an amnesty, but failed to tranquilize the city, for the people attacked the Capitol in July 1339, expelled one senator, threw the other into prison, and made Jordan Poncelli-Orsini and Stephen Colonna rectors of the city. At the entreaties of the Romans, who now hoped to establish their republic by means of democratic institutions, prosperous Florence sent two experienced statesmen to instruct the ancient mother city in the arts of popular government, and many marveled at the change of times and circumstances. According to the Florentine model, taxes were imposed, and thirteen priors of guilds, a gonfalonier of justice, and a captain were appointed. But the pope protested against these innovations, ordered the rectors to resign their authority, appointed vicars, and then on March 1, 1340, made Tibaldo of S. Eustachio and Martin Stefaneschi senators for six months. In order to win over the hungry populace he sent 5000 gold florins for distribution; and indeed the city soon showed itself again ready to recognize his dominion. For Benedict XII was a strong, upright, and peace-loving man, and was determined to curb the tyranny of the hereditary nobility. He also defended the oppressed provinces of the church against the arbitrary depredations of their rectors. The new senators now acted with energy against some of the leading men, such as Francesco de

Albertescis of Caere and Anibaldo of Monte Compatri; but Berthold Orsini and Jacopo Savelli snatched the guilty out of the hands of justice, forced their way into Rome, and seized the church of Aracoeli. The senators vanished from the Capitol, when Berthold and Paul Conti proclaimed themselves captains of the people. But as the pope sent a nuncio empowered to make use of spiritual censures, these captains were banished, and order was restored. Ursus of Anguillara and Jordan Orsini then assumed the senatorial authority.

Such were the conditions of Rome during the long absence of the pope. The unfortunate people saw all their attempts to obtain peace and impose a check on the barons frustrated, and sought for some one who would deliver them from their intolerable misery. A memorable festival, the coronation of a poet on the Capitol, took place precisely at this terrible period, and contributed to awake ancient memories, and to fashion out of them singular events.

XIV

*From Notary to Dictator:
Cola di Rienzo*

*Cola di Rienzo first appears in history as a representative of the
Roman Republic at Avignon, where he came to know Petrarch
(1343). His antiquarian knowledge and oratorical skill, and his
burning hatred of the aristocracy, won him a place with the most
fervent republican factions. His outspoken complaints at the
papal court against outrages by nobles invited the wrath of the
great families.—*EDITOR.

THE new senators, Matthew Orsini and Paul Conti, immediately
brought suits against [Cola]; but the pope, who wished him well,
put a stop to these proceedings. Clement VI showed himself
more complaisant to the Roman democracy than to the patrician
houses. We are acquainted with the grounds that induced the
Avignonese popes to adopt this policy; they all strove to satisfy
the Roman people, in the hope of pacifying the reproaches
brought against them, on account of their absence from the seat
of the apostles. In Cola, Clement recognized a man that might
be useful to him. The poor plebeian begged for the post of notary
in the civic camera, which carried with it the salary of five gold
florins a month, and the pope gave it, with the most flattering rec-

From book XI, ch. 5, secs. 2 and 3.

ognition of his virtues and learning, on April 13, 1344. With
this official appointment began Cola's public career in Rome,
whither he returned after Easter of the same year.

The son of Lorenzo or Rienzo had not yet invented the myth that
he was a bastard of the Emperor Henry VII, but was known as
the legitimate child of a tavern keeper in the region Regola,
where his mother Maddalena helped to earn a scanty livelihood
by washing and carrying water. He was born about 1314. The
poverty of his parents afforded him no means for the cultivation
of his distinguished abilities. From the death of his mother until
his twentieth year he lived with a relative at Anagni—"a peasant
among peasants," as he himself lamented. About 1333 or 1334
he returned to the city, on the death of his father, and had here
opportunity of educating himself by study. The young Roman
owed more to self-instruction and to the writings of the ancients
than to the professors of his native city, to whose decayed university he may nevertheless have resorted. His letters show
that he was intimately acquainted with the Bible and the Fathers
of the church, even with canon law. He was versed in Livy,
Seneca and Cicero, Valerius Maximus and the ancient poets; they
formed his Latin style, endowed him with eloquence, nourished
his intellect with magnificent imagery, and filled him with long-
ings after the ideals of antiquity. He was often heard to exclaim,
"Where are those good old Romans? Where is their lofty rectitude? Would that I could transport myself back to the times
when these men flourished." The ignorant inhabitant of the region stared at the youth, who was of handsome aspect, and
around whose mouth a whimsical smile was wont to play as he
explained ancient statues and reliefs, or read the inscriptions on
the marble slabs scattered through the city. It was these ostenta-
tious inscriptions—ghostly voices, which, in the midst of ruins,
spoke of a great world that had completely passed away—that
stirred his poetic imagination and incited the man to believe
himself in the place of these heroes and consuls, and to adorn
himself with attributes and titles, which, in the silence of his
dreams, he may long before have appropriated. It was, moreover,

the histories of antiquity, in the study of which he steeped himself, that in him, as in Petrarch, removed the barriers between past and present, and fired him with such enthusiasm "that he resolved to translate into practice that which he had learnt in reading." And from the depths of his dreamy nature, on the soil of antiquity, in the tragic silence of Rome, and in the midst of the misery of an enslaved population, arose a marvelous genius— one of the most remarkable products of the Middle Ages.

. . . .

Important events throughout the rest of Italy made a deep impression on public opinion in Rome, and prepared the way for coming events. On September 18, 1345, Andrew, the youthful husband of Queen Joanna, had been murdered in Aversa, and his brother Lewis of Hungary organized an expedition to Naples to avenge his death. The fall of the Angevin monarchy was fruitful of consequences. The kingdom had hitherto been the basis of the temporal position of the papacy in Italy, and the support of the entire Guelf party; the national principle had rested on its power, as had been plainly evident in the time of Henry VII and Lewis the Bavarian. It now fell into anarchy; the papacy and the Guelf party lost their support in Italy; a power was extinguished which had served as a factor in the cause of unity and order as far as Rome and the Romagna, and the gates of the country were thus left open to attacks from outside. While Italy trembled at the thought of an invasion of the Hungarians, the German Werner had already formed his Great Company, which sacked and ravaged Tuscany and Lombardy. A time of terrible misery was at hand, and the unfortunate nation sighed for a savior as in the days of Dante and Henry VII. A solitary and brilliant example of the love of freedom raised the hearts of patriots. This was the revolt of the Florentines, who banished the duke of Athens in 1343, soon after installed a democratic government, removed the nobility from all civic affairs, and conferred the authority on the guilds. The old patrician communal constitution in the cities fell to pieces about this time. The nobles were excluded from the communes, and, even in the smaller republics, the guilds with their priors obtained sole power. Of this, Todi offers a memorable example. The Umbrian city reformed its statutes on December 6, 1337, and gave utterance to the following principles:

> Since (owing to the work of the enemy of the human race, who sowed dissension among the citizens) the commune of Todi has in past times been continually troubled by civil war and by many expenses, and since we recognize that every city, every country, every place which is ruled by the people and men of the people and artisans, enjoys peace and rest, therefore we, invoking the name of Jesus Christ, of the glorious Virgin Mary and of S. Fortunatus, resolve by this just law, which shall endure for all time, that the city of Todi and its territory in general and in particular shall be ruled by popular institutions and by the people, by the popolani and the artisans, and that the people, the popolani, and the artisans of this city shall possess all government, every kind of jurisdiction, of custody and authority, the entire criminal and civil imperium, and the power of the sword.

The collapse of feudalism produced discontent and a desire for novelty among the Italians. Men sought after new forms of government, established and changed them in a moment. The republican constitution, with its feverish activity, was a constant experiment with a view to an artificial equilibrium. In Rome also the artisans were striving, though less successfully, for power. Since the beginning of the fourteenth century they had formed thirteen guilds, recognized by the state, under consuls, who assembled in council on the occasion of every important resolution of the republic. Several letters of the popes in Avignon are courteously addressed to the consuls of the merchants, to the agriculturists, and to the remaining guilds (*artes*). It is possible that even at this time they may have had meeting places on the Capitol. In every revolution these guilds formed the elements of a popular government, although the time of the rule of the "popolani" in Rome had not yet arrived. The hereditary nobility still maintained their exclusive right of eligibility for the Senate, and the inorganic juxtaposition of two political bodies side by side was consequently seen in Rome—the government of the people with the "good men" on the basis of the guilds, and that of the nobility with two senators at the head of the state. Had this nobility been an actual civic power, especially had it been a monied power, it would have thrust the plebeians out of the republic, as in Venice. Its strength, however, was crippled by the circumstance that its territorial possessions were partly situated in remote districts, by its family feuds, and finally by the authority of the pope, in whom the populace found protection. The citizens stood in increasingly solid organizations opposed to the aristocracy. In addition to the corporations, their ancient constitution by regions under captains gave them a permanent bond; while in their very midst the class of the *cavalerotti*—that is to say, the wealthy citizens of the ancient houses of the popolani, who served on horseback in the civic militia—founded a new aristocracy. The time was near when in Rome, as in Florence and other cities, the victory of the popular party over the ruling families must be decided.

When Cola di Rienzo prepared to execute his scheme for the overthrow of the nobility, the sufferings of the people had become insupportable.

> The city of Rome was sunk in the deepest distress. There was no one to govern. Fighting was of daily occurrence; robbery was rife. Nuns, even children, were outraged; wives were torn from their husbands' beds. Laborers on their way to work were robbed at the very gates of the city. Pilgrims were plundered and strangled; the priests were evildoers; every sin was unbridled. There was no remedy; universal destruction threatened. There was only one law—the law of the sword. There was no other remedy than self-defence in combination with relations and friends. Armed men assembled together every day.

It was the month of May 1347. Robert Orsini and Peter, son of Agapitus Colonna, who had previously been provost of Marseilles, and had then returned to secular life, now ruled the Senate. The Roman militia, under Stephen Colonna, had gone to the neighborhood of Corneto, the granary of Rome, to procure corn, and Cola hastened to profit by the absence of Rome's most powerful baron. He had initiated Raymond, bishop of Orvieto, the spiritual vicar of the pope, into his plans, for so just appeared the grounds of the revolution that this prelate promised it his support. The movement was thus placed beforehand under the authority of the church.

On May 19, heralds paraded the city and invited the unarmed populace to a parliament on the Capitol, when the bells should give the summons. Only the initiated understood the signal. At midnight Cola heard mass for Whitsunday in S. Angelo in Pescheria, where the conspirators had assembled. He placed himself and his work under the protection of the Holy Ghost, by whose mystic power he believed himself inspired. On the morning of Whitsunday he left the church in full armor, his head only uncovered, and surrounded by his fellow conspirators. Three great banners were carried before him: the red and gold banner of freedom, with the image of Rome; the white banner of justice, with S. Paul, the sword-bearer; the banner of peace, with S. Peter; a fourth banner, that of S. George, being old and tattered, was carried in a coffer on a lance. The revolt formally began with a procession to the Capitol; but few armed men protected the way. The papal vicar walked beside Cola with uncertain step, and the bishop and the demagogue ascended together to the palace of the Capitol. Cola mounted the tribune; he spoke with fascinating eloquence of the servitude and redemption of Rome. He assured his audience that he was ready to sacrifice his life out of love for the pope and for the salvation of the people. A thousand voices shouted applause. Here one of the conspirators belonging to the Mancini family read a series of decrees, which ordained that every murderer was to be punished with death; every false accuser with the penalty that had fallen on the accused; that sentences must be executed in fifteen days; that proscribed houses must be pulled down, but should revert to the camera; that each region of the city should provide one hundred men on foot and twenty-five on horse, each of whom should receive a shield and a reward from the state; that widows and orphans, convents and religious institutions should be supported by the state; that a guardship on the coast should protect the merchants; that the public taxes should belong to the civic camera; that all fortresses, bridges, and gates should be defended by the rector of the people; that no aristocrat should

274

occupy a fortress; that all places in the civic territory should receive their rectors from Rome; that the barons should be obliged to preserve the safety of the roads, to refuse shelter to any bandit, and to supply corn to Rome; that a granary should be established in every region. The parliament passed these wise laws with tumultuous applause. It conferred the full signory of the city on Cola, with unlimited authority, as reformer and conservator of the republic, to make peace and war, to punish crimes, to appoint to offices, and to promulgate laws.

The new dictator modestly invited the papal vicar to become his companion in office, whereby the popular government would be assured of the pope's recognition. Rome seemed under the power of an irresistible spell. The senators fled; many nobles left the city; not a drop of blood was shed. The people met in constant deliberation. In another parliament Cola assumed the title of "tribune," because, being a man of the people, he wished to restore the fame of the ancient tribunate. A white dove hovered accidentally over the assembled crowd, and Cola flattered himself that this was a symbol of the divine sanction to his appointment. The idea of the tribunate had been consecrated by antiquity, and was intelligible to all. Cola could therefore assume the title without exciting ill will; but he added to it by pompous epithets, which revealed his fantastic mind. He called himself Nicholas, by the authority of our most merciful Lord Jesus Christ, the severe and clement, the tribune of freedom, of peace and justice, and the illustrious redeemer of the Holy Roman republic.

The news quickly spread throughout Italy and across the Alps that the republic of Rome was delivered from its tyrants, and its ancient freedom restored by a wondrous hero.

XV

Cola against the Aristocracy

EVENTS in Rome took the aristocrats by surprise. Stephen Colonna, it is true, hastened from Corneto to the city, but was unable to do anything beyond vent his anger in words. The tribune sent him his command to leave Rome; the aged hero tore the document in pieces, and exclaimed, "If this fool provokes me further, I will throw him from the windows of the Capitol." The bell sounded an alarm, the people assembled in arms, and Stephen, accompanied by a single servant, fled to Palestrina. The tribune confined all the nobles to their estates, garrisoned all fortresses and bridges of the city, and spread terror by the strictest justice. Feeling himself in full possession of power, he summoned the nobles to do homage on the Capitol; they came trembling, as they had formerly come at the bidding of Arlotti; the younger Stephen Colonna himself appeared with his sons, and even Raynald and Jordan Orsini, the Savelli, Anibaldi, and Conti. They swore to the laws of the republic, and placed themselves at its service. The college of judges as well, the notaries and the guilds, did homage to the tribune, and his rule in Rome was thus recognized by all classes.

In none of the other revolutions had it occurred to the heads of the city to send letters announcing their accession to government outside the sphere of the city itself. Cola, however, thought

From book XI, ch. 6, secs. 1, 2, 3, and 4.

of Rome in its relation towards Italy and the world. His envoys carried letters to all communes, princes, and despots of Italy; even to the Emperor Lewis and the king of France. In these letters the tribune pointed out to the cities of the Roman province that Rome, liberated by him, had at length found peace and law; he exhorted them to address thanksgivings to God, to seize arms for the extirpation of all tyrants, and at an appointed time to send two syndics and a judge to Rome, where a general parliament would take counsel concerning the well-being of the entire Roman province. These letters were written with intelligence and dignity. From a higher point of view, Cola wrote to the cities of Italy, and exhorted them to join in throwing off the yoke of the tyrants, and to form a national brotherhood, since the deliverance of the eternal city was also that of "the whole of sacred Italy." He further invited them to send deputies and judges to a national parliament in Rome on August 1. The great and truly ingenious scheme of making Italy into a confederation, with Rome as its head, was here expressed for the first time, and its novelty and boldness filled the world with admiration. Thus, at the very beginning of his reign, Cola di Rienzo displayed lofty national ideas in sight of his native country It is probable that, immediately after the revolution, Raymond, the papal vicar, sent a despatch to his master, whose recognition was above all things necessary to Cola. As to the tribune himself, not until the beginning of June does he seem to have notified his elevation to power to the pope. The simple bishop of Orvieto cut but a sorry figure beside the tribune, like Lepidus beside Octavian: all letters are written by Cola alone, and not in one single political act is his colleague in office mentioned by a word.

While his messengers, bearing a silver wand, scoured Italy, the tribune established his government in the Capitol. With the exception of the removal of the senators, the constitution was not changed; the great and little Council, the Thirteen, the College of Judges continued to exist. From motives of prudence Cola required only a three months' term of office for himself, but the Romans scarcely heard him speak of his retirement when they swore they would rather perish than that he should withdraw from the government—a result that he had foreseen. He appointed a syndicate, however, for the administration of his office. He had coins struck immediately, and brought engravers from Florence for the purpose. He surrounded himself with a military escort of devoted men—the first care of tyrants as well as of champions of liberty. Three hundred and ninety cavalerotti, citizens on horseback, splendidly equipped, and a militia of foot soldiers numbering thirteen banners with one hundred men to each, were appointed to defend his government. His person, like that of Pisistratus in former days, was moreover protected by a bodyguard formed of one hundred youths from his quarter Regola, who, armed with lances, invariably preceded the son of the tavernkeeper on the bank of the Tiber, as, mounted on a white horse, clad in vesture of white silk with gold fringe, and a royal banner waving over his head, he rode through the city. The armed militia gave emphasis to his justice, and justice was Cola's greatest merit. He punished without respect of persons. A Cistercian monk found guilty of some crime was beheaded; a baron of the house of Anibaldi suffered the same fate, and an ex-senator the ignominy of being hanged on the very Capitol where he had formerly ruled the republic in pomp and splendor. This was Martin Stefaneschi, lord of Portus, nephew of two cardinals, namely, Anibaldo of Ceccano and the celebrated Jacopo Stefaneschi. His crime was that of sacking a vessel which was on its way to Naples, bearing the revenues of Provence. The tribune's bailiffs tore the ailing exsenator from the arms of his young wife; and the despairing widow, looking from the loggia of her palace, might soon after have beheld the body of her husband swinging in the air. The execution spread mortal terror among the nobility. The palaces in Rome, like those of the foreign embassies at a later time, were then asylums for criminals of every kind; the tribune, however, caused a robber to be seized in the dwelling of the Colonna and executed. Barons expiated any lawlessness suffered on their estates by heavy fines. Several were lodged in the dungeon of the Capitol. Even Peter Colonna, the banished exsenator, was led on foot to prison by constables. Corrupt judges, wearing lofty miters on which their crimes were inscribed, were exposed in the pillory. An Augean stable of abuses, of corruption, perjury, fraud, of falsehood and deceit, was to be cleansed, and no one was better acquainted with the desperate condition of the Roman administration than the former notary of the civic camera. The beneficent institution of a tribunal of the peace checked the enmities in the city; for judges taken from the people assembled in a palace, on the summit of which waved the banner of S. Paul, and reconciled the parties either by exhortations or by the barbarous *jus talionis*. Cola could boast that he had reconciled 1800 citizens who were at deadly enmity with one another. The exiles were recalled; the destitute received liberal assistance. A strict system of police punished adulterers and gamblers. The servile use of the title of Don or Dominus given to the nobility was prohibited; henceforward the pope alone was to be addressed as Lord. It was forbidden to affix the arms of barons to houses; only those of the pope and the Senate were allowed to remain. The palisades with which the nobles entrenched their houses were swept away; it was decreed that the materials were to be employed for the restoration of the Palace of the Senate, and each exsenator was compelled to pay a hundred gold florins towards the new building.

A well-ordered administration increased the revenues of the civic camera by the hearth tax (*focaticum*), the feudal rent of subject places, by the annual dues which isolated towns such as Tivoli, Toscanella, Velletri, and Corneto had to pay in money or grain, by the dues on bridges, roads, rivers, and finally by the monopoly of the salt works of Ostia. According to an ancient statement the hearth tax for every chimney amounted to 26 denarii, or to 1 carlin and 4 denarii. Cola computed the proceeds of this tax for the whole civic territory, from Ceprano to the river Paglia, at 100,000 gold florins, the revenues of the salt monopoly at about the same, and finally 100,000 gold florins as the proceeds of the tolls and city fortresses. It is true that the correctness of these statements is doubtful in spite of the size of the civic territory. The tribune suppressed the tolls on the roads, which the barons had formerly appropriated, and restricted the tax on articles of consumption (*gabella*), which had produced a large sum, more especially in Florence. On the other hand, the hearth tax was rigorously imposed. All vassals of the city paid it readily, the Prefect John of Vico excepted. At the same time, Cola gained many places by his magnanimity. Toscanella was allowed to commute the yearly tribute of 1000 pounds of gold for 100 pounds of wax for the church of Aracoeli, and Velletri received back its independence. Wise laws regulated market prices and filled the granaries. Corn was also brought from Sicily, and even the desolate Campagna began to be cultivated under the tribune. The roads, which were now safe, were animated by commerce and traffic. The peasant again cultivated his fields unarmed, and the pilgrim, heedless of danger, again wended his way to the sanctuaries of Rome. A religious spirit pervaded the emancipated people, as it pervaded the British nation in the time of Cromwell; civic virtue, which had been quenched by crime, revived under the rays of liberty and peace.

The fame of the man who had achieved such great results in so short a time spread through the world. That the distant sultan in Babylon trembled in fear of the tribune was an amusing fiction narrated by sailors; but it was probably no exaggeration when one of Cola's envoys announced on his return, "I have carried this wand of embassy publicly through woods and along roads; countless men have knelt before it, and kissed it with tears of joy, because the highways are now free from robbers." During the first months of his rule Cola deserved to be the idol of Rome, and to inaugurate a new era of republican liberty. The people saw in him a man elected by God. No one yet censured the vain pomp in which the tribune of the people appeared whenever he traversed the city. On the festival of SS. Peter and Paul he rode to the cathedral on a powerful charger, clad in green and yellow velvet, carried a scepter of glittering steel in his hand, and was surrounded by fifty spearmen. A Roman carried the banner with his coat of arms above his head; another bore the sword of justice before him; a knight scattered gold among the people, while an imposing train of *cavalerotti* and officials of the Capitol, of *popolani*, and nobles either preceded or followed him. Trumpeters blared through silver tubes, and musicians played on silver cymbals. The dignitaries of the cathedral, ranged on the steps of S. Peter's, greeted the dictator of Rome with the strains of the *Veni Creator Spiritus.*

Meanwhile answers arrived to Cola's letters. The pope, who at first had been alarmed, was tranquilized, or at least appeared to be so. True he complained that the constitution had been changed without his intervention; he acquiesced, however, in the revolution, and confirmed Nicholas and Raymond as rectors of the city. The messenger returning from Avignon brought Cola a casket inlaid with silver, on the lid of which were represented the arms of Rome, the tribune, and of the pope. Clement's amiable letter produced great satisfaction. Deputies from the cities daily arrived to attend the national parliament. Their presence filled the Romans with self-consciousness, while it strengthened Cola in the belief in his mission and power. The Capitol seemed indeed to have become the political center of Italy. True that some of the despots in Lombardy had at first received the tribune's letters of invitation with contempt; they nevertheless soon declared themselves ready to send deputies to the national parliament. Lucchino, the tyrant of Milan, exhorted Cola to maintain the new constitution, but to proceed against the barons with caution; the Doge Andrea Dandolo and the Genoese offered their services in respectful letters; Lucca and Florence, Siena, Arezzo, Todi, Terni, Pistoja and Foligno, Assisi, Spoleto, Rieti and Amelia called the tribune their illustrious prince and father, and expressed the hope that the change in Rome would redound to the welfare of Italy. All the cities of the Campagna and Maritima, of the Sabina and Roman Tuscany did homage to the Capitol by solemn embassies, while hostile parties from a greater distance brought their quarrels before the tribune, seeking his decision.

Nothing bears clearer witness to the power which the revered name of Rome still exercised than the recognition which Cola di Rienzo obtained from almost all the lords and cities of Italy, whose communes were guided not by enthusiasts but by serious statesmen. Far and wide the belief was cherished that the Roman republic would arise in its ancient splendor, and already there glimmered a magic ray of long extinct paganism, whose spirits only seemed to await the word of the enchanter burst from their graves. There was, moreover, no sincere Christian who did not regard the sojourn of the popes at Avignon as a crime against the sacred city. Its deliverance from the power of the tyrants, and the security now assured to the pilgrims, were regarded as universal concerns. The revolution so successfully accomplished consequently appeared a great event, which would probably be followed by the return of the papacy and the restoration of the empire. It is only fair to acknowledge that Cola di Rienzo with genius grasped and expressed the ideas of his time. Dante would undoubtedly have greeted the new savior of Italy under the mystic image of the "Veltro." The tribune's conception of the lex regia, of the inalienable majesty of Rome, on which the empire rested, entirely harmonized with the principles of the *monarchia*, in which a great poet had explained that the Roman people, as the noblest on earth, had been chosen by God through wonders and historic deeds for the government of the world. Although he never appealed to it, Cola was doubtlessly acquainted with Dante's treatise. But in Henry VII and Lewis the Bavarian, the Ghibelline idea had proved impracticable; for no foreign emperor had been able to heal dismembered Italy. A gifted man now arose in deserted Rome, restored the republic, and neither as Guelf nor as Ghibelline, but as Roman tribune, offered the Italians the salvation which the Ghibellines had sought in vain from the German emperor, the Guelfs in vain from the pope. A third idea now woke to life, that of a confederation of Italy under the guidance of Rome, the sacred mother. The thought of the unity of the nation was openly expressed for the first time, and Italy conceived the hope of rescue and restoration by her own means.

Petrarch, who now took the place of Dante as the representative of the Italian national spirit, affords the best proof of the magic influence of Cola on his age, and of the current of ideas of antiquity with which it was permeated. When this one Roman of the most obscure origin, he wrote afterwards, arose, when he ventured to take the republic on his weak shoulders, and to support the tottering empire, Italy stood erect as if by a stroke of magic, and the terror and renown of the Roman name penetrated to the ends of the world. The crowned Roman citizen, the reviver of classic learning, whose mind was filled with dreams of Scipio and Brutus, shared with Dante the principles of the *monarchia*, and saw, amid the degenerate Roman populace, the only source of universal dominion; in the ruin-heaps of Rome the lawful seat of both emperor and pope. These views were pushed to their furthest issues by the Italian hostility towards the continued sojourn of the popes in Avignon. When the wonderful tribune arose on the Capitol, Petrarch greeted him as the man whom he had long sought and at last found, as the political incarnation of his own thought, as a hero who had sprung armed from his own brain. From Avignon he addressed enthusiastic congratulations to Cola and the Roman people. He sacrificed his love for the house of Colonna to freedom and his native country. All the great men, from whose ranks popes, cardinals, senators, and generals had issued in previous centuries, only appeared to him as foreigners, as descendants of former slaves of war, as Vandals who destroyed the grandeur of the city, as usurpers who had appropriated the monuments and rights of the republic; in short, as an invading caste of robbers, who ruled in Rome as in a conquered city, and maltreated the genuine Roman citizens as their slaves. "Prudence and courage," exclaimed Petrarch, "be with you, since power you will not lack, not only to maintain freedom, but also to recover the empire. Every one must wish Rome good fortune. So just a cause is sure of the approval of God and the world." He wished Cola success, called him the new Camillus, Brutus, and Romulus; said that not till now were the Romans true citizens, and exhorted them to honor their deliverer as a messenger of God.

The enthusiastic approval of a man honored as a genius by the whole world inflamed Cola's imagination, and strengthened him in all his dreams. He caused Petrarch's letter to be read aloud in parliament, where it produced a great impression. He himself invited the poet to leave Avignon, and adorn the city with his presence, as a jewel adorned a ring. Instead of Petrarch, his promised festival ode appeared. He dedicated his finest poem

283

to the freedom of Rome and its new hero. The Roman revolution found its poet in Petrarch, as all subsequent revolutions have also found their poets of liberty. And as he stood in splendor on the Capitol, in sight of the world, Cola reached the summit of his fortune. . . .

When Cola summoned the Italians to send deputies to Rome, his object was to constitute a parliament for the whole of Italy, and to assemble it on the Capitol. The idea was magnificent, and worthy of a statesman of the first rank; neither was it impracticable, since the time was sufficiently favorable for Italy to assume an independent form. The pope was far away, the emperor far away, the empire almost dissolved; Naples in a state of anarchy, the Roman nobility subdued, the middle class dominant in the majority of the republics; enthusiasm for freedom, hatred of the tyrants, the feeling of patriotism, and the spell of Rome prevailed in distant spheres. During the five centuries that followed, the Italian people never beheld a conjunction of historic circumstances so favorable to the scheme of nationality as now in the days of the tribune. Under similar conditions a man of Cromwell's genius would have brought a great revolution to a successful issue; to a gifted actor the task was impossible. Cola di Rienzo was endowed with fascinating talents and brilliant ideas, but was devoid of true creative power, and was formed for neither a lawgiver, a statesman, nor a hero. He indulged in general theories; he was capable of forming these theories with logical sequence into an imposing scholastic system of thought; but he was unpractical, spiritless, and weak when face to face with the world of realities. The summit of glory and splendor on which he stood turned his head; vanity mastered his weak judgment, and his unrivalled imagination—an imagination which the greatest poets of all ages might have envied—caused him to see the actualities of life through a charmed medium. Cola also as a revolutionary stood under the influence of theology, and therein was entirely the contemporary of Dante. He applied to himself all the hopes concerning the messiah of Italy, all the dreams of enthusiastic monks concerning the reign of the Holy

Ghost. He believed that he—the obscure man so suddenly raised to power—was in political matters a second S. Francis, who would restore the tottering empire as the saint had restored the tottering church. But the man of the people from Assisi, like every popular tribune of antiquity, would have rejected the companionship of the vain demagogue. The fear of opposition, nay, even of practical action, crippled his power of will. His national program of creating a united Italy, with Rome for its center, was so audacious that he shrank before it. The question occupied the minds of men in Germany, Italy, and Avignon, although they failed to grasp its entire significance. Was it to the advantage of the world, the pope, and the emperor, of the republics and despots of Italy, that Rome, the cosmopolitan city, should be united to Italy? Even at the papal court the full significance of the problem was scarcely better understood than in Italy; nevertheless, opposition was immediately raised to Cola's schemes. Municipal hostility awoke in the cities. The small number of republics (twenty-five) which sent legates to Rome shows how strong was this opposition. The Florentines hesitated to despatch plenipotentiaries, fearing that their autonomy might thereby be diminished, and Cola was obliged to pacify them by the assurance that such was not his intention. And instead of the Italian parliament being summoned to Rome with an exclusively national aim, he already explained, from motives of fear and vanity, that its primary object was his own elevation to the dignity of knighthood and his coronation as tribune.

In ancient times the *Feriae Augusti* had been celebrated on August 1, and in the Middle Ages the day was (as it still is) kept as a popular festival, on which the chains of S. Peter were exhibited. The tribune had consequently chosen it for his own fete. On the eve of the solemnity the Lateran was the scene of a fantastic assemblage. The legates from the cities, the foreign knights, Cola's wife and mother-in-law, surrounded by a brilliant company of noble ladies, behind them two youths, who carried a gilt bridle (a symbol, perhaps, of moderation), the gorgeous cavalry from Perugia and Corneto, who twice threw their silken garments among the people, the tribune himself, clad in white silk embroidered in gold, the papal vicar beside him, preceded by the sword-bearer, and followed by the standard-bearer and a sumptuous retinue, appeared to the strains of music. The curious ceremony by which Cola received the dignity of knighthood, in the presence of the highest clerical dignitaries of Rome and the envoys of the Italian communes, imports a character borrowed from the romances of Amadis and Parcival into the political history of the city. Nevertheless, we must judge the solemnity according to the character of the Middle Ages, when, not at courts only but also in republics, the honor of chivalry was conferred by the most curious ceremonies, so that we hear of knights of the banquet, of the bath, of the banner, of the battlefield, of the shield, and of honor. In the evening the tribune with his escort dismounted at the baptistery of the Lateran and boldly plunged into the ancient basin, where, according to legend, the Emperor Constantine had washed away his paganism and leprosy. Cola here cleansed himself of the stains of sin in fragrant rosewater, while the vicar of the pope pensively surveyed the desecrated font of Christianity. Cola's bath was soon enough reckoned as one of his chief offenses; but the ingenious knight put the question, whether the bath which had been allowed to Constantine, a pagan afflicted with leprosy, was not still more permissible to a Christian who had cleansed Rome from the leprosy of tyranny; whether the stone basin was holier than the temple trod by the foot of the Christian, or than the body of Christ of which he partook? The knight of the bath, clad in white, lay down to rest on a couch, which had been erected under the porphyry columns of the ancient baptistery, and, although troubled by the fear of the collapse of his temporary bed, passed the night in slumber. In the morning he clothed himself in scarlet and mounted to the jubilee loggia of the Lateran. The syndic of the people and other nobles here invested him with the girdle and gold spurs, while the solemn chants of the mass ascended from the church. Henceforward, Cola called himself candidate of the Holy Spirit, the Knight Nicholas, the severe and clement, the deliverer of the city, the zealot for Italy, the friend of the world, the Tribunus Augustus.

He combined the festival which concerned his own person with the political acts which he had already prepared. After a short address to the people he caused a decree to be read from the same loggia by Egidius Angelerii, the notary of the Capitol. In accordance with the thoroughly theological spirit of the tribune, he desired that this curious edict should be promulgated from the same place where Boniface VIII had bestowed the jubilee blessing on the world, and that it should operate as a blessing of Rome on the universe—a strange whim of intellectual madness, in which the papal benediction *urbi et orbi* was caricatured. The decree stated that Cola, having bathed in the basin of the glorious emperor Constantine, to the honor of God the Father, Son and Holy Ghost, of the princes of the Apostles and S. John, to the glory of the church and of the pope, for the good of Rome, of holy Italy and the world, desiring that the gifts of the Holy Spirit should be poured out upon the city and Italy, and that he might emulate the magnanimity of ancient emperors, declared as follows: That the Roman people, according to the sentence already pronounced by the judges, were again in full possession of the jurisdiction over the whole world, as in antiquity; that all privilegia, which had been granted to the prejudice of this power, were already revoked; that in virtue of the dictatorship conferred upon him, and that he might not be niggard of the gifts of grace bestowed by the Holy Ghost, he pronounced the city of Rome the head of the world, and the foundation of Christendom; that at the same time he declared all the cities of Italy free, and presented them with the Roman citizenship; further, that the imperial monarchy and the imperial election belonged to the city, to the Roman and Italian people; accordingly, he invited all prelates, the emperors-elect, the electors, kings, dukes, princes, counts, margraves, peoples and cities who claimed any right to the election, at the coming Whitsuntide to appear at the sacred Lateran before him and the plenipotentiary of the pope, as well as of the Roman people, with the proofs of their claims. Failing which, he would proceed against them as the law and the inspiration of the Holy Ghost required. More especially he cited Lewis duke of Bavaria and Charles king of Bohemia as

287

emperors-elect, also the dukes of Austria and Saxony, the margrave of Brandenburg, the archbishops of Mainz, Tréves, and Cologne.

The Romans, accustomed to all the spectacles of history, blunted to the distinctions between the sublime and the ridiculous, filled with pride of ancestry, imbued with the dogma of the eternal supremacy of Rome, living and breathing an atmosphere of dogmatism, neither laughed at this edict, nor at the figure of the crazy tribune, who with drawn sword pointed in three directions in the air and cried, "This is mine." They loudly shouted their approval. The absurd proclamation appeared as the ultimate consequence of the claims of the city to the imperial majesty, with which she had formerly confronted Conrad, the first of the Hohenstaufens. Not to forget was the destiny of the Romans. The thought of the ancient world monarchy, which the writings and monuments of the past kept alive, and the gigantic shadow of the ancient empire, under which Rome lay, were esteemed realities by the later generation, and we may say that the history of the city in the Middle Ages was frequently nothing more than a continued funeral oration over the splendor of the ancient city. The errors and theories of Dante and Petrarch in their theological age explain or excuse the insane dreams of the tribune. For both poets extol the Romans as the political people elected by God to the monarchy, as the Hebrews had been the religious people elected to monotheism; and like the Hebrews, the Romans acknowledged their historic mission as not already accomplished, but to be continued through all time. History had yet to perform a long task before men should be released from the dogmas of the past, and even down to latest times mankind has occasionally returned to bathe in Constantine's mystic font.

The vicar of the pope was taken by surprise. On hearing the edict, the dismayed bishop stood there, in the words of Cola's naïve biographer, like a man of wood. He raised a protest in the name of the pope, but the voice of the notary was overwhelmed in a flourish of trumpets, as the speech of the prisoner on the scaffold is drowned by the rolling drums.

The festival was closed by a sumptuous banquet in the Lateran, where Bishop Raymond, seated beside the tribune against whose folly he had just protested, helped to desecrate the marble pontifical table. The foreign envoys, the nobles and citizens, the women, supped at other tables, and the populace held their rejoicings in front of the Lateran, where the bronze horse of Marcus Aurelius poured streams of wine and water through its nostrils. Popular games and tournaments were celebrated both this and the following day, and since ancient times Rome had witnessed no similar festival. The envoys brought valuable gifts to the tribune; even the Roman barons and citizens offered presents. The Colonna alone failed to appear; the Gaetani were declared under the ban, and Petrucius Frangipane was brought from Civita Lavinia and thrown into prison.

On August 2, Cola celebrated on the Capitol the festival of the unity of Italy, or the fraternity of the cities. He presented to the envoys large and small banners bearing emblems, and placed gold rings on their fingers as symbols of their marriage with Rome. To the Florentines, whom he wished to distinguish, he gave the banner of Italy, with the figure of Rome between those of Italy and Faith. They refused, however, to receive it, fearing lest it might be regarded as a sign of enfeoffment. Envoys of other cities also only accepted the symbols under condition of preserving the rights of their republics. Pisa sent no representative at all.

Ideas, opinions, and forms are so deeply rooted in human nature that they repeat themselves at distant intervals, and unite the present with the past. The festivals of fraternity during the French Revolution in Paris appeared in truth an imitation of the August festival of the tribune of the people in Rome. Cola now sent forth envoys to the pope and the kings, to inform them of the great events that had taken place, to deliver his citations to the German princes, and to exhort the rulers of France and England, whose bitter enmity was injurious to Christendom, to make peace, above all, to announce to all lands that the illustrious tribune was resolved to institute a new and peaceful system in the world. Such was the curious course adopted by the unsuccessful convocation of the first national parliament of Italy. Nothing practical was achieved or created; a political idea of the highest national importance was destroyed by its fantastic alliance with the idea of the world monarchy, and only revealed itself in symbolic and theatrical scenes.

Cola di Rienzo, however, had already done more than enough to challenge the papacy, and had now to dread the consequences of his provocation. He had also challenged the authority of the emperor, but the thought of imperial opposition caused him no dismay.

The audacious citation of the emperor was merely the consequence of the humiliation of the crown of Charles the Great, which Lewis the Bavarian had first taken from the Roman people, and then, out of fear of the pope, had not ventured to wear. And in truth the appearance of this democratic emperor in Rome helps to explain the absurd edicts of the Roman tribune. Afraid that Clement VI would revive the proceedings instituted by John XXII, and in spite of the decrees of Rense, Lewis had offered humble submission to the pope. The attempt at reconciliation failed, and the pope succeeded in setting up a rival king in Germany, where many violations of the law had caused the elector-princes to renounce the Bavarian. The rival chosen was Charles of Moravia, son of John, king of Bohemia, and grandson of Henry VII. Before his election he had already promised in Avignon (April 22, 1346) to act as the submissive creature of the pope, without extracting any advantage from the declaration of the independence of the empire, which, with the prospect of the imperial crown in view, had not been acknowledged by the voice of Bohemia. Charles was elected by his faction, headed by his great uncle, Baldwin of Treves, at Rense, on July 11, 1346, to the joy of his father, that restless king of Bohemia, the blind hero, who met his death on the field of Crècy on August 26 of the same year. Charles was crowned in Bonn on November 25, and was immediately after recognized by the pope, to whom he renewed his vows on April 27, 1347. The contempt of all greatminded men was excited by the utter degradation to an empty title of the authority of the empire by the promises of its head, who, before his entrance into Italy, had undertaken to submit his person to the sanction of the pope, to remain in Rome only for the day of his coronation, to leave the city immediately after, and never again to enter any territory of the church. The degradation also partly explains Cola's foolhardy actions, which appear as satires directed against an empire that had fallen so low. In fact, the candidate of the Holy Ghost showed more courage than the candidate for the imperial crown, when, amid the deplorable decay of the empire, he explained that all its prerogatives of majesty had reverted to their source, the Roman and Italian people.

. . . .

Cola's actions were of a nature to make him appear the most dangerous of all revolutionaries in the eyes of his benevolent patron, the pope. That Clement did not earlier proceed against him was due to the universal admiration that the tribune evoked, and to the fear of the exalted ideas which had taken hold of the Roman people, also in part to the distance of Avignon. The fulfilment of the tribune's designs would not only have destroyed the *dominium temporale* [temporal lordship of the popes], but would have overthrown all legal relations between church and empire. He leaned on no party, was neither Guelf nor Ghibelline, but on the contrary appealed to the Italian nation. He looked away from the German emperor; he required the pope to make his residence in Rome, and at the same time proclaimed Rome the capital of united Italy, to whom the rest of the republics, "the ancient children" of the city, were to sacrifice their municipal spirit. He asserted that Rome and the church were one, as, according to his view, so were the empire and Rome. He thereby expressed the opinion that the city was the source and essence of the universal monarchy and of the two world powers, and openly protested against the opinion that where the pope was there was the church. After the example of Lewis the Bavarian, Cola—had he succeeded in attaining to actual power—would have restored the papal election to the Roman people. For the first time the voice of Rome terrified the pope within the strong walls of Avignon; he now recognized that other matters than the reformation of civic government on democratic lines were discussed on the Tiber, that Rome's antagonism to Avignon was a national principle, and that the exile of the popes gave birth to a movement that threatened the church with schism and the papacy with the loss of its historic position in Italy.

A lofty idea was contained in Cola's curious dreams, and a logical method in his delusions. As was natural in his time, he sought for the legal foundation for the transformation of Italy in the dogma of the majesty of the Roman Senate and people. After having proclaimed this sovereignty and the unity of Italy in his decree of August 1, and having declared that he held all Italians as free Roman citizens, he resolved to summon the entire country to reconstitute itself in the form of a national Roman empire. According to his scheme all Italians should have the right of electing their emperor by a plebiscite, which was to be exercised in Rome by twenty-four electors appointed by themselves. The emperor to be elected after Whitsuntide of 1348 was to be an Italian patriot; thus the ancient unity of the nation would be restored by a Latin Caesar, Italy rescued from the divisions which tore her asunder, and delivered forever from the ignominious rule of "unworthy foreigners." Neither was this view far removed from the Guelfs; for they also maintained that the imperial election belonged to the Roman people, and through them to all the communes of Italy, who shared in the right of Roman citizenship and Roman freedom, and that only through the church, and in the name of the Roman people, was it transferred to the German elector-princes. On September 19 Cola appointed two doctors of law, the Knight Paul Vajani of Rome, and Bernard de Possolis, a native of Cremona, as his envoys, and sent them with plenary powers to the cities and lords of Italy, in order to gain their adhesion to his memorable plan. The gifted tribune hoped to reach an exalted aim, little thinking that only through the labyrinth of the sins and sufferings of another five hundred years was the way to be prepared for its realization. He wished to inscribe the new articles of confederation of a free and united Italy on tables of bronze, and, according to ancient custom, to place them in the Capitol, which he fancifully called the

"Holy Latin Palace." Among the friends of the Italian nation on whom the imperial election might fall, he undoubtedly thought of himself, and already dreamed of transforming the title of Tribunus Augustus into that of Imperator Augustus. His envoys travelled through Italy; a great thought was propounded to the nation, which was not ready to receive it. It undoubtedly remains the imperishable glory of Cola de Rienzo that he ventured to express these national ideas in his age; as it remains a reproach to the Italians that at a time when the papacy was in banishment, and the empire at its lowest ebb, they proved incapable of creating a political nation.

Meanwhile the pope resolved to proceed against the audacious demagogue. The French cardinals dreaded the return of the papal curia to Rome, if the city became free and powerful. Every prelate shrank from the thought of Italian unity, or the restoration of an Italian empire, which would have endangered the independence of the papacy. All the cardinals, especially the relations of the Orsini and Colonna, demanded that proceedings should be instituted against Cola, who had already completely thrust aside his colleague in office, the papal vicar Raymond. As early as October 7 the pope gave the legate Bertrand de Deus, who was then in Naples, power to depose Cola and to appoint new senators. On October 12 he sent the cardinal a letter, in which he enumerated all Cola's offenses, and ordered him to leave the tribune in office, if he retracted, confined himself to his jurisdiction in the city, and promised obedience to the church; otherwise, to depose him, and possibly bring a charge of heresy against him. The legate was to fix a period within which the Romans were to renounce Cola under threat of the interdict; he was to distribute money and corn among them, though not in such abundance as to make them arrogant. He was to withhold the bull of jubilee, which was, however, to be promulgated as soon as the Romans should make submission. The Sabines were to be forbidden to obey Cola, or to form any alliance with Rome. And since some asserted that Cola was already under the ban, Clement had caused duplicates of the letter to him to be drafted, one of which addressed Cola as already excommunicated, the other as still a member of the church, so that, according to circumstances, the cardinal could give him one or other. These documents show the serious consternation of the pope, his fear of the power of the tribune or of the Romans, his extreme prudence. More than seventy Roman nobles received letters with the request that in any event they would aid the legate.

Cola, learning of the hostile feeling at Avignon, wrote in detail to Clement VI, enumerated all his services, justified his actions, and lamented that the pope rewarded him with prosecutions for all the good that he had done, when a courier would have been sufficient to persuade him to retire from his office, had this been required. His enemies meanwhile assembled on all sides, and the tribune had manfully to defend against their attacks.

. . . .

On December 3 the pope issued a violent bull against the Roman people, stigmatizing Cola as a criminal, a pagan, and a heretic, and exhorting the Romans to thrust him from among them. Among the crimes with which the tribune was charged was that of wishing to overthrow the church and empire, for he had asked the cities of Italy to vote for a fresh imperial election. He was further accused of having in his delusion aimed at the imperial crown, untroubled by the danger to which he exposed the Romans, upon whom he thus invoked the wrath of all Germans and of the church. He had imprisoned priests, had usurped the rights of the church, had by his edicts commanded all Roman prelates to return to the city, and had even presumed to declare that Rome and the church were one. But Cola had fallen even before the bull reached Rome. The approaching jubilee was in sight of the greedy Romans; the pope might deprive them of it, and they had to choose between freedom, which only exacted sacrifices, and subjection, which promised abundance. The growing peril diminished Cola's courage day by day; he was terrified by gloomy dreams of the fall of the Capitol; the hooting of an owl, which was heard in the ruins, and refused to be driven away, roused his fear and horror. He suffered from giddiness, and frequently fainted. An accident expelled him from the Capitol.

By the terms of his treaty, Lewis of Hungary was permitted to raise cavalry in Rome. A Neapolitan baron, notorious for his crimes, John Pipin, count of Minorbino, was in the city with his brothers acting as recruiting officers. Cola, who had already cited him before his tribunal on account of his robberies, detested him, but was now obliged to tolerate him out of regard for the king of Hungary. The count joined Luca Savelli in a conspiracy to which the cardinal-legate was not a stranger. The bailiffs of the tribune attempted to post a citation against Savelli on the doors of the church of S. Angelo. The Neapolitans prevented them. Thereupon Cola summoned the count of Minorbino before his tribunal. Pipin barricaded himself near the church of S. Salvator in Pensilis in the Circus Flaminius. He ordered the bells of S. Angelo to be rung, and raised the cry, "The people! The people! Death to the tribune." At the summons of the bell of the Capitol only five companies rallied round Cola; the populace and the Orsini belonging to his party remained away. He sent a German captain against the barricade erected by the rebels; the captain fell. The tribune believed that all was lost. The liberator of Italy trembled before a few Hungarian lances. His diseased imagination beheld the entire city in revolt, although so far was this from being true that had he acted with prompt resolution he might easily have quelled the rebels. His heart failed him; he no longer possessed the courage of a child; he could scarcely speak. He renounced the insignia of his tribunate; he laid the silver wreath and the steel scepter as votive offerings on the altar of the Virgin in Aracoeli. He took leave of his friends, lamenting that, after a good reign of seven months on the Capitol, he was obliged to abdicate, driven away by the jealousy of the wicked. He wept; the bystanders, those who saw him descend, the populace, the better citizens wept. But no one held him back. With drums beating, banners waving, accompanied by armed men, the tribune of the people descended from the Capitol, and withdrew to the Castle of S. Angelo, where he shut himself up. The whole of Rome was in consternation. A beautiful dream had faded into nothing, after only seven months of such exaltation as the city had not experienced for long years. It was December 15, 1347, when the rule of Cola di Rienzo reached its noiseless end. The tribune of the people had given the Romans, sunk in their deep abasement, a classical carnival spectacle, had displayed the splendor of the ancient world in a magnificent triumphal procession before their eyes. Now came disillusion, and with it reality in the prosaic form of the restoration of the vindictive nobility returning to their homes.

XVI

Cola's Restoration and Death

THE tribune's retirement was so little expected by the aristocrats that not until three days had elapsed did they venture into the city, now without a head. That he sought no vengeance on his enemies does honor to the heroic spirit of the aged Colonna [whose family had been almost extinguished in battle with Cola]; Cola's civic institutions were allowed to stand, his relatives suffered no persecution, S. Angelo, where he remained under the protection of the Orsini, was not attacked. Immediately afterwards, Bertrand de Deus made his entry into the city, of which he took possession in the name of the church. He revoked all the decrees of the tribune, restored the ancient forms of government, and made Berthold Orsini and Luca Savelli senators. Luca represented the party of the Colonna, since Stephen no longer undertook the burthen of the senatorship. The old man, crushed by misfortune, stood beside the grave of his son and grandson. Of his honored race, scarcely any remained but Stefanello, son of the slain Stephen. He himself disappears from the history of the city, in which for more than half a century he had played so prominent a part. He died probably in the year 1348.

After the legate had set in order the civic government, he returned to Montefiascone, cited Cola as a heretic and rebel before his tribunal, and placed him under the ban. The tribune's

From book XI, ch. 7, secs. 1, 2, 3, and 4.

most zealous adherents, such as Cecco Mancini, his chancellor, were involved in the same suit. But the sudden restoration of the papal authority was not sufficient to tranquilize the excited city, where democratic passions flowed in strong currents, where Cola's friends were still numerous, and where only a few miserable remains of the nobility reappeared. Soon after his fall the extribune had gone to Civita Vecchia, the citadel of which was still commanded by his nephew Count Mancini; but when the count deserted to the legate, Cola again retired to S. Angelo. It was scarcely known where he was. The new senators had him depicted head downwards on the Capitol; he replied in his accustomed manner from his hiding place. One day a painting was discovered on the church of S. Maddalena near S. Angelo, representing an angel treading serpents, dragons, and lions under foot. But the allegory no longer took effect. Cola recognized that his time was over for the present; he dreaded the artifices of the Orsini, who contemplated surrendering him to Avignon upon favorable conditions, as Count Fazio of Pisa had sold the antipope to John XXII. On learning that the king of Hungary had victoriously entered Naples on January 24, he escaped from Rome in the beginning of March, and amid many dangers made his way to the kingdom, where he hoped to find protection with his allies. The pope immediately demanded the surrender of the fugitive from King Lewis. But Cola's fortunes and place of abode were known only to report. It was said that he desired to return to Rome with Hungarian troops, and that he had placed himself in alliance with the great company.

This dreaded horde of mercenaries was commanded by Werner of Uerslingen, grandson of the duke of Spoleto, and had long been the scourge of the Italian provinces. After having entered the service of Lewis of Hungary, and been dismissed from it in Naples, Werner had formed a company of 3000 men, German soldiers and other adventurers, and had undertaken a raid into Latium. The citizens of Anagni slew his envoys, who, with insolent effrontery, had demanded blackmail. Werner forthwith appeared before the ill-fated home of Boniface VIII, stormed its walls, slaughtered its inhabitants, sacked and burnt the city.

This crime inaugurates the terrible period of the erant companies of mercenaries without fatherland and without religion; for their home was the temporary camp, their divinity fortune, and their law the sword. The utterly disorganized kingdom of Naples, which had swarmed with brigands since ancient times, was the nursery of these predatory condottieri. In Naples were educated all the German mercenary leaders of renown, Werner, Conrad Wolf, the count of Landau, Count Sprech, and Bongarden. The massacre at Anagni might now show the Italians that the ideas of the fugitive tribune had been great and patriotic; for the national confederation, which he had striven to organize, would have prevented the incursion of foreign mercenaries. Rome now trembled before Duke Werner. Had the terrible leader made himself master of the city, he would probably have fulfilled the impious motto inscribed on his coat of arms: "I am Duke Werner, leader of the great company, the enemy of God, of pity, and of mercy." But the city was this time spared the disgrace of falling into the hands of a band of mercenaries, for Werner left Latium. The Roman militia barred his way through Tuscany, and the cities here formed the first league against this company, a league which soon after entered the service of the church.

The hopes which Cola placed on the king of Hungary were vain. Rome had no value for Lewis; and four months after his entry into Naples he returned to his native land, in fear of the pestilence which raged in southern Italy. The extribune, wandering in the Abruzzi, was pursued by the excommunications of the church. The pope commanded his legate to form an alliance with Perugia, Florence, and Siena, to frustrate Cola's plans for return. On the recall of Bertrand at the end of 1348, the new cardinal-legate Anibaldo, a member of the family of the counts of Ceccano, ratified all the sentences issued against him, and placed him as a heretic under the ban. The unlucky fugitive, however, cherished one satisfaction; this was the state of wild anarchy to which the city had reverted, after having enjoyed peace and order under his government. Disunion prevailed among both people and nobility; family wars both within and without; robbery and crime in every street. The new senators having proved incapable, the pope commanded a non-Roman to be made senator. Whether he was obeyed or not is uncertain, for so great was the confusion that prevailed after Cola's flight that events in the city are veiled in obscurity for upwards of a year. The year 1348 was undoubtedly terrible, owing to the Black Death which devastated the West with unprecedented violence. All contemporary chroniclers have described this plague, and Boccaccio has immortalized its memory in the introduction to his novels. It had been brought to Italy in the usual way from the East by Genoese vessels in the autumn of 1347, and no precautions having been taken against it, its devastations were unbounded. More than 80,000 died in Siena and its territory; 500 fell daily at Pisa; in Florence three out of five, in Bologna two-thirds of the population were buried. The consequences were a complete revolution in the relations of property in all such places as had been depopulated by the plague, a rise in prices and wages, a deep-rooted distress, endless quarrels about property, immorality and debauchery, and a sudden revolution in the forms of life. The loosening of the hitherto recognized bonds of society had a distastrous effect on the civic spirit in the republics, and the pestilence of 1348 weakened these bonds perhaps even more than the tyranny and brigandage of which it was the ally.

The silence of chroniclers shows that Rome suffered less than other cities. Nevertheless, she did not entirely escape, and the flight of marble steps to Aracoeli, erected in October 1348, still serves as a monument of the plague. It was destined to convey believers to the church where the image of the Virgin was preserved, to which the Romans ascribed their immunity from the pestilence, now as in previous centuries. Repeated earthquakes increased the indescribable misery in many cities of Italy. On September 9 and 10, Rome was so violently shaken that the inhabitants forsook their houses and dwelt in tents for weeks. The basilica of the Twelve Apostles collapsed; the gable of the Lateran fell; S. Paul's was transformed into a heap of ruins; the upper half of the celebrated Torre delle Milizie was overthrown; the Torre dei Conti suffered grievous injury; and the Colosseum, like other ancient buildings, cannot have escaped.

All these horrors terrified the people and increased their longing for the indulgences of the jubilee, which appeared to their
clouded fancy as the purification of the world from demoniacal
influences. As compensation for the pompous spectacle of the
temporal sovereignty of the Eternal City, which had just been
presented by the tribune to the Romans, the pope now offered
them the spectacle of the western pilgrimage, and this brought
the greatness of the church again before their eyes, while by
real advantages it consoled them for the vanity of their dreams.
Indeed, after Cola's fall no better method of securing Rome remained to the pope. And since the throng of pilgrims demanded
a firm government, safety of transit, and abundance of provisions,
he appointed Gerald de Ventodur from Limoges, lord of Den-
zenat, to be senator extraordinary for the entire year. He also
entrusted Anibaldo of Ceccano and Guido of Boulogne-sur-Mer
with full powers as cardinals of the jubilee.

From Christmas of 1349 onwards the roads of Italy were
thronged with bands of pilgrims. Entire parties frequently biv-
ouacked round fires during the frosts of night. If the statement of
Matthew Villani, that the number of pilgrims in Rome during
Lent amounted to 1,200,000, appears incredible, the more moderate estimate of 5000 persons who daily entered and left the city
must approach the truth. Rome itself was one huge inn, and every
householder a host. As always, there was a dearth of hay, straw,
wood, fish, and vegetables, but more than abundance of meat.
Complaints were made of the avarice of the Romans, who prohibited the importation of wine and corn in order to raise the
prices. The impoverished city was again enriched for several
years by the money of the West.

Among the pilgrims there were probably many who had visited Rome during the jubilee of 1300. They could now survey
the changes which half a century had wrought. They had on the
previous occasion seen the last great pope of the all-ruling church
and received his blessing from the loggia of the Lateran. There
was now no longer any pope in Rome; the sacred chair had already stood in a corner of France for nearly fifty years; and the
chief person being absent, the festival of expiation was incom-

plete. When the pilgrims made their way to the three great basilicas—a journey of eleven miles—they must have been appalled to find them in ruins. S. Peter's was abandoned and utterly neglected; S. Paul's had been destroyed by the recent earthquake; the Lateran was tottering; the deserted streets were filled with innumerable traces of the civil war; ruinous palaces, overthrown towers, decayed monuments ravished of their marbles. Deathlike silence reigned on the hills, where stood churches crumbling away with age, roofless and without priests, and deserted convents where goats pastured in the grass-grown courts.

> The houses are overthrown, the walls come to the ground, the temples fall, the sanctuaries perish, the laws are trodden underfoot. The Lateran lies on the ground, and the mother of all the churches stands without a roof and exposed to wind and rain. The holy dwellings of S. Peter and S. Paul totter, and what was lately the temple of the Apostles is a shapeless heap of ruins to excite pity in hearts of stone.

Thus Petrarch exclaimed when he visited the city in the autumn of 1350. The spider wove its web over ruined Rome as in the days of S. Jerome.

. . . .

Scarcely was the year of jubilee ended when anarchy more frightful than ever broke over Rome. The government of the new senators Peter Sciarra and Jordan, son of Poncellus, was devoid of energy. The nobles ignored every law, took brigands and bravos into their pay, and filled the city and country with deeds of crime. Jordan left the Capitol when one of his fortresses was attacked, and Luca Savelli seized the power, expelling Ponzio Perotto the papal vicar. There was no longer any government; the republic seemed at an end. The pope was bewildered. . . .

[Pope Clement VI,] who had formerly been Cola's loyal protector, and who was a man of liberal disposition, did not desire his death, and the extribune remained in honorable custody, though with sentence of death hanging over his head. He consoled himself in his gloomy solitude with the books of Livy and Holy Writ, and would thus have passed the remainder of his life in the tower of Avignon or of Villeneuve, had the caprice of fate not suddenly brought him again into the light of day.

Clement VI died and Innocent VI ascended the sacred chair. Resolved to restore the state of the church, the new pope confided the difficult task to Cardinal Albornoz. His glance also fell on Cola. The prisoner greeted the change on the throne as a turning-point in his own fortunes, and may therein have recognized the fulfilment of Fra Angelo's prophecies. His noble intellect, indefatigable in invention, immediately formulated new ideas; he now became a Guelf; he addressed supplications to the new pope, and offered himself as his instrument to deliver Italy from all tyrants, and restore her natural unity under the authority of the sacred chair. Innocent VI believed that Cola could be of use to the church; he absolved him from all its censures, gave him an amnesty, released him from prison, and handed him over to Cardinal Albornoz, that the cardinal might profit by his experience in Italian affairs and his influence over the Romans. Thus a great statesman and a gifted dreamer left Avignon for Italy to quell the tyrants.

.   .   .   .

Cola raised new troops, made Riccardo Imprendente of the house of Anibaldi, lord of Monte Compatri, his captain-general, and caused Palestrina to be again invested. All went well. The Colonna were reduced to extremities, and their fall seemed certain. Had Cola acted with moderation, he would probably have ruled for years as senator, but the demon of ambition and want of money drove him to dangerous measures. He imposed a tax on articles of consumption. In his tyrannical jealousy he caused (and this was his most wicked deed) a noble and beloved citizen, Pandolfuccio, son of Guido, formerly his envoy in Florence, to be beheaded. He seized now one man, now another, and sold them their freedom for the sake of the ransom. No one dared any longer open his mouth in council. Cola himself was unnaturally excited. He laughed and wept at the same moment. The temper of the people showed him that a conspiracy was formed against his life. He raised a bodyguard, fifty men from each region, to be at hand at the first summons of the bell. The army before Palestrina demanded pay, and murmured that it had not received it; in his distrust he deposed Imprendente and appointed new captains. This conduct estranged Imprendente also, and his followers. It must have been at this juncture that a man who afterwards became famous in Europe appeared before Cola, Gianni di Guccio, a spurious French prince and a pretender to the crown of France, whose fortunes constitute one of the most remarkable romances of the Middle Ages, and are interwoven with Cola's last days. When Gianni, whose cause the senator seems to have espoused, took leave of him on October 4, to bear his letter of introduction to the legate at Montefiascone, he was warned at the Porta del Popolo by a Siennese soldier to get away quickly, for the senator's life was in danger. The spurious prince immediately returned to inform Cola, who dismissed him with letters in which he conjured Albornoz to send him aid, for a storm threatened to break over him. The cardinal forthwith ordered the cavalry to horse, but it was already too late. Such at least is the tradition, although no contemporary document exists to confirm the statement.

On October 8 Cola was awakened by the cry, "Popolo, Popolo!" The regions of S. Angelo, Ripa, Colonna, and Trevi, where the Savelli and Colonna dwelt, hurried to the Capitol. Its bell was silent. Cola at first did not recognize the importance of the revolt, but when he heard the cry, "'Death to the traitor who has imposed the taxes,'" he understood the danger. He called his people to him; they fled; judges, notaries, guards, friends, all sought safety in flight; only two persons and his kinsman Luciolo, a furrier, remained with him. Fully armed, the banner of Rome in his hand, Cola stepped on to the balcony of the upper hall of the palace to address the people. He made a sign for silence; the people cried him down, in fear of the spell of his voice. Stones and missiles were thrown at him; an arrow pierced his hand. He unfolded the banner of Rome, and pointed silently to the gold letters, "*Senatus populusque Romanus*," that they might speak for him— a trait of true greatness, the finest perhaps in the life of the tribune. He was answered with the shout, "Death to the traitor!"

304

While the populace set fire to the wooden fortifications, which surrounded the palace like palisades, and strove to enter, Cola let himself down from the hall into the court under the prison. Luciolo from above made treacherous signals to the people. All was not yet lost; the hall was in flames, the staircase fell in, the assailants consequently could not easily force their way inside; the forces of the Regola might have had time to come up, and the temper of the people might have changed. The first door was on fire, the roof of the loggia fell in. Had Cola with high courage but stepped among the raging multitude to receive death at the hands of his Romans on the Capitol, he would have ended his life in a manner worthy of an ancient hero. The piteous way in which he staggered out of the Capitol shamed even his contemporaries as even now it shames every one possessed of manly feeling. The tribune threw aside his armor and official dress, cut off his beard and blackened his face; he put on a shepherd's cloak, placed a pillow on his head, and thus hoped to steal through the crowd. To all whom he met he shouted in a feigned voice, "Up! at the traitor." As he reached the last gate one of the people laid hold of him, saying, "This is the tribune!" His gold bracelets betrayed him. He was led to the steps of the palace below the lion's cage and the image of the Madonna, where the Senator Berthold had formerly been stoned, and where Fra Monreale, Pandolfuccio, and others had received their death sentence. There stood the tribune surrounded by the people. All were silent. None ventured to lay hands on the man who had formerly delivered Rome, and moved the world to admiration. His arms crossed on his breast, he looked about him and was silent. Cecco del Vecchio thrust his sword into his body. The mangled and headless corpse was dragged from the Capitol to the Colonna quarter, and was hanged outside a house close to S. Marcello. Two days the appalling figure remained; once in life the idol of Rome, now the target for the stones of street boys. By command of Jugurtha and Sciarretta Colonna, the remains of the Tribunus Augustus were burnt by Jews on the third day, on a heap of dry thistles in the mausoleum of Augustus. The scene of the last act of this curious tragedy had been specially chosen in mockery of Cola's pompous ideas concerning antiquity. His ashes were scattered like those of Arnold of Brescia.

The long series of men who, dominated by the spell of the Eternal City and by the dogma of the Roman monarchy, fought for the restoration of a past ideal, closes with Cola di Rienzo. The history of the city has shown the connected succession of these men and the ideas of the time have explained the necessity for the existence of the last tribune. On the confines of two ages, in the excitement of the dawn which preceded the renascence of classic antiquity, Cola di Rienzo stands as the historic off-spring of the antagonism of Rome to herself and to the time, a contradiction which drove him insane. His fellow sinners are in fact Rome, Dante, Petrarch, Henry VII, the emperors, the popes in Avignon, and the century itself. His fantastic scheme of once more gathering the peoples in the absence of the pope round the ancient Capitol, and of reerecting the Latin empire of the world, awoke for a moment the enthusiastic belief in the idea of universal Roman citizenship. It was also the farewell of mankind to these ancient traditions. A life-giving reality took the place of this delusion: the spirit which, by means of Romano-Greek learning and art, effected its own deliverance from mediaevalism. Herein lies the serious importance of the friendship between Petrarch and Coli di Rienzo. The former awoke classic antiquity in the intellectual kingdom after its restoration in the political sphere had vanished with Rienzo as a dream. In the world of history as in that of nature there are mirages from distant zones of the past; such and the most curious of all was the appearance of the tribune of the people. The combination of thoughtfulness and folly, of truth and falsehood, of knowledge and ignorance of the time, of grandeur of imagination and pusillanimity in action makes Cola di Rienzo, the heroic player in the tattered purple of antiquity, the true representative and image of Rome in her deepest decay. His story has endowed forsaken Rome with an imperishable glamor of fantastic poetry, and his successes appeared so enigmatical that they were ascribed to the aid of a demon. Even Raynaldus, the annalist of the church, believed in the diabolical arts of the tribune, but every intelligent person who believes in the power of ideas among men, is able by that power to explain Cola's influence. His personality was sufficient to draw the first men of the time within its spell. The pope himself and the emperor, kings, populace, cities and Rome all fell under his magic charm. The fascination by which some men take the world captive is due to the fact that they understand the mystic secret of the age. A dark delusion cannot of itself exert this fascination. There must be concealed within it some real thought, which suddenly shines forth and, striking on a receptive mind, awakes enthusiasm, which again perforce shrouds itself in the old delusion.

The time in which Cola di Rienzo appeared was filled with the fervent desire of liberty and the hope of a messiah, and bore the germ of a new spirit in its bosom. No wonder that Italy held the gifted Roman for her hero and savior, when he boldly unfolded his flag on the Capitol. He was indeed the prophet of the Latin renascence.

The strange appearance of Cola has such distant perspectives both in the past and the future, and presents such stern traits of tragic necessity, that it offers more material for the contemplation of the philosopher than the long and noisy reigns of a hundred kings. His magnificent ideas of the independence and unity of Italy, of the reform of the church and of the human race, are sufficient to outshine his political follies and to save his memory from obscurity. No century will ever forget that the plebeian, crowned with flowers on the ruins of Rome, was the first to shed a ray of freedom on the darkness of his time, and, with prophetic glance, to show his native country the goal which she was not to attain until five hundred years had passed.

III

TERRITORIAL PRINCIPALITY

I

Revival of Papal Authority

FROM the middle of the fourteenth century onwards the errant soldiery [wandering mercenary bands] constantly acquired greater preponderance. France, released from its war with England, and dismembered Italy were the natural theaters for their activities. Contemporary historians could not understand how it happened that so many men of the higher nobility, so many brave warriors, joined these brigand hordes; nor could they comprehend how these companies rose, as it were, afresh in a single night, and traversed unpunished the fairest provinces. They explained this symptom of a disease organic to society as due to the influence of the planets or as a divine judgment. The contemporary world, in which the great institutions of the Middle Ages—empire, church, feudal monarchy, chivalry, the patrician constitutions of the cities—fell to decay, was in a state of dissolution and in search of a new social form. The bands of mercenaries were the proletariat of European society, which was breaking out of its ancient grooves. Chivalry, formerly the splendid association in which manly vigor and custom found their legitimate forms, had been overpowered by the growing culture and prosperity of the burgher class; its ancient spirit disappeared, and the knight degenerated into the errant soldier of fortune. The same middle class ousted the hereditary aristocracy from the re-

From book XII, ch. 1, sec. 3.

publics; whence it followed that the idle nobles sought occupation in military affairs and henceforth appeared as condottieri; as did even the Colonna, Orsini, and Savelli of Rome. The fall of the aristocracy, the conservative class which rested on hereditary landed property, was at the same time one of the main causes of the dissolution of the ancient communal constitution. For it robbed the communes of the spirit of chivalrous honor and of military energy, the loss of which could not be replaced by the burgher class, consisting as it did of workers, and resting on the movable power of capital. After Rome and Florence had expelled the nobility, the defensive force of the two republics gradually declined. Industry and prosperity made the citizens useless for defense; they hired mercenaries like the communes of antiquity in the time of the decline of Greece. Tyrants set up as rulers with the aid of these same mercenaries. Thus a lawless condition of brute force and despotism was everywhere produced. While the states now lay prostrate, society formed leagues for attack and defense. The spirit of association was all-powerful both in a good and a bad sense. The same means offered ruin and salvation. This is the age of leagues of both a political and a social nature, the military brotherhoods, the societies of knights, the confederations of cities, confraternities of every tendency, and in every country of Europe.

This state of things began in exhausted Germany with Henry VII; in Italy with the exile of the papacy and the fall of the Neapolitan monarchy; in France with the war of succession with England, which almost annihilated the kingdom of Philip le Bel. By reason of its relations with the whole world, Italy was more especially the arena for the mercenaries of all nations. The mercenaries of Navarre and France; the English, who had been drawn thither by the wars; the Germans, who through the relations of the empire had constant dealings with Italy; the Poles and Bohemians, who had accompanied Charles IV; the Hungarians, who came to Italy with the house of Anjou, all streamed into the country in crowds, especially when a treaty of peace threw them out of employment. For nowhere was there a standing army. The war

312

of the church against the Visconti, the hostilities between Montferrat and Milan, between Siena and Perugia, constantly offered the mercenaries fresh occupation. Every signor and every city required their services. They themselves were errant military states, admirably ordered. The leaders of these *barbuti* (as they were called on account of their helmets), clad in mail from head to foot, were surrounded by a council of four captains for the cavalry (*cavalieri*), and by an equal number for the infantry (*masnadieri*). Important affairs, moreover, were, according to republican custom, submitted to the parliament of all the corporals. Constables, marshals, corporals, formed various grades in this military association, according to the *bandiere*, or squadrons into which the company was divided. There were judges and notaries, and treasurers, who distributed the booty and salaries and administered the finances. A troop of women, kidnapped nuns and willing courtesans, accompanied these bands, at whose approach all fled in terror, and who left famine and pestilence behind. Their motley camp was a market, where the spoils of convents and cities were sold by a crowd of merchants, while great Italian banks stood in commercial relations with the captains, who deposited their plunder at interest. The companies held negotiations with princes and republics according to diplomatic forms, as equal with equal. They received their representatives at the little council of war or in great parliament; they sent procurators and orators to the states; they received and drew up in documentary form treaties to which every captain added his seal in lead or red wax. The main object of all these negotiations was solely the extortion of money. When Cardinal Albornoz through envoys requested the Count of Landau to leave the State of the Church, the condottiere replied with unabashed candor:

My lords, our manner of life in Italy is universally known. To rob, plunder, murder those who resist, is our custom. Our revenues depend on mortgages in the provinces which we invade. Those who value their lives buy peace and quiet by heavy tribute. If therefore the signor legate wishes to dwell at unity with us and to secure tranquillity to all these cities, then let him do like the rest of the world, that is to say, pay, pay! Take this answer to your master quickly; for I will not guarantee that nothing unseemly shall happen to your most revered persons, if I find you still here an hour hence!

The great cardinal with blushes did frequently what all the world did—purchased immunity from the brigands.

While Landau's company flourished, the mercenaries of another German adventurer, Hans of Bongard, whom the Italians called Annichino, were no less dreaded. At the same time Englishmen also appeared in Italy; for in 1361 John of Montferrat led "the White Company" from Provence against Galeazzo Visconti. The pope had even given money to this company in order to be rid of it, and enable it to march against Italy. Besides a thousand other scourges the White Company brought the plague with them. They consisted chiefly of English, Gascons, and Germans under the command of Albert Sterz, who was soon after joined by Otto, Duke of Brunswick, in the service of the same margrave. In 1364 a Habsburger, Count John, also entered Italy as a mercenary leader. With Ambrogio Visconti (bastard of Bernabò) he commanded the company of S. George. From far and near the pope, the legates, the princes and cities of Italy summoned foreign mercenaries into the unhappy country. Albornoz himself had hastened to Hungary to procure mercenaries from King Lewis, and Charles IV was incessantly requested to provide them. In 1364 the Englishman John Hawkwood, "the falcon in the wood," who had come to Italy with Sterz, placed himself at the head of the English company. The Pisans first took him into their pay; afterwards he became the most celebrated of all the mercenary leaders and was for years the friend of Florence. The republic, which refused a grave to Dante, erected a monument in honor of the brigand in her cathedral.

Owning neither towns nor territories, these companies of freebooters were already more powerful than the little Italian states, and the fate of the country lay within their hands. It was only the absence of any national tie that hindered them from acquiring the actual sovereignty of Italy, as it had been acquired by mercenaries in the time of Odoacer. Their brilliant model was the earliest mercenary band of a political character, that great company of Catalans, whom Roger de Flor had led against Byzantium, and who had conquered the dukedom of Athens in 1311. As early as 1349 Florence had attempted to form a league against these freebooters. Albornoz had incessantly striven for the same object, but not until after the conclusion of peace with Bernabò was the pope able to take more vigorous measures. On September 15, 1364, Urban V exhorted Florence, Pisa, and all the Italian communes to unite in expelling the bands. The common danger once more offered the Italians the opportunity of uniting in a league; but party passions and weakness prevented its formation. All that took place were some isolated attempts at deliverance. In order to render the White Company innocuous and to prevent its alliance with the company of the Star, Albornoz and Queen Joanna formed a contract with the former, which, under the command of the knight Hugh Mortimer, numbered 5000 horse and 1000 foot. They pledged themselves, in return for 160,000 gold florins, to serve the church and Naples for six months against all enemies, especially Annichino, and to spare the State of the Church and the kingdom for five years. The treaty was only partially successful. Annichino stood with 10,000 armed men in Tuscany, where he took Vetralla in March 1365. Rome trembled before him. The White Company, which was to be under the conduct of Gomez Garcia, a nephew of the cardinal, as captain-general of the church and Naples, showed itself refractory. Gomez secretly left the camp and went to Orvieto. The English pursued him. Had they formed an alliance with Annichino, things would have gone badly for the state of the church. But Gomez had already come to an understanding with him, and Annichino surprised the English near Perugia, and completely routed them. These events show how hopeless was the condition of Italy.

The emperor had come to Avignon in May of the same year, where he had formed a plan with the pope for the extirpation of the bands. They wished to remove them from France and Italy, and to turn them against the Turks. The pope charged Albornoz to persuade them; but the mercenary leaders mocked at both emperor and pope. During the winter Annichino's company held itself entrenched in Sutri, and devastated the Sabina and Tuscany with fire and sword. The following year the Campagna suffered a like fate at the hands of Hawkwood's company, which pushed from Naples across the Liris. Roman envoys implored the pope to return and to save the capital of Christendom from ruin. On April 13, 1366, Urban V issued a bull of excommunication against the companies, the scum of all nations, who were in the act of thrusting the church, the kings and princes from their respective countries, and there establishing their permanent seat. He required the mercenary leaders to disband their forces within a given time, and to surrender the occupied cities. He forbade all princes and republics to employ them in their service, and all nobles and communes to serve under their banner. He pronounced infamous all members of a company down to the fourth degree. In his despair he called on the emperor, the princes and bishops, the cities and peoples of the world to unite for the extirpation of these terrible hordes, and promised plenary absolution in return.

The bull was read from every pulpit in Italy, and the condottieri answered it in derision with fresh outrages. These soldiers of fortune were aware that their power was far too great to be shattered by an excommunication, and that neither tyrants, republics, nor even the church herself could dispense with their services. They scarcely feared the league which had been formed by the pope, knowing too well the seeds of decay which every alliance of the kind bore within it. On September 19, 1366, the Italian league was concluded by a congress of the cities in Florence, under the presidency of the papal legate. It embraced the State of the Church, Naples, and Tuscany; the Roman people, however, who had sent no envoy, were also to enter it. But the league was dissolved December 1367, because envious Florence protested against the emperor's taking part in it.

II

The Pope Returns to Rome

*In 1367 Pope Urban V (1362–70) returned to Rome, a city ruined by constant warfare and neglect and beset with poverty. He undertook some work of restoration on churches and engaged in sumptuous diplomatic interviews with the Emperor Charles IV and with the Byzantine Emperor John Palaeologus, who was seeking military support against the Turks. Difficulties of life persuaded Urban and his court to return to Avignon, despite the prophesy of Saint Birgit of Sweden that the pope would die if he left Italy. The prophecy was soon fulfilled. Urban's successor, Pope Gregory XI, continued efforts to restore public order in the states of the church, and, in 1376–77, he himself returned to Rome.—*EDITOR.

WHILE Rudolf of Varano ably defended Bologna against the [papal army under Cardinal Robert of Geneva], the Florentines showed themselves ready to be reconciled with the church. As early as April, they had accepted the mediation of the Romans; they also listened to the admonitions of the emperor and of the kings of France and Castile, but answered them with the courage and conviction of their right. They pointed to the massacre at Faenza, the work of a cardinal; they pointed to history, which

From book XII, ch. 2, sec. 3.

reminded the world of the ancient Guelf loyalty of Florence to the church; they laid bare the wounds of Italy to the eyes of Europe, and never had a country more justification for rising against its oppressors in a Sicilian Vesper. The commercial power of the Florentines was at stake; their connections were scattered over every kingdom in the world, where the inventive children of the republic carried their wares, their products, their arts, their learning, and their civilized modes of life. In June 1376 they sent envoys to Avignon, among them S. Catherine [of Siena]. A pious maiden of the people, invested by a powerful republic with the character of an envoy, presents a strange spectacle. The saint from Siena had already frequently exhorted Gregory XI to return to Rome and reform the church, and had openly explained to him that the apostacy of Italy was due solely to the priests, who were sunk in worldliness and vice, and to the impious pastors. She now spoke at the papal court with gloomy zeal in favor of peace, but the terms of the Florentines and those of the pope remained irreconcilable.

The exhortations of the inspired priestess may nevertheless have contributed to strengthen Gregory's resolution to depart. In 1375 he had issued a bull which commanded all bishops to remain in their sees. It is said that one day he asked a prelate, "Lord Bishop, why do you not go to your see?" to which the bishop answered, "And you, Holy Father, why do you not go to yours?" The reply made a deep impression on the pope. His relations, his father, the Count of Beaufort, the French cardinals (who were twenty-one in number against five Italians), the king of France and the king's brother, the duke of Anjou, in vain besought him to remain.

Avignon recognized that the papacy was departing for ever, and with the papacy the splendor of the city. The dismay was great. As Gregory mounted his horse on September 13, 1376, the animal refused to bear him, and its restiveness was held to be an omen. Six cardinals remained behind, as garrison of the now deserted papal fortress, which inevitably awaited an antipope. On September 22 Gregory arrived at Marseilles. On October 2 he embarked with the Curia; the fleet consisted of galleys from

318

Naples, Spain, Provence, Genoa, Pisa, Ancona, and the knights of Rhodes, under the command of the celebrated prior of the brethren of S. John, Fernandez de Heredia, who had just been elected grandmaster of his order. The voyage to Genoa and thence onwards on October 18 was unfortunate; the sea was stormy, some vessels were wrecked, the Bishop of Luni was drowned; no good was foreboded.

When the Florentines learnt that Gregory XI had set forth, they wrote to the Romans. They warned them against deceptions; told them that they did not even yet believe the pope would return to Rome. Should he, however, come, he would not appear as an angel of peace, but as a general to carry the war into Roman territory. They exhorted Rome even now to unite with them for the deliverance of Italy, in order that the pope, if he came, might be forced to give peace to the country, or if he did not come, that the universal voice should call him to a free and tranquil Italy. The Romans paid no heed to their invitation; a solemn embassy from the capitol invited Gregory XI to return, and offered him the signory of the city, which impatiently awaited him.

The pope sailed along the Italian coast amid continuous storms. His train landed in the harbors and spent the nights in the towns along the shore. On November 6 they anchored off Pisa, on the seventh at Leghorn, where they remained nine days on account of the storm. They touched at Elba and Piombino, Orbetello on Cape Argentaro, and lay before Corneto on December 5. On stepping ashore the pope was received with rejoicings by an innumerable crowd, as Urban V had been received nine years before, but no Albornoz now appeared with the keys of a hundred conquered cities; no envoys of republics offered homage; no princes with trains of soldiers showed themselves. With a faint heart Gregory set foot on the ecclesiastical state. He took up his abode in Corneto, meaning to stay some time, but above all to assure himself of his reception in Rome. And this he did by treaty with the republic. The cardinals of Ostia, Portus, and the Sabina, who had received full powers, concluded a treaty with the city on December 21, as follows: As soon as the pope landed at Ostia, Rome conferred the full *dominium* upon him, under the same conditions that had previously been offered to Urban V; the city made over to the legate all bridges, gates, towers, and fortresses, the whole of Trastevere and the Leonina. The pope promised to let the executors of justice and the four councillors of the *balestrieri* continue in office and retain administration of the civic revenues. But these magistrates must tender the oath of fidelity, and the pope had the right of reforming the corporation. On landing at Ostia the guild were to meet him, accompany him to S. Peter's and then retire to their private dwellings, where they were to remain. In vain the Florentines strove to dissuade Rome from this treaty with the church. On December 26 they again wrote a fiery letter to the *banderesi;* in it they said that the pope, whom they awaited with such longing, would bring them nothing but the ruin of liberty and the dissolution of their corporation. These bold republicans wrote that even if he restored the city to its ancient splendor, overlaid its walls with gold and gave Rome back the ancient majesty of the empire, not even then ought he to be received by the citizens were these advantages to be purchased with the loss of their freedom. They again implored the Romans to hold out for their rights as long as the oppressor was not within the walls of the city, and they offered the aid of their entire army.

Gregory XI celebrated a joyless Christmas at Corneto. He had sent back all the galleys except three or four from Provence, which he retained for his protection, since the prefect of Civita Vecchia rendered the sea insecure. On January 1 he sent cavalry against Viterbo: they were defeated by the prefect of the city, who took 200 of them prisoners and sent the news of his victory to Florence. After five anxious weeks Gregory finally left Corneto on January 13. He sailed past Civita Vecchia, which recognized the signory of the prefect, and landed at Ostia on January 14. The sight of this coast, which is so melancholy and deserted that Dante placed the entrance to the nether world of the Christians at the mouth of the Tiber, must have made a dismal impression on the pope and his court. Here it was that in former days their compatriots the Provençals had effected their ominous landing under Charles of Anjou. A long chain of causes and effects linked the disembarkation of the first Angevin and the last Avignonese pope.

In the evening the Romans in great numbers appeared to greet him. In conformity with the treaty, they made over to Gregory the *dominium* of the city. There were rejoicings and dancing by torchlight to the music of instruments. The following day the pope embarked to sail up the Tiber to S. Paul's. It was night; crowds went to and fro with lights and torches; the pope remained on board. Not until the morning of January 16 did he step ashore. The whole of Rome had come to S. Paul's. Horsemen in splendid array, carrying banners, pranced here and there amid the braying of trumpets. The solemn entry took place on January 17, 1377, for on the festival of the Cathedra of S. Peter the sacred chair was to be restored to the cathedral of the apostles. The procession took its way through the venerable gate of S. Paul, through which a pope had never before entered. The Gothic hero, Totila, however, had formerly forced his way through its portals to the city, and 110 years before Gregory's time Charles of Anjou made his entry by the same route.

Gregory XI came with a force of scarcely 2000 men under the command of Raymond of Turenne; but even this escort was too warlike to satisfy S. Catherine, who, like Petrarch, demanded that the pope should come to Rome bearing only the crucifix and accompanied by the chanting of psalms. A crowd of white-clad mountebanks, dancing and clapping their hands, preceded the pope when he left S. Paul's. This curious spectacle might have afforded material to a satirist for caustic reflections on the return of the Avignonese to Rome. But in the fourteenth century the sight of a pope, who, in the most solemn moment of his life—a moment imperishable in the history of the world—was preceded by dancing buffoons, scarcely created the effect that had been produced in his time by the Jewish king, grimacing and dancing before the ark of the covenant. The magistrates of the city on horseback, the militia, and the archers escorted and surrounded Gregory's triumphal procession. He rode a richly caparisoned palfrey, under a *baldacchino*, which was upheld by the senator and other nobles, while the banner of the church was carried in advance by Juan Fernandez Heredia. The count of Fundi of the house of Gaetani and several Orsini were seen in the procession.

The choir of the clergy received the pope at the gate of S. Paul; the keys of the city were given him. The procession wound through that memorable quarter of Rome which leads between the Tiber, Monte Testaccio, and the Aventine, through the Marmorata to the Capitol and S. Marco, whence Gregory XI proceeded onward by the Via Papalis through the Field of Mars to S. Peter's. These regions were as deserted in his time as in the present day. Monte Testaccio was surrounded by a piazza used for the public games. With the exception of a few mills and houses, the Marmorata was as forsaken as it now is, and was only marked by a few more ancient ruins, for instance by the Arch of Lentulus. On the deserted Aventine still rose the fortress of the Savelli, of which now nothing is left but the remains of the wall that surrounded it. The ponderous towers on the Capitol and near S. Marco still invested this part of Rome, which is now covered with splendid buildings, with a warlike aspect. The Romans had veiled the streets with motley draperies, and even the roofs were covered with rejoicing crowds, which threw flowers on the path of the Holy Father, who at length came to restore the papacy to the city for ever, and for ever to deprive her of her freedom.

It was afternoon before the procession reached S. Peter's, which sparkled with the radiance of 18,000 lamps. Exhausted, the pope could at last cast himself in prayer before the apostle's grave. The great work was accomplished; the seventy years' exile was ended. As we now stand before the monument of Gregory XI in the church of S. Francesca Romana on the Forum, we are reminded of this solemn moment by the sight of the reliefs which adorn the tomb. Gregory rides under a *baldacchino*; cardinals on handsomely bedecked horses, and noblemen in armor follow; from the gate of S. Paul, the walls of which are falling to ruin, stream the people. Rome herself advances in the form of Minerva. A saint, the Sienese maiden, walks at the right of the pope, and seems to conduct him into Rome; the papal chair hovers in clouds over the Eternal City, and through the air an angel carries the insignia of the papacy, the tiara and the keys of Peter.

322

III

A Stranger in His Own See: Gregory XI

GREGORY XI entered the Vatican with the firm determination of restoring Rome. But was it possible to accomplish the work under conditions so unfavorable? The thought of Florence robbed him of sleep. This republic incessantly goaded Italy to save the liberty which she believed to be threatened by the pope. She therein showed herself a prophetess; for her independence was to perish in after times at the hands of a pope who was her own citizen. The horrors committed by the mercenaries in the service of the church afforded terrible corroboration of the complaints of the Florentines. On February 1, 1377, Cesena, which had hitherto remained faithful to the church, and where the cardinal of Geneva dwelt, rose in despairing resistance to the Bretons, who formed its garrison; 300 Bretons were slain, when the legate, furious with anger, summoned the English from Faenza and commanded them to punish the town. The order was mercilessly fulfilled. About 8000 inhabitants escaped to the neighboring towns; the bodies of some 4000 murdered citizens covered the streets. A cry of indignation reechoed throughout Italy against the church, which had consecrated her return with massacres in Faenza and Cesena. The Florentines called on all the princes of Christendom to have pity on Italy.

From book XII, ch. 3, sec. 1.

These events also had their effect in Rome. Gregory here found himself deceived in his expectations, for the city gave him by no means the full power, but wished to maintain her freedom under the rule of the banderesi, and was encouraged in her wish by the Florentines. The Romans desired that the influence of the pope should be checked by the rebellion in the State of the Church, by Florence, and the city prefect. The nobles made use of the presence of the Curia in order to reestablish themselves in Rome. Luca Savelli and the Count of Fundi conspired with 400 of their associates against the popular government, but their plan—of which the Curia could scarcely have been ignorant—was shattered. The pope now appointed as senator Gomez Albornoz, nephew of the great Egidius, an experienced general, on whose energy he staked his hopes. He himself went in May to Anagni, which recognized the signory of Honoratus Gaetani, Count of Fundi. Here, in the native town of Boniface VIII, Gregory XI could review the painful history through which the papacy had passed between the fatal attempt of Nogaret and his own return from Avignon. He remained at Anagni until November 5, 1377, busily occupied with the war against his enemies, and with negotiations for peace.

Fortune favored him. One member after another deserted the league of the Florentines. Rudolf Varano, their captain-general, was enticed to the side of the pope, and in July 1377 Bologna purchased the continuance of her autonomy by the recognition of the papal authority. True that the Florentines had not lost courage; they nevertheless sent envoys to the pope. Their conditions were such as could not be accepted. They refused to restore the ecclesiastical property and to revoke the decrees against the Inquisition and the papal forum. They demanded that all rebels against the church should remain six years in statu quo, with full liberty to form alliances against anyone, and as indemnity they offered the pope, in the name of the league, only the annual sum of 50,000 gold florins for six years. When Gregory XI refused these conditions, Florence reproached him for having, with unchristian severity, refused to give peace to Italy. On September 21, 1377, the courageous republic once more exhorted the Romans to join the league, promising them 3000 lances and the aid of Bernabò.

Under the government of Gomez Albornoz, however, the Romans had become reconciled to the pope, and had entrusted him to conclude peace with the prefect of the city. Francesco of Vico deserted the Florentine league and made terms with the Capitol. The deed was drawn up at Anagni on October 30, 1377; and on November 10, three days after the pope's return to the city, was ratified by the general council of the Romans. The document clearly reveals the constitution of the republic at the time; the general council was summoned by the Senator at the time, Guido de Prohynis, a Provençal, with the consent of the three conservators, the two executors of justice, the four councillors of the guild of archers, and the three captains of war. The consuls of the merchants and husbandmen, the thirteen captains of regions, further twenty-six good men and one hundred and four councillors of the city, eight for each region, were united as general council, and this committee of the people concluded the deed of peace.

The costly war in the end was more severely felt by the pope than by Florence. Both adversaries desired peace. It thus happened that through the intervention of the king of France, and even that of Bernabò, whom Gregory had succeeded in winning to his interests, a congress was held at Sarzana. But the negotiations there were soon shattered by the death of the pope.

Death alone prevented Gregory XI from following the example of his predecessors and escaping to Avignon. He always regarded his removal to Rome as a painful sacrifice. As he wrote to the Florentines, he had left his beautiful native country, a grateful and pious people, and much else that he valued; he had closed his ears to the opposition and entreaties of kings, princes, and cardinals, and had come to Italy at danger, difficulty, and expense, with the firm resolve to repair all that the rectors of the church had neglected, and he found himself bitterly deceived in every expectation. The thought saddened his every hour. On his deathbed he is said to have repented of having listened to the prophecies of pious women, and come to Rome to plunge the church into the abyss of a schism. This schism he foresaw. For the first conclave to be held in Rome since the time of Benedict XI must necessarily be held amid the bitter conflicts of the French and Italian parties, and amid the same conditions must also be decided the greatest question of the time—whether the papacy should again become Roman and Italian, or remain French and foreign. We may imagine the affliction of the ailing Gregory, who saw a chasm, which he had no power to bridge over, yawning before him. For never has a dying pope experienced, like a dying king, the joys or the sufferings excited by an already chosen successor. Sick to death, Gregory issued a bull on March 19, in which he commanded that on his departure the candidate elected by the majority of cardinals in, or out of, conclave, in Rome or elsewhere, should be recognized as pope, in defiance of the opposition of the minority.

While Gregory lay hopelessly ill, cardinals as well as people were seized by deep dismay. The former already discussed the new election, the latter the means of averting the election of a Frenchman and procuring that of a Roman. Owing to the removal of the papacy to Avignon, the Romans had lost even the last remains of influence over the papal election; the canon laws of the church had deprived them of these remains, but they themselves ever strove to enforce them when opportunity offered. And opportunity now presented itself. The Sacred College numbered at this time twenty-three cardinals, of whom six had remained at Avignon, one was absent at the congress at Sarzana, and sixteen were in Rome. Of these, seven were Limousins, four were French, one was a Spaniard, and four were Italians; namely, Francesco Tibaldeschi of S. Sabina, called the cardinal of S. Peter, a Roman like Jacopo Orsini of S. Gregorio; further Simon de Brossano of SS. Giovanni and Paolo, a Milanese; and Peter Corsini of S. Lorenzo in Damaso, a Florentine. The foreigners consequently formed the majority, but were themselves divided, jealousy severing the Frenchmen and Limousins. It was soon evident that no Ultramontane could hope for a majority.

All these matters were discussed while Gregory XI lay at the point of death. But before he passed away, the senator, the magistrates, the captains of the regions, several of the clergy and respected citizens came to the cardinals at S. Spirito, and represented the wishes of the Roman people. They explained that it was necessary for the welfare of Italy that a Roman, or at least an Italian, should be elected pope, who would make his dwelling in Rome, would restore the city and the State of the Church. The cardinals gave them fair words, exhorted them to take measures for the peace of the city in order to avert a popular rising. In fear the Ultramontanes brought their valuables to S. Angelo, which was commanded by a French castellan. The excitement was feverish. Scarcely ever had the death of a pope been awaited with the like suspense. All were aware that the moment of Gregory's departure marked a crisis in the history of the world.

He died on March 27, 1378, The pontificate of the last and most unfortunate of the Avignonese popes was brief and sad. Nothing but struggles against the storm, his moral and physical sufferings were alike severe. Grief and infirmity had rendered Gregory XI an old man at the age of forty-seven. The dead was borne to S. Peter's, where the first obsequies were solemnized; the following day he was carried to S. Maria Nuova on the Forum, of which he had been cardinal and where he had wished to rest. Rome remained everlastingly grateful to him for having brought the sacred chair back to the city. After two hundred years a later generation erected a sumptuous monument in the church where he sleeps, and this monument immortalizes his one glorious action.

IV

The Pontificate of Urban VI (1378-89)

*Fearing that the cardinals would elect a French pope who would take the Curia back to Avignon, the Roman mob demanded the election of a Roman, or at least an Italian, as pope. Under great duress, the conclave elected Urban VI, the first step toward the Great Schism. Gregorovius largely ignores the history of the French line of popes, that did return to Avignon, and concentrates on the Roman line.—*EDITOR.

THE city of Rome, at this time ruled by its authorities under altered forms, was entirely devoted to Urban VI, the representative of the national Roman papacy. He appointed senators and even nominated other magistrates for such time as he pleased. The bishop of Cordova was consequently able to assert that Rome had never been so obedient to a pope. Beyond some nobles and Queen Joanna [of Naples], Urban no longer beheld an enemy in Italy. And even these adversaries were now to be vanquished by Charles of Durazzo. Charles came to Rome with an army in 1380, a man thirty-five years of age, short, fair, active, a friend of learning and poetry, of gentle manners but inspired with the

From book XII, ch. 3, sec. 4.

ambition of the Angevins. Urban made him standard-bearer of the church and senator, whereupon the prince installed Fra Raymond of Montebello, prior of the order of S. John in Hungary, as his vicar on the Capitol. In order to arm Charles for his undertaking, the pope plundered the Roman churches and church estates; splendid vessels, massive images of saints, were carried to the furnace, and a vast sum was thus accumulated. Charles remained in Rome until the summer of 1381. On June 1 he received the investiture of Naples, on the following day the crown. In token of recognition he promised Francesco Prignano, surnamed Butillo, nephew of the pope, to confirm him in the possession of Capua, Amalfi, Salerno, Fundi, Caserta, and Sorrento; Urban, of his papal authority, having already endowed his uncouth relative with these principalities, the fairest portion of the monarchy.

Leaving the Florentine Lapo of Castiglionchio, a learned friend of Petrarch, behind as his vicar, Charles quitted Rome for Naples. Jacopo Gaetani, the brother and mortal enemy of Honoratus, followed his banner. The unfortunate kingdom was again the scene of a war of conquest, kindled by the caprice of a woman and a pope's thirst for revenge. Hungarians, Bretons, Germans, French, Italians fought for years for and against Durazzo and Anjou, for and against Urban VI and Clement VII. The death of Charles V had detained in France the adoptive son of the Queen, and Joanna's only support was her valiant husband Otto of Brunswick. Otto sought in vain, like Manfred in former times, to make a stand against the enemy on the Liris. Charles defeated him at S. Germano on June 28, entered Naples soon after and besieged the Queen in the Castell' dell' Uovo. Her husband, who was hastening to her relief, being taken prisoner, Joanna surrendered to the victor on August 25. In the spring of the following year, Lewis of Anjou, already crowned king by the antipope, appeared on the scene of action at the head of a French army and accompanied by the Count of Geneva, by Amadeus of Savoy, and several noble lords. Never had a stronger force appeared against Naples, and this decided the fate of the imprisoned queen. By command of Charles of Durazzo, Robert's granddaughter was strangled with a silken cord in the castle at Muro, in May 1382, and her remains were exposed to public view for seven days in S. Chiara at Naples. Thus did the unfortunate woman expiate in her old age the crimes of her youth.

In his desire for revenge Lewis now crossed the Abruzzi and entered the kingdom. Urban, fearing for Rome, took Hawkwood into his service, and the Romans flew to arms. They would probably have renounced the pope had the Angevin appeared before their walls. He did not, however, enter Roman territory, and only some cities in the State of the Church, Corneto, Todi, Amelia, Ancona, in fear declared in his favor. But the power of his troops was soon shattered by Charles's tactics, and the flower of his army wasted by illness and fatigue. The war of the two pretenders was meanwhile so lame and ineffective, that the impatient Urban resolved to go to Charles in person; and henceforward the life of the pope is closely interwoven with the war of succession in Naples. Urban VI at the head of mercenary bands, instigated solely by thoughts of hatred and temporal sovereignty, one of the most repulsive figures among the popes, has scarcely any higher claim to regard in history than that of a general or pretender to a crown.

Six cardinals opposed the journey; but he nevertheless resolved to make it, since he wished to remind Charles of the principalities promised to his nephew. He secretly left Rome, where the pestilence was raging, on April 19, 1383. Had the Romans known of his intention, they would assuredly have detained him. He remained one month at Tivoli, two at Valmontone. He then went to Ferentino, S. Germano, Suessa, and Capua. Charles greeted him with displeasure at Aversa, where he kept him for five days shut up in his beautiful castle, in order to extort his desires. Naples received him with pomp in the beginning of November, but here also the king immediately conducted him to the Castello Nuovo. And not until after a treaty concerning the nephew's fiefs had been negotiated through the intervention of the cardinals, and until Urban had promised not to interfere in affairs of state, did Charles allow him to take his seat in the cathedral. The pope soon found himself in strained relations with the king, his ungrateful creature. Wherever Urban VI appeared, appeared also the furies of dissension, his constant attendants. Charles wished him to leave the country, and the pope began to assume the airs of a feudal superior. No one heeded him, and never before had reverence for the vicar of Christ fallen so low. In June 1384 he left Naples, to retire in his anger to Nocera, a town that belonged to his nephew. And here in the fortress where in former times Helena, Manfred's widow, had met her death in prison, Urban fixed his seat.

After having but just returned to Rome, the papacy now seemed to be removed to the kingdom of Naples, and Christendom looked affrighted on the actions of two popes, of whom one at Avignon, the other at Nocera, each surrounded with a senate of cardinals, led an existence darkened with hatred. The history of this period, especially of the sojourn of Urban VI in Naples and Nocera, displays a barbarism of manners and conduct that is truly appalling. The differences between Urban and Charles waxed greater every day. Urban did not leave Nocera, not even when in September 1384 the duke of Anjou died at Bari, transmitting his rights to Joanna's kingdom to his little son Lewis. The brave prince had seen the failure of his enterprise, equipped at such immense cost; had watched the leading nobles die around him, and his army dwindle. His death gave Charles fresh power; he now treated the pope with less regard, and the pope repulsed with violence every attempt at intercession. The king, suspecting that he cherished the foolish scheme of placing his nephew Butillo on the throne, requested his return to Naples, but Urban answered with contempt. Among the cardinals were some who disapproved of his enigmatic conduct, or whom Charles had bribed, and all had been unwilling to go to Nocera. Since this part of the country swarmed with predatory bands and brigands, and since even the road to Naples was not safe, they feared for their own persons, while their sojourn in the fortress, the resort of the most infamous society, was insupportable. Every educated man must have shrunk from the sight of the savage faces that frequented the castle; captains of mercenaries and corsairs, spies in the pay of Charles, mendicant priests, cunning lawyers, the rude clergy of the district constantly came and went. What detained the pope?

331

Why did he not return to Rome? His whim savored of insanity. Charles wished to be rid of him at any cost. The cardinals hated him. The question of deposing him was privately discussed and submitted to legal opinion.

But Cardinal Orsini of Manupello whispered to Urban that a conspiracy was on foot against him, and the pope caused six cardinals who had opposed his journey to Naples to be seized and let down into a cistern, on January 11, 1385. According to the opinion of Dietrich of Niem, they were all blameless and learned men. The historian of the schism, an eyewitness of their prolonged sufferings, describes them with the sympathy of a humane observer. They languished in a damp subterranean vault, loaded with fetters and tormented by hunger, cold, and loathsome vermin. The inhuman nephew accompanied their groans of anguish with savage laughter, while the Holy Father paced the terrace of the castle to and fro, reading his breviary aloud, by his presence to urge the ministers of torture to greater energy. The entire Curia was struck with horror and indignation. Some cardinals who had remained behind in Naples, among whom was Pileus of Tusculum, deserted Urban; they issued letters to the clergy in Rome, in which they spoke of the necessity of a general council.

Aflame with anger, Urban hurled sentence of excommunication and deposition on the king and his wife Margaret, an amazon worthy of the time. He laid Naples under the interdict, and cherished dreams of placing the crown on the brainless head of his nephew. But Charles now sent troops against him. The same Alberigo who had gained the victory at Marino, now, as grand constable of Naples, besieged him at Nocera. With the sound of trumpets it was proclaimed from the walls of the town that whoever surrendered the pope dead or alive should receive a reward of 10,000 gold florins. The head of Christianity was thus proscribed like a brigand chief. And like a general of mercenaries the pope defended himself. He is described as going three or four times to the window, a bell in one hand, a torch in the other, and with a countenance burning with hatred, cursing the army of the king which stood below.

The town of Nocera had fallen, but the fortress, though sore pressed, still held out. On July 5, Raymondello Orsini, son of the Count of Nola, first an adherent of Durazzo, then leader of such Angevins as still remained in arms, came to the relief of the starving pope. The count opened a way through the besiegers and entered the fortress. But longer resistance was impossible. Urban had already sent messengers to Antonio Adorno, the doge of Genoa, and ten galleys had arrived in the harbor of Naples to take him on board. On July 7 he left Nocera, accompanied by Raymondello and surrounded by rapacious mercenaries, Italians, French, Bretons, and Germans, who were ready to sell him at any moment if he did not yield to their demands. He carried the captive prelates with him in his hurried flight. Worn out with suffering and in chains, they were scarcely able to sit their horses. One of them, the bishop of Aquila, excited Urban's suspicions; the pope caused him to be put to death, and he was left lying by the wayside like a dog. The company rode in horror and fear of death to the coast at Salerno. Here a part of the troops rebelled. The pope bought his release. With 300 German and Italian lances, he proceeded to Benevento, thence like a bandit hurried across mountains, heaths, and rivers, under the burning August sun, to reach the Adriatic coast, where the cities held to the Angevin. The hunted members of the Curia longingly scanned the ocean's furthest distance, until at Trani they one day descried the Genoese sails on the horizon. The fugitive band threw themselves exhausted on the shore, greeted with shouts by the sailors, who received their ferocious pope as their ancestors had formerly received Innocent IV.

Urban sailed from Bari to Messina, then by Corneto to Genoa, where he landed on September 23. His roughness irritated the authorities and people of the republic, with whom he was immediately at strife. The Doge, the chief citizen, and the clergy urged him to liberate the wretched cardinals as he had promised. An unsuccessful attempt at flight aroused his anger. He immediately caused the cardinals to be put to death. Whether they were tied in sacks and thrown into the sea, or strangled, or buried alive is unknown. The English cardinal, Adam Aston, on the urgent remonstrance of his king, was alone restored to freedom. Two others, who had not been imprisoned, Pileus, bishop of Tusculum, and Galeottus of Pietramala, had already deserted to Avignon. The hideous deed took place on the night of December 15, 1386. In the morning the insane Urban took ship and sailed for Lucca. Thence he intended to return to Naples with an army.

A sad event had reduced everything in the kingdom to confusion: Lewis of Hungary had died on September 11, 1382, without leaving a male heir. The malcontents had summoned Charles of Durazzo, who had crossed to Dalmatia in September 1385, to snatch the Hungarian crown from the head of Maria, Lewis's youthful daughter, and the betrothed of Sigismund, brother of Wenceslaus. The barons of the country crowned Charles in Stuhlweissenburg; but on February 7, 1386, he was stabbed by a brutal Hungarian in presence of the widowed Queen Elizabeth. Royal women thus avenged Charles's murder of a queen, their cousin, and the hand of fate turned against a usurper. Terrible is the dark working of Nemesis in the house of Anjou, a house founded in the blood of the Hohenstaufens. Within the space of a few decades the gory shades of the young Andreas, of Queen Joanna, and of Charles of Durazzo stand side by side. Poison hastened the end of the king, already seriously wounded, and he died on February 24. He left under the guardianship of Margaret two young children, Ladislaus and Joanna, whose fate afterwards gave them a worldwide celebrity.

Charles's death plunged his country into immediate anarchy. The Angevin faction wished to summon the heir of Duke Lewis from France and to set him on the throne, and the pretenders to the crown put forward by both parties were thus children under age, Ladislaus on one side and Lewis of Anjou on the other. Otto of Brunswick had pronounced in favor of Lewis. The husband of Joanna, who had previously obtained his liberty and had gone to Avignon, now returned with troops, and entered Naples on July 20, 1387, while Margaret, the fugitive widowed queen, shut herself up with her children in impregnable Gaeta.

Urban VI was at this time in Lucca, whence he went to Perugia, solely occupied with the thought of conquering Naples for his

nephew; he consequently recognized neither of the two pretenders. It was not until August 1388 that he left Perugia with 4000
spearmen, chiefly English, and advanced through Umbria. A fall
from his mule warned him. An aged hermit appeared before him
and said: "Thou wilt go to Rome, willingly or not; in Rome thou
wilt die." His excited imagination beheld the form of S. Peter hov-
ering over him as if showing him the way to Rome. The Romans
would forcibly have prevented his going to Naples, had not their
military strength been less than that of the pope. Urban was carried to Tivoli in a litter. He halted at Ferentino, whence he wished
to force his way into Neapolitan territory. The unpaid mercenaries had for the most part deserted him, and the fact induced
him to accept the invitation of the Romans and return to the city
in September.

Rome had meanwhile suffered severely from the war. Her enemies and those of the pope, the prefect, Count Honoratus, the
Orsini, the errant bands had devastated the Campagna, while
Catalan pirates laid waste the Maritima. Hunger and pestilence
were familiar guests in the city. It was steeped in filth and abject
poverty. Not even the entire independence to which the Capitol
had attained during Urban's long absence atoned for such a depth
of decay. After the senatorship of Charles of Durazzo had expired
according to agreement with the conquest of Naples (and in this
case also his invasion was a repetition of that of the first Anjou),
senators had governed Rome in succession until 1383, when the
conservators and *banderesi* assumed the sole government. They
had waged incessant war on Francesco of Vico; but finally this
tyrant—one of the most violent members of a family distinguished
by violence—fell victim to a revolt in Viterbo, when the populace
tore him in pieces. As early as May 10 the cardinal of Manupello
had been able again to take possession of Viterbo in the name
of the church, and this success was an additional ground for Urban's return to Rome, where he was received with honor.

His attendant Furies, however, immediately began their game
of dissension. The pope wished to subjugate the Capitol and of
his own authority to appoint a senator. The people consequently
made an armed attack on the Vatican. But a few days afterwards

the excommunicated *banderesi* were seen approaching S. Peter's barefoot, a cord round their necks, wearing the shirts of penitents and carrying burning tapers in their hands. They knelt before the penitentiary, who, seated on a high episcopal throne, touched their heads with a rod. Urban VI thus always showed himself a man of energy. Rome hated him, but nevertheless obeyed him more submissively than other popes.

Urban had meditated on the most efficacious means of reducing the Romans to subjection; he proclaimed that the jubilee should be celebrated every thirty-three years, and would have fixed it for 1390, had he not been overtaken by death. He passed away on October 15, 1389, in S. Peter's, where he lies buried. The virtues which this Neapolitan is said to have possessed—energy, love of justice, and simplicity of life—were distorted into contrary excesses by his savage disposition. Rude energy and coarse strength are not qualities that redound to the praise of a priest, and we cannot extol Urban for having possessed them. A pope at the end of the fourteenth century had no claim to the lenient judgment which his predecessors, living in barbarous ages, should receive from posterity. We do not therefore venture to palliate the diabolical nature of the man by alleging the party passions called forth by the schism which had just begun, although these passions were the causes of his fury. The judgment of contemporaries remains valid; namely, that Urban VI was a rude and inexorable tyrant. Dietrich of Niem, who knew him well, says, however, in his praise, that he was never guilty of an act of simony, never trafficked with spiritual dignities, yet on his death left more money than he had found in the treasury.

V

Papal Despotism,
Roman Anarchy,
and Neapolitan Force

Pietro Tomacelli, cardinal of S. Anastasia, a Neapolitan, was elected in Rome on November 2, 1389, and consecrated as Boniface IX on November 11. He was still young (only thirty), was a man of strong will, matured judgment, and blameless life. Aware of the errors of his predecessor's policy, he hastened to recognize the house of Durazzo and release it from the ban. His legate crowned the boyish Ladislaus as king of Naples in May 1390, and the Roman church again turned for support to this kingdom, its ancient vassal state.

A pope who was able to seat himself on the throne with the bull of jubilee in his hand, was secure of great advantages. The festival announced by Urban VI was celebrated in 1390, and although the schismatic nations [i.e., those loyal to the line of popes at Avignon] bore no part in it, pilgrims streamed from Germany, Hungary, Bohemia, Poland, and England to long desecrated Rome. The festival of the sacred jubilee had become a monetary speculation of the pope, who sent agents into every country and dispensed indulgences for the price of the journey to Rome. These

From book XII, ch. 4, secs. 1 and 2.

shameless agents collected from various provinces more than 100,000 gold florins. Money had become the great mainspring of the hierarchical financial establishment in Rome, which, to the mockery of Christendom, still called itself the church; for without money the war for her existence could not be carried on. The most deplorable abuses waxed daily; simony and usury were practiced unabashed. Contemporaries describe Boniface IX as a man of exceedingly defective education but of acute intelligence, as avaricious and unscrupulous beyond measure. During his pontificate he gave every ecclesiastical office for money or its equivalent, and enforced payment for every petition that he granted. He did not even scorn a few gold pieces, his maxim being that a little fish in the hand was worth a whale in the ocean. His relations, his avaricious mother and his two brothers incessantly accumulated wealth.

Boniface, like his predecessor, was also compelled to sell ecclesiastical property and to mortgage the treasures of the churches. In his desperate straits, and in order to reduce the number of his adversaries, he conferred a multitude of vicariates in the state of the church on magistrates and tyrants. After January 1390 he appointed Albert of Este vicar for Ferrara, Antonio Montefeltre for Urbino and Cagli, the Malatesta for Rimini, Fano, and Fossombrone, Lewis and Lippus Alidosi for Imola, Astorgius Manfredi for Faenza, Ordelaffo for Forli. On Fermo and Ascoli, and even on powerful Bologna, he conferred the vicariate in city and territory for twenty-five years. Inasmuch as these nobles and republics for a yearly tribute entered into this relation with the pope, they recognized his supremacy and pledged themselves to hold his enemies their enemies, his friends their friends. The dismemberment of the State of the Church into small hereditary states was consequently hastened. And Boniface IX in this wise acquired money and even found himself recognized once more as territorial ruler in the State of the Church, which no pope had done for a length of time. In a few years, by intelligence and energy, he regained the most influential towns, Perugia, Spoleto, Todi, Viterbo, Ancona, Bologna, to all of which he more or less secured their autonomy.

Soon after the jubilee the general feeling in Rome became hostile towards the pope; for the conservators and *banderesi* still maintained the freedom of the republic. No senator is anywhere to be found during this year. Disputes between the Curia and the conservators, who wished to render the papal court subject to their forum, produced causes of dissension. On September 11, 1391, Boniface consequently concluded a treaty with the Roman commune, by which the latter promised to recognize the immunity of the clergy, not to burthen the Curia with taxes, to restore the walls of the city and bridges, to contribute to the recovery of the Tuscan estates of the church, and to exhort all Roman barons to join an offensive and defensive league with the pope and the city. On March 5, 1392, he made a further treaty with Rome for the purpose of carrying on the war against the enemy in the patrimony. Both parties pledged themselves to equip a certain number of horsemen in order to fight the city prefect, John Sciarra, Galassus, and the bastard John of Vico. The pope emphatically declared that all the territories which these tyrants had seized, with the exception of Viterbo, Orchio, and Civita Vecchia, should belong to the Roman people. The Romans, who were speedily undeceived, readily lent their militia to fight against John Sciarra, who had seized Viterbo in 1391, and against the French companies in the pay of the antipope. They thus strengthened the pope, who well knew how to make use of their services. But they rose in 1392; weapon in hand, they forced their way into the Vatican, and, before the very eyes of the pope, dragged from the palace the canons of S. Peter's, who had refused to sell the property of the basilica, which the Romans had demanded for the purpose of defraying the expenses of the war. Boniface, insecure in the city, consequently seized the opportunity offered him by Perugia to leave Rome and then to force the city to recall him under favorable conditions.

Perugia, torn asunder by the factions of the Beccarini and Raspanti, invited the pope to appease the disturbances by his presence. The city offered him the full signory, and he went thither in October 1392. He remained a year, successfully occupied in recovering the Marches. Ancona, Camerino and Jesi, Fab-

riano and Matelica yielded submission. Even the prefect of the
city, sorely harassed by the Roman militia, sued for peace, and
the already repentant Romans ceded the dominion of Viterbo to
the papal legate. Meanwhile, in the summer of 1393, Boniface
left Perugia, where a revolution had broken out, and Biordo de
Michelotti had set up as tyrant, and went to Assisi. Roman envoys here urgently invited him to return, for the people dreaded
that he might establish his seat in Umbria—a fear that the pope
had already foreseen. He declared himself ready to return, but
under conditions which he sent to Rome. Their tenor was as follows: the pope should henceforth elect the senator, or if not, the
conservators invested with senatorial power should tender him
the oath of fealty. The senator should be restricted in his office
neither by the *banderesi* nor by any other magistrates. The Roman people were to undertake to keep open the roads to Narni
and Rieti, and out of the taxes of the Ripa and Ripetta to maintain a galley for the protection of navigation. The clergy and the
papal court were to be subject only to their legal forum, that is
to say, the courtiers of spiritual condition to the jurisdiction of
the auditor camerae; those of the secular to the marshal of the
pope; the Roman clergy to his vicar. Pope, cardinals and all were
to be exempt from tribute and taxes. The magistrates were not
on any pretext whatever to lay claim to the property of churches,
hospitals, or pious institutions in Rome. Two good men were to
be annually appointed as officers for the distribution of relief,
one by the pope, the other by the people. One thousand well
equipped horsemen were to be provided as escort for the return
of Boniface IX, and 10,000 gold florins to defray the expenses of
his journey. The pope sent these articles from Assisi to Rome,
where a council of one hundred citizens for each region and the
general council assembled with the magistrates to discuss them.
The parliament in presence of the cardinal of Todi and the abbot of S. Paul's concluded the treaty on the Capitol on August 8,
1393, accepting, and swearing to the conditions.

This memorable document remained in essentials the foundation for succeeding times of the political relations between the
pope and the city of Rome.

Boniface now returned at the end of 1393, and was received

with honors. He did not at first irritate the people by the appointment of a new senator; at least no such appointment is mentioned in the acts of the time. Meanwhile the treaty just concluded appeared to the demagogues injurious to the rights of the people. The discontent broke forth as early as May of the following year, and was chiefly caused by the *banderesi*, whose power Boniface had set himself to destroy. His own life was threatened, and it was solely due to the intervention of the young King Ladislaus that the danger was averted. In the autumn of 1394 Ladislaus came with a large military force to Rome, where he released the pope from his dangerous position.

At the same time, Clement VII died at Avignon on September 16, 1394. Boniface was thus released from an opponent who had incessantly disturbed Rome, while a long desired possibility of ending the schism presented itself. Since the chief necessity was now to prevent the election of a successor to Clement VII, the University of Paris hastened to prevent the cardinals at Avignon proceeding in the matter. But as early as September 26 the cardinals elected from their midst the Spaniard Peter de Luna as pope, and on October 3 seated their candidate as Benedict XIII on the schismatic throne at Avignon. All attempts made by synods and universities, and even by kings, to quell the schism were frustrated by the irreconcilable claims of the two disputants. The world was already growing accustomed to two churches and to two popes, with their so-called "obediences."

Benedict XIII at once strove to harass his Roman rival by enemies in the state of the church. Two tyrants stood in arms in Umbria, Biordo de Michelotti of Perugia, who had made himself master of Assisi, and Malatesta de Malatestis of Rimini, who had subjugated Todi. Honoratus of Fundi remained the most dangerous enemy in Campania. He sent letters to the Romans, inciting them to renounce Boniface and recognize Benedict. Some nobles, John and Nicholas Colonna and Paul Savelli, whose families had remained buried in unhistoric oblivion for nearly half a century, contemplated seizing the civic dominion. The people of Trastevere raised a revolt, which was, however, suppressed, and the region was punished by the loss of its civic rights. That Boniface was enabled to subdue repeated conspiracies was owing entirely to King Ladislaus. The great successes which this prince began to achieve over his opponents in the kingdom of Naples facilitated the subjugation of Rome and Campania to the pope. In the spring of 1397 Honoratus himself made peace with him, and soon after the Colonna also sought absolution.

The pope, who had firmly resolved to overthrow the popular government in Rome and to break the power of the guilds, now that that of the nobility had long been broken, at length succeeded in his object by adroitly utilizing a revolution which had been suppressed. In 1398 the Roman people agreed to the abolition of the *banderesi* and to the appointment of a senator; the prospect of the gains of the approaching jubilee of 1400 also played no small part in the complaisance of the Romans, whose avarice frequently proved traitor to their liberty. After the senatorial office had remained unfilled for several years, the pope appointed Angelus de Alaleonibus of Monte S. Maria in Giorgio as his vice-senator. But a great part of the people were seriously irritated. In concert with the count of Fundi a scheme was formed for the restoration of the government of the *banderesi*. The leaders of the conspiracy were Peter Sabba Juliani, Peter Cenci and Natolo Buci Natoli, all three former conservators. The revolution was to break out in August, and Count Honoratus was to attack the gate of S. Giovanni during the revolt. But the vigilance of the vice-senator frustrated the design, and the heads of the conspirators fell beneath the axe of the executioner on the steps of the Capitol. In the midst of the horrors of this execution Boniface IX became actually master of Rome. The rule of the *banderesi* was now for ever abolished; the dominion of the guilds disappeared, the societies of the archers and shield-bearers lost the political power which they had preserved for nearly fifty years, and the earlier system of administering Rome by a foreign senator appointed every half year by three conservators of the civic chamber was restored under the strengthened authority of the pope. Freedom took leave of the Capitol.

The revolution which Boniface had accomplished in the summer of 1398 forms an epoch in the civic history of Rome. From it we may trace the downfall of the republican independence of the Romans, who, after long efforts to form a permanent political state, renounced the task in despair. After the military nobles had been overthrown by Cola di Rienzo, the power of the citizens was also shattered, owing to their lack of internal cohesion. In 1398, for the first time, Rome recognized full *dominium* of a pope. On July 11, 1398, Boniface IX had appointed Malatesta Galeotti de Mallatestis of Rimini Senator for six months. The Romans at first opposed the appointment, but after the events in August no longer showed any resistance. The pope at the same time made Galeotti captain-general of the church, hoping by his means to repress all further attempts at revolt. Henceforward, until the death of Boniface, an uninterrupted series of foreign senators governed the subjugated republic.

In order to safeguard his power, Boniface IX caused the ruinous fortress of S. Angelo to be restored and provided with a tower. The Vatican palace was likewise converted into a stronghold, after the model of the papal fortress at Avignon; the palace of the senators on the Capitol, which had been destroyed in the fire under Cola di Rienzo, was rebuilt and fortified, in spite of the murmurs of the Romans, who complained that their communal palace was converted into a papal citadel. This structure was merely built of bricks, and was so rude that at a later time Flavius Biondus, ashamed of its aspect, lamented that this once magnificent Capitol no longer presented anything worth seeing beyond the church of the Franciscans in Aracoeli. Boniface also tried to restore ruined Ostia, in order to protect the entrance to the Tiber against Provençal and Catalan corsairs. He consequently removed the city of Ostia from the jurisdiction of the cardinal-bishop and placed it under the papal authority. The mouth of the Tiber again served as a station for some galleys, and again, for the first time after a long interval, a papal fleet makes its appearance. The pope appointed Gasper Cossa of Ischia as its admiral. His energy thus showed itself great and royal. But are ships of war, armies, and fortresses the objects which should form the care, and on which should repose the fame, of a high priest of religion?

The transition from the fourteenth to the fifteenth century could not be celebrated either in Rome or in the world, rent asunder as it was by the schism, as a festival worthy of mankind. Boniface IX, taking his place on the jubilee loggia of the eighth pope of the name, in order to invoke the blessing of heaven on the faithful, only called forth the curse of a second pope [in Avignon]. In spite of the speedy repetition of the indulgence, many pilgrims came to Rome even from France. The companies of flagellants also reappeared to call mankind, which was sunk in hatred and quarrels, to repentance. These companies first arose in Provence. Five thousand in number, they came to Genoa. Men and women, young and old, clad in white cowls, a red cross on their heads, they marched in twos and twos, preceded by choristers chanting hymns. They were called the Whites (Bianchi). Twenty-five thousand flagellants came from Modena to Bologna, where the population, donning the white habit, proceeded to Imola and encamped upon the field, and the bishop celebrated mass. The phenomenon was soon repeated throughout the whole of Italy. Thirty thousand Bianchi produced a movement of fanaticism even in Rome. False prophets announced the approaching end of the world; false miracles deceived the crowds, and scandals of every kind were practiced. The deluge having subsided, left pestilence as its dregs behind. The pope prohibited the companies of the Whites. But the masked confraternities which walk in procession through the cities of Italy to the present day still exist to remind us of these institutions of the Middle Ages.

The condition of Rome at this period offers but a barren subject to the historian. The sight of Boniface IX in the fortified Vatican, where, surrounded by lances like a secular prince, he led an anxious existence, amid storm and distress of every kind, carries us back to far remote times. He valiantly fought and conquered his enemies, but these enemies were only insignificant rebels, and his victories were not worthy of the papacy. Its great historic ideal of culture lay piteously shattered.

.   .   .   .

VI

Rome, Pawn of Territorial Principalities

THE death of a pope during the schism offered a favorable opportunity for the tranquilization of strife, since, by refraining from
holding any fresh election, one camp at least might have shown
the world that it earnestly desired peace. The fourteen Roman
cardinals were indeed doubtful whether or not they should give
a successor to Innocent VII. But self-seeking and fear drove them
into conclave on November 18, in order that the Roman church
should not be left without a visible head. They here signed a
solemn declaration that if any among them was created pope, he
should endeavor to effect a union and for its sake would renounce
the tiara. They moreover explained that they only elected a new
pope in order that he might act as "procurator" of the union. The
elected candidate was also to pledge himself not to appoint any
new cardinal.

On November 30 the choice fell on the cardinal of S. Marco,
the Venetian Angelo Correr, who ascended the sacred chair on
December 6, 1406. Gregory XII in his first consistory declared
that he would conscientiously abide by his oath. He assured his
hearers, "that to speed the union" he "would hasten over sea and
land; if by sea, even in a fishing boat, if by land, even with a pilgrim's staff." Thus spoke a man of eighty, whom the cardinals
had probably only elected because, according to human belief,

From book XII, ch. 5, sec. 1, 2, and 3.

ambition is generally changed into abnegation in the neighborhood of the grave. But they were deceived. A moment of trembling authority always seems so precious to old men wearing the
purple that their wearied selfishness reacquires the vigor of
youth. Gregory XII entrusted Leonardo Aretino with a letter to
his rival, in which he invited him to a joint abdication, and the
Spaniard, Peter de Luna, answered in a like spirit. Emissaries
went to and fro to arrange a meeting. Christendom demanded a
council with ever increasing urgency, for the church sank into
deeper ruin with each succeeding year. Annates, tithes, reservations, indulgences, and dispensations had drained the West by a
system of shameless robbery. The priestly office was everywhere
sold; the prelates accumulated enormous sums without ever visit-
ing their spiritual seats. Simon Magus was ruler of the church
and the apostolic camera resembled a Charybdis. The schism
had enormously increased the evil. In every country noble-
minded men fought against this terrible state of affairs and demanded a council. About 1393 Nicholas of Clemange, rector of the
Paris Academy and for many years secretary to the court of
Avignon, wrote his treatise, *On the Ruin of the Church*, or concerning her corrupt state, in which he enumerated all the evils
with which she was deformed, and traced these corruptions back
to their source, the avarice of the pope and clergy with regard
to temporal things. While he urged reform he gave utterance to
the significant saying: "The Church must first be humiliated and
then re-erected." The papacy had forfeited its moral elevation
and position. It had vanished like the empire, and was severed
into two divisions, each of which owed its crippled existence
solely to the protection of powerful monarchs. The great papacy
of Hildebrand and Innocent [III] sank to be an object of critical
investigation throughout the world, for kings, parliaments and
synods, the universities and public opinion rose as so many tribunals to subject to examination in the two contending popes the
papal office itself, in the contending cardinals the rights of the
Sacred College. The decretals, the fundamental laws of the
popes, were destroyed, and from this critical examination there
reissued once more powerful that Ghibelline or monarchical

right, in virtue of which the highest secular authority, the emperor, received the faculty of judging and deposing a pope by a council.

Benedict XIII and Gregory XII, constrained by the will of France, had concluded a treaty in Marseilles, by which they pledged themselves to hold a congress at Savona in September 1408. But both feigned a desire that they did not feel. Gregory, old and weak, was ruled by his nephews, with whom he spent his days in childish gluttony, and squandered the tithes which he extorted under pretext of the union. Ladislaus, moreover, opposed the reconciliation; the king of Naples had everything to gain by the continuance of the schism; while its tranquilization, and possibly a French pope, might deprive him not only of the protectorate over Rome, but also of his crown; for Lewis of Anjou, under the protection of his relation the king of France, still asserted his claim. As it now appeared that a congress to bring about the union would really be held, Ladislaus formed the scheme of preventing it by seizing Rome by a master stroke. The Romans had recognized the supremacy of the new pope, and had accepted at his hands John de Cymis from Cingoli as senator. They were consequently unfriendly to Ladislaus, although several barons desired his arrival.

At the king's instigation the Colonna with Neapolitan troops forced an entrance into the city through the broken walls by the Porta S. Lorenzo, on the night of June 17, 1407. Gregory XII immediately fled to S. Angelo. His condottiere, Paul Orsini, however, arrived the following morning from Castel Valca, entered the Vatican, joined the Corrers, the nephews of the pope, and hastened to meet the enemy at the gate of S. Lorenzo. John and Nicholas Colonna, Antonio Savelli, Jacopo Orsini, Conradin of Antioch fell into the hands of the victor. Rome lighted bonfires. The Colonna bought their release from the Orsini, but less privileged barons were beheaded on the Capitol, among them Galeotto Normanni, the "Knight of Liberty," Richard Sanguigni, and Con radin of Antioch, a descendant of the Hohenstaufens and the bearer of a name that was fatal to himself.

Dietrich of Niem maintains that Gregory XII was acquainted

with the king's design, that he purposely fled to S. Angelo in order to make it appear that he was besieged there, and that his journey to the congress might thus be prevented. If he actually cherished the hypocritical intention, it was frustrated by the attitude of the Romans and the independent will of Paul Orsini. Gregory had taken this brave man into his pay as captain of the State of the Church, and assigned him the revenues of the Romagna and other provinces. In recompense for his services he had bestowed upon him the vicariate of Narni, but had no money wherewith to satisfy his claims. He was even forced to pawn his valuable papal crown to the Florentine bankers, a disgraceful transaction, which may, however, serve to illustrate the degradation of the papacy of the age. Paul Orsini terrified the helpless Gregory by his demands, still more by his increasing influence. The wealthy general, a member of the foremost Guelf family in Rome, was now a second Ricimer. This induced Gregory to leave the city. A pope fled before a condottiere. He appointed Cardinal Peter Anibaldi Stefaneschi of S. Angelo as his vicar-general, and on August 9, 1407, went with his Curia to Viterbo, thence to repair to the congress at Savona, or so at least he announced.

Gregory's departure took place contrary to the will of the Romans, who dreaded the tyranny of the powerful Orsini, or foresaw the inevitable confusion in which the ambition of Ladislaus must involve them. For the rest, Paul remained with some thousand men as chief captain of the church and defender of the city, while the magistrates of the Capitol obeyed Cardinal Peter; the Senator John de Cymis had resigned his staff of office into the latter's hands, and the three conservators administered the Senate.

Gregory XII with eight cardinals went from Viterbo to Siena in September, where he was met by the French envoys and those of the other pope. Savona now seemed to him unsafe; he requested that the congress might assemble at some other place, but in vain. Insincere negotiations were carried on by both sides, and Gregory's avaricious nephews attained their object—the prolongation of the schism.

While the pope remained absent, and the State of the Church

resembled a property without a master, the king of Naples attempted to make himself ruler of Rome. Here all was terror and confusion. On January 1 the cardinal-legate imposed a tax of 30,000 florins on the clergy of the city; they met in the Convent della Rosa and resolved neither to pay anything nor to celebrate mass. The magistrates imprisoned several priests; the others yielded to force. Massive images of saints and vessels were melted down, for so the pope commanded. Famine set in, processions were made, the handkerchief of S. Veronica was exhibited, but no bread was forthcoming. The increase of taxation irritated the people, robbery was rife in every street, a procession of 100 pilgrims was massacred by the soldiers of the Orsini. Many Romans now longed for Ladislaus, from whom they hoped for order and abundance. The king with a powerful army was already in motion. In these circumstances the cardinal-legate held it fitting to restore the ancient power to the people. On April 11 he reinstated the *banderesi*, received from them the oath of fidelity in the Vatican, and gave them the banner. Amid the sound of trumpets, the popular magistrate then made his entry into the Capitol, on the steps of which he was respectfully greeted by the captains of the regions. Thus was democratic rule restored in Rome for the last time; the people, however, soon enough recognized that it had become incapable of maintaining freedom.

A few days after, the king appeared before Rome with a numerous force, while his galleys anchored at the mouth of the Tiber. Paul Battista di Giovio, a Roman captain, held the fortress of Ostia for the church, but, being badly provisioned, it capitulated as early as April 18. On April 20 the king removed his camp to the neighborhood of S. Paul's. With him were distinguished captains, the count of Troja, the count of Carrara, Gentile de Monterano, the two Colonnas, Battista Savelli and Migliorati. The last, banished from Ancona by Gregory XII, had taken Ascoli and Fermo and given them to Ladislaus, whose service he had entered immediately after. The king caused a bridge of boats to be placed across the Tiber. Paul Orsini remained in Rome with 1400 horse and with foot soldiers; the walls of the city had been strengthened by barricades; a successful defense was not impossible, since the Romans had frequently overcome much greater difficulties. But they were crippled by famine, disunion, and treachery, and the rapid conquest of Rome by Ladislaus shows that the civic republic had expired. In the beginning of the fifteenth century, none of the three principles through whose struggle with each other a great party life so long had been preserved, remained vigorous. Everything was in process of dissolution; the aristocracy as well as the middle class, the municipal spirit, the imperium, and the papacy. Owing to the schism, Rome had even fallen into the humble position of a provincial city. She might consequently become the prey of the first successful conqueror, without her fall producing any perceptible change in the world. This want of self-reliance in itself explains her incapacity for resistance. Her defense, moreover, was entrusted to a general of condottieri, whose services were open to the highest bidder. Paul Orsini carried on negotiations with Ladislaus, who offered him gold and honors in return for the surrender of Rome. The Romans, learning of these negotiations, denounced Orsini as a traitor to his country, and themselves hastened to avert the ruin that threatened. Envoys of the people appeared in the royal camp, and on April 21 a treaty was concluded, by which all fortresses and the Capitol were made over to Ladislaus, and the popular government placed the authority in his hands. The *banderesi* immediately resigned; Janottus Torti, the senator appointed by the king, ascended the Capitol, and Neapolitan troops entered the city.

The kings of Naples—Normans, Swabians, the Angevins—all directed their ambitious gaze towards the fortress of the Capitol; the danger for the popes was consequently great, and in their secular history there is perhaps nothing more surprising than the fact that, from the beginning, they had been able to reduce the only monarchs in Italy into vassals of the church. These Neapolitans occasionally rose to the honor of becoming senators of Rome, but none of them succeeded in grasping the scepter of Caesar. Ladislaus, the conqueror of the city, was more powerful than any of his predecessors, and a great future seemed to open before him. In the monastery of S. Paul, where he made his abode, the young monarch arrayed himself for his magnificent entry, as his ancestor, Charles of Anjou, had done in the same building. He entered Rome on April 25. But as S. Angelo still adhered to the pope, he made his way through Trastevere, riding under a *baldacchino* upheld by eight barons, accompanied by the Romans bearing palm branches and torches. The pealing of bells and bonfires in the evening announced the saddest of all festivals, the fall of Rome under the authority of a king. He made his dwelling and remained at S. Crisogono. The same day Paul Orsini, now the servant of Naples, departed for Castel Valca; the gates and bridges of the city were surrendered, the latter being walled up by the king's command. He forthwith arbitrarily elected a fresh set of conservators, captains of regions, and other magistrates; the constitutional liberty of communal election had already been set aside by Gregory XII and Cardinal Stefaneschi. The places also in the city territory, Velletri, Tivoli, Cori, and others, did homage to the king and received his castellans. Envoys from Florence, Siena, and Lucca appeared to congratulate him on his triumph over Rome and to form an alliance with him. His troops entered the Patrimony and Umbria, where Perugia, Todi, Amelia, Orte, Rieti, Assisi immediately recognized him as signor. He thus annexed the provinces of the State of the Church to his Neapolitan kingdom.

The monarchy of Italy and the imperial crown itself floated before his audacious brain. He had the motto, *"Aut Caesar aut nihil* [Caesar or nothing]," embroidered on his mantle. It is said that he coveted the title of king of the Romans, but that the people refused it, explaining that they had a Caesar already. Their king was Rupert of the Palatinate, a prince who must have been ashamed of the conquest of Rome. But another German perhaps felt the disgrace more deeply than he. Dietrich of Niem, who had left the city before the entrance of the Neapolitans, addressed a letter of admonition to Rupert, in which he took upon himself the mission of Dante and Petrarch, and exhorted the indolent king of the Romans to remember the glory of the German emperors, to gird his loins with the sword and to restore the empire.

The senator ruled the city for Ladislaus with iron severity;

every attempt at revolt was punished with the axe. But no excess was committed. The magnificent person of the young king, whom the whole of Italy began to regard as the man of the future, won the people to his side, and the abundance of food which he provided, as also his strict justice, were the best supports of his power. Occupied with schemes for the conquest of central Italy, he remained in Rome until June 24, 1408. Before he left he ordered the foremost barons, among them the Colonna and Savelli, to remain at a distance from the city until his return. As guardians of the city, he appointed the senator, his marshal, Christopher Gaetani, count of Fundi, the conservators, and captains of regions. Leaving the count of Troja with troops behind for a time, he returned to Naples.

In other circumstances the conquest of the city by Ladislaus would have been an important event. Even Benedict XIII had formed the audacious design of making himself master of Rome, and of seating himself as Roman pope on the throne which his rival left vacant. He consequently sent Genoese galleys to the mouth of the Tiber, but this fleet only left Genoa the same day that Ladislaus made his entry to Rome. Gregory XII was by no means dismayed by the usurpation of the king. If acquainted with the designs of his rival, he would undoubtedly have wished that Ladislaus rather than Peter de Luna should occupy Rome. When his legate appeared before him as a fugitive in Lucca, he received him without reproaches; on the contrary, with such proofs of recognition as to occasion the belief that the cardinal had acted according to the pope's commands. It was said that with his sanction Paul Orsini had betrayed Rome and occupied the State of the Church; and, in truth, so little indignant was Gregory with Ladislaus, that he raised no protest, but still allowed his nuncio to remain with the king. The conquest of Rome and the Patrimonies afforded him and his nephews a pretext for preventing the work of union.

The arts which the two popes employed, each for the purpose of stigmatizing the other as the sole cause of the continuance of the schism, while they were only unanimous in preventing the union, presents an offensive spectacle of intriguing selfishness. The deluded world was tired of the sight, and at last tore the artful net in which the church was entangled. After the failure of the proposed congress at Savona, the popes had made reciprocal advances; Benedict XIII had come to Porto Venere, and Gregory XII had gone from Siena to Lucca, where he had sought protection from Paul Guinigi, signor of this city. They exchanged embassies, proposals, and reproaches. What one wove the other destroyed. What one proposed the other overthrew. Never was a more shameless game played with the deepest needs of humanity. Gregory XII, entirely devoid of means, without mercenaries but such as the Corrers had collected, raised a cry over the galleys which stood at command of his rival. For the shrewd Benedict XIII leaned on the power of Boucicault, the governor for the French king in Genoa; and Gregory, not without reason, complained that he could not go to the seaports which the congress had proposed, since these were unsafe. When Benedict now undertook the vain expedition with Genoese galleys against Rome, the enterprise offered his rival a welcome pretext for breaking off negotiations. The cardinals, the envoys of France, Venice, and the Florentines assailed him every day; a preaching friar in Lucca denounced him as a godless breaker of his word; the pope ordered the bold orator to be imprisoned, and refused any longer to discuss the union.

Meanwhile Benedict XIII lost his earlier support. In January 1408 the French king by edict commanded that, unless the schism were ended by Ascension Day, no obedience should be rendered to either pope. Benedict, on the other hand, issued a bull threatening excommunication, which provoked the French parliament and the University of Paris into declaring him deposed. His adversary triumphed for a moment; forgetful of the oath by which he had promised to appoint no new cardinal, he made four. This step excited the anger of his college of cardinals, whom he had already in suspicion surrounded with armed men and confined like prisoners. The cardinal of Liége secretly left Lucca on May 11, and, vainly pursued by Paul Correr with cavalry, betook himself to Castel Libra Fracta in Pisan territory. Amid violent tumult he was followed by six other princes of the church, who remembered the fate of the cardinals of Urban VI. They all assembled at Pisa, where, in appealing to a council, they adopted the only practical course that could save the church. The shout of "Council" resounded instantaneously throughout the world, conditions had become ripe for it, and for the moment both rivals were disarmed. Benedict XIII, defenseless in Genoa as in Avignon, embarked at Porto Venere on June 17, and fled to his home at Perpignan, where he had summoned a council for November 1. The unyielding Spaniard henceforward defied his fate with a spirit that in a nobler cause would have made him appear great. In his strength of will and astuteness, Peter de Luna was in fact an unlucky successor to Hildebrand and Alexander III, appointed to fill a wrong place and to live at a wrong time in the world's history, where his rare energy was uselessly thrown away.

The French cardinals had deserted Benedict XIII. Encouraged by the king of France and the opinion of the University of Paris, they had gone to Leghorn. Here for the first time the two hostile colleges saw and associated with each other, and henceforward formed the elements out of which sprang the council. This they unanimously demanded, and appointed to meet at Pisa on March 25, 1409. Gregory XII, seeing the danger before him, also convoked a council, which was to meet at Whitsuntide the following year at a place yet to be determined in the province of Aquileja or Ravenna; and Christendom, which so long had vainly sighed for a council, was now confronted with the prospect of not one but three. Gregory now wished to leave Lucca and return to Rome. He demanded that Ladislaus should send troops to escort him, but the suspicious Florentines raised an armed protest. He resolved to go to the Marches, where he could place himself under the protection of his adherent, Carlo Malatesta; but Baldassare Cossa seemed as though he would refuse him passage. From the time of Boniface IX, Cossa had remained as legate in Bologna, where he had constituted himself ruler. Faithlessly and by violence he had annexed a part of the Romagna; and while the State of the Church fell to pieces, he remained there an independent tyrant. Innocent VII had not ventured to deprive this intriguing Neapolitan of the legation of Bologna, but had threatened to do so, and it was consequently said that the cardinal caused him to be poisoned by the bishop of Fermo. As Gregory XII now wavered, Cossa did everything to hasten his fall. The prospect of the papal crown stood before his ambitious gaze. He soon became the soul of all the negotiations that concerned the council. He openly severed himself from Gregory, and formed an alliance with the Florentines against Ladislaus, who was still able to support the latter pope, and was the only prince who would prevent the union. Gregory XII had meanwhile gone from Lucca to Siena, with which Ladislaus was in alliance. He here excommunicated Cossa and the other princes of the church who had deserted him, and created new cardinals. At the beginning of November he went to Malatesta at Rimini and held negotiations with Ladislaus.

The king, threatened by the events which were shaping themselves at Pisa, was resolved to uphold Gregory. In his necessity the pope—and the action was unprecedented in the annals of the church—had ceded to him Rome, and even the entire State of the Church, for the trifling sum of 25,000 gold florins. In consequence of this agreement Ladislaus set forth in March 1409 to march by Rome to Tuscany, and, if possible, to dissolve the council. He came to the city on March 12. He remained sixteen days in the Vatican. On March 28 he advanced with Paul Orsini to Tuscany, turned back, curiously enough, on account of bad weather, and on April 2 again marched out toward Viterbo. He took Cortona, and proceeded to Arezzo and to the neighborhood of Siena; but the league of the Florentines and Siennese, which had been brought about by Cossa, set a limit to his progress and delivered the Council from every danger. Finally, the election of a new pope changed the condition of affairs.

The council had been opened at Pisa on March 25, 1409. This illustrious Ghibelline city had but now closed her once splendid career as a free republic. After a heroic resistance, which embellished her fall, she was not conquered by the swords of the Florentines, but for vile money was betrayed to her hereditary enemy by her Doge Giovanni Gambacorta. As Milan also lay powerless, the

Florentines took the foremost place in Italy next to the Venetians. Under their protection the prelates and envoys of kings, princes, and peoples, even plenipotentiaries of universities, and more than a hundred magistrates of both civil and canon law, assembled—a significant sign of the new power which learning, now become independent in Europe, had acquired. Rupert's ambassadors also appeared to defend the rights of Gregory XII, who was still recognized in the German empire. The Council of Pisa, summoned by cardinals without intervention of the pope, forms an epoch in the history of the church. From the canonical point of view it was an act of open rebellion against the pope, and from the first it found itself involved in the most glaring inconsistencies. The twenty-three cardinals who convoked it had refused obedience to their pope, on one side to Gregory XII, on the other to Benedict XIII, and consequently they required that these popes should recognize them as their accusers and judges; they finally formed a college of judges, each side of which held the other as schismatic. But Christendom represented by deputies beside these cardinals, recognized a revolutionary decision, and for the first time all classes rose to form a tribunal, which cited the papacy before it. The theory of the celebrated Gerson, that the church was church even without the pope, and that the pope was subject to the council, obtained recognition at the council of Pisa. This was the first real step towards the deliverance of the world from the papal hierarchy; it was already the Reformation.

The synod constituted itself as a Christian congress, as a legal and ecumenical council, which represented the visible church. On the memorable day of June 5, 1409, it pronounced the sentence that Benedict XIII and Gregory XII, as schismatics and heretics, were excommunicated and deprived of every spiritual office. The council proceeded to the election of a universal pope. Forced by the assembly, the cardinals pledged themselves that whichever of them issued from the conclave as pope was not to dissolve the council until the reform of the church had been carried through. Cossa, who perceived that his time had not yet come, may have preferred provisionally to be the master of a pontiff appointed to stop a gap; he proposed an old man of seventy, of blameless life and feeble will, and Alexander V was proclaimed pope on June 17.

The pope created by the council was neither a Frenchman nor an Italian, but with prudent discernment had been chosen from a nationality indifferent to all. Pietro Filargo was a native of the island of Candia, which belonged to the Venetians; himself of obscure origin, he had no nephews. It was said that he had known neither father nor mother. As a beggar-boy he had been brought up on the island by Italian Minorites; then, having entered their order, he had travelled to Italy, England, and France, where he educated himself in science, like the English beggar who had risen to fame as Adrian IV. As protégé of Galeazzo, who invited him to Lombardy, and for whom he carried on negotiations with Wenceslaus for the title of duke, Filargo became bishop of Novara, Brescia, and Piacenza, patriarch of Grado, archbishop of Milan, and was made cardinal of the Twelve Apostles by Innocent VII. On July 7, 1409, he took the papal crown, and thus, after more than seven centuries, a Greek again ascended the sacred chair, the last pope of this nationality having been John VII, in 705.

Meanwhile Benedict XIII at Perpignan and Gregory XII in Cividale had held synods, and each had protested against the Council of Pisa and its pope. Each by bulls demanded that Christendom should recognize himself as legitimate head of the church, and each still found recognition—one in Aragon and Scotland, the other in Naples, Friuli, Hungary, and Bavaria and with the king of the Romans. Christendom had now three popes, each of whom claimed legality, and who excommunicated one another. Of Alexander's rivals the weakest was Benedict XIII, who was beyond reach and harmless in a fortress in distant Spain. Gregory XII, on the contrary, was under the protection of the most powerful monarch of Italy, to whose territory he soon repaired. The first task of the pope elected by the council must consequently be that of crushing Gregory—a task which could only be accomplished by an expedition against Ladislaus himself.

Alexander V excommunicated the king and set up a pretender; for already the youthful Lewis of Anjou had hastened to Pisa to assert his rights to Naples, and already had united with Florence, Siena, and the cardinal-legate in a league against Ladislaus. The king was immediately forced to quit Tuscany, where he left Paul Orsini behind with troops; the allied army then set forth, led by Malatesta de Malatestis, under whom served Sforza of Attendolo and Braccio da Montone, captains with whose names Italy soon resounded. With them were Cossa himself and Anjou. The defection of the Orsini to their side opened the roads into the State of the Church, so that all the country to the gates of Rome did homage to Alexander V.

The allied army appeared before the city on October 1. Here the count of Troja and the Colonna lay in strong positions, while Janottus Torti held the Capitol, and S. Angelo under Vittuccio Vitelleschi remained neutral. The Neapolitans had banished many citizens, even sent some as prisoners to Naples; the pressure of their arms consequently forced the Romans to energetic resistance. True, the allies were able to force an entrance to the portico of S. Peter on October 1, whereupon the fortress opened fire on the Neapolitans and raised the flag of Alexander V. They did not, however, succeed in entering the city, but withdrew on the 10th, crossed the Tiber near Monte Rotondo, and attempted an attack on the northeast side. It failed, as did other repeated attacks, and the unexpected resistance of Rome seemed to threaten the failure of the whole costly enterprise. Lewis of Anjou and Cossa returned discouraged to Pisa, while Malatesta and Paul Orsini continued the siege. Ladislaus consequently committed a great mistake in failing to come in person to deliver Rome.

On December 23 Malatesta encamped near S. Agnese, and the same night Paul Orsini again entered the Borgo. The count of Troja here hoped to annihilate him, but himself suffered a defeat near the Porta Septimiana, which closed Trastevere. This decided the fate of the city. For here Alexander's party only waited the first opportunity to rise, and Malatesta had entered into correspondence with Cola di Lello Cerbello, a respected Roman, to whom he offered large sums of money if he incited the people to revolt. On the eve of S. Silvestro the cry, "Long live the

358

church and the people," was raised in the regions Parione and Regola, and was reechoed throughout Rome. Paul Orsini immediately entered Trastevere with Lorenzo Anibaldi; on New Year's morning, 1410, with others of his house, he crossed the Bridge of the Jews to the Campo di Fiore, where he found the people assembled, pronounced the Neapolitan rule at an end, and installed new officials. The same day Malatesta and Francesco Orsini also entered. On January 5 the senator laid down his arms on the Capitol; the Neapolitan guards at the city gates did the same, though not until after a brave resistance. The Porta S. Paolo was especially strong, almost a fortress in itself, as is still evident, and for the first time in Rome's history the tomb of Caius Cestius was transformed into a bastion with breastworks. The chronicler of Rome saw with surprise a great gun mounted on Monte Testaccio, which directed its fire against the Porta S. Paolo. This and the Porta Appia fell on January 8. On February 15 the Gate of S. Lorenzo and the Porta Maggiore were taken by assault, and, after Ponte Molle had surrendered on May 1, the entire city did homage to Alexander V.

Nothing now prevented Alexander from responding to the summons of the Romans and taking his seat in S. Peter's. He had announced a new council to deal with the reform in three years, had left Pisa and gone to Pistoja, intending to proceed to Rome. But the astute Cossa induced him to remain in Bologna, and the characterless pope yielded to the orders of the cardinal to whom he owed the tiara. On February 12 an embassy of the Romans presented him with the keys and the banner of the city, with the urgent request that he would enter Rome as its ruler; the Florentines also expressed the same desire. Alexander V received the *dominium* from the hands of these envoys, and on March 1 confirmed by charter the liberties of the Roman commune. The form of the government of the city and the most important magistracies at this time are revealed by this document. They were as follows: A foreign senator, who remained in office for six months; a foreign captain and judge of appeal with two notaries; a chamberlain; the thirteen captains of regions; a civic council of thirty-nine men; sixty constables; a protonotary; four marshals; two chancellors; two syndics of the Roman people; two secretaries of the Senate; two tax collectors (*gabellarii*); an overseer of the customs for the salt (*dohanerius salis*); two syndics for all officials; two overseers of the buildings (*magistri edificiorum*).

The pope had sincerely intended soon going to Rome, but death overtook him at Bologna on May 3, 1410. If we may credit malicious rumor, this pope also was hastened on his way to eternity by Baldassare Cossa. According to the belief of contemporaries, Alexander V was a liberal and learned man, but a good-natured glutton, and without a will of his own. On the sacred chair he found himself reduced to such straits that he was reminded of his early days; and speaking of himself said, "As bishop I was rich; as cardinal poor; as pope a beggar."

The most influential of the cardinals had now only to desire the crown in order to obtain it. He made an apparent resistance to his election, but had he not gained the votes of the conclave by fear and gold, they would have been extorted in his favor by the swords of his mercenaries. Moreover, Lewis of Anjou, who was preparing for his expedition against Ladislaus, supported the elevation of Cossa, from whom he promised himself the possession of Naples. The eighteen cardinals assembled in Bologna elected the dreaded man on May 17, and on the 25th crowned him as John XXIII in the cathedral of S. Petronio.

Baldassare Cossa was descended from a noble Neapolitan house. In his youth he and his brothers are said to have followed the lucrative occupation of corsairs. He afterwards became a distinguished soldier, and then went to the University of Bologna, where he led a dissolute life. Boniface IX had made him archdeacon and had brought him as his chamberlain to Rome. In the Curia, where fortune appears in portentous form, he had utilized his office to acquire wealth by indulgences and other means of usury. He had become cardinal of S. Eustachio, and had finally returned as legate to Bologna, where he shrank from no measures to retain dominion over the Romagna. His contemporaries unanimously pronounced him as great a man in all secular matters as he was ignorant and useless in spiritual. Nor were there wanting voices of indignation called forth by the election of a pope who had acquired his reputation not by any service but by many crimes, whose sacred dignity was disgraced not only by his past, but also by the suspicion of having been the murderer of two popes.

Shortly before Cossa's elevation, Rupert, the blameless but also inglorious, king of the Romans, died on May 18. John XXIII consequently hastened to send his nuncios to Germany, in order to procure the election of Sigismund, king of Hungary and brother of the dethroned Wenceslaus. In him he hoped to gain an assistant against Ladislaus. Sigismund was elected king of the Romans at Frankfort on September 20. True that on October 1 another faction put forward the aged Margrave Jobst of Moravia, a member of the same house of Luxemburg. But he died as early as January 8, 1411, when Sigismund once more was unanimously elected at Frankfort on July 21. He immediately recognized John XXIII as lawful pope.

Rome rendered homage without hesitation, and accepted Ruggiero di Antigliola of Perugia, the senator whom he had appointed. Meanwhile Paul Orsini as captain of the church, eagerly continued the war against the adherents of King Ladislaus. Several cities surrendered to him, even the Colonna offered peace; Battista Savelli also made submission. John XXIII consequently found himself in tranquil possession of the city and its territory, while his rival Gregory XII in Fundi or Gaeta found an asylum under the protection of King Ladislaus. In order to further the expedition against Naples, Lewis of Anjou came to Rome on September 20. On December 31 he went hence with Paul Orsini to Bologna, where he urged John XXIII to accompany him to Rome. The Romans also invited the pope to return.

The army was equipped from the proceeds of the taxes from the provinces and the treasuries of the churches, and the services of the most celebrated captains of the time, Paul Orsini, Sforza, Gentile de Monterano, Braccio of Montone, seemed to assure victory to the Angevin. The expedition left Bologna on April 1, 1411. John XXIII and all the cardinals were accompanied by Lewis and several French and Italian nobles, and followed by the main body of the army. On April 11 they reached S. Pancrazio; the following day, amid the rejoicings of the now subdued Romans, the pope made his entry into S. Peter's, where the magistrates, carrying tapers, appeared before him to do homage. On April 23 he consecrated the banners, which he committed to the Angevin and the Orsini; and a few days later the pretender, accompanied by the cardinal-legate, Pietro Stefaneschi, with 12,000 horse and numerous infantry, proceeded to the conquest of Naples along the same road that Charles I, Charles of Durazzo, and so many other conquerors had taken.

Unhindered, he entered the kingdom near Ceprano. The brilliant victory at Rocca Secca on May 19, 1411, would have cost Ladislaus the throne had the victor made use of it. The king escaped with difficulty. He collected his troops at S. Germano, astonished that he was allowed time to do so. "The first day after my defeat," he said, "the enemy had me in his hand, the second he had my kingdom, the third he had neither my person nor my kingdom." From the field of battle Lewis sent to Rome as trophies the flags that had been captured of the king and Gregory XII. John XXIII received them with transports of joy. The festival which he celebrated is significant of the spirit of the papacy of the age, from which the priestly character had entirely disappeared. John had these flags erected in S. Peter's, in order that they might be seen by the whole of Rome; they were then torn down, and, while the pope advanced in procession through the city, they were dragged behind him in the dust. Such was the form in which the head of the holy church showed himself fourteen centuries after Christ. Terrible news, however, soon arrived; the battle near Rocca Secca had been no such day as Benevento or Tagliacozzo; for the defeated king soon stood with a fresh army in the field and in such a strong position that his enemies did not venture to attack him. Penury ruled in their camp; they were severed by discord; the Angevin accused Paul Orsini of treachery, because he had not pursued the king. The unfortunate pretender returned to Rome as early as July 12, with a victorious but shattered army. He embarked at the Ripa Grande on August 3, in order once more to return to Provence without a

crown; not one of the disillusioned Roman barons offered him
an escort of honor.

The failure of the great enterprise was fatal for John XXIII,
for the power of Ladislaus remained unbroken. The king gained
the Florentines by the sale of Cortona; they consequently abandoned the league with the pope, who was further weakened by
the defection of Bologna. This city, which Cossa had ruled so
long as tyrant, scarcely saw him leave its walls as pope, when it
raised the old cry, "The people! The people!" expelled the cardi-
nal-vicar, and reasserted its freedom. These various events inspired Gregory with fresh courage. What did it avail that his
adversary again excommunicated Ladislaus and preached the
crusade against him? The king could appear before Rome without encountering any great resistance, and the people were irritated by excessive taxation. The mercenaries were not to be
trusted; the captains Sforza and Orsini were at variance, and
might become traitors any moment. The Pope, filled with suspicion, consequently entrenched himself in the Vatican and
united the palace with S. Angelo by a walled-in passage. Gallows
and the headsman's axe punished the malcontents on the Capitol, where Riccardus de Alidosiis had ruled with severity as
senator since August 27, 1411. Rome remained obedient, but the
infidelity of the captains of the mercenaries placed John XXIII
in no slight perplexity.

Sforza d'Attendolo, now in the service of the church, was the
younger rival of Paul Orsini. The celebrated condottiere, who derived his name from his herculean strength, was a native of Cotognola in the Romagna, where he was born about 1369. He had
rapidly risen from obscure beginnings. It is said that as a
youth he had earned his living with a mattock; that, disgusted
with his humble fate, he one day threw his tool against a
lofty oak, resolving that if it fell he would remain a peasant, if
it stuck in the tree he would take service under one of the captains
with whose renown the youthful imagination of Italy was then
fired. The peasant's son mounted a horse and in time became
grand constable of Naples and father of the Duke of Milan. The
wars of the popes in Naples gave Sforza opportunity of displaying

his military and political genius. John XXIII, rendered increasingly anxious by the fear of Ladislaus, summoned both his captains to Rome as council of war. They quarrelled. Sforza, whom Ladislaus had already won to his side, left the city with his company, and pitched his quarters on the Algidus in June 1412. The pope sent a cardinal with 36,000 gold florins to persuade him to return, but the defiant captain soon openly entered the service of the king, and advanced to Ostia, where he assumed a hostile attitude. The pope exposed the traitor in effigy on all the gates and bridges of the city, hanging to the gallows by the right foot, a peasant's axe in right hand, in the left a scroll which said, "I am Sforza of Cotognola, a traitor who, contrary to honor, have twelve times broken my faith to the church."

The defection of Sforza, the revolt of the prefect of Vico, who held Civita Vecchia with the help of the Neapolitans, the apostacy of other barons, and the irritated mood of the Romans finally compelled John to change his policy and with diplomatic skill to draw the king into the net of his intrigues. As early as June, papal envoys negotiated a peace. The same Cossa, who had been the most eager advocate of the Neapolitan enterprise, now declared himself ready to betray the Angevin, if Ladislaus betrayed Gregory XII. He offered to recognize him as king, to make him standard-bearer of the church, to pay him large sums of money for the release of Cossa his relation, and to surrender Ascoli, Viterbo, Perugia, and Benevento as mortgages. In return Ladislaus was to recognize him as pope, to place one thousand lances at the disposal of the church, to persuade Gregory XII to resign, or banish him from the kingdom. Ladislaus evidently dreaded the repetition of the Angevin enterprise; the king of France exhorted him to renounce Gregory. He was threatened by Sigismund, king of the Romans, whom, as pretender to the throne of Hungary, he had made his enemy, and who, being a strong man, intended to assert the claims of the empire in Italy, and he therefore resolved to form a compact with John XXIII. The unexpected treaty of peace was concluded at Naples in June 1412, and was proclaimed in Rome on October 19. It was dishonorable to both sides. In order to save appearances, the king convoked a synod of bishops and magisters in Naples; this assembly immediately discovered that Gregory XII unlawfully called himself pope, and was manifestly a heretic. Ladislaus now would have had no scruple in selling his protégé, and it was only the flight of the betrayed pope that saved him from this last disgrace. The aged Gregory was at his wits' end when one day, to his extreme surprise, he received the command to leave the kingdom as soon as possible. But the accidental arrival of two Venetian trading ships in the port of Gaeta helped him in his need. On October 31 he embarked on one of these vessels with his few friends or relations, among whom was his nephew, Cardinal Condulmer, afterwards Eugenius IV, and, in deadly terror of corsairs and enemies, sailed through the two Italian seas until he reached the coast of Slavonia. He was thence transported by another vessel to Cesena, where Carlo Malatesta appeared and offered him an honorable escort and an asylum at Rimini. The successor of the celebrated lords of Rimini was the sole but powerless prince who espoused Gregory's cause. His unswerving loyalty—judge the motives that inspired it how we may—commands respect, and shines all the more brightly in contrast with the disgraceful treachery of Ladislaus.

The treaty with John was, moreover, a very important step towards the tranquilization of the schism; for Gregory XII thus forfeited his last support of political importance, and events soon followed that compelled John XXIII also to appear before [the Council of Constance,] the tribunal that was to judge all three popes.

VII

Anarchy under
Pope Innocent VIII (1484-92)

The Council of Constance (1414–18) healed the Great Schism by deposing all three claimants to the papal throne. Under the guidance of Emperor Sigismund, the council elected Pope Martin V, obliging him to undertake general reform of the church. But the reform program was never enacted. The popes concentrated their efforts on dismantling the remnants of republican government in Rome and establishing the papal government as a territorial principality. Factionalism continued to hamper their efforts, however, and the work was far from complete toward the end of the fifteenth century, in the pontificate of Innocent VIII.— EDITOR.

THE death of Sixtus IV was the signal for the insurrection of the adverse party, which had been so long suppressed. Rome was filled with wildest tumult. Hell seemed to be let loose. Friends and enemies, barons, citizens and cardinals barricaded their houses, while the people, in their indignation at the grasping rule of Sixtus's nephews, sacked the palace of Riario near S. Apollinare and plundered the granaries and the banks of the Genoese moneychangers....

From book XIII, ch. 4, sec. 1.

The Campagna lay in ruins, and nothing was to be seen but the charred remains of cultivated places and troops of beggars and robbers. Revenge and deeds of violence of every kind, the consequences of these wars, form the stamp of Roman society from the days of Sixtus IV onwards; and it is not perhaps merely because we possess the minute diaries of two Romans for precisely this period, that this society appears in such an extraordinary state of brutalization. Rather is it that the Italian character in general, in the last thirty years of the fifteenth century, displays a trait of diabolical passion; tyrannicide, conspiracies, deeds of treachery are universal; a criminal selfishness reigns supreme, and a terrible doctrine is evolved, that the end justifies the means. We read with a shudder of the wholesale massacre of the Neapolitan barons, concerning which, after some feeble remonstrances, the weak pope remained timidly silent. But the massacre excites less horror than the fact that it only produced fear; nowhere indignation. The time of the desecration of the Christian religion was also the epoch of the struggle for the formation of monarchies in Europe. The same traits of fiendish cruelty and egotism are seen in England during the Wars of the Roses, in France under the dominion of Lewis XI, in Spain in the fanaticism of the wars against the Moors. In the history of the papacy and of the papal nephews the same spirit becomes still more appalling than at the court of Lewis XI or Ferrante.

Innocent VIII, having unchained anarchy in the last disastrous war, was no longer able to curb it. Vainly he issued edicts against the assassins and robbers. Each morning revealed the horrors of the night, bodies of men who had been stabbed lying in the streets. Pilgrims and even ambassadors were robbed outside the gates of the city. The judges were either powerless or corrupt. The pope's family unblushingly sold justice. The vice-chamberlain, asked why the malefactors were not punished, answered with a smile, in presence of the historian Infessura, "God wills not the death of a sinner, but that he should live and pay." Criminals, if insolent, were hanged in the Torre di Nona, but were released when they could pay a sum of money to the papal Curia. Murderers without difficulty obtained a safe conduct from the pope, which allowed them to roam the city with armed men in order to defend themselves against vengeance. Francheschetto Cibò had made a formal treaty with the vice-chamberlain, by which every fine above 150 ducats came to himself and only the smaller fell to the Camera. Everyone mocked at justice, and everyone had recourse to the aid of armed men. When Bernardo Sanguigni was stabbed by a Frenchman in the house of Grechetta, a celebrated courtesan of the time, more than forty armed youths sprang from the Palazzo Crescenzi to avenge his death. They burned the house. More than 2000 people took part in the uproar.

At this time every palace was a fortified camp; the dwelling of every cardinal, with the entire quarter that surrounded it, an asylum. These wide and lofty houses still resembled fortresses and were provided with little towers. The heavy portal was closed by an iron-cased door, which, when barred, was not easily forced. It opened into a vaulted entrance hall, which led to a great pillared courtyard with steep stone staircases and loggie on the upper floors, where, as also in the spacious chambers, the cardinal could accommodate several mercenaries armed with muskets. Even artillery was to be found in these palaces. When criminals obtained protection from a cardinal, his "family," weapons in hand, defended them against justice. One day, some young Romans having wounded the followers of Cardinal Ascanio, the cardinal's family sallied forth publicly with projectiles and wounded more than twenty people in the streets. The captain of the Curia, Savelli, intended to execute a criminal in the neighborhood of the palace of Cardinal Balue; from his window the cardinal prohibited the execution, the spot being within the district of his jurisdiction. The executioner failed to obey, and the cardinal ordered his retainers to attack the court of justice. They sacked it, destroyed the documents and released all the prisoners. The Cardinals Savelli and Colonna hereupon sent troops against their colleague by night; the pope summoned the combatants to his palace, when they heaped insults on one another. The entirely secular and princely form which the College of Cardinals in general had assumed is especially characteristic of the time of the Renascence. The power of the cardinals, increased by the accumulation of benefices and by alliance with foreign courts, had become so great that it threatened to subjugate the papacy. They appear in Rome like revivals of the senators of antiquity. Almost all, like the pope himself, were surrounded by a Curia or by nephews. They walked or rode about the city in warlike attire, wearing costly swords at their sides. Almost every cardinal kept several hundred servants, and this household could be augmented by bravi. Added to these were the partisans among the populace, who obtained their living at the cardinal's court. Almost all these princes of the church had their factions, and they vied with one another in displaying their magnificence, more especially in cavalcades and in the carnival festivities, when at their own expense they equipped triumphal cars with masques, troops of singers and comedians. The cardinals at this time cast into the shade the Roman nobility, whose parties, however, they espoused.

Innocent had persuaded the Orsini and Colonna to conclude a truce. At first inclined to take the part of the Colonna, he afterwards turned to the side of the Orsini. In 1487 he acquired the hand of Maddalena, a daughter of Lorenzo Medici and of Clarice Orsini, sister of Virginius, for his son Franceschetto, who had returned empty handed from the Neapolitan war. And the Orsini family thus recovered its lost influence. Lorenzo had also married his son Piero to Alfonsina, daughter of Robert Orsini, lord of Tagliacozzo and Alba, in March 1487. Madonna Clarice, with her son Piero, and a magnificent retinue of several hundred persons on horseback, came to Rome with the bride on November 3, 1487, and the marriage was celebrated in the Vatican on Sunday, January 20, 1488. It entailed the most important results, results which paved the way for the Medici to the papacy. Lorenzo himself, who saw the power of his house tottering in Florence, drew closer to the church. He immediately rendered it an important service, by helping it to recover possession of Orsini. Boccolino dei Gozzoni had set up as tyrant in this city in April 1486; deprived of support by the peace with Naples, he held negotiations with the Turks, whom he invited to seize the Pentapolis. The pope sent troops against him under Cardinal Julian, and took Trivulzio into his pay. The bold rebel bravely defended himself for a year, until Lorenzo's representations induced him to sell Orsini to the church for 7000 ducats.

The change in the policy of the Vatican gave rise to a misunderstanding between the pope and Cardinal Julian, who had retired to Bologna as early as September 1487. Hitherto he had been omnipotent; now the influence of his enemies the Orsini threatened to oust him from power. In general the fortunes of the nephews of Sixtus IV began to sink. Girolamo, who had been able to retain Forli and Imola on the death of his uncle, fell under the daggers of assassins, who had conspired to slay the tyrant, on April 14, 1488. They threw his naked body from the window of his palace into the street, when the Forlivesi rose and sacked the castle of their lord. It was believed that the pope had been privy to the conspiracy and that he hoped to make his own son signor of Forli. In fact the liberated city invoked the protection of the church, and her envoys were hospitably received. Innocent, however, showed little confidence in the appeal; he was restrained by fear; and the hopes of the Forlivesi were defeated by the energy of the widow of the murdered man. This amazon defended the fortress with the courage of a hero. True, the papal governor of Cesena entered Forli, but Giovanni Bentivogli and Gian Galeazzo sent troops to the relief of the countess. The papal forces were taken prisoners, the murderers of the tyrant were quartered, and on April 28, 1488, Ottavio Riario, son of Girolamo, was proclaimed lord of Forli. Italy was soon terrified by another violent death; Galeotto Manfredi of Faenza was murdered in his palace by his own wife Francesca Bentivoglio. The people elected as their signor Astorre, the little son of the slain lord.

It was said in Rome that, in despicable weakness, and contrary to his given promise, the pope had abandoned Forli like Aquila. His moderation may have been due to consideration for Cardinal Julian, a relation of the Riarii. Julian however had returned to Rome and was again the most influential adviser of the pope. The Cibò were men of too little character to dispute the foremost place in the Curia with Cardinal Rovere. They were satisfied to acquire the ordinary favors of fortune, without interfering in the political affairs of the papacy like the Borgia or Riarii. The same year Innocent married his grand-daughter Donna Peretta, a daughter of Teodorina and Gherardo Uso di Mare (a Genoese merchant, who was also papal treasurer), to Alfonso del Carretto, Marquis of Finale. To the indignation of all religious people, the marriage festival was celebrated with great splendor in the apartments of the Vatican when the pope took part in the banquet in the company of women.

VIII

The Borgias

ALEXANDER VI closed the fifteenth and opened the sixteenth century, and here the reader of the present history will congratulate the writer, that after long wanderings amid the ruins, the sufferings, the errors and the scattered works of the human race during a period of eleven hundred years, he has at length reached the end of the Middle Ages. He will recognize with joy the laws by which mankind is guided onwards to an ever greater degree of perfection. The fifteenth century was richer in acquisitions than its predecessor; it witnessed the development of learning and art, saw Europe renew her intellectual youth, beheld the rise of a new world—here America and there India—to which Vasco de Gama had discovered the passage by sea at the end of the century. With the sixteenth century mankind entered on more elevated missions. While in Germany were already born the men who were to carry out the great Reformation, which had hitherto been invariably refused to Christendom, the center of gravity of the European world rested essentially in the Latin nations. Portugal and Spain, France and Italy were in advance of the German races, partly in culture and partly in political maturity. The principle of life was no longer the Latin church, but Latin culture, its political aim the national monarchy. For of all the powers of the time, the church—owing to the fault of the papacy, which had

From book XIII, ch. 5, sec. 3.

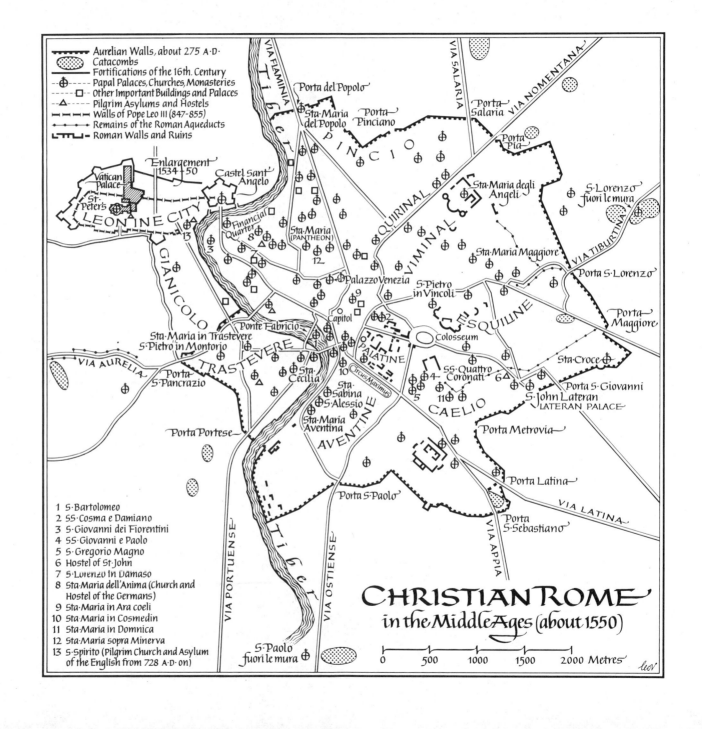

become a political institution—had reached the depth of decadence, and the church alone threw a gloomy shadow across the light that illumined the world. It is only with shame that Christendom reads the bull of jubilee, in which Alexander VI invites it on a pilgrimage to Rome, and only with horror that any man of conscience can look on the unclean hand of the Borgia, as he held the silver hammer, with which on the Christmas Eve of 1499 he opened the door of entrance to S. Peter's.

Nevertheless pilgrims, especially Bohemian converts, came in sufficient numbers to iniquitous Rome, where even in the person of Borgia they revered the head of a church, whose miraculous powers, according to the belief of the faithful, could not be destroyed by the godlessness of her priests. Among the pilgrims was one of the noblest women of Italy, Elisabeth Gonzaga, wife of Guidobaldo of Urbino. Genuine piety brought her to Rome, in spite of the remonstrances of her brother-in-law, the Marchese Francesco. She dwelt in the palace of Cardinal Savelli, under the protection of the Colonna, but only remained a few days in Rome, and left the city on Easter Eve. The sight of the pilgrims gladdened a pious Camaldolese, a friend of Lorenzo de' Medici, who rejoiced that in the midst of such moral corruption there were still thousands who had not perished in Sodom. It is a striking testimony to the severance between faith and morals, that on Easter Sunday 200,000 people knelt in front of S. Peter's to receive the blessing of Alexander VI. The pilgrims in Rome might form their own experience of the nature of the Curia, and carry back to their homes the knowledge they had gained. They beheld the splendor and heard of the crimes of the Borgia, and their respect for the papacy could scarcely be increased, when they saw a beautiful woman come as a pilgrim from the Vatican palace to the basilica, attired in magnificent clothes, riding on horseback, surrounded by a hundred other women on horseback also, and when they learnt that this was Madonna Lucrezia, the daughter of the pope. The accounts of Candia's murder, tales of Vanozza, Julia Farnese and other women formed assuredly topics of current gossip in Rome, where in all ages foreigners have been entertained with the genuine or fictitious mysteries of the faith. These pilgrims, however, willingly offered their Easter gifts, unconcerned by the reflection that their money only served to defray the sins of Rome. The moral conscience of the world, although so gravely offended, still awaited the breath of the spirit that was to give it the knowledge of wrong and the strength of indignation. Indulgences were sold in every country, and papal agents trafficked in remission of sins.

Fortunately for Caesar the year of jubilee coincided with his enterprise in the Romagna. The pope also added to the revenues by the tithes for the Turkish war, to which he exhorted Christendom, since [Sultan] Bajazet was making preparations for conquering the Venetian cities in the Morea. These tithes were imposed for three years on all clergy, of every rank, and in every country, and an estimate was taken of the revenues of the members of the Curia and the cardinals. The bonfires, which the pilgrims saw blazing in Rome on January 14, 1500, announced that the pope's son had become master of Forli. This fortress had been attacked by the French on the 12th. Its chatelaine was conveyed a prisoner to Rome, where her life would have been brought to a speedy close in S. Angelo, but that her heroism touched the hearts of the French. They effected her release after eighteen months. Catherine Sforza Riario, since 1498 the widow of her second husband Giovanni Medici, and mother of the afterwards celebrated condottiere of the name, chose a convent in Florence as her asylum. In a letter to the signory of the republic, the pope himself introduced her as "his beloved daughter in Christ."

The joy in the Vatican was scarcely interrupted by the sudden death of the cardinal-legate Juan Borgia, who fell a victim to fever at Fossombrone on January 14, or, as rumor said, to poison administered by Caesar, to whom he was superfluous. His remains were brought to Rome and buried unostentatiously in S. Maria del Popolo. The cardinal had been at variance with the pope, and, it was asserted, was an avaricious man, who practiced usury. Caesar had now become master of Imola, Cesena and Forli. Nor did the Venetians hinder his further progress, since they themselves were harassed with the Turkish war and required the pope to aid them with tithes. For even before the expedition of Lewis XII the banished Duke of Milan had set the Turks in motion against Venice. During his exile the duke had engaged Swiss to help him to reconquer his states at a favorable opportunity. As early as December 1499 the king had returned from Lombardy to France, bringing with him the rightful heir to Milan, the youthful son of Gian Galeazzo [Visconti]. Under the governor Trivulzio, the French by their rapacity and insolence aroused the indignation of the Lombards, who themselves recalled their banished tyrant. He came at the end of January with his brother Ascanio and at the head of an army of mercenaries. After having unexpectedly lost his realm, he recovered it, as it were by magic; and as early as February 5, 1500, was able to reenter Milan. This sudden restoration and the war, which broke out on the Po between the reinstated duke and the generals of Lewis XII, who were taken by surprise, compelled Caesar's French auxiliaries to leave the Romagna, and forced Caesar himself to renounce further conquests for the time.

He went to Rome. He made his splendid entry on February 26 with a part of his troops, which consisted of Italians, Gascons, Swiss and Germans under the command of Vitellozzo, who stood in his pay. He was received by all the cardinals and magnates, also by the foreign ambassadors. Clad in black satin, a gold chain round his neck, Caesar Borgia rode to the Vatican, surrounded by a hundred Gascons dressed in black, and followed by an escort of honor. The pope received the Duke of Valence, the conqueror of Forli, with delight. The son threw himself at the father's feet and addressed him a discourse in Spanish; Alexander answered in Spanish, which was the language of his heart. He gave no audiences that day; he wept and laughed at the same moment. In reward of his performances, he made Caesar standard-bearer of the church, an office that had been filled by the murdered Gandia. On April 2 he solemnly conferred the banner and baton of command upon him in S. Peter's. He also presented the fratricide with the Golden Rose. In flattery and fear Rome celebrated festivals of rejoicing. Never had the Carnival amusements been so magnificent. The triumph of Julius Caesar was represented in the Piazza Navona with eleven gorgeously decorated carriages, in honor of the pope's son, who audaciously adopted Caesar's motto as his own. In the midst of these festivals the news arrived that, on February 24, the Infanta Joanna of Spain had borne a son to the Archduke Philip of Austria, and that the boy had received the name of Charles. The national church of the Germans, S. Maria dell' Anima, was decorated in honor of the birth of the child, the future great emperor Charles V.

If the restoration of Sforza clouded the joy of the Borgia, the fear which it occasioned vanished on the receipt of the tidings that all was at an end in Lombardy. Lewis XII had sent a fresh army under La Tremouille against Milan, and Sforza, betrayed by his own Swiss, had fallen into the hands of the French at Novara on April 10. Seldom has history shown so many changes of fortune, seldom have so many terrible tragedies been crowded into so short a space. Fall and restoration, flight and return, victory and defeat chased one another like specters across the stage of Italy. The whole country reeked of blood, and trembled in dread of the fate which the accumulated guilt of centuries seemed to have invoked. Cardinal Ascanio was taken prisoner near Rivalta by Venetian cavalry under Carlo Orsini. Alexander demanded his release, but the signory of Venice surrendered him to the king of France. With a band of captive prelates, whose feet were tied together under their horses, the proud cardinal was conveyed back to Milan, whence he was removed to the tower at Bourges. Ascanio now received the reward of his share in the election of Borgia to the papacy. Conscious of the justice of his punishment, he bore his fate without complaint, and assuredly deemed himself fortunate that in a French prison he had escaped the poison of the Borgia. The sight of his fall shows the uncertainty of fortune; but far more dreadful was the fate of his brother. During the ten long years that elapsed until his death, the murderer of his nephew, the traitor to his country, pined in a gloomy dungeon of the fortress of Loches in Berry, in his hideous solitude a prey to the furies of conscience, whose stings no single redeeming thought served to allay. This frivolous but highly cultured man had been driven to crime by the lust of power. His history offers one of the most terrible examples of evil entailed on a whole nation by the ambition of a prince.

Fortune was now the slave of the Borgia. For Lewis XII could no longer detain his troops for the conquest of the Romagna. The father's coffers were filled with the wealth amassed in the jubilee, and this wealth served to acquire troops. The boldest plans were conceived. Pilgrims to the jubilee were stupefied by the intoxication of the iniquitous city, where, as in antiquity, the bacchanalian atmosphere was at the same time saturated and poisoned by suffering. When, after gazing on the image of the Savior depicted on the Handkerchief of Veronica, these pilgrims returned to the city across the Bridge of S. Angelo, they saw on high a row of men, who had been hanged on the battlements of the fortress, among them the physician to the hospital of the Lateran. This man had long been accustomed to shoot passersby with arrows at daybreak in order to rob them, and to poison wealthy patients, pointed out to him by the confessor to the hospital. And when from the sacred basilica the pilgrims came forth on the piazza on the floral festival of S. Giovanni, they beheld the pope's son seated on horseback at the steps of S. Peter's, hurling lances against bulls within a wooden enclosure. With herculean strength, such as Pipin's, he severed the head of one of these animals from the body at a single blow, and all Rome stood in admiration of his brutal strength.

Meanwhile the pope was attacked by fever. Roman satire composed a dialogue between him and death, which again spared him in an accident that followed. On the afternoon of June 29 he was sitting in a room in the Vatican, when a sudden storm burst over the palace, and a chimney fell through the roof, carrying with it people from the upper floor and killing Lorenzo Chigi, brother of the celebrated Agostino. The datary Ferrari and the chamberlain Gaspar sprang into the recess of a window, shrieking, "The pope is dead!" The cry reechoed through Rome, and Caesar may well have turned pale! The city rose in momentary confusion; several Spaniards fled to S. Angelo; the citizens rushed to arms; messengers hurried to the exiles to tell them that now was the time to return and take vengeance on their enemies. But meanwhile cannons announced from S. Angelo that the pope was still alive. He was found sitting among the *débris,* protected by a curtain, but with two wounds on his head, and was carried out. On July 2 he caused thanksgivings to be offered to the Virgin, with whose special protection he believed himself favored. His natural force was inexhaustible. "The pope," said Popo Capello, in September 1500, "is seventy years old; he grows younger every day, his cares do not last a night; he is of cheerful temperature and only does what he likes; his sole thought is for the aggrandizement of his children; he troubles about nothing else."

The wounds on Alexander's head were not yet healed, when a terrible tragedy was enacted before the jubilee pilgrims. At eleven o'clock on the night of July 15, as the young prince of Bisceglie left the Vatican to return home, he was attacked and stabbed at the steps of S. Peter's. The murderers escaped among a band of horsemen, who carried them off to the Porta Portese. The prince staggered to the pope. "I am wounded," he said, and he named the murderer. His wife Lucrezia, who was present, swooned. The prince was carried to the neighboring palace, which he made his abode, that of the cardinal of S. Maria in Porticu. The mysterious way in which Burkard relates the tragedy (we seem to be dealing with specters) leaves a sinister impression, and art would never have veiled the horror more transparently than prudence has done in this case.

> The illustrious Don Alfonso, duke of Bisceglie and prince of Salerno, was seriously wounded on the evening of July 15, but since he determined not to die of the wounds then received, he was strangled in his bed on August 18, about the first hour of the night. His remains were carried to S. Peter's. They were followed by Don Francesco Borgia, treasurer of the pope, and his family. The physician of the dead prince, and a certain hunchback with whom he had associated, were brought to S. Angelo. They were examined by inquisitors, but were soon released, since the man who had entrusted them with the commission went unpunished, and he was well known.

There is another account of the bloody deed, which openly mentions Caesar as the murderer. Round the wounded man were his wife Lucrezia and his sister, the Princess Squillace. In fear of poison they prepared his food, and from the same suspicion the pope caused him to be guarded by sixteen men. One day he visited the invalid unaccompanied by Caesar. Caesar also came once and said, "That which did not take place at noon will take place in the evening." People actually believed that they saw a demon pass to and fro. The pope, the women, almost the entire court knew that Caesar would kill the prince—no one could save him. For of what was the terrible man not capable who had stabbed the Spaniard Pedro Caldes, Alexander's favorite chamberlain, under Alexander's very mantle, so that the blood spurted into his, the pope's, face? Caesar returned another day; he entered the room, where the already convalescent prince stood up; he forced the terrified women to leave it, he called Michelotto, the minister of his bloody acts, who strangled Bisceglie. The prince was buried at night. Caesar openly acknowledged that he had murdered him, because Bisceglie cherished designs against his life. The terrible deed was everywhere discussed through the city, but only in secret and terror. The bodies of murdered men were daily found in the streets, and others, even prelates of high position, disappeared as it were by magic. Caesar now ruled the pope himself. The father loved his son but trembled before him. Lucrezia also (she had a son by Alfonso, who was called Rodrigo) was obliged to submit to the commands of a brother who had made her a widow. He temporarily ousted her from the Pope's favor. He had deprived her of Sermoneta, for "she is a woman," he said, "and cannot defend it." Certain it is that Alexander sent his daughter to Nepi only at Caesar's desire. Lucrezia left the city on the last day of August, attended by 600 horsemen, to recover her equanimity, which had been shaken by the death of her husband. Such, at least, are the terribly laconic words of Burkard. If Lucrezia loved her husband, then was her fate indeed tragic, and the girl must have revolted at the thought that she was nothing but the victim of her brother's deadly will. Caesar got rid of Alfonso, not on trifling personal grounds, but rather because he wished to set free the hand of his sister, in order that he might form an alliance—favorable to himself—with the house of Ferrara, at a time when the connection of the Borgia with Naples had lost all value.

The dead were quickly forgotten, for the living had enough

to do. More money was required. Twelve new cardinals, among them six Spaniards, whom the pope, or rather his son, had created, paid for their hats in handing a sum of 120,000 ducats over to Caesar. With the most barefaced candor Caesar explained to the Sacred College that these cardinals were necessary because he required money for his war in the Romagna. Among these new slaves of Caesar were his brother-in-law d'Albret, Ludovico and Juan Borgia, and Gian Battista Ferrari.

With French aid he first drove his former brother-in-law from Pesaro in October 1500, then Pandolfo Malatesta from Rimini, and encamped before Faenza. The lord of this city was Astorre Manfredi, a youth of seventeen, whose beauty and virtue had made him the idol of his people. The inhabitants of Faenza defended the city for months, until on April 25, 1501, hunger forced them to an honorable capitulation. Caesar promised indulgence to the citizens, and free exit to Astorre, but immediately broke his oath by sending the unfortunate boy to the dungeons of S. Angelo.

Alexander now created his son duke of the Romagna. In making the largest province of the sacred chair a patrimony of his house, he remained untroubled by the thought that this province, made hereditary in the Borgia dynasty, must entail the ruin of the entire State of the Church. No opposition was raised by the Sacred College; poison and sword had reduced the cardinals into a trembling choir of servants or flatterers of father as well as son. The college was purposely filled with Spaniards. The duke desired nothing more ardently than to make Bologna the capital of his territory. He carried on correspondence with the Mariscotti, but the vigilance of Bentivoglio and the protection which he received from France frustrated Caesar's plans, and he was obliged to remain satisfied with Castel Bolognese and a body of auxiliaries, whose number was stipulated by treaty. The Mariscotti expiated their conspiracy on the scaffold.

Imola, Forli and Pesaro, Rimini, Faenza, Cesena and Fano formed his dukedom for the present. To these territories he hoped to unite the whole of central Italy. Spoleto was already in the hands of the Borgia; a bull had already deprived Julius Caesar

Varano of Camerina. The duke's progress was checked, however, by the jealousy of France. His attempt against Florence was also unsuccessful. The fruitless war with Pisa exhausted the republic; in 1499, repulsed by the already almost conquered city, the Florentine general Paolo Vitelli had atoned for his misfortune by his death, when his brother Vitellozzo in revenge joined the Medici. These exiles had invariably been defeated, but nevertheless continued to threaten their ancestral city, and even formed an alliance with Caesar Borgia. Reinforced by the auxiliaries of Bentivoglio and in concert with Piero Medici, Vitellozzo and the Orsini, some of whom with other nobles had become his condottieri, the duke entered Florentine territory in May 1501. For after having vainly made war on the Orsini, the Borgia now adroitly utilized their services, in order to expel other nobles, and then to reward these allies in their peculiar fashion. The audacious demands of the duke, who sent this secretary Agapito Gerardini to Florence, more especially his desire to restore the Medici, terrified the signory. They purchased their exemption in taking Caesar "in condotta" at a salary of 36,000 ducats, but without any obligation as to actual service, and pledging themselves not to protect Jacopo Appiano of Piombino. For Caesar immediately directed his attention against this noble. Some places within Appiano's dominions, even Elba and Pianosa, made submission to Caesar, but Lewis XII commanded him to halt, and Alexander recalled him. He left a portion of his troops under Giampolo Baglioni and Vitellozzo before Piombino, and hurried to Rome, which he entered on June 13, 1501.

Lewis XII proceeded to carry out his enterprise against Naples. Too weak to accomplish it without the consent of Spain, he had made Ferdinand [the Catholic, king of Aragon] his associate in an abominable crime. The secret treaty, which was concluded at Granada on November 11, 1500, by the two monarchs, one of whom was called the most Christian, the other the Catholic, is one of the most disgraceful documents of those cabinet politics, which, under the sanction of the pope, were now inaugurated in the history of Europe. The fact that he invited another monarch to become his rival was moreover a clear testimony to the incapacity of Lewis XII. The two kings promised each other to attack Naples simultaneously, and so to divide the kingdom that Calabria and Apulia should fall as a duchy to Spain, the remaining provinces with the capital as a kingdom to France. The pope was to be asked to confer the respective investitures, and as he hated Frederick [of Altamura, king of Naples] and was entirely devoted to Lewis on Caesar's account, his consent was undoubted. Moreover, the alliance between France and Spain rendered the Roman barons defenseless against the attacks of the pope.

The overthrow of Aragon was accomplished, like so many falls in the history of dynasties, in the person of an innocent prince. Frederick was beloved by his people. His reign would have assured them a period of prosperity, had it been possible to remedy the evils which the feudal nobility had brought on the kingdom. The king still remained ignorant of the treaty, but not of the preparations of France. Fear and weakness impelled him to seek an alliance with the Turks, which however was never effected. Although he feared the claims of his relation, the powerful king of Spain, he hoped for his protection. With the aid of the Colonna, he believed that he could resist the French army on the frontier.

The French under Aubigny arrived in the neighborhood of Rome, and in June encamped beside the Acqua Traversa. The envoys of France and Spain explained to the pope the contents of the treaty between their masters. The premeditated robbery was cloaked under the hypocritical name of religion, for the monarchs alleged as the essential reason of the war against Frederick the fact that he had invited the Turks to Italy. The conquest of Naples was merely the introduction to the great Crusade against the Crescent.

Alexander proclaimed Frederick deposed as a traitor to the kingdom, and agreed to the partition of Naples between the two kings, who, in return, were to take the oath of vassalage to the church. If this act suffices to show Alexander's treachery, at the same time it diminishes the credibility of such witnesses as try to prove the pope a great statesman. He evidently cherished the wily intention of driving the two powers into fierce war with one another, and in consequence foolishly hoped that he might be able to make Caesar [Borgia] king of Naples.

On June 28 the French army, which was joined by Caesar Borgia with some troops, set forth for the conquest of Naples. On their march the forces destroyed Marino and other towns of the Colonna, for this house remained faithful to Aragon, which had decided in its favor the long dispute with the Orsini concerning Alba. The sudden fall of Naples was only the repetition of the melancholy past, but it was rendered more deplorable by the treachery of Spain towards its kinsman. Frederick had appealed to Gonsalvo for aid, and, on the General's treacherous demand, had surrendered to him the fortresses of Calabria and Gaeta. As soon as the French entered the kingdom, the Spaniard threw aside his mask, and Frederick retired to Capua in utter dismay. Fabrizio Colonna held this fortress for him, while Prospero commanded in Naples. Capitulation was discussed, but, in the midst of the negotiations, the enemy stormed the walls, and on July 24 Capua suffered the terrible fate of a conquered city. Fabrizio was made a prisoner. Caesar offered immense sums to the French general if he would either put him to death or surrender him into his power, but the noble-minded John Jordan Orsini rescued his hereditary enemy, who was allowed to purchase his freedom.

The frightful carnage at Capua disarmed all who still remained in arms for the last of the house of Aragon. Frederick shut himself up in Castel Nuovo, while all Naples shouted the name of France. He held parley with Aubigny and went first to Ischia. Among the unfortunate fugitives assembled in the castle of the island, one woman above all was calculated to awaken pity. This was that Isabella [del Balzo, Frederick's wife] who had suffered the ruin of the houses of both Milan and Naples, and who now beheld the fall of the last remains of the greatness of her ancestors, while she bewailed the fate of her own son, a prisoner in France. Aghast with horror at the treachery of his relation, Frederick in despair resolved to seek an asylum for himself and his children with the less criminal of his enemies. Lewis XII gave him the duchy of Anjou and an annual pension. The melancholy days which he passed in France were alleviated by the devotion of the companions of his exile, among whom was the poet Sannazaro. Frederick of Aragon died at Tours on September 9, 1504.

Before leaving Naples he had sent Don Ferrante, his eldest son, to Taranto. The town surrendered to Gonsalvo on condition that the little prince should be allowed to journey to his father, but the treacherous Spaniard disgraced his name by breaking his solemn oath. He sent the boy a prisoner to Spain. There Frederick's son died childless, but not until 1550. Such was the tragic end of the house of Aragon, which during a century had filled the history of Naples and Italy with more crimes than virtues. Like Anjou, the house was foreign to the country, but speedily became nationalized. The court of Aragon had been conspicuous from the time of Alfonso for the protection extended throughout the beauteous kingdom to learning and art. And not until the fall of the Aragonese did the country sink into its miserable servitude under foreign dominion. The house of Aragon also vanished in Spain. For the perfidious Ferdinand left no male descendant to inherit the crown. His son John had already died on October 1497, and already Charles [V] was born to the house of Austria, a child on whom an unparalleled degree of fortune was to bestow the heritage of half the world.

IX

Caesar Borgia

THAT in Cola di Rienzo Petrarch saw the hero of his ideal can never redound to the poet's dishonor; but the homage which Machiavelli has dedicated to the execrable Caesar Borgia still darkens the memory of the great founder of statecraft. The book of *The Prince*, as a product of experimental science applied to affairs of state, has no less claim to be regarded as the most terrible witness of the corrupt age to which it belonged than the historic figure of Caesar Borgia himself. There is no stronger contrast than that between the *De Monarchia* of Dante, a treatise of ideal politics dedicated to the emperor who according to the poet's view was the God-summoned savior of Italy, and *The Prince* of Machiavelli, dedicated to a petty and predatory Medici. We may thereby measure the distance that the intellect had traveled from deductive scholasticism to inductive experience. Machiavelli's program was condemned with theoretic indignation, but practically was eagerly accepted as a political gospel by popes, kings, and statesmen of Europe. The denial of Dante's ideal of humanity avenged itself among the Italians by their incapacity for the reform of society. If the error of their long-cherished hopes concerning the mission of Henry VII, Cola, Lewis the Bavarian, Ladislaus of Naples, and even Charles VIII is pardonable, because explicable by history, nothing so clearly

From book XIV, ch. 1, sec. 2.

demonstrates the depth of their moral and political misery as the fact that one of their greatest thinkers put forward Caesar Borgia as the model of the prince of his time. Machiavelli's *Principe* does not, like the *Politics* of Aristotle, institute an inquiry into the best state, but into the qualities and crimes which must be possessed and practiced by a prince who is to govern a new state (*principe nuovo*). His prince in the main is not the absolute ideal of the regent, but the man in the given conditions of the Renascence. Since Italy was now utterly demoralized, she could only find her savior in a despot, who would unscrupulously adopt any means to attain his end, that of exterminating not only secular but spiritual feudalism, and would found a modern system of monarchy, a national and united state. Machiavelli, who despaired of moral power in society, discovered this political grandeur in Borgia, and it hovered before his mind in his *Principe*. But are we therefore justified in asserting that he believed a Caesar Borgia could ever be the founder of a united Italy? In this case Machiavelli must have lost all understanding of the conditions of power at the time, and especially of the nature of the papacy. He hated it and the hierarchy as the source of the perpetual corruption and dismemberment of his native country. "We Italians," he said, "have to thank the church and the priests that we have become irreligious and wicked, but they are guilty of a yet greater evil, which has been the cause of our ruin. It consists in the fact that the church has kept and still keeps our country severed. In truth no country has ever been united or fortunate which did not obey a republic or a prince, as France and Spain do now. The reason, however, that Italy does not enjoy a like constitution, that she is not governed by a republic or a prince, is due solely to the church. For the church, having made her seat and possessed a temporal sovereignty here, was neither sufficiently powerful and strong to unite the rest of Italy under her scepter, nor on the other hand weak enough to forfeit her temporal dominion by invoking in her dread a potentate who would defend her against the mighty ones of Italy."

The disastrous condition of his country made Machiavelli, the one-sided politician, forgetful of the greatest creations of the intellect which were due to the individualization of its cities and provinces, and which could never have arisen had Italy been already united in the twelfth century. The same disunion caused him to substitute for the Guelf theory of confederation the Ghibelline idea of monarchy, since only the latter could set aside the temporal papacy, and shatter the spell of the Middle Ages. In this matter Machiavelli saw so clearly that he may be called a prophet. The progress of history has entirely confirmed his theory, for Italy has at length transformed herself into a monarchy with Rome for her capital, a city which, after having been held by the pope for a thousand years, she has now wrested for herself. New and united Italy has arisen in accordance with Machiavelli's program. But if in Caesar Borgia he saw only the instrument, who, in extirpating the tyrants in the State of the Church, and paving the way for its secularization, might serve towards the future union of Italy, nevertheless in his time hopes such as these must necessarily have been shattered by the nature of all political and ecclesiastical conditions, especially since the Italians did not take part in the reformation of the church. It was only the successors of Alexander VI who reaped the benefits of Caesar's policy, namely the monarchical unity of the State of the Church. Julius II could therefore already speak of the "extraordinary services" of the duke of the Romagna. For he himself inherited the results of this policy, and founded the papal monarchy, which, as the same Machiavelli says, began to appear formidable even to France. Without averting foreign rule, with which on the contrary it formed an alliance, it checked the formation of an Italian national state for more than three hundred years. These facts may show whether even that, the best result of the crimes of the Borgia, was indeed worthy of praise.

X

Julius II,
the Ornamentation of Rome,
and the Fragmentation of Christendom

WITH the fifteenth century a new period of magnificence dawned for the city. She became once more that which she had ceased to be since the ruin of the Roman empire—the classic city of the world. On the eve of its fall the papacy enthroned itself in splendor and majesty; the center of gravity of all the political relations of Italy and Europe lay in Rome. The secularization and wealth of the church created or heightened a feverish activity in all arts and learning. As in the times of Augustus and Trajan artists, poets, musicians, rhetoricians and scholars gravitated thither. The finer spirits of an epoch of culture flourish as a rule in unison—a law which Sallust has already noticed. And with the beginning of the sixteenth century, the overflowing intellectual life of the Italian nation reveals itself like a Bacchic triumphal procession, then droops and fades.

For only two decades was the city of Rome the classic theater of this splendid culture, the center which in the main gave form and color to the European mind. It filled the place which under Lewis XIV Paris afterwards assumed. In Rome however there was no combination of creative forces to exercise an influence on Italy,

From book XIV, ch. 2, sec. 1.

such as Paris exercised on France. Even in the sixteenth century creative intellects lived and flourished in every Italian city. Milan, Florence and Venice, Bologna, Parma and Ferrara, even smaller cities surprise us by their independence and wealth, more especially in the province of the creative arts. It is a national phenomenon. Rome however attracted the choicest spirits of Italy into her service; in Rome they found the widest field for their energies and the highest tasks for their genius.

In the atmosphere of world history that wrapped the city around, in its monumental and ideal sublimity, the artistic mind was enabled to discard its provincial limitations and acquire an impress of greatness that was essentially Roman. Even things ecclesiastical assumed greater proportions owing to the cosmopolitan idea of the papacy, and the specifically Christian element was less narrowing in an age when ancient culture was absorbed in Christianity. The papacy, which for some time before had been the pioneer of culture, was antiecclesiastical and worldly. The sumptuous vestments in which it arrayed itself concealed from no one the deep-seated malady of the church. Nevertheless we must now acknowledge that, in view of the needs of culture, the sole merit of the popes of that age is precisely their cult of pagan antiquity. After the age of the Renaissance the popes were no longer able to achieve anything great, anything of importance in universal history. Mankind however would have been deprived of many creations of art had the ascetic Platonism of Savonarola or the iconoclastic ethics of the first reformers prevented those popes indulging their tastes. After so many saints, their predecessors, had darkened and scourged the world with dogmas and penitential discipline, they had the courage or the taste to invite Christianity to assist at Olympic festivals.

It is perhaps one of the strongest proofs of the imperfection of human nature, that in almost every great epoch of culture the Beautiful reaches its greatest perfection side by side with the decay of morals and political life. Our statement finds confirmation in the history of the Greeks and Romans, and in modern times in that of the Italians and French. The theory does not hold good to an equal degree in the case of the Germans. Creative artistic energy probably requires a sensuous atmosphere, electrified by passion; this atmosphere, which is created by the currents of the time, remains sunny and clear in the higher realms of genius; while in the lower it shows itself merely as a precipitate of vulgar vice, and is fatal as a moral pestilence. Among the artists of the most corrupt age in Italy, there were such ideally beautiful natures as Raphael and the stoic Michelangelo; and beside the prostitution of talent exemplified in Pietro Aretino, Vida the writer of hymns and the serious-minded Flaminio; among princes the noble Guidobaldo of Urbino and his wife Elisabetta Gonzaga. Nor did the Saturnalia of Rome last for ever. The nobler efforts of this magnificent luxury of the Renaissance outlived the storms of the time, and as monuments of the licentious and worldly papacy stand the Cathedral of S. Peter and the Vatican with its masterpieces of pagan as of Christian art.

Under Julius II the Renaissance became an artistic classicism. Art had become the impress of the age as of the national spirit of Italy. It was now just as in antiquity the expression of a civilization;—the monumental expression of that perfection of general culture to which mankind had attained. It surprises us now as a phenomenon, for it has passed away, and according to the laws of the intellectual cosmos, the Renaissance of the Beautiful will probably only reappear after an interval of centuries. The art of our times is but the afterglow of that of the fifteenth century. As among the Greeks of the age of Pericles, art among the Italians at the beginning of the sixteenth century was an ethical consciousness, beauty a national sense; it was cultivated nature. Society, religion, life, invention, learning, poetry, were all governed by artistic form.

Julius II did not love art as an enthusiast of the Beautiful, but as a great character who possessed a decided taste for plastic form. With genuine Roman ambition he wished to give monumental expression to his reign, we may say to the spirit of his papacy, in sublime artistic creations. The fullness of the time supplied him with men of genius of the first rank. It was only necessary to see and summon them and they came, and rendered him and themselves immortal. Augustus would have deemed himself fortunate had Bramante, Michelangelo, and Raphael worked for him at one and the same time. These great masters were for Julius II the instruments by which he attained his desire of immortality, which indeed they have procured him. Apart from them in time he would have vanished amid the ordinary horde of commonplace popes and princes, without leaving a trace in history. For it is these creative intellects alone who have given his character and name human interest, and still link them to humanity.

He had imbibed from the time of his uncle Sixtus the Rovere passion for building, and we have seen how he had already gratified his taste while still a cardinal. The disturbances of his reign and the expensive character of his political enterprises prevented him accomplishing the transformation of Rome to the degree that he had intended. He continued Sixtus IV's work of widening the streets. The Via Giulia, that of S. Celso, the Judaeorum, the Via delle Botteghe Oscure and the Lungara were restored by him. His architect Bramante provided him with the plans, while Domenico Massimi, Geronimo Pichi and others were his aediles.

The Via Giulia still bears the name of the pope. It was intended to lead from the Ponte Sisto to the Vatican, and in fact to pass over the ancient triumphal bridge by S. Spirito, which Julius meant to restore. The new street was to be adorned with the most magnificent buildings and even by an immense palace for the Roman tribunals. This Palatium Julianum, which was never finished, was afterwards pulled down to the remains of the blocks of travertine, which we may still see near S. Biagio della Pagnotta. In the same palace Bramante wished to erect a circular Corinthian building, but this, too, was never finished. It served for a long time for the representation of comedies, until in 1575 it was demolished by the Brescians to build their Church SS. Faustino e Giovita. The Via Giulia acquired an animated aspect as early as the time of Leo X, and in the sixteenth century became the favorite quarter of Rome. Palaces with richly ornamented facades dating from the time of the Medici still remain here.

The whole of this district, especially that of the Banks, was filled with stately buildings as early as the time of Sixtus IV.

In causing the ancient church of S. Celso to be pulled down, and a new church to be erected, Julius gave it a wider area. Bramante also soon after built the papal mint, where the silver pieces called Giuli were first struck in 1508. The inscription of 1512, which extols the services of the pope in the language of the ancient emperors, may still be read in the Via de' Banchi. Agostino Chigi, his minister of finance, had a private bank in the same street opposite the Palazzo of the Alberici (Cicciaporci), which was afterwards built by Giulio Romano. Further on, in the Palazzo Borgia, the chancery of that time, dwelt Galeotto the cardinal-nephew, who had enlarged and decorated the magnificent building of Alexander VI.

The other great street which Rome owes to Julius II is the Lungara. He caused it to be made in a straight line, and intended to continue it along the Tiber to the Ripa Grande. People began to build houses, but, nevertheless, the Lungara showed no signs of animation. The Riarii and Cardinal Farnese had country houses and gardens at the end of the street, and there Agostino Chigi built a villa, which, under its later name of the Farnesina, has acquired a worldwide renown.

The Siennese family of the Chigi had come to Rome in the time of Sixtus IV with Mariano, who grew rich in exchange transactions. He acted as banker to the Borgia. His son Lorenzo was killed in the accident in the Vatican, when the life of Alexander VI was endangered by the fall of a roof. The other sons Agostino, Gismondo, and Francesco, had received their training in the banking house of the Spanocchi, to which Agostino himself succeeded in 1509. His business prospered owing to his extensive enterprises and his relations with the Curia. He had already been banker to Alexander VI, and afterwards became financial adviser to, and the confidant of, Julius II. Julius gave him a lease of the alum mines at Tolfa, and that of the salt marshes at Cervia, which proved so fruitful a cause of war to the popes. In September 1509 Julius received him into the Rovere family. Chigi's wealth increased to such a degree that his income was estimated at 70,000 ducats, an enormous sum at that period. He owned a hundred vessels on the seas, and had houses of business in Lyons,

London, Constantinople, Amsterdam, and even in Babylon. He was held in honor in the east; the Sultan called him "the great Christian merchant." His credit was unbounded. He ruled the money market of his time. Even Venice awarded him citizenship. On his arrival there the council did homage to him, gave him a magnificent reception, and made him take his place beside the doge. Several princes obtained loans from his house. He lent pope Julius 40,000 ducats without interest, receiving as security the tiara of Paul II. Owing to his wealth this highly cultured man was the most magnificent patron of art in Rome.

The architect of his villa, which was begun about 1509, is believed to have been the gifted artist Baldassare Peruzzi, who, born in Siena in 1481, came to Rome shortly before the death of Alexander VI. Peruzzi was a compatriot of Chigi, and by him employed on his villa. Nevertheless, a recent art critic has striven to prove that the plan of this celebrated house was designed not by Peruzzi but by Raphael. Chigi wished for a simple villa of noble proportions and graceful style, and the building became the model of an unpretending country seat of refined taste. It was a dwelling-house in the outskirts of Rome—a suburbanum—and, on account of the limited space on the banks of the Tiber, the gardens, which were considered so beautiful, could not have been of great extent. Peruzzi covered the exterior of the building with paintings in chiaroscuro, of which no trace remains. He painted the story of Perseus and the Medusa in the gallery of Galatea, while Sodoma decorated the upper story with the beautiful frescoes of Alexander's marriage with Roxana. In his villa Chigi wished to have no reminiscence of the Christian religion, but only subjects belonging to the joyous realm of ancient poetry. He engaged Raphael's services, and the Galatea and the celebrated frescoes, depicting the myth of Cupid and Psyche, were thus called into existence. With Raphael also worked his pupils, Giulio Romano and Francesco Pecci; further, Giovanni da Udine and Sebastiano del Piombo. Chigi's house became one of the most beautiful monuments of the time, and marked an epoch in the history of art. The fortunate merchant found himself in possession of a pearl without equal, which may well have excited the envy of contemporary princes. Poets described the wonders of his villa. True, that the artists of Greece or imperial Rome would have smiled at the enthusiasm it excited, but so needy had mankind become that it appeared a marvelous creation; and so miserably provided with beauty is our public and private life even now, that the villa still enjoys an almost undiminished fame. Chigi also filled it with works of art, statues, pictures, valuable medals and gems, and there lived a life of splendor until his death, which took place within it on April 10, 1520. His family experienced the common lot of the uncertainty of fortune; and after being crippled with debts under Paul III, they returned to Siena, and became extinct in 1580. The villa was sold by auction, and bought with all the statues it contained by Cardinal Alessandro Farnese; in the course of time it fell to the dukes of Parma, and was called Farnesina.

Only half a century divided the Farnesina from the palace of Paul II, with which the new architecture in Rome had begun, and yet the architectural distance between the two buildings seems to place them more than a century apart. The buds of modern art, which began to unfold in the time of Mino and Pontelli, had developed more richly. Grace and joyous sensuousness were the requirements of the new generation. The popes also rendered homage to this taste, and were able to bestow great proportions on their monumental undertakings. Julius II in particular completed a part of the legacy bequeathed by Nicolas V in the reconstruction of the Vatican, and carried it out in his own courageous manner. In Rome he found the most gifted architect of the time. Bramante, who was born at Castel Durante in the Duchy of Urbino in 1444, had begun his career in the Romagna and continued it in Milan, where he executed several ecclesiastical buildings for Ludovico Sforza. The fall of Sforza seems to have driven him to Rome about 1499. He here studied the antiquities, of which he made several plans, not only in the city, but also at Hadrian's Villa near Tivoli, where the first excavations were now made. By the application of the laws of antiquity he founded a new era of architecture in Rome. His buildings are characterized by nobility of proportion, severe beauty, classic grace and a purity

of form that verges on bareness. Alexander VI, whose architect
was Antonio di Sangallo, scarcely employed Bramante. But Cardinals Carraffa, Castellesi and Riario commissioned him to build
their palaces and churches. The building of the Cancellaria, the
Church of S. Lorenzo in Damaso, of the Palazzo Castellesi were
prolonged until the reign of Julius II, and the cloister of S. Maria
della Pace, which Carraffa had entrusted to Bramante, was only
completed in 1504. Under his guidance a German architect is said
to have finished S. Maria dell' Anima, the foundation stone of
which had been laid on April 11, 1500, by the imperial envoy
Mathias Lang. Although ascribed to Giuliano di Sangallo, its
finely proportioned but bare facade has all the characteristics of
Bramante's style. In the early part of the sixteenth century
Bramante built the round temple in the courtyard of the Church
of S. Pietro in Montorio, an elegant trifle in imitation of the antique, and having the appearance of a model. The architect had
already entered the service of Julius II.

It is strange that the celebrated Florentine Giuliano di Sangallo,
who had formerly built the palace beside S. Pietro in Vincoli, the
fortress at Ostia and the palace at Savona for Julius II, was not
permanently kept in Rome by this pope. On his election Giuliano
at once hastened to him and probably received employment, but
soon afterwards he became architect to the Florentines, and, if
Vasari's statements be correct, even quarrelled with the pope on
account of the rebuilding of S. Peter's, which he himself had suggested, but the execution of which had been given to Bramante.
Giuliano went to Florence, and only returned to Rome in 1512,
where he did not acquire any prominent position. Neither did his
brother Antonio, his fellow-worker in the palace at Savona and
architect to Alexander VI, rise to eminence in Rome during the
reign of Julius II. He designed here the domed church of S.
Maria di Loreto on the Forum of Trajan, which was begun in
1507. But not until later did the distinguished architect rear
himself an imperishable monument in the Palazzo Farnese.

All the designs conceived by Julius II, the construction of
streets and quarters, the rebuilding of the Vatican and the erection of the new cathedral, were entrusted to Bramante. He even

employed the Umbrian architect as engineer of the fortifications at Bologna and the siege works of Mirandola. The same master also designed plans for a great number of palaces not only in Rome, but also in the State of the Church.

Julius wished to connect the Belvedere with the Vatican in such wise that the intermediate space should be filled with a combination of halls, courts and palaces. With this aim Bramante drew a classic design; a magnificent court between the Belvedere and the Vatican; the upper part of which was to form a garden terrace, the lower a place for tournaments. This piazza was to be surrounded with a beautiful portico with three rows of pilasters one above the other, and to end in huge niches, an upper one of the Belvedere, a lower one with rows of seats for the spectators at the games. Nicholas V had already entertained the idea of a secular theater in the Vatican, and would have had classic comedies represented there. Julius II would probably instead have given the Romans combats with animals and tournaments. Even later popes had games of chivalry celebrated in the court-yard of the Belvedere, although not in the theater, as Julius II had intended. Stirred to enthusiasm by Bramante's designs, Julius was impatient to see the rise of these magnificent buildings, and with characteristic haste urged them onwards. He even ordered the work to be continued during the night. But as in the case of Nicholas V, death stepped between him and his project. Only one portico connecting the Belvedere with the Vatican was finished, and this was so hurriedly executed, that as early as the time of Clement VII the walls required a support. Under Sixtus V, who in building his library rendered impossible the execution of Bramante's design, the open loggia was walled up. This gallery now serves for the great collection of Christian and ancient inscriptions. Pius VII finally added the Braccio Nuovo to the library.

The celebrated work of Bramante, the "Court of Damasus," the triple arcades of which are the most successful imitation of the antique, was also begun under Julius II. Bramante has therein given an unequalled example of vigor, lightness and grace. The loggia was finished by Raphael according to Bramante's design.

The grandest of all Julius II's conceptions was that of the new cathedral of S. Peter. He revived the idea of Nicholas V, which no pope hitherto had ventured to carry out. In spite of the violent opposition of the cardinals and of mankind in general, who wished to preserve the venerable basilica of the apostles, he ordered the cathedral to be rebuilt in the classic style. Bramante submitted the plan for his approval. A Greek cross with ponderous tribunes at the end of the arms, a majestic cupola over the center between two belfries, a simple and dignified porch resting on six columns. The foundation stone was laid by the pope on Saturday in Albis, April 18, 1506. Walking in procession from the high altar of the ancient church through the chapel of S. Petronilla, the old man fearlessly descended a ladder to an abyss-like opening that had been excavated beside the foundations. He was accompanied by only two cardinal-deacons, the master of the ceremonies and a few other persons. A goldsmith, apparently Caradosso, brought an earthenware vase containing twelve medals, which had been recently struck, two being large gold pieces, the others of bronze, with inscriptions referring to the ceremony. These were buried in the ground. The foundation stone of white marble, four palms long, two wide, and five fingers thick, was placed beside the foundation wall, and the consecration of the building ended the ceremony.

Among the spectators of the scene there was no one who could have remained unaware of its significance. Every man of intelligence must have told himself that this new foundation stone was also the keystone of a long period of the Roman church. He must have turned a glance of reverent farewell to the ancient cathedral, in regard to which the life of Christian nations had been one continued pilgrimage, and within whose venerated halls hovered the associations of twelve centuries of history. The ancient cathedral was now to pass away, as the ancient empire of Constantine and the ancient basilica of Sylvester had passed. The new era erected a new cathedral for an altered race, and must not Julius II have asked himself what would be its import in the coming centuries? Had the sibyl of Augustus appeared to him on this solemn occasion to reveal the fate of the Roman church in the near future, he would have turned away in horror. But in 1506 the power of the sacred chair seemed to the pope to rest on pillars more solid than those over which Bramante's cupola was to soar, and no suspicion lay further from his mind than the thought, that behind the veil of time already stood the forces of an incalculable revolution that would rend in twain the cathedral of the Roman church.

Everyone knows that the taxes for the building of S. Peter's, which Julius already demanded from Christendom, and which his successor allowed to degenerate into usurious traffic, were the first actual causes of the German reformation. The historian of the Council of Trent was thereupon justified in his remarkable confession:

> The material structure of S. Peter's was thus responsible for the fall of a great part of his spiritual building; since in order to collect all the millions consumed by the colossal work, the successor of Julius II was obliged to resort to means that gave rise to Luther's heresy, and this has made the church the poorer by many more million souls.

In fact the German reformation, which turned away half of Catholic mankind from S. Peter's in Rome, already stood close to the foundations of the new church, and it is merely a vain compensation for the other half to see, in the finished cathedral, the spirit of heresy represented in the form of a hideous demon, on whose neck is placed the foot of the founder of the Jesuit order. New S. Peter's was no longer that which it ought to have been, and what old S. Peter's had been, the temple of the universal church, but only the center of those races—for the most part Latin—who remained faithful to the papacy. Almost from the first hour the history of its construction is accompanied by the apostasy of the evangelical provincial churches (chiefly German), from the Roman papacy, and by the firm establishment of a modern culture on foundations as immovable as the fundamental laws of intellectual liberty can be. The plan of the gigantic cathedral of the Catholic church was conceived even before the Reformation, but the Lutheran heresy probably contributed in no slight degree to inflame the zeal of Popes Julius and Leo. It is justly called the fortress of Catholicism. Who can think of S. Peter's in Rome apart from the papacy?

The work of building was protracted throughout the reigns of twenty popes, until on November 18, 1626, Urban VIII was able to consecrate the finished structure, on the date when, according to legend, Bishop Sylvester had blessed the ancient Church of S. Peter. The history of its building consequently embraces that of the fine arts from the time of their classic perfection to their decadence, their ruin and their second renaissance; from Bramante, Raphael and Michelangelo down to Maderno, Bernini and Fontana, nay, even down to Canova and Thorwaldsen, who erected within it the monuments of the latest renaissance.

Bramante worked for eight years in S. Peter's, during which time the ancient church was partially demolished. In their eager haste pope and architect showed so little reverence for the past that they allowed most of the monuments, mosaics and the antique columns of the ancient building to be destroyed. Michelangelo indignantly remonstrated against the vandalism shown by Bramante. Even beautiful tombs of the time of Mino, even the monument to the very father of Renaissance culture—Nicholas V —were broken in pieces. We may now see the remains of these monuments, in the crypt of the Vatican, the subterranean museum of the ruined antiquity of S. Peter's and also of the papacy. These vaults contain an invaluable, if mutilated series of historic memorials, which, beginning with the tomb of Junius Bassus, ends with the coffin of Alexander VI. They are the catacombs of the papal history, where the traveler gazes on the stone face of a bygone time, and the taper's light falls on the mosaics of the eighth century, on sculptured forms resembling idols, on fragments of inscriptions, such as that of the Donation of Matilda, on the imperial grave of Otto II, on pagan sarcophagi, in which repose spiritual despots, on stone coffins, and above them on the dismal outstretched forms of popes, who during life ruled men like gods, and who with the age to which they belonged lie buried deep below the Cathedral of S. Peter.

Bramante built the four colossal piers of the cupola, but soon after his time it was found necessary to strengthen the foundations. He also began the tribune of the nave and that of the south transept. This was all that either he or Julius II beheld of the structure. For the great architect died on March 11, 1514, and appropriately found a grave in the crypt of the cathedral which he had founded. According to his dying wish, Raphael succeeded him in the direction of the work, at first in conjunction with his friend Giuliano di Sangallo, and the aged Fra Giocondo of Verona, after 1518 alone. The substitution of a Latin cross designed by Raphael, for the Greek cross originally intended, was a blunder. Bramante's idea, however, triumphed after repeated vacillations. After Raphael's death Peruzzi adopted a new design, which was considered the most beautiful of all made for S. Peter's, and reverted to the Greek form. After him Antonio di Sangallo again adopted the long nave; and once more Michelangelo designed another Greek transept; but although, by the express orders of the pope, the building was continued down to the beginning of the seventeenth century on the lines of the original plan, Paul V acquiesced in the alterations proposed by his architect Maderno, by which S. Peter's finally received the form of a Latin cross. The fatal result of this decision is that the dome, the audacious work of Michelangelo, has never received full justice.

The traveller who stands for the first time in front of S. Peter's must admit that a Gothic cathedral is the ideal of a church, and perhaps that Christianity itself is there expressed in a clearer and more historic aspect than in this world-famous building. In the interior the masses of the piers, the arches and barrel-vaulting suggest immensity but not infinity. We breathe no air of sanctity, and that spell of mystery, with which the ancient and simple basilicas of Rome and Ravenna are filled, is entirely absent. In S. Peter's the language of religion is translated into the modern, secular and profane style of a period of soulless splendor. The wealth of magnificent mosaics is here spread with astounding lavishness over walls and vaults, but these mosaics—chiefly copies from paintings belonging to the period of the material redundance of art—produce a merely decorative effect and exercise no religious influence such as their legitimate predecessors in ancient basilicas. And yet this gorgeous theater of the modern cult of the Catholic religion was conceived and built in the proportions of a universal church; and thus it stands unique in the world.

If in their cathedrals and basilicas bygone generations had given expression to their ardent longing for divine salvation, S. Peter's on the other hand shows a triumphant consciousness of the actual possession of a great culture, in the acquisition of which the Christian church had borne so great a part. In fact this colossal structure sprang up out of the Renaissance, in the medium of the secular culture, to which paganism and Christianity had combined to give a new and universal form. It is the memorial of that neo-Latin culture, a monumental metamorphosis of the secularized spirit of the church, the last great act of the papacy. If Rome perished and a silent waste stretched round S. Peter's, this gigantic cathedral would afford to posterity a more convincing witness to the all-ruling power of the papacy and of the cosmopolitan idea of the church than the pyramids of Egypt of the power of Rhampsinitus and Cheops.

In S. Peter's is embodied the universality, which in the history of culture corresponds to the cosmos of the church. It is the crystallization of the collective modern culture of the Italian Renaissance. The Byzantine, Roman and Gothic churches are all stamped with the individual impress of a more or less limited religious past. Although S. Peter's also necessarily bears the features of the culture of its time, nevertheless this is so universal that no one specifically historic or national element predominates over the others.

XI

Paganism at the Court of Leo X

Upon the death of Julius II (1513), the cardinals elected Giovanni de' Medici as pope. He took the name of Leo X (1513–21). Leo's ecclesiastical career began at the age of fourteen, when Pope Innocent VIII made him a cardinal. Carefully educated in Florence by the great humanists Poliziano, Pico della Mirandola, Ficino, and Bibiena, he early became a great patron of art and literature.—EDITOR.

GREAT was the part played by the papacy in Renaissance culture, the magnificent flower of an epoch in the world's history, after the expiration of which the Italian intellect naturally sank back in exhaustion from the feverish exertion to which it had been roused. The influence of the popes on the civilization of mankind stood in exact proportion to their harmony with the requirements of the time. It was greatest in the Middle Ages, when all intellectual life lay under the spell of theology; it was powerful towards the close of this period, when the popes surrendered themselves to the humanistic current of the century, when the spirit of classic antiquity, the invigorating gulfstream of culture, again flowed through the world of thought. Had the popes hurled the anathemas of their predecessors against pagan culture, or

From book XIV, ch. 4, sec. 1.

those of their successors against the tendencies of rationalism, they would have checked an entire civilization. It was however the last time that the papacy was able to assume an attitude of perfect harmony with the culture of the period. After the Council of Trent the Counter-Reformation, the Inquisition, and Jesuitism erected, so to speak, a Chinese wall around it, so that it lost connection with the progress of the time. A glance at its present position reveals to what a depth of torpidity and isolation the papal hierarchy has sunk in the midst of the living world.

No pope abandoned himself so unreservedly to the tendencies of his age as Leo X. He was so entirely permeated by them that his name has been given to his period, although his intellect, which was merely receptive, did not in any way endow it with the impress of his ideas. For no spark of native genius, no true creative power dwelt in this pleasure-seeking feminine nature. On succeeding to rule, Leo said to his brother Giuliano, "Let us enjoy the papacy, since God has given it to us." And to no more worldly sentiment could a pope have given utterance than this epicurean speech. The mainspring of his life was sensuous enjoyment of the full possession of contemporary culture, with which he was intoxicated. The monks with their ideals of poverty and mendicancy he held in contempt. He had no religious prejudices. His toleration sprang from his classic culture, and this was based on no other principles than those of beauty and enjoyment. Painting, poetry, eloquence, and music, these national endowments of the Italians, under Leo became the powers of the intellectual luxury of the time.

Pallavicini has bitterly upbraided him because he surrounded himself entirely with poets instead of theologians, and preferred the fables of paganism to the doctrines of Christianity. The German Reformation raised no complaint against the elegant classic culture of the papacy, but the exclusively pagan tendency of the Italians undoubtedly demanded as its antithesis the renaissance of Christianity. The task of reforming the two intellectual tendencies of the age, the world of faith and that of knowledge, was too great for any single people. It was divided between Italy and Germany, and never have the national intellects of these two countries shown themselves more free and independent than in these achievements in the history of culture.

In Leo's age paganism seemed entirely to discard the vesture of Christianity, in which as imagination, sense of form and polytheism, it had always survived among the Latins. Could a Roman of Cicero's time have been present in the sixteenth century at the festival of one of the saints of the church on whom the epithet of *Divus* had been bestowed, he would scarcely have discovered anything unfamiliar in his surroundings. In Roman sepulchral inscriptions God is again Jupiter; Dante had already called him Sommo Giove—and heaven again Olympus. The conservators of Rome, who restored a cistern on the Capitol, inscribed on it like ancient Romans, "We have founded the vessel, do thou fill it, O Jupiter, with rain, and be gracious to the presidents of thy rock." The cardinals were called senators, the saints simply gods (*dii* and *deae*), and the deifying title of *Divus*, as that of *Optimus Maximus*, is usually bestowed on the popes. When Leo ascended the throne the poet Janus Vitalis announced that Jupiter had again descended from Olympus to Rome, and that Leo Medici as Apollo would cure all the maladies of the time. Neither had Julius II been dismayed when one Good Friday a preacher had likened him to Zeus, and compared Christ to Decius or Curtius. In his elegy on Bibiena, dedicated to Pope Leo, Valerianus thus addresses the shade of the cardinal:

> We do not seek to inquire to what part of Olympus thy immortal virtue has led thee on a golden quadriga, but when thou wanderest through the heavenly worlds to look on the heroes, then forget not to implore the King of Heaven and all the other gods, that, if they would enjoy their worship here on earth, to add to Leo those years of which the godless Parcæ deprived Giuliano Medici and thee.

With equal naïvete Cathaneus relates that he had erected a tumulus on the shore to his friend Johannes Bonifacius, who had been drowned, and that in a loud voice he had three times invoked him by name. We shall presently see that on Leo's death the Romans even ventured publicly to sacrifice a bull in the Colosseum to the hostile gods.

Paganism oozed through every pore of Catholicism, in the form of art and religion, of Platonic philosophy and Ciceronian eloquence. Under the hands of Bembo and Sadoleto even the papal bulls adopted the style and phrases of antiquity. Among the Latins the Christian religion had become petrified into a pagan service of the senses and of formulas. The absence of all deep philosophical power in the national intellect of Italy served as a means of defense to the Roman church, which could thus survive her secularization, although she could not have outlived her spiritual regeneration. From the Platonic school at Florence, which was dissolved in the beginning of the sixteenth century, issued theistic and pantheistic ideas, but no definite rationalism. From this Platonism Italian art erected an ideal enthusiasm for the Beautiful, and this was its most living influence; it took the place of religion in the Renaissance; Plato became the apostle of the Beautiful. The sight of the unutterably depraved priesthood, or the knowledge that the papal power made the greatness of Italy impossible, may have driven patriotic thinkers such as Machiavelli to unbelief, while the influence of the ancient philosophy possibly filled others with contempt for the doctrines of the church, or the admiration of paganism produced an aesthetic and sceptical tolerance. The barriers of Dante's Paradiso were removed; the beloved pagans were transplanted into the glory of the heaven of the blessed, where they exchanged greetings with the Christian successors to their splendor.

Sceptics appeared in the liberal schools of Bologna and Padua, who denied the existence of a heaven beyond, while astrology, in affirming the influences of nativity, destroyed belief in the freedom of will. The celebrated head of the Italian sceptics was the Mantuan, Pietro Pomponazzo, and from his school issued the most renowned scholars of the time. Although in 1513 the Lateran Council found it necessary to proclaim belief in the immortality of the soul as an article of faith, Pomponazzo in one of his writings ventured to assert that it was impossible to give rational demonstration of this doctrine, and that it had never been maintained by Aristotle. Thirty years later Pomponazzo would have been burnt for this assertion, but he was now merely punished

405

with censures. Bembo protected his pamphlet from condemnation, and he died highly honored at Bologna in 1524. In his youth Leo X had been initiated in debates on Plato's doctrines on the soul; it is said that as pope he once praised the acute arguments with which an opponent of the theory of immortality defended his views; and even if this and other sneers, attributed to Leo and his friends, at "the profitable fable of Christianity," be untrue, they serve at all events to show the atmosphere that prevailed in the Vatican.

Scepticism reigned universally. Accommodating itself to the prevailing culture, however, it remained diplomatically veiled from sight. Priests laughed among themselves, as in former days the augurs in ancient Rome, and allowed their hands to be reverently kissed by smiling laymen. We can form no opinion, however, as to how far scepticism would have developed into rationalism in Italy, since free inquiry was soon stifled or suppressed by the Inquisition. Generally speaking, among Italians the desire for truth was not the result of their desire for learning. In Italy, the hierarchical despotism, united to sensuality and the longing for the Beautiful, with the gross superstition of the lower classes and the unbelief of the upper, produced a distaste for the labor of thought and the moral struggles by which it is accompanied. After humanistic culture had emerged from the stage of enthusiastic discovery, it became an intellectual luxury, without giving rise to any deeper effect on the ethical life of the nation. It did not morally rejuvenate itself, and in this lies its weakness even at the present day.

In the age of Leo culture in short was preeminently secular. In the Middle Ages it consisted essentially in theological and legal discipline; but now philology, rhetoric, poetry, archaeology, and natural science gained the upper hand. The treasures of Italian learning were greater then than now. In relation to the time and its progress, they were probably equal to those of Germany at the present day. The church, however, sought to gather learned men and learning itself within her priesthood, as in the Middle Ages she had striven to gather them within the fold of monasticism.

In Leo's time, after the purely secular patronage of arts and letters exercised by the Medici in Florence had been transformed into a spiritual patronage in Rome, scholars and poets found more powerful protectors in the Vatican and among the greater prelates than in princes and republics. The series of writings dedicated to popes and cardinals is very numerous. This servile relationship already condemned scholars and poets to silence on many subjects. They might be cynics and pagans, but not free-thinkers. The papal censorship of the sixteenth century after Leo X persecuted not the abominable works of Aretino, but the writings of the serious-minded Flaminius, and Sadoleto's treatise on the Epistle of Paul to the Romans was placed on the Index.

Scholars and poets went to the Curia in search of offices and benefices, and here took orders as apostolic secretaries, canons, and bishops. The most celebrated literati were priests; such were Bembo, Sadoleto, Giberti, Canossa. The famous poet Bernardo Accolti was apostolic secretary; the renowned poet Vida died a bishop; the celebrated Latin historian of Rome, Paulus Jovius, was a bishop also; writers of novelle like Bandello, and a hundred poets of the time, were bishops or papal scriptors or abbreviators. The most horrible of all authors, Pietro Aretino, even entertained hopes of the cardinal's purple.

In Roman society the finest culture was more especially found within the higher circles of the clergy. The period of the Renaissance is also the golden age of the clerical aristocracy, who reveled in the possession of Rome. The Roman state had become a state of monsignori, and to the monsignori literature also essentially belonged. After the time of the Borgia the Roman nobility, if not serving in the army of the pope, the emperor, Spain or France, sank into that debasing condition of indolence and fossilization, deprived of all political activity, from which it is only now beginning to emerge. Of the ancient families of the city, the richest at this time was the Massimi; its head Domenico dwelt in princely splendor in his palace in Parione, where he gave magnificent banquets; but we do not hear that he encouraged learning or art, although Lelio, a member of his house, was one of the greatest scholars in Rome. There was no longer, as in Petrarch's days, any great Maecenas among the Roman barons, and if among the nobility several men of exquisite culture, such as the Mellini, Cesarini, Altieri, the Porcari, and Valle, were found, they stood for the most part in immediate connection with the prelates. The state, wealth, luxury, and culture, all had been usurped by the priests. The cardinals possessed larger incomes than the greater nobles, the annual revenues of many amounting to 30,000 ducats and upwards.

Among the middle class some bankers were conspicuous owing to their wealth, and if we expect the Massimi, wealth lay mainly in the hands of some Italian immigrants or German merchants such as the Welsers and Fuggers. The aristocracy of money, which had raised the house of Medici to the papal throne, was represented in Rome by Agostino Chigi. This distinguished man was on intimate terms with Leo X, and we may say was as much his patron as his favorite. The most celebrated scholars, poets and artists enjoyed his princely liberality. The Spanocchi, who kept a bank of exchange, were also respected on account of their wealth and their patronage of the noble arts. Bindo Altoviti was conspicuous as a Maecenas. His family had come from Florence, and owing to the marriage of Rinaldo to Clarentia Cibò, sister of Innocent VIII, had risen to power in Rome. Antonio Altoviti, who married Dianora, daughter of this Rinaldo, was master of the Mint under Innocent VIII, acquired wealth and bought houses beside the Ponte S. Angelo. His son Bindo, born in 1491, restored the ancestral dwelling about 1514, and this deserted and picturesque palace still remains beside the bridge. Raphael painted the Impannata for Bindo, Michelangelo presented him with the cartoons of his Sistine pictures, and Benvenuto Cellini executed his bust in bronze.

Diplomacy, which, with the cardinals' courts, was so prominent a characteristic of Roman society in the sixteenth century, had not yet attained prominence in the time of Leo X. The magnificent cavalcades of the ambassadors indeed enlivened Rome with scenes of theatrical splendor; it was merely owing to accident, however, if envoys remaining for a longer period, those especially of Italian courts, made their houses centers of society. This was done by Castiglione, the envoy of Mantua and Ferrara; by Alberto Pio of Carpi, ambassador at Rome first of the emperor, then of France, and afterwards by Gasparo Contarini and Jean du Bellay.

The higher ranks of Roman society presented a variety of circles, the center of which was almost invariably a clerical Maecenas. First of all was the comprehensive circle of the pope. Then the smaller coteries of the Cardinals Riario, Grimani, Bibiena, and Alidosi, of Giulio Medici, Caraffa and de Saulis, of Petrucci, Farnese, Castellesi and Soderini, of Sanseverino, Gonzago and Egidius of Viterbo. These men exercised a patronage similar to that of the great nobles in ancient Rome. Each according to his inclination protected learning or art. In the time of Clement VII the young cardinal Ippolito Medici supported 300 poetasters in his palace. There were also the circles of the Chigi and Altoviti, of Castiglione and Alberto Pio, of the art-loving Baldassare Turini and of Sigismondo Conti of Foligno. Even Raphael, who had now risen to wealth, appears as a Maecenas. On his visits to the Vatican he was followed by a troop of clients who provoked the laughter of the recluse Michelangelo. Raphael lived like a great noble in his palace in the Borgo, as his countryman Bramante had lived, as Sangallo lived and as Bernini was to live afterwards.

In the circles that surrounded these patrons of art and letters a satirist would have discovered all the characteristics portrayed in the pictures of manners given by Horace and Juvenal, Ammianus and Jerome. At the banquets of the pope and cardinals he would again have discovered the flatterers, hypocrites and parasites, who with outstretched necks extolled the pictures, statues, libraries and collections of their patrons, and would have listened to the rhetoricians, who lauded their greatness to the skies. In truth the Rome of Julius II and Leo X resembled on a reduced scale the Rome of the Roman emperors. Satires and novelle give us a picture of the city in these days; but no one ventured to appear as the Juvenal of the Renaissance.

In this paganizing society of witty and pleasure-loving men there was only one deficiency, the absence of noble women. This was so acutely felt that the arrival of Giuliano Medici with his wife excited universal joy. "God be praised," wrote Bibiena, "for we want nothing here but a court of women." In the time of Innocent VIII and Alexander VI illustrious women were boldly invited to banquets at the Vatican, but after the Borgia the popes rarely ventured on such a step. No good woman could have moved voluntarily and at ease among the monsignori, as women moved at the courts of Ferrara, Mantua and Urbino. It was with good reason that Veronica Gambara formed her brilliant circle at Bologna. When Vittoria Colonna afterwards came to Rome, she lived mainly in a convent. Bianca Rangone also, for whom Leo X built a summerhouse in the Borgo, led a retired life. The presence of Isabella Gonzaga at theatrical representations in the Vatican was, however, observed.

In Roman society the place of noble women, was filled by mistresses and courtesans. Before he became cardinal Bembo lived openly with the beautiful Venetian Morosina. Leo X showed no hesitation in attending the marriage of Agostino Chigi with his mistress Francesca, another beautiful Venetian. Refinement of life produced a revival of the institution of hetaerae.

Aretino celebrated a Roman courtesan, who could repeat a hundred passages from the classics and knew by heart all Petrarch's poems and Boccaccio's tales. The celebrated Imperia of Ferrara in the time of Julius II shone like a star, whose rays dazzled the senses of all the monsignori. Her dwelling in the Banks, which is described by Bandello, may be regarded as a salon, thronged by the most intellectual men. Hangings, pictures, vases, nicknacks, choice books, beautiful Renaissance furniture lent such magnificence to her rooms, that the noble Spanish ambassador one day spat in the face of a servant, because he could find no other place suitable for the purpose. Imperia accompanied her own verses, or those of her adorers, on the lute; she was a pupil of Strascino, for whose finest poem, "On Venery," she had probably supplied the material. This youthful Phryne was celebrated by Blosius, Beroaldo and a hundred other poets, and even the grave Sadoleto was reputed her admirer. She died only twenty-six years old, and received honorable burial in the Chapel of S. Georgia. Her epitaph records as her title of honor the great name of a Roman hetaera, of which she had been entirely worthy, and her beauty, rare among mankind. Becadelli's theory that courtesans occupy a more useful place than pious nuns was acted on in Rome. As the surname Romana had been given to the last saintly Roman woman in the time of Eugenius IV, so with equal national pride people now talked of a Cortisana Romana. Intellect in women, clothed in physical beauty, was celebrated with the feeling of antiquity.

We should inspire disgust did we attempt to depict the unbounded vice of Roman society in the corrupt times of Leo X or to lift the veil from the mysteries of the priesthood. The moral corruption of an age, one of the best of whose productions bore the title of "Syphilis," is sufficiently known, but the classic vices of Greece and the East were not first introduced by the Renaissance, nor was the priesthood more depraved than lay society, nor Rome more corrupt than Genoa, Venice or Paris. In the capital of the church, however, immorality necessarily appears more revolting and also more dangerous than elsewhere.

In the midst of this corrupt priesthood we may observe a germ of moral reaction in a society of pious men, which was productive of great results at a later period. This is the Oratorium Divini Amoris [Oratory of Divine Love], of which the priest Julius Dathus of SS. Silvestro e Dorotea in Trastevere was the head. In this society Christendom sought refuge from the whirl of pagan pleasures in the time of Leo X. It was joined by Giampietro Caraffa and his friend Gaetano Tiene. The ardent zealot Caraffa, nephew of Cardinal Olivieri, had already been chamberlain to Alexander VI and was made bishop of Chieti under Julius II; under Leo X he acquired distinction at the Lateran Council and obtained renown as nuncio in England and Spain. Sadoleto, Contarini, Giberti, Aluigi Lippomanno, Latinus Juvenalis, Tullius Crispoldus, Bonifacius a Colle belonged to this oratory, which became the foundation of the order of the Theatines.

Even before Luther or Hutten, Savonarola had described Rome as a sink of iniquity. Did we however only possess the picture of the city drawn by a single reformer, it would undoubtedly be onesided. Luther only beheld the profane because he only sought for the sacred Rome. Erasmus fell under the spell of the same city, and while Luther said that he would not take 1000 florins not to have seen corrupt Rome, Erasmus acknowledged that only Lethe could wash out its sweet remembrance. Erasmus first came in February or March 1509, and spent some months with men of learning, such as Scipio Carteromachus, Sphaerula, Julius Camillus, Beroaldo, and with cardinals such as Grimani, Riario, Medici and the cardinal of Nantes. Rome as the theater of the world and its culture fascinated the greatest scholar of the time. Monuments, art and collections, libraries, the wealth of learning and intellect, the grandiose style of life, all filled him with admiration. As a satirist it seemed to him a great European carnival, where worldly vanity went masked in spiritual attire, where were represented all lusts and desires, all intrigues and crimes, their magnet the Vatican, and thirst for gold, honors and power the forces that moved them. Sailing on this tumultuous sea he seemed to behold Sebastian Brand's overcrowded Ship of Fools; and, in fact, soon after his arrival in London in 1509, he wrote his celebrated *Praise of Folly* in the house of Thomas More.

As a Christian he was astonished at the bold and glaring coloring borrowed from paganism by the Roman religion, of which nothing remained that was not false, and whose formerly revered temple had been transformed by the ambition and rapacity of the priesthood into a European banking house and a retail market for diplomas of favors, indulgences and objects of superstition. As a man of the world, however, Erasmus could not feel otherwise than at ease in the courts of cardinals, and above all he had to acknowledge that in this corrupt Rome were found the most liberal form of intercourse and the most exquisite courtesy. In the age when in his *Cortegiano*, Castiglione drew the ideal courtier, ancient urbanity was revived, and even if only the mask of inward corruption, it must have enchanted every northerner.

The papacy, learning, antiquity, art, all linked Roman society in correspondence with the world. In Rome the most important matters of the time were discussed, or actively taken in hand; cosmopolitan politics, cosmopolitan literature, for in the Renaissance of Latinism we may speak of such a thing, the arts, poetry,

412

the rising drama—above all, science. The wealth of intellectual life flourished here in the morass of vice. It is, however, only just to admit that alongside of sensuality and avarice, pride and self-importance, hypocrisy and falsehood, conspicuous virtues were seen; generosity, friendship and benevolence, respect paid to talent and love of all that was beautiful. In nobler natures even unchastity was accompanied by a liberal humanity, which was the true flower of the culture of the Italians. . . .

XII

The Condition of Rome under Leo X

IN spite of the many public and private buildings, the city of Leo X in nowise presented a beautiful or even a habitable aspect. The popes were unable to rebuild the whole of Rome, and during their long period of rule there was never a time in which the city did not produce the impression of decay. The character of ruinous desolation and enchanted desertion, over which hovers the melancholy spirit of the past, as over no other city in the world, still constitutes the especial charm of Rome. All that was new was isolated and disconnected. Magnificent palaces with frescoed facades stood in streets that yawned with waste spaces or among the gloomy dwellings of the Middle Ages. This contrast entirely corresponded to the spiritual character of the city. The sacerdotal element thrust the civic out of sight. Convents, encircled with great walled enclosures, occupied vast tracts of the city and prevented the rise of other buildings. The cosmopolitan character of Rome was also a hindrance to architectural individuality. People had only to compare Florence, Genoa, Venice and even the smaller cities of Italy with Rome in order to perceive that the city did not bear the stamp of organic growth that springs from the national spirit. Leo X exerted himself to enlarge, and to introduce

From book XIV, ch. 4, sec. 5.

414

some plan into, the labyrinthine streets, but his intention could not be carried out by edicts. Entire quarters of the city, such as the district Monti, parts of Trevi and Colonna, of Campitelli and Ripa, were left in their savage state, and have thus in great part remained until recent times.

For centuries the Field of Mars had been the true center of the city, and here building had been most actively carried on. Leo invited Tuscans to make their abode in this quarter, more especially where the three streets, which had long existed and which end in the Piazza del Popolo, had by his commands been put into better order. One of these, the present Ripetta, was at this time called after him the Leonina. But it, too, was broken by waste spaces and vineyards, especially where it adjoined the Corso. And at this time there was scarcely a street in Rome, not even the Via Giulia, that could be called finished or complete.

The population increased. The growth of modern cities is due essentially to the development of prosperity by commerce and industry among the middle classes, and also to immigration. The former of these sources can never have had any influence on the growth of Rome. The mass of the Roman people lived mainly on the requirements of the priesthood, or as even in ancient times on the concourse of foreigners. While the rest of Italy was alight with the flames of war, Rome enjoyed tranquility under Leo X. Many Italians consequently came to the city as to a haven of safety. Since the time of Sixtus IV even Slavonians and Albanians had established themselves on the Ripetta, and after Julius II a numerous colony of Lombards settled in the Field of Mars. Genoese, Florentines, even Spaniards and Germans, natives of Flanders, Lorraine and Burgundy ensconced themselves from Trastevere far into the Campo Marzo, in quarters whose centers were formed by their national churches. Several of these national names still survive in the names of streets. Art and learning, the church, the papal court yearly attracted crowds of newcomers, who arrived to seek their fortunes in Rome as in the times of the ancient emperors. If some only appeared and vanished with the flow and ebb of fortune, others remained in the city and became Romans. According to the statement of Francesco Vettori, the population of Rome increased by a third during the reign of Leo X, and before the disasters of 1527 was estimated by Jovius at 85,000.

But in spite of all, the Roman people were among the poorest in Italy. Prelates and courtiers, papal nephews and adventurers may have accumulated temporary fortunes, but the wealth of the middle classes and the stationary wealth of Rome remained insignificant. The civic nobility and the great burgher class fell more and more to decay. Hundreds of senatorial families, whose names are registered in the Fasti of the Capitolian magistracy, or who belonged to ancient noble houses, still dwelt in their historic quarters, but contemplated with sadness their inevitable ruin. Incessant wars had devastated the country round Rome; the Borgia had made terrible clearances among the nobility and had introduced arbitrary changes in their property. The restorations effected on the death of Alexander VI did not suffice to repair these losses. Colonna and Orsini it is true still remained the foremost feudal families of Rome, and still regarded themselves as independent princely houses, but in the statistics of the Italian dynastic princes of Leo's time, the estimate of their revenues would barely have amounted to 25,000 ducats. The Conti and Gaetani, the Savelli and Anibaldi, the Frangipani, Pierleoni, Astaldi and Cenci, in short the entire historic nobility of the city, had fallen very low. Even families comparatively fortunate, such as the Farnesi, Altieri, the Valle, Massimi and Cesarini, owed their better circumstances to merely accidental causes.

In the beginning of the sixteenth century Marcantonio Altieri, who, as one of the conservators during the illness of Julius II, had been the negotiator of peace with the barons, compiled a work, in which he represents some noble Romans as bewailing the utter ruin of the civic families.

Rome, formerly the Queen of the Universe, has sunk so low, that to the Romans their own city must appear like a desolate and gloomy den. From the quarter Monti as far as Cavallo, Trevi, and to the quarter of the Conti, are missing the Cerroni, Novelli, Paparoni and Petrucci, further the Salvetti, Nisci, Cagnoni, the Lupelli, Pirroni and Venettini; the Dammari, Foschi and Pini, the

Masci, Capogalli, Mantaca and Carboni, the Palocchi, Acorari, Pedacchia and Valentini; the Palelli, Arcioni, Migni, Capomastri, Subbatari, Negri; then the Mancini, Scotti, Infessura, Diotajuti, Boccamazi, Cenci, Tasca, Portii; the Calvi, Lalli, Buonsignori, Grifonetti, Frangipani and Marcellini. All these families, owing to their property, numbers and antiquity, formerly so celebrated and magnificent, are now either entirely or in part ruined. As regards the rest of the unfortunate city, of the many seats founded in former days for the pleasure of the nobles, how many are there that have now so entirely vanished from sight, that we can scarcely discover traces of the porticoes, where we were formerly received. But why should we speak of palaces, when a glance at the streets is enough? For we must sorrowfully admit that the greatest and most prosperous part of their inhabitants, many honored and honorable men with their families, have disappeared. Who can survey without profound sorrow the once glorious Piazza Colonna, formerly inhabited by the fathers, children and grandchildren of the Buffalini, not to mention the Cancellieri, Treiofani, Tetellini, the Normandi, Sbonia, Valerani, Vari, Carosi, the Sorici, Ceretani, and Boccacci, the Juvancolini, Palosci, Jacobazzi, the Capoccini, the Signorili, and other countless respected families of the neighborhood? They have now almost entirely passed away, and in their place we find merely a mean and degraded rabble.

The speakers in the dialogue surveyed yet other quarters and districts of Rome, such as Pigna, Piscina, Piazza Giudea, Campitelli, in which they deplored the ruin of almost every illustrious family. We would rather remain silent, says the dejected Altieri, concerning the rest of Rome, so that we may not add to our grief by the enumeration of all the families that have fallen to decay in this great city, especially since we lack the genius and means to restore them. A Pierleoni recalls the former greatness of his family, in whose palaces Pope Urban II had found an asylum, and which was now sunk in misery. A Capoccia paints a like picture of the past glories and the present impoverishment of his noble house, and the proud Altieri acknowledges himself to have fallen so low that he is obliged to engage in agriculture and to associate with the humblest class. He consoles his companions in misfortune with references to the common fate which, in this century, had befallen the greatest families of Italy, such as the house of Aragon, the Sforza and Malatesta, the Ordelaffi and

Montefeltre, all of whom within a short space of time had been killed, scattered or reduced to beggary in the most piteous manner. They must, therefore, comfort themselves with the sentence of Pindar concerning the uncertainty of fortune, and accept in patience the inexorable fate.

Such is the picture which Romans themselves draw of the decay and ruin of the most illustrious class of the Roman people even in the most extolled age of the city, and we have quoted it here in order to correct exaggerated accounts of the prosperity and splendor of Rome at this period. A few years later Altieri penned his description, the terrible misfortune befell her that effaced even this picture of the Eternal City.

XIII

Aftermath of Catastrophe

*After the brief pontificate of Adrian VI (1522–23), Giulio de'
Medici became Pope Clement VII (1523–34). A man of humane
education, he had served his cousin, Leo X, as adviser, and reaped
among the rewards of service the archbishopric of Florence and
a cardinalate. As pope he followed disastrously ambiguous diplomacy, allying now with Francis I of France, and again with
Francis's enemy, the Emperor Charles V. His treacherous re-
alignment with Francis, by joining the Holy League of Cognac
(1526), brought Bourbon and the imperial troops to Rome. In
the following sections, Gregorovius describes the consequences of
the terrible sack that ensued.—*Editor.

PESTILENCE raged in Rome and the troops grew riotous; from
England and France arose threatenings of war. Prince Philibert
in consequence wished to make peace with the pope. But the
army would not hear of treaties. The greater part of the pillagers
were again in a state of beggary, and many others in weariness
and satiety even committed suicide. The prophet of Siena, whom
they kept with them, had prophesied truly when he said: "Dear
comrades, now is the time, rob and take all that you can find;
you must, however, yield everything up again; the property of

From book XIV, ch. 7, secs. 1 and 2.

priests and the spoils of war go as they come." Soldiers, in possession of more than 30,000 florins, loudly clamored for their arrears of pay. They demanded the pope as hostage, and permission to sack S. Angelo, in which they believed that the treasures of the world were collected. Orange tranquilized the mutineers by promising to yield himself as security for their demands, and so strangely had circumstances altered, that the pillagers, choked with their spoils, found themselves in yet worse condition than their enemies in S. Angelo.

Even before the withdrawal of the allied army, Clement had summoned Lannoy from Siena to Rome to afford him the support of his authority; for Lannoy still remained faithful to the pope, and was still carrying on negotiations with friends and enemies, with the allies and the imperialists at the same time. When the viceroy arrived on May 28 the soldiers threatened to murder him, and he fled from Rome. A mile outside the city he met Moncada, the duke of Amalfi, del Vasto, Alarcon and Don Enrico Manriquez, who had come from Terracina with a few thousand men, and with them he returned to Rome the same day.

No one paid heed to him any longer; Philibert conducted the negotiation by means of plenipotentiaries. When on May 31 the prince was wounded by a shot from S. Angelo, whence the besieged continued firing on the trenches, the imperialists threatened to storm the fortress and to kill the pope and cardinals. Cannon had already been planted on Monte Mario and trained on S. Angelo. A mine, which reached the foundations, had also been laid from the gate of the fortress, and if driven to extremities the troops threatened to blow up the pope and all the cardinals and prelates.

On June 1 the pope sent Schomberg to the imperialists; he also —and this was his bitterest resolve—sent for Cardinal Colonna. He compared Colonna—his most uncompromising enemy—to the lance of Achilles, which wounded and healed at the same time; he appealed to the Cardinal's compassion and magnanimity and asked him for assistance. Together they bewailed the sufferings of Rome and their own imprudence which had caused them. Pompeo now strove to alleviate these sufferings, and henceforward assisted the pope in raising the money which he had to pay. Clement was finally obliged to consent to a treaty, for it was impossible that he could remain more than a week longer in S. Angelo, where hunger and pestilence were raging. He beheld almost all his states lost to him, with the exception of Umbria, which was protected by the allied army. Venice profited by the misfortunes of her ally to reoccupy Ravenna and Cervia. Gismondo Malatesta had entered Rimini; Alfonso was advancing against Modena. Even Florence, upon which the pope bestowed more than half his care, had forced Cardinal Passerini and Ippolito and Alessandro to leave on May 16. Filippo Strozzi and his wife Clarice, to whom the elevation of these Medicean bastards had always been a thorn in the side, had borne a conspicuous part in this revolution. The republic was restored in Florence, and on June 1 Niccolo Capponi, son of the celebrated Piero, was made Gonfaloniere. To their misfortune the Florentines renewed their alliance with the king of France.

On June 5 Clement concluded a treaty with the imperialist envoy Giambartolomeo Gattinara, and surrendered to Charles's mercy. He undertook to pay the army 400,000 ducats in three instalments, and gave as securities the archbishops of Siponto and Pisa, the bishops of Pistoja and Verona, and his relations Jacopo Salviati, Lorenzo Ridolfi and Simone Ricasoli. He promised to surrender Ostia, Civita-vecchia, Modena, Parma and Piacenza as pledges, and to reinstate the Colonna in their rights. Until the payments were discharged he was to remain with the cardinals in S. Angelo, and then to go in freedom to Naples or further, in order to conclude the peace with the emperor. Renzo Orsini, Orazio Baglione and the foreign envoys were to have free retreat from the fortress.

On June 7 the papal garrison left S. Angelo, and Alarcon entered with three companies of Germans; Italians and Spaniards. This officer might boast that within the space of two years he had been jailer both of the king of France and of the pope. The remainder of the Swiss guards were allowed to withdraw and were replaced by 200 landsknechts under Schertlin. "There," wrote this officer, "we found pope Clement with twelve cardinals in a small room; we took him prisoner; there was great lamentation among them; they wept bitterly; we were all moved." The 400 Italians under Renzo, who was accompanied by Alberto Pio, also departed with the honors of war, although the landsknechts suspected that they carried with them the papal treasures. Both these forces took ship for France at Civita-vecchia. The release of the pope himself depended on the fulfilment of the treaty; his restoration in Rome on the will of the emperor. With a stroke of the pen in Madrid, Charles V might have put an end to the State of the Church. A first instalment was with difficulty raised by loans; new money was coined out of gold and silver vessels; the clamorous landsknechts were paid with crosses, chalices and other valuables of the church. The pope had his tiara melted down by Cellini; and Clement seemed to throw the whole of his grandeur into the crucible. There were difficulties, however, in the way of the surrender of the fortresses, which had been stipulated by treaty, Clement himself having given the commandants secret orders not to surrender. Ostia alone was occupied by the imperialists. Doria refused to leave the harbor of Civita-vecchia until he had received the sum which was owed him; Francesco de Bibiena occupied Civitacastellana in the name of the league; neither Parma nor Piacenza would receive the imperial envoys Gattinara and Lodron. Unhindered by Lodovico Rangone, brother of Guido, Alfonso had already entered Modena on June 6.

The condition of Rome was terrible. The city seemed to be inhabited by specters. La Motte having embarked for Spain, Don Pedro Ramires acted as governor; 24,000 men were still quartered in the city, half of them Germans. In constant insurrection, they angrily demanded their pay, and upbraided their officers as traitors who had deceived them. The Viceroy and del Vasto were obliged to seek safety in flight. Philibert himself was too young and inexperienced to fill the difficult post. Charles's advisers urged that a new generalissimo should be sent to Rome. The emperor gave the post to the duke of Ferrara, but the duke refused to become the general of mutineers.

On June 17 Ferrante Gonzaga went with the cavalry to Velletri. For since in Rome the famine was great and the pestilence deadly, the Italian troops wished to take up their quarters on the Campagna. More than 3000 landsknechts perished, even distinguished officers such as Claus Seidenstücker and Count Christof of Eberstein. When the state of things became unendurable, the officers persuaded the army to move to its summer quarters. A small sum of money was raised to tranquilize the clamorers; three captains were appointed as custodians of the hostages in Rocca di Papa, and on July 10 the troops departed for Umbria; the Germans led by Bemelberg and Schertlin, while Philibert marched with 150 horse to Siena to hold the city for the emperor. The places on the Campagna, which the pope by briefs had ordered to afford quarters and supplies to the troops, beheld with horror the approach of these hordes. With the courage of despair, little Narni, the ancestral home of Gattamelata, put cowardly Rome to shame. Men and women defended the walls; but the Germans under Schertlin and Antoni of Feldkirchen attacked them on July 17, and the unlucky fortress was destroyed by fire and sword. That Todi escaped the like fate was solely due to the fact that it was occupied by the duke of Urbino. Terni was imperialist, and in its hereditary hatred had even aided in the destruction of Narni. Spoleto, strong and capable of defending itself, sent bread to the camp at Aquasparta, but demanded payment. The Germans returned to Narni, the Spaniards to Terni and Amelia. Heat, penury and discontent rendered their camp a veritable hell. Fever carried them off in hundreds. And when on September 1 Caspar Schweger held a review of the landsknechts at Narni, it was found that they only numbered 7000.

Messengers from Milan arrived in Rome. Leyva, who was sorely harassed there by the league, requested immediate help, and it was said there that the pope was not fulfilling the treaty. The leaders in despair sent envoys to Lannoy at Naples, demanding that he should come in person to give his advice and take command of the unmanageable populace. He declined, and sent del Vasto as mediator. The state of things in Umbria was everywhere desperate, even in the camp of the allies, which, under the duke of Urbino and Saluzzo, remained at Pontenuovo to protect Perugia. The troops suffering from hunger grew rebellious, and sacked and burnt the unfortunate district. The duke himself quarrelled with the other generals, and was distrusted not only by Francis I, but also by the Venetians, whom Guicciardini had stirred up against him. The signory threatened to detain his wife and son, who were then in Venice, as hostages, until the Proveditore Pisani restored peace between them. Anarchy reigned in Perugia. Orazio Baglione, Urbino's protégé, caused his cousin Gentile and other members of the family to be murdered. And against the imperialists, who had seized Camerino, the allies could only venture on petty skirmishes in the district of Terni, whither the landsknechts had advanced, while the Spaniards and Italians encamped near Alviano and Castiglione della Teverina.

Clement passed hideous days and nights, buried alive, as it were, in the terrible fortress of S. Angelo in the scorching heat of summer, helpless, deserted and surrounded by savage soldiery. He dwelt with the cardinals in the so-called Maschio of the fortress; the Spaniards quartered below. So closely was the pope guarded, that scarcely anyone was permitted access to his presence. He had not been allowed to retain silver to the value of ten scudi. Two cardinals died in S. Angelo; the usurer Armellino, who was killed by the loss of his wealth, and the brilliant Ercole Rangone, who died of privation or pestilence.

From his prison the pope sent letters to Charles V and the European powers imploring his release. The imperialists offered to conduct him to Gaeta, but he declined. They allowed him, however, to send Alessandro Farnese to Madrid. This cardinal, afterwards Paul III, left S. Angelo, but abandoned his mission; and the pope in consequence confided it to Salviati, cardinal legate to the court of France. But neither did Salviati consider it prudent to place himself in the power of the emperor; he left his negotiations to the nuncio of Spain, the unfortunate Castiglione, who was utterly crushed by the disastrous fate of Rome. The State of the Church, the very government of the church itself, had ceased to exist; the cardinals living outside Rome were scattered; Venice wished them to assemble in Bologna under Cibò's guidance, but the meeting did not take place.

Meanwhile the capture of Rome was variously judged in the world at large. The adherents of the emperor greeted with joy the fall of the papacy; the Lutherans were triumphant because Babylon had fallen, as prophecies had long since foretold; and not only those who were in secret friends of the Reformation, such as the Spaniard Juan Valdez, but even sincere Catholics recognized a divine judgment in the misfortunes of Rome. England and France did not so much compassionate the pope as they dreaded the greatness of the emperor. These two powers—the nuncios Gambara and Salviati were active at one and other court —concluded a treaty at Westminster on April 30, and renewed it on May 29, with the object of liberating the pope. In the summer Wolsey crossed to France. The English statesman passionately urged on the conclusion of the league. He pointed out to the king that the fall of the pope was his personal concern, especially since it endangered the dissolution—ardently desired by Henry—of his marriage with Catherine of Aragon. Wolsey proposed that he should assemble the cardinals absent from Rome at Avignon, and take in hand the deliverance of the church, in which assembly he hoped to play the leading part. He was appalled by the suggestion that the pope might be removed to Spain, and the papacy become Spanish.

The league, or rather France, was prepared for war, and as early as the end of July 1527 Odet de Foix, lord of Lautrec, crossed the Alps to Italy. It was with reluctance that the brave marshal undertook the command on the scene of his former reverses. He had never been fortunate in Italy; severely wounded at Ravenna, defeated at Bicocca, he had been driven from Lombardy. His brother had fallen at Pavia. He himself was never to see France again. The Venetians also marched against Milan, and the flames of war burst forth afresh in this territory. Its defense was a difficult task for Leyva, the imperial governor, owing to want of means.

Charles himself had only received the news of the catastrophe of Rome at the end of June. The cruel sack of the city appalled and mortified him. He forbade all rejoicings at the birth of his son Philip, and ordered public mourning. Nevertheless he secretly rejoiced at the good fortune that had delivered the pope himself into his hands. He made no haste to set him free. Not until July 26 did he write to the Romans; he lamented their misfortunes and promised to restore the honor and splendor of the Roman name. But it was only after a strangely long interval that he sent Quiñonez and his chamberlain Don Pedro de Veyre to the pope. On August 2, he wrote to the king of England, that the pope was the author of the entire disaster, since he had urged Francis I to violate the peace and had provoked a new league and the war. The papal enterprise against Naples had made it necessary for the imperial army to march to the defense of the kingdom: against his wishes and those of the generals the troops had gone by way of Rome. He regretted the atrocities that had been committed, he was guiltless, but he recognized therein the just judgment of God, who desired to punish the crimes of the guilty.

Emperor and pope stood facing a crisis, such as history has but seldom witnessed. The relations between the temporal and spiritual powers might now suffer a radical change. Had not the time come utterly to abolish this papal immunity, which dated from Charles the Great, and which had been so fatal to Italy, the empire and the church itself? It seemed as if by an edict the emperor might make Rome again the capital of the empire, conduct the pope—as the Reformation desired—back to the Lateran as a mere bishop, and finally reform the church by means of a council. A revolution of incalculable extent must have followed owing to the secularization of the church property in Europe, and the fall of the papal dominion or of the ecclesiastical state would probably have entailed the ruin of the church in patriarchates and national churches, which could only have obtained union in a federative constitution.

Questions of this kind forced themselves on the mind of the emperor and his servants. An anonymous correspondent wrote to him from Rome on June 8.

We expect that your Majesty will give us accurate instructions, so that we may know how you intend governing Rome henceforward, and whether some form of apostolic chair is to remain or not. I will not conceal from your Majesty the view of some of your servants, who hold that the sacred chair in Rome should not be utterly and entirely abolished. For in such case the king of France could immediately install a patriarch in his dominions, and refuse obedience to the Apostolic See, and England and every other monarch might do likewise. It therefore appears advisable to your Majesty's servants that the sacred chair should be kept in such subjection that your Majesty could always dispose of and rule it.

On May 31, from Prague, the Archduke Ferdinand, now also king of Bohemia and Hungary, announced to his brother the capture of Rome, and exhorted Charles not to release the pope until everything had been adjusted by a peace, else would Clement deceive him as he had deceived Francis I; he also advised the emperor to think of a council. And that Charles might force the captive pope to convoke a council in order, by the imperial power, to reform the church, and thus make himself its true head, was what the powers of the league most dreaded. England and France agreed not to recognize any council as long as the pope remained "a slave in the power of his godless enemies." Ghibelline ideas revived the more strongly when backed by the German Reformation. And if Dante's dream of a world monarchy could ever have been realized, it might have been realized now. The prudent Lannoy, it is true, advised the emperor to make peace and to liberate the pope, but he also wrote that now was the time to think of the reform of church discipline by a council. According to the advice of the Chancellor Gattinara, even Florence and Bologna should be united to the empire. To restore the imperial power over Italy, but to release the pope, was the view taken by Spanish statesmen. The Spanish clergy ardently took the side of the pope.

Charles V, cold and prudent, withheld his opinion. He determined to await the report of Veyre, whom he had made viceroy in August and had sent to the pope with instructions which clearly expressed his ideas. He explained that the fall of Rome was a divine dispensation intended to lead to the peace of the world and the reformation of the church. He wished the pope to be brought to Spain, but if this could only be done by force, then was it his intention to restore him to the sacred chair by means of the viceroy. The pope's liberty, however, was only to extend to the discharge of his sacred office; and before he received even this, he must give the emperor security against any further deception. And finally he would oblige the pope to summon a council.

Clement VII found himself in the same position as Francis I at Madrid. He too was reduced to stipulate for his liberty on conditions that would condemn him to powerlessness in the future; he too received in prison letters warning him to remain steadfast and not allow himself to be forced to any unworthy step. In such terms the king wrote to him on September 14, holding out hopes of his speedy release. It was with suspicion, however, that the pope watched the languid operations of the league in Lombardy; he already suspected Lautrec's designs on Parma, Piacenza, and even on Bologna. On September 16, Cardinals Wolsey, Bourbon, Salviati, Lorraine and Sens wrote to him from Compiègne. They feared the actual occupation of the State of the Church by the emperor; they protested against all the decrees with which, under pressure of the temporal power, the pope might infringe the rights of the church.

Clement was now harassed by the return of the imperial troops from Umbria on September 25. The allies, indeed, who occupied Narni in their rear, endeavored to advance into the Sabina, where the Spanish cavalry remained beside the Orsini fortresses of Monterotondo and Mentana; but their plan of attacking the imperialists and cutting off their retreat by destroying the bridge over the Anio was betrayed. The army of the league made no attempt to deliver Rome, and was in so disordered a condition that the imperial forces would have had no difficulty in driving it back to the walls of Florence. The landsknechts took up their quarters in Rome with greater insolence than ever, they robbed and made prisoners, destroyed palaces and houses, the entire city seemed threatened with destruction. They angrily demanded the fulfilment of the treaty with the pope, and would have strangled him had he fallen into their hands. Alarcon, who defended him, believed that in these tumults he perceived the hand of the ambitious Cardinal Pompeo. Scarcely a semblance of government did this general with Morone and the Colonna maintain in Rome, while Orange still remained in Spoleto. The troops no longer obeyed his commands. The hostages stipulated for in the treaty of June, namely, the archbishop of Siponto (afterwards Julius III), the archbishop Bartolini of Pisa, the datary Giberti, Bishop Antonio Pucci of Pistoja, a nephew of Cardinal Lorenzo, and the Florentines, Ridolfi and Salviati, were surrendered by the pope to the Germans in the great hall of S. Angelo. A touching scene took place, all burst into tears. Alarcon conducted the hostages to the Campo di Fiore; they were then handed over to the landsknechts, and confined in the Palazzo del Cancellaria. Thence they were frequently dragged, chained together in couples, to the meetings of the landsknechts on the Campo de Fiore, and there menaced by the sight of newly-erected gallows.

Meanwhile Veyre had landed at Gaeta at the end of September. He here learnt of Lannoy's death, which had taken place on the 23rd of the month at Aversa, and he communicated his instructions to Moncada, who was now acting as governor in Naples. On September 30 he sent the emperor an account of the condition of Italy, which he found in such a critical state that he urgently counselled him to make peace, especially as Lautrec's enterprise had restored the pope's courage. He then went to Rome in order to arrive at some decision with Clement. He regretted to find the pope still in S. Angelo instead of in the security of Gaeta; in Rome he was exposed to the ferocity of the landsknechts. Vessels were kept ready on the Tiber, that in case of need he might escape to Ostia and the sea.

Veyre, his avowed adversary, would have imposed upon him the severest terms, nay, would have deprived him of all temporal authority; and Seron the chancellor and representative of Moncada, would have done the same; the pope, however, had already gained other imperial counsellors to his side. Quiñonez he won by the promise of the purple; Morone with the investiture of the bishopric of Modena for his son. Even Pompeo was gained, not so much by the grant of the Legation of Ancona, as by the knowledge that the pope, with whom he had been at such bitter enmity, would finally be restored by the emperor. In consequence of the division of views Veyre went to Moncada in Naples. Time pressed; it was necessary to remove the army from Rome, since Lautrec already threatened the Neapolitan frontier. The pope urged him to advance rapidly and become his liberator; he must, it is true, form a treaty with the plenipotentiary of the emperor, but he might obtain more favorable conditions under the pressure of the approaching French army. Francis I had made the pope's imprisonment a pretext for setting the powers again in motion. The alliance between him and Henry VIII, concluded on August 18, which had been joined by Venice, Florence, and Sforza, threatened to place all the acquisitions of the emperor again at stake; and in July Charles was already aware that Wolsey, his deadly enemy, had formed the scheme of dissolving the marriage of the king of England with Catherine of Aragon, and of thus severing Henry for ever from Spain.

The treaty with the pope was settled in S. Angelo on October 31, and was signed on November 26. According to it the emperor pledged himself to restore Clement to liberty, and even to give him back the State of the Church, on condition of his neutrality; for which Clement was to give Ostia and Civita-vecchia as securities, and Cardinals Trivulzio, Gaddi and Pisani as hostages. He was, however, to pay the sum owing to the army at fixed dates. A general peace was then to be concluded, and a council was to provide for the reformation of the church. In order to raise the required sum the imperial ministers were given faculties to sell the estates of the church in the kingdom of Naples, and on November 21 Clement created some cardinals for money.

Thus vanished the possibility of giving to the world a new form, from which the papacy should be excluded. It was apparently within the power of Charles V to abolish the papacy, to make Rome once more an imperial city, and thereby unite Italy under his scepter. A Spanish dynasty would then have ruled the entire country, and would have taken as firm root as the Aragonese had taken at Naples. The prolonged sufferings of Italy, which succeeded the times of Charles V, the sacerdotal dominion perpetuated through long centuries, and the crippling of the national state by the spiritual power, which spread its tentacles like a polypus throughout the entire system, may well lead to the opinion that Charles V was to blame for not rising to the great task, nay, for even shrinking before his own greatness. But such reproaches are vain. History develops in accordance with organic laws; every political event is the result of conditions, and it is only superficially that the acts of potentates appear free. In the year 1527 the Ghibelline idea of the abolition of the State of the Church reappeared in the political world; it heralded a future necessity, but Charles V lacked the power to carry it out. Nor was the power possessed even by Napoleon, who for a moment reestablished that universal Caesarism in Europe which Charles V was obliged to renounce. That age was not ripe for the great revolution which must necessarily follow the abolition of the temporal papacy. Only today has mankind become ready to receive it; only now has the thousand years' dominion of the pope in Rome vanished away like a shadow, consumed by the spirit of the age, blotted out by the mere will of the Italian people, and with the expressed or unexpressed consent of all those European powers who formed a league against Charles V for the rescue of the papacy. The emperor, of orthodox and Catholic belief, feared not these powers alone, but also the religious passions of Spain and Sicily, the might of the Inquisition, and also the revolutionary character of the German ecclesiastical schism. The council of state in Spain urgently demanded the release of the pope. Charles resolved to reinstate him, but so humbled and with temporal power so limited that he could no longer prove dangerous. The emperor hoped to attain his object in the treaty of November.

The north of Italy was already devastated with the horrors of war. True, that Leyva defended Milan and other cities with admirable courage, but Alessandria and Pavia, which Lautrec in revenge subjected to terrible ill-treatment, as well as Genoa, fell into the power of the French. Bologna was in the hands of the league, and the roads to Rome and Naples already lay open to the French. The pressure of their arms also weighed upon Ferrara. Duke Alfonso, allowing himself to be won over by the great promises of France and the pope, joined the league at a congress in Ferrara on November 15. He was always French at heart, and was now to be permanently bound to France by Renée, daughter of Lewis XII, whose hand was promised to his son Ercole. Federigo Gonzaga also immediately renounced the emperor in favor of the league.

In accordance with the treaty the imperial troops were to leave Rome as soon as they received the stipulated sum of money. But the payment of this was no easy matter. The landsknechts, before whose fury the leaders were obliged to fly to the Colonna at Rocca di Papa, threatened to murder their hostages, who, however, thanks to the aid of Cardinal Pompeo, successfully escaped on November 29 from their fifty-two days' imprisonment. With the assistance of the Spaniards encamped beside S. Maria del Popolo, they fled from Rome on horses kept ready for them, and in this wise Giberti, one of the authors of all the mischief, regained his liberty.

The pope was still so closely guarded in S. Angelo that William Knight, the envoy of the English king, who amid many dangers had arrived secretly at Rome, could not gain access to him and was obliged to take his departure. After Clement had surrendered Cardinals Cesi and Orsini to the German captains, and with the aid of Pompeo had paid a part of the sum owing, he demanded his release. It was fixed for December 9. But as Moncada and Veyre made difficulties, he gained the consent of Luigi Gonzaga, colonel of the imperial cavalry, and Morone to a secret departure. On the night of December 8, 1527, disguised, borne in Morone's litter and surrounded by Morone's servants, he quitted S. Angelo. Gonzaga received him on the Field of Nero; on horseback he hurried past Cesano to Viterbo, and safe and sound reached the strong city of Orvieto after seven miserable months. He arrived on the night of December 10, accompanied by five cardinals. Not until he had made himself known was he allowed admittance. A few days after his departure, S. Angelo was handed over to the papal troops under Carlo Astaldi, and the spiritual government was restored in the city.

The pope established his quarters in the deserted episcopal palace of Orvieto, where Cardinal Ridolfi was bishop. On January 11, 1528, Clement thanked the emperor for his release and professed himself willing to remain loyal to him, in the confidence that Charles would restore the prestige of the papacy. Meanwhile he regarded Lautrec as his real deliverer, and by letter thanked both him and King Francis. Soon after his arrival the duke of Urbino, the marquis of Saluzzo, Federigo da Bozzolo and Luigi Pisani hurried to Orvieo to congratulate the pope on his deliverance, in effecting which they had been so lamentably unsuccessful. The brave Federigo Gonzaga died at Todi immediately after leaving the pope. Clement bewailed the loss of one of the last of the celebrated condottieri who had done honor to the Italian name. In truth the military renown of the Italians now vanished, and if among them any appeared endowed with the talents of a general, it was to serve under the banner of the emperor. Nothing could have been more painful to Clement than his meeting with Francesco Maria. Even had the duke been guiltless of treachery, the indignity suffered at his hands must be vividly present to the pope's mind. Clement, however, received him with every honor, and so accomplished a diplomatist was the pope, that he even held out hopes of a marriage between the duke's son Guidobaldo and Catherine de Medici.

All the heads of the league besought him openly to declare in its favor. Lautrec, who had entered Bologna on December 19, sent to him Guido Rangone, Paolo Camillo Trivulzio, and the young Vaudemont. Gregorio Casale, who, though a Bolognese, had long been in the English service as diplomatist, exhorted him in behalf of England, and Stephen Gardiner and Fox soon arrived bearing the same commission that Knight should have formerly borne to S. Angelo; namely, the demand for the papal sanction to the ominous divorce, which was soon to become the ground of England's separation from the Roman church. The English envoys were surprised at the pope's pitiable position in Orvieto, where he found himself as badly provided for as ever in S. Angelo. The apartments which he occupied were ruinous and destitute of necessaries; the bed and furniture of his sleeping-room were barely worth twenty nobles; famine and dire penury reigned in Orvieto.

Francis I sent Longueville with congratulations and the explanation that the league was resolved energetically to continue the war. After the conquest of Naples, a ruler acceptable to the pope was to be placed on the throne. With his accustomed ambiguity, Clement resorted to his old artifices; he professed himself neutral, but listened to proposals and imposed conditions. One of these was the surrender of Ravenna and Cervia, for scarcely was he released from the fortress, when he sent the archbishop of Siponto to Venice to demand the surrender of these cities. This surrender he made—at least diplomatically—the necessary condition of his joining the league. Venice, however, refused to listen to the proposal.

Clement, always the prey of his suspicion, was angry that Francis I should have taken Florence and Ferrara under his protection; he refused to recognize the articles which had been agreed upon with Alfonso, and, as before, demanded Modena and Reggio. With distrust he saw Parma and Piacenza in the power of Lautrec, and the marshal himself in Bologna, whence, pending the issue of the negotiations between France and Charles V, he hesitated to depart. The negotiations failed, in spite of the moderation of the emperor, who even offered to renounce Burgundy in favor of peace, and on January 28, 1528, the ambassadors of the powers assembled in Burgos declared war. France was encouraged in this course by the early progress made by Lautrec.

The pope wished the marshal to take the road by Rome; Lautrec, however, chose the shorter route from the Romagna to the kingdom. To their misfortune, the Florentines had sent troops to join him, namely, 4000 men of the *Bande Neri*, under Orazio Baglione. The marshal was accompanied by a papal nuncio, Pierpaolo Crescenzi. His march had the effect of restoring to Clement the possession of Imola and Rimini. Scarcely had Lautrec crossed the Tronto on February 10, when the barons of the Angevin party rose throughout the kingdom. It now behoved the imperialists to deliver Naples, which was threatened, and the troops hurried thither from Rome. After furious struggles they resolved to follow the exhortations of Ferrante Gonzaga and Moncada's summons. The pope sent 40,000 gold florins from Orvieto, mostly under the pretext that the money was given by the Roman magistrates, and Lautrec consequently reproached him that he was equipping the enemy for the march on Naples. From Galera, where he had spent the winter, Orange came to Rome, and then hurried to Naples, whence he brought some money on February 9 to appease the German landsknechts. Del Vasto persuaded the Spaniards voluntarily to depart. The ranks of the imperial troops were greatly reduced; of the leaders, several of the foremost were missing. Melchior, Frundsberg's youthful son, had died of the pestilence on January 13. A review showed only 1500 cavalry, 4000 Spaniards, upwards of 2000 Italian infantry, and 5000 landsknechts. After a sack which had lasted nine months, these terrible forces left Rome on February 17, 1528, to march to Naples. And scarcely had they departed by the Porta S. Giovanni when the Orsini Amico of Arsoli, the leader of a band, and the abbot of Farfa, burst into the city at the head of a hastily collected mob. The Trasteverines, the inhabitants of the Regola, and those of Monti, banded themselves together. They attacked the stragglers of the army, slew or threw them into the river; they even strangled patients in the hospitals and robbed what was left to rob. All the houses of the Jews were sacked.

The retreating army carried with it Bourbon's remains in a leaden coffin, in order to remove them from the vengeance of the Romans. They were afterwards interred in a tomb at Gaeta. In revenge for the attack of the Orsini the imperialists burnt Rocca Priora and Valmontone. Leaving their artillery at Montefortino under the custody of Giulio Colonna, they advanced into Neapolitan territory.

A terrible war again scourged Lombardy and Naples at the same time. The French under S. Pol and the Venetians under Urbino attacked the imperialists, while Leyva defended Milan, supported by landsknechts who had been led to Italy by Duke

Erich of Brunswick. The Romans trembled before this new danger, for it was said that these troops were to advance to Naples. They turned for advice to Casale, the English envoy at Orvieto. They contemplated equipping 4000 men, destroying the bridges across the Tiber and defending the city, which Count Nicolò of Tolentino commanded for the pope. They even hoped for aid from the abbot of Farfa. Their best defense was perhaps the arid desert to which the Campagna had been reduced for miles round the city.

Lautrec was victorious in Neapolitan territory until April, when the war resolved itself into the bloody siege of the capital. The city was defended by Moncada with all the foremost generals, Orange, Don Ferrante, Orbina, Alarcon, del Vasto, Bemelberg and Schertlin. The opening movements turned in favor of the French; on April 25 they won a naval battle under Filippino Doria; Moncada and Ferramosca were killed in the engagement, also the Marchese del Vasto; Ascanio and Camillo Colonna, Seron and several other nobles were made prisoners.

Clement watched with anxiety the progress of this war, on the fortunes of which depended his resolutions. Famine drove him from Orvieto to Viterbo on June 1. He first made his abode in the ancient fortress, then entered the palace of Cardinal Farnese at the Porta Romana. On June 8 he made this cardinal legate for Rome and Campeggi legate for England; whereupon the imperial envoy at once raised a protest against the possibility of annulling the royal marriage.

Clement must have shuddered at the sight which Italy presented on all sides. From the Alps to the Faro the country was one single battlefield for Spaniards, Germans, French, and Italians; the condition of its towns and districts resembled that which prevailed during the Gothic war. If he compared his reign with the reigns of Leo and Julius II, he was obliged to confess that he had lost what they had won; Modena and Reggio, Ravenna and Florence had vanished; Rome was a heap of ruins. He was himself disgraced, deprived of all respect, of all power, a plaything of the rival parties. In the history of the church there is scarcely any pope who was so utterly miserable as Clement VII, nor any whose misfortunes excited so little compassion. If he inquired into the causes of his misfortunes, the venerable Egidius of Viterbo could have told him that they were none other than the corruption of the papacy owing to its political distortion.

He continued his oscillating policy, wavering to and fro according to his wont; for misfortune, as Guicciardini remarks, had not quenched his inclination to falsehood and artifice. Since the papacy still remained a principle of such importance that the political balance of Italy could not be adjusted without it, each of the powers besought his adhesion. He held negotiations with all, and to all held out hopes. The league demanded that he should excommunicate the emperor and pronounce him forfeit both of Naples and the empire. Francis I would then install Angoulême his third son as king in Naples and marry him to Catherine Medici. The surrender of Ravenna and Cervia, on which the pope made his adhesion dependent, was vainly urged by the Vicomte Turenne on the republic of Venice, whose ambassador Contarini had arrived at Viterbo two days after the pope. But Clement still remained undecided; he was awaiting the results of Lautrec's enterprise in Naples. Through his envoy Gianantonio Muscettola the emperor again exhorted him to form an honest alliance with him and renounce the friendship of France. The king of England pressed for the dissolution of the marriage. Did he refuse Henry, he offended the powerful defender of the faith, who was so zealous against Luther; if he yielded to his will, he insulted the emperor. Clement was weak enough to send the cardinal legate Campeggi with the bull desired by Wolsey to the English court in July; he was instructed to show it to the king alone, yet not to publish it, but on the contrary to burn it.

A French fleet meanwhile lay off Corneto. Renzo, who had arrived in it, laid siege to Civita-vecchia, when the pope, in defiance of his neutrality, aided him with munitions. The fleet sailed to Naples, and Renzo's son alone continued the siege of Civita-vecchia.

The unexpected turn of the Neapolitan war finally determined the mind of the pope. Lautrec's success turned to lamentable defeat. Pestilence raged in both camps; the pillagers of Rome as well as their opponents were decimated by sword and disease. Veyre fell; the Roman Tibaldi and Orazio Baglione were killed;

437

Luigi Pisani, the nuncio Crescenzi, Camillo Trivulzio, the lord of Pomperan, the young Vaudemont, all died of pestilence, and on August 15 Lautrec himself fell a victim. The unfortunate Marshal was buried under a sandheap in his own tent, in the vineyard of the duke of Montalto before Naples; he was afterwards disinterred by a Spanish soldier, who carried him on his shoulders through the entire city and kept him in a cellar, in the hope that some Frenchman would redeem the body. The nuns of S. Chiara, whose convent had been founded by King Robert, bought it in pity, and gave it honorable burial in their church. The Romans also honored the memory of Lautrec as the deliverer of their city from the imperialists; and by a decree of the Senate his obsequies were celebrated in the Lateran.

The besieged army, in a state of disorganization, was led by Saluzzo and Navarro to Aversa. The celebrated Navarro, who had risen from the condition of servant to be grand-admiral of Spain and the first engineer of his time, and had then renounced his country, was made a prisoner and met a miserable death, strangled as it would appear in Castel Nuovo. The *Bande Neri* under Ugo Pepoli were annihilated, and Saluzzo and Rangone surrendered at Aversa in the beginning of September. The former died of his wounds at Naples, the other obtained his liberty and went to Rome. Seldom has a war been so fatal. The pitiable remains of the French army staggered like ghosts along the roads, carrying white sticks, the signs of beggary, or died penned like animals in the royal stables of the Maddalena. Others were dragged in detachments to Rome, where they were provided with food and allowed to encamp outside the walls. "The French," said Reissner, "have never had any luck in Naples; and their hands have never been cleansed from the innocent blood of Conradin, the last young prince of Swabia."

The yoke of Spain now pressed with iron severity on the kingdom of Naples. Philibert, the viceroy of Charles, and his counsellor Morone punished the nobles of the Angevin party with confiscation of their property, imprisonment and death. Several great nobles died on the scaffold, among them Federigo Gaetani, son of the Duke of Traetto, and Enrico Pandone, Duke of Boviano.

On the same marketplace where in former days Conradin had been executed, the prince of Orange from a balcony draped in black watched the murderous work. The entire kingdom was turned into a scene of terror and a pestilential graveyard. Thus Spain erected her dominion, and thus Charles again triumphed over the league, especially since Andrea Doria deserted the French service for that of the emperor and restored freedom to his native city Genoa in October 1528.

For once it had been a lucky star that pointed out the right path —the path of neutrality—to Clement. The victory of the emperor (it was only in the Abruzzi and on the coasts of Apulia that a desultory warfare was still prosecuted) left him no choice but to show himself submissive towards Charles, and, as Charles desired, to return to Rome. The emperor promised him to supply the famished city with corn from Sicily, to help him in every way, and even to restore Ostia and Civita-vecchia. The pope shrank from the thought of Rome; he feared the return of Orange and his savage troops; the state of the city and Campagna were also calculated to inspire terror. Throughout Latium, the Sabina and Tuscany, war raged between the Orsini and Colonna on account of a disputed succession. Vespasiano, husband of the beautiful Giulia Gonzaga, had died on March 13, 1528, leaving by his first wife Beatrice Appiani, an only daughter Isabella, and the hand of the wealthy heiress had been promised to the young Ippolito Medici. The pope ordered the estates of Vespasiano to be occupied. In his service Sciarra Colonna penetrated to Paliano, where Giulia and Isabella were at the time, but Sciarra was attacked and taken prisoner by the abbot of Farfa. A furious war between the Orsini and Colonna—Ascanio and Prospero raising claims to Paliano—was the result of the quarrel when several towns, even Tivoli, Anagni and Rieti, were laid waste. Clement sent to Paliano the brave Luigi Gonzaga, who banished the abbot of Farfa and reinstated his sister Giulia in her property. She rewarded his services by the secret treaty with the rich heiress Isabella, which the pope, although reluctantly, was obliged to approve.

In the beginning of October, Clement decided to yield to Muscettola's urgent entreaties and return to Rome.

XIV

Clement VII's Return to Rome

CLEMENT left Bologna in ill humor on March 31, 1530, and returned to Rome on April 9. After having experienced the most astounding changes of fortune within a brief space of time, he found himself once more amid the ruins of the city, ruler of the State of the Church. But this restoration, which he owed to the favor of the emperor, only slightly soothed the pain produced by the consciousness, that the great period of the all-ruling papacy had for ever passed away, and that never again could it shake off the fetters of the dominant power in Europe. The Reformation was victorious in Germany as in Switzerland, and the divorce of Henry VIII threatened to sever England also from the papacy. Already in July 1529 the pope had brought the suit before the Roman tribunal as the emperor had requested. On November 30 of the same year Wolsey died soon after his disgrace. The powerful cardinal fell because he had been unable to procure the dissolution of the king's marriage, and with him fell his political program, based on the alliance between the pope, England and France against Charles V.

Instead of profiting by the interval which he had purchased by the peace with the emperor to fulfil his highest duty as supreme head of the church, and to stifle the flames which had broken out within her, Clement VII only strove to evade this duty and

From book XIV, ch. 7, sec. 5.

to avert the council of reform which the emperor continued to demand. His most pressing concern was the subjugation of his native city, and this he carried out with a cold-blooded cruelty that is truly appalling.

The death struggles of the republic throw a more sinister shadow over the ungrateful papacy and especially over Clement than that produced by the fall of Rome itself. The terms of peace of Cambray and Bologna had abandoned the republic to her own feeble resources. Condemned like a heretic by the pope, she was surrendered to the secular arm of the emperor, who gave the first proof of his loyalty to the alliance by acting as executioner in Clement's service. Florence, the last representative of the national freedom of Italy, fought both potentates with heroic courage, and her overthrow sealed the political ruin of the country.

After the fall of the Gonfaloniere Capponi, and his death on October 18, 1529, there remained no longer any statesman of insight and energy. The talents of the Strozzi, Soderini, Carducci, Alemanni and Vettori were insufficient to reconcile the parties, to control the intrigues of the Medici, or to save the state. In the republican army, formed mainly of a few citizens unused to warfare and of untrustworthy mercenaries, one Florentine fired with antique patriotism, Francesco Ferrucci, is alone conspicuous. The greater number of the officers were foreigners, among them several Romans, such as Mario and Giampolo Orsini, the son of Renzo of Ceri, Giulio Santa Croce, Stefano Colonna, and for a time even the abbot of Farfa, until, won back by the pope, he returned to Bracciano. The foremost general was that Malatesta Baglione, in whom the Florentines reposed confidence, simply because his father had been executed by order of Leo X. He soon proved a traitor; for already, through the treaty of Perugia, we saw him in the power of the pope.

On October 24, 1529, Orange opened first on S. Miniato, the fortifications of which had been skilfully designed by Michelangelo. In consequence of the peace with Venice, the besieging army was strengthened by several thousand Spaniards, Italians, and Germans, under Felix of Werdenberg, and the fate of the city

441

was now decided. In a transient return of religious enthusiasm, Florence, in her distress, had appointed Christ her standard bearer. Fra Benedetto da Fojano fired the people by his discourses, as Savonarola had done in former days. The republic in desperation defended itself for months. All the villas, which lay like a wreath of joyous life round the beautiful city, had been laid waste by the Florentines themselves. They had, moreover, to lament the ruin of many more distant places, which were burnt by the enemy, the pope impassively looking on. The endurance of Florence and the deliberation of Philibert drove Clement to despair, and filled him with suspicion of the emperor, France and Venice, while the costly war exposed him to the hatred of the world. It was with difficulty that Pucci, Salviati and others raised supplies. Clement found himself in the position of Leo X during Leo's war with Urbino. He, too, contemplated raising funds by a wholesale creation of cardinals. Grammont, the French envoy in Rome, dissuaded him, and in the name of humanity admonished him to spare his native city. The wretched pope replied with a sigh, "O, that Florence had never existed!" On June 8, 1530, he gave the cardinal's hat to the French statesman, after having previously bestowed the same dignity on the chancellor Du Prat, in order to acquire his goodwill and that of King Francis.

Spaniards, German landsknechts, bands of Calabrese under Maramoldo, and other rabble collected by the pope from the Romagna under Ramazotto, covered the Florentine territory and surrounded the city, where hunger and pestilence reigned. The fall of Volterra, which surrendered to Alessandro Vitelli, was avenged by Ferrucci in the harsh punishment he inflicted on the Etruscan city, which he reconquered and valiantly defended; but the important town of Empoli was lost, and Malatesta secretly frustrated the measures for the relief of Florence. In the battle of Gavinana, on August 3, Ferruccio fell in an attempt to relieve the city, and the prince of Orange was also killed by a shot from an arquebus. The same avenging hand of fate which had struck Bourbon before besieged Rome, and Moncada before besieged Naples, now fell on Orange in sight of besieged Florence. It had fallen too on Girolamo Morone, who died of illness at S. Cas-

siano near Florence on December 15, 1529. Philibert, a fair handsome man with blue eyes, intrepid and ambitous of great deeds,
was not thirty years of age. It is said that he had hoped to become duke of Florence, and to win the hand of the much wooed
Catherine Medici, who—still a child—was detained as hostage by
the Florentines during the entire siege. The body of the celebrated
prince, naked, and hanging across a wretched mule, was carried
from the battlefield (it was that of Cataline at the foot of the
Apennines) to Pistoja, precisely as the remains of Caesar Borgia
had been removed from the field of Viana.

Florence, a prey to hunger and pestilence, torn asunder by factions, ensnared in the wiles of Malatesta's treachery, was now
forced to capitulate. On August 12, 1530, a treaty was concluded
with Don Ferrante Gonzaga, Philibert's successor in command,
and with the papal commissary Bartolommeo Valori. The city
undertook to purchase the withdrawal of the imperial army with
a sum of 80,000 gold florins, and to leave it to the emperor within
four months to decide on its future form of government. Nevertheless the Medicean party immediately put forward a government of twelve men, who inaugurated their reign by the confiscation of the property and the murder of their opponents. The
siege had reduced the flourishing city, which numbered 70,000
inhabitants, to poverty, and besides 22,000 who had fallen in battle, several thousand citizens had died of hunger or pestilence.
Such was the end of the illustrious republic, which for centuries
had represented the Italian national spirit in a political system,
constantly changing but always full of vitality, and in the noblest
creations of genius. Florence fell only three years after Rome, and
at the hands of the same soldiers of the emperor, who threw
Italy into fetters. If the cruel fall of Rome in 1527 causes us to
shudder, nevertheless her fate was in some degree a well-merited
punishment; but Florence, even if also ripe for her end, was not
guilty to the same degree. In the hour of her heroic death, she,
the last representative of Italian independence, adorned herself
with the laurels of Dante, with all the noble names and virtues
of her past. Pope Clement VII, the cowardly bastard of the degenerate house of Medici, plunged the dagger in her heart. With

Florence expired not only the freedom of Italy, but the most brilliant period of Italian culture. Henceforward Spain was able to rule in tranquility the enslaved country.

On October 28, in an edict promulgated at Augsburg, the emperor in his clemency conceded an amnesty to the Florentines, their regents for all time were to be the Medici, and their elected head Alessandro his future son-in-law. Thus by the will of Charles V was this bastard race planted on the ruins of Florence, and the most ardent wish of Clement VII was attained.

As in the times of Justinian, the scourge of the devastating elements followed on war and pestilence. On October 7, 1530, Rome suffered one of the worst inundations of the Tiber on record. Nearly 600 houses and some bridges, among them the Ponte Sisto, were destroyed. The pope, just returned from Ostia, unable to reach the Vatican, was obliged to seek shelter in the palace of Ridolfi on the Quirinal, where he remained two days. The loss of property was immense, and the exhalations left by the flood produced a fresh outbreak of pestilence. "The pope however let those weep who wished to weep, and, uninstructed and unheeding, continued his political projects for the aggrandizement of his house."

Riveted in the fetters of Spain, which with his wonted cunning and weakness he shook from time to time, owing to the grace of the emperor his position as an insignificant prince in Italy, as formerly Herod in Judea owed his to Augustus, the timid spirit of Clement VII shrunk to utter nothingness in his latter years, and his most important concern was in truth the aggrandizement of the house of Medici. Fearing Spain and Charles V, whom, as may well be imagined, he never forgave for the insult inflicted on him in Rome, he strove to undermine the imperial power by strengthening that of France, which could as little forgive its own defeat. But he was careful to avoid provoking the emperor, in whose hands lay the fate of the Medici. He willingly recognized the elevation of Ferdinand of Hungary and Austria as king of Germany and the Romans, when, in spite of the opposition of the Protestants, the emperor's brother was elected at Cologne on January 5, 1531, and crowned at Aachen on January 11. In the summer of the same year the emperor yielded to the request of

Clement VII, and through his ambassador Muscettola and Nicholas Schomberg, the representative of the pope, installed Alessandro as regent of Florence. On July 5 the bastard entered the unfortunate city. By this act of favor Charles soothed the pope's indignation, evoked by the sentence pronounced in April, when in the name of the empire the duke of Ferrara had been confirmed in possession of Reggio, Modena and Rubiera. The long-continued and disastrous attempts of the popes to seize these territories by artifice and force were consequently frustrated. Nevertheless, even during times of peace Clement still continued his cunning intrigues against Ferrara.

On April 27, 1532, the republican constitution was abolished in Florence and Alessandro Medici created duke. In July 1532 the pope sent Ippolito, his other nephew, as legate to Hungary, where, after having tranquilized Germany by the religious peace of Nuremberg of July 23, the emperor at length undertook the campaign against the Turks. This Crusade had been decided on at the Diet of Regensburg, and with 8000 Spaniards, and also papal troops, Antonio Leyva departed from Italy to join it.

But as Soliman without hazarding a decisive battle retired to Turkey, and the German imperial army refused to prosecute the war in Hungary, Charles returned to Spain by way of Italy, where he wished to hold a second meeting with the pope in Bologna. The aim of this congress was to secure Italy against the ceaseless designs of Francis I, to settle the question of the divorce between Henry VIII and Catherine, and to decide on convoking a council to reconcile the Protestants to the church. It was with reluctance that Clement obeyed the behest of the all-powerful emperor; coming from Perugia in the middle of winter, he arrived at Bologna on December 8, 1532, and soon after received Charles. The ill humor was great on both sides. The emperor was too well acquainted with the papal policy not to know that, provided they had a favorable opportunity, Clement and the Italian states formerly belonging to the league would ally themselves with France against him. Under pretext of the danger threatened by the Turks, he succeeded in forming an Italian league, in which the pope, the emperor, Sforza, Alfonso, Florence, Genoa, Siena

445

and Lucca pledged themselves to a six years' alliance, the aim of which was to safeguard Milan against the machinations of France. The republic of Venice alone refused its adherence.

More than all else Clement feared the council. The emperor had continued to demand it ever since the first congress at Bologna, for to him it was of vital importance that an end should be put to the schism in Germany, which while it weakened his power strengthened that of France. Already, in consequence of the league of Smalkald and urged thereto by necessity, the Protestant princes had determined on the momentous step of seeking protection from the hereditary foe of the empire. It was therefore necessary that Francis I should prevent the council being summoned, in order that the schism in the Empire might be prolonged; and Clement VII was too astute a diplomatist not to recognize that the pressure which Turks and Protestants brought to bear on the emperor would present opportunities advantageous to himself. Many other topics besides the Lutheran question might be discussed at a council; if not that of the stain attached to his birth, at any rate his nepotism, the ruin of Rome and the cruel subjugation of Florence. The remarkable letters to Charles of the cardinal and bishop of Osma, Garcia de Loaysa, confessor to the emperor and after May 1530 his representative in Rome, show clearly how greatly the pope feared a council and how adroitly he evaded it; "the most mysterious man, more full of ciphers than any other in the world." Clement was undoubtedly well pleased when Grammont, the French ambassador in Rome, opposed the endeavors of May and Loaysa, the imperial ministers, to summon a council. And although on January 10, 1533, Granvella, May and Covos, councillors of the emperor, met in Bologna to confer with a junta of cardinals, and Clement wrote to the German electors, that it was his most earnest wish that the ecclesiastical council should assemble as soon as possible, the expression of this wish was nothing more than words. The conditions which he proposed for the council could never be accepted by the Protestants.

Ever suspicious of the emperor, who measured the greatness of the Medici drop by drop, and who still delayed sending his little daughter Margaret to Italy, Clement finally accepted the family alliance offered him by France. The pawn which he moved in this political game of chess was the young Duchess Catherine Medici, whom after the fall of Florence the pope had caused to be brought to Rome. The emperor, in accordance with Granvella's advice, wished to marry her to Francesco Sforza and thus detach the pope for ever from France. But Francis I had already made at Calais a treaty with the king of England, the object of which was to prevent the pope from throwing himself entirely into the arms of the emperor. In his anxiety to recover Milan, Francis lowered himself so far as to ask for the hand of the daughter of Lorenzo de' Medici for his second son Henry of Orléans. The pope showed timidity in accepting the proposal, which was made to him by Grammont and the duke of Albany in 1531. He carried on negotiations with France at the same time as he was discussing with the imperial ambassador the project of his niece's marriage to Sforza. The emperor, who did not believe Francis I serious in regard to the proposed marriage, was at length startled by hearing of his consent, with which Cardinals Tournon and Grammont hastened to acquaint the pope in Bologna. It was now too late for Charles to prevent the marriage. After having received the pope's promise to pronounce the ecclesiastical censure on Henry VIII on account of his adultery, the emperor left Bologna on February 25, 1533, the day after the Italian league had been signed, to proceed to Spain by way of Genoa. He was accompanied by Alessandro Medici. A few days later Clement returned to Rome.

The formation of the new league gravely irritated the French court; the pope, however, represented that it was to the advantage of the king, since its result would be to disperse the Spanish army in Lombardy; and he gave it to be understood that between his promises to the emperor and their fulfilment much might intervene. His ambition exulted in the thought of having gained a husband of the house of Valois for his niece. He prized this stroke of fortune more highly than the marriage of his nephew to an illegitimate daughter of the emperor, although by no means dissatisfied with Charles's promise that the nine year old princess should immediately be sent to Italy and married to Alessandro at a fitting time. He contemplated bestowing Reggio, Modena, Rubiera, Pisa, Leghorn, Parma and Piacenza as a marriage portion on Catherine.

In November 1531 he had arranged a meeting with King Francis, and the suspicious Charles was unable to prevent the interview. The Congress of Nice was to follow that of Bologna, in order, as Clement intended, to show the world that his sole object was peace with all the powers; for in this meeting the Turkish war, the settlement of the English divorce question and affairs of general importance were to be the only subjects of discussion. The emperor did not allow himself to be deceived. He was perfectly aware that the question at issue was the restoration of Genoa, Milan, and yet other territories to the crown of France by the marriage of Catherine de Medici.

Clement left Rome with ten cardinals and several prelates on September 9, 1533. Travelling through Umbria and Tuscany without touching Florence, he reached Porto Pisano, where he embarked in Albany's fleet on October 4, the richly dowered bride having shortly before been taken to meet her uncle on the coast of Nice. On October 12 he landed at Marseilles. Here the meeting with Francis had been arranged to take place, since Charles of Savoy, in fear of the emperor, had refused to hand the fortress of Nice over to the pope. After the days of terror in Rome, after all his dreadful experiences, Clement VII celebrated in Marseilles the royal honors to which the house of Medici was raised. He dwelt in the immediate neighborhood of King Francis, as formerly in Bologna in that of the emperor. The king and Queen Eleanor, sister of Charles V, the princes and nobles of France, the envoys of foreign powers, a thousand lords, knights and noble women, finally the papal court surrounded the youthful pair, whose marriage was performed by the pope himself. Eight and thirty years later the curses of mankind were to fall on Catherine's head, for the far-off consequence of this union was to be the massacre in Paris, the night of S. Bartholomew, which was sanctified by the prayers of a Roman pope. The festivals at Marseilles, the banquets, prolonged for days, on the shores of that radiant sea, were intoxicating to the senses; and this was the spectacle which the pope offered to the world in place of a council.

In order to avert the council the king's aid was necessary. Amid the tumult of revels and tournaments king and pope in private discussed the future of Italy. True that Clement pledged himself not to assist Francis by treaty towards the reconquest of Milan and Genoa, but he also promised not to hinder him in their recovery, and it was assuredly only death that released him from the inevitable consequences of the congress of Marseilles.

On his return to Rome on December 10, 1535, he believed himself to have reached the summit of his statecraft, since the alliance between his house and the two great powers, between which he had invariably oscillated to and fro, seemed to him the most efficacious means of preserving the balance between them, while at the same time it assured a brilliant future to the house of Medici. He was not deceived on the second point at least, for Catherine ascended the royal throne of France, and for two centuries the Medici ruled Florence. Within a few years, however, death removed the two bastard nephews, for whose sake Clement VII had destroyed the liberty of his native city. The brilliant Cardinal Ippolito died as early as August 10, 1535, at Itri, in Campania, of fever, or of poison administered at the instigation of Alessandro. The vicious Alessandro himself was murdered at Florence on January 5, 1537, by Lorenzino Medici.

Clement VII did not live to see the death of his nephews. Falling ill soon after his return, he lingered for some miserable months, tortured by memories, by the fear of a council and by the melancholy spectacle presented by Germany and England. For after his final judgment on Henry VIII's divorce and his threat to pronounce the anathema on the king, England severed herself from the Roman church.

On September 23, 1534, Clement wrote from his deathbed a letter of farewell to Charles V.

Most beloved son in Christ! In this my severe and constant illness, of which your Majesty has probably already been informed, since, although my strength for a while seemed to be restored, I have now relapsed into greater danger, I feel myself near my end and shall not unwillingly take leave of life. Concerning, however, the peace of Italy and Christendom and the establishment of the apostolic chair, all of which I mainly owe to your grace, and now leave behind me, I am no little concerned, for I know not what times may follow, nor of what mind may be my successor. Besides these public affairs I am also troubled by the thought of my native Florence, where I saw the light, and by that of my nephew Duke Alessandro, since I fear that the position, which your magnanimity has bestowed on him, may be destroyed by those enemies who are encouraged by the circumstance that his marriage with your daughter has not yet taken place. But your fidelity and goodness, dearest son, do not allow us to fear, that the love which emanates from your magnanimity, will ever be diminished through you; on the contrary I regard as already accomplished that which your conscientiousness has determined. Impelled therefore by the special love which I bear to your Excellency, and feeling that I am beloved by you, I address you by means of this letter and its bearer with almost my last voice. I send to you my beloved son the Protonotary Carnesecca de' Medici, my private secretary, to whom I am accustomed to impart all my cares, the thoughts of my soul and my most secret concerns. I earnestly entreat you out of regard to me to receive and listen to this man, who is very dear to me by reason of his fidelity and virtue, and I implore you by the heart of Our Lord Jesus Christ, in this my last hour, that your Majesty will maintain the same disposition towards the Holy Church and the welfare of the whole of Christendom, and I recommend to you in all times the dignity of the sacred chair and the peace of Italy, which mainly depend on the power and rectitude of your Majesty. I also recommend to thee personally my nephews Cardinal Ippolito Medici and Alessandro, who is thy servant, and in respect of the dukedom of Penna and also in particular thy Majesty's subject, that thou in the same goodness, with which thou hast taken them under thy protection, may further keep them, for I can leave behind no greater assurance than the trust in thy unbounded goodness and favor. In this confidence I willingly depart this life, and do not doubt that thy Majesty in virtue of thy great goodness and in memory of me will keep these my nephews in thy perpetual protection.

We may honor the steadfast affection which Clement VII bore to his relations, but must at the same time wonder that the last thought of a pope, who had witnessed so many striking events of worldwide importance, should be dedicated to the fate of two insignificant nephews. Clement passed away on September 25.

"He died," says Guicciardini, who despised the pope, "hated by the Curia, distrusted by the princes, leaving behind a hated and oppressive rather than a pleasing memory, for he was considered avaricious, a man of little sincerity and by nature averse to doing good." "Clement," says Jovius, "lacked the faculties of magnanimity and generosity; his nature took pleasure in parsimony and dissimulation; he was not cruel or malicious, but hard and narrowminded. He hated no one, for he loved no one." "For upwards of a century," says his confidant Francesco Vettori, "no better man than Clement has sat on the Sacred Chair; he was not cruel, or proud, or addicted to simony; neither avaricious nor sensual. . . . Nevertheless the disaster took place in his time, and others who were filled with vices lived and died, as the world goes, in prosperity."

On the head of Clement VII instead of on that of Alexander VI fell a storm of misfortune, heavier than was deserved by the guilt of this weak and timid man; a man of little heart and no great passion; who of the exalted duties of the priesthood fulfilled only the traditional observances, and whose entire reign was absorbed in politics, petty or grand. The punishment, which avenged the disorders, the worldly ambition and the sins of the papacy under his predecessors, fell on him as the heir of all the accumulated corruptions of the Curia and church. It is only just to say, that Clement VII was so entangled in the labyrinth of inherited evils, that some superhuman power would have been required to effect his release. It was solely the influence of the Reformation that opened a loophole to his successors. Ascending the sacred chair amid the storms of a new epoch, an epoch which was to transform the world, he encountered the political tempest, armed only with the feeble arts of the diplomatist educated in the school of Leo X, and Machiavelli's *Prince*, in order to afford, if ever a pope did so, proof clear as day, that the corruption of the church as of the state arose from the combination of religion with politics, and to show that priests are called to stand by the altar of the church, but not to political rule. His pontificate was fraught with ruin both to the world and to Rome. We may therefore call him the most unfortunate of popes. He beheld at one and the same time the fall of the historic greatness of the papacy, the destruction of the unity of the Catholic church, and the extinction of Italian liberty under foreign rule.

Had this pope of the downfall been a greater character, he would have stood forth at least as a tragic figure in the history both of his country and of the papacy. For Clement VII was the last pope whom circumstances summoned to defend the liberty of the Italian people against the restored imperial authority and against foreign dominion, as his great predecessors on the papal throne had defended it in ancient times. He failed pitiably in the fulfilment of this exalted task, and finally abandoned it from petty motives of domestic policy, to form an alliance with the same victorious power that reduced Italy to servitude. To this alliance Florence fell the first sacrifice, and the restoration of a national political system in Italy was thereby rendered impossible for centuries. With Clement the papacy itself also failed in this great aim and failed for ever. Owing to the foreign rule, which Alexander VI had introduced into Italy, and which Clement VII strengthened and sealed, the papacy, deposed from its high national position, hurled from the summit of its universal spiritual power by the Reformation, finally ousted from the new life of culture and reduced to intellectual torpor by the Counter-Reformation, surviving henceforth only as a ruin, and quaking at every breath of freedom in the world of politics or science, formed an alliance with almost every despotic power and with every retrograde theory, in order to preserve its temporal state and its spiritual authority.

The tomb of Clement VII in S. Maria sopra Minerva, where it stands opposite the monument of Leo X, is the last milestone of a long series of the papacy and the city of Rome, the history most full of passion, the most glorious and most sublime in the annals of mankind.

Conclusion

CLOSE OF THE HISTORY
OF THE CITY OF ROME
IN THE MIDDLE AGES

Close of the History
of the City of Rome
in the Middle Ages

THE task of the historian of the city of Rome in the Middle Ages is ended; he has reached his goal. As from the summit of a lofty mountain which he has arduously climbed, he can turn his gaze backwards over the long and dark periods he has traversed, and forward to succeeding times, to that boundary where the future is shrouded in mystery from the present. If it be the task of the historian to reveal the form of the times, he must await the verdict of thinking men, as to whether he has succeeded in doing more than trace in shadowy outline the features of the mysterious past.

The spirit of the Middle Ages is indeed frequently more perplexing than that of classic antiquity, to the ruins of which its history is linked. Entire territories within it are steeped in darkness, over which chronicles and documents scarcely shed a ray. The Middle Ages are the development of the Western races, by the influence of the principles of the Christian religion operating on the foundations of ancient culture; they are the great factory and the treasure house of all the ideas of our culture. The farther we are separated from them, the more mysterious and deserving of reverence do they appear. The sublimity of their ideals and the fervor of their religion, the grandeur of their world-embracing system, the visionary subordination of the earthly to the spiritual, the many-sided forms of their life, the profound antagonism between the supernatural and the actual world, and their destructive but at the same time fruitful struggle; all these things exhibit a cosmos of ideas and phenomena, whose essential nature seems veiled in mystery. Several incidents in the mediaeval world, which formerly appeared clear, are now blurred to our altered vision; many that looked dark to bygone generations are illuminated for us by the light of reason. Ideas and dogmas, rights and laws, belief and mode of thought, church and state have changed their places in the intellectual system, or have sunk below our horizon, and this transformation is history itself. Is it given to the historian to retrace with safety its many tortuous paths, correctly to perceive the laws of its movement, to secure to the times of which he treats their true posthumous value, and from the ruin of facts to raise up the spiritual picture of the past as its indestructible, because ideal, actuality? Here, where I must take leave of the history of the city of Rome—the work which has filled with enjoyment seventeen years of my life—I once more feel acutely the whole weight of my task. Out of the ruins of the centuries, the historic march of which is for us interrupted by arid voids, I had the audacity to seek to glean it from the Roman soil. My work is merely an imperfect fragment; but such as it is, I gratefully and reverently lay it as a votive offering at the feet of Rome.

The idea of the work was suggested by the overwhelming spectacle of the monumental grandeur of the city, and perhaps by the presentiment which made itself obscurely felt at the time, that the history of the Roman Middle Ages would soon reach its perfect close in the downfall of the papal dominion, and that, after a long-continued period of spiritual rule, the city of Rome approached a second metamorphosis—that of her resecularisation. While writing this history, I was an eyewitness first of the restoration of the papacy after its merely momentary fall in 1848, then of the great Italian revolution, which produced the last catastrophe. These events aided my work, quickening my perception of the fundamental ideas and the historic current of the Roman past, while at the same time they opened to me many of the archives of Rome and Italy, which apart from this revolution would scarcely have been accessible.

I began my task in 1855, and ended it in 1871, at the time when the fall of the papal temporal state had become an accomplished fact. No more significant or appropriate moment could indeed have been found for the completion of the history of the city of Rome in the Middle Ages.

Friendly critics of the work have suggested that I should continue the history down to present days on the same lines as those on which I have endeavored to deal with the Middle Ages—from its documents. I am therefore obliged to say that I do not desire to undertake this new task, and to give my reasons therefor.

The period from the death of Clement VII onwards offers but scant materials to the historian of the city, and these materials deal almost exclusively with the history of the papacy, restricted, as it was, within ever-narrowing limits of moral influence. During these three centuries the city of Rome could neither be an active factor in the history of the West, nor a mirror reflecting the movements of Europe. The historian would consequently find it difficult to bring the great currents of universal history into relation to the city of Rome, or to discover the hidden survival of those great fundamental thoughts that determined the character of the Roman Middle Ages. By these thoughts I mean, besides the papal power, the principle of the civic republic, and the idea of the empire.

From the time of Charles V's coronation until the end of the eighteenth century, the popes ruled Rome in such perfect tranquility, that during this period of the political extinction of Italy, as well as of the torpor of the papacy, they enjoyed their happiest but most inglorious term of government. The imperial idea, like the municipal principle, rested in oblivion, until the ancient struggles were reawakened by the French revolution. From this moment, when a fresh chain of national, social and intellectual revolutions began, until present days, the author who continues the history of the city of Rome will have to describe the death strug-

457

gles of the political papacy; and in his hands the revivified picture of Rome will take shape as the tragedy of the ruin of the State of the Church and of the present form of the papacy. He will have to depict the dreamlike awakening of the republic on the Capitol at the end of the eighteenth century, and the gigantic shadow of Caesarism, which in Napoleon suddenly rose over Rome and the world, while the legitimate imperial authority of the German emperors vanished. He will describe the sudden fall of the colossus of Caesarism, and the restoration of the papal power by the Congress of Vienna, and will relate how a violent conflict of secular impulses immediately arose against this spiritual restoration. He will set forth how each of the three leading ideas, that determined the history of the city of Rome, were supplanted in turn by the impulse of nationality. He will show how the national-political idea, which was first conceived by Cola di Rienzo, but which was by him interwoven with ancient Roman legal conceptions and ecclesiastical scholasticism, shook off its mediaeval character. He will prove how this severance from every tie with the ancient ideas of the empire, the church and the municipal republic, and, in general, how the radical estrangement of the modern theory of the state and European politics from the old theological conception of the universe, have given the victory to the principle of nationality.

The spirit that rules the history of the world has unburdened itself before our eyes in a storm of disasters, and has brought with it so much of destruction and of creation, that even although the latest developments may have produced only phases of transition and problems instead of permanent forms, still a new era for Europe begins with the years 1870 and 1871. The reader who has followed the history of Rome in the Middle Ages holds in his hands the threads of a historic web, which embraces both the Latin and the German world, and the center of which is Rome; he will therefore recognize the perfect sequence of historic cause and effect which has resulted in events such as those of present times.

The Ghibelline ideas of the development of the church, the struggle of the spirit of reform against the papal hierarchy, the efforts of the papacy to acquire universal spiritual supremacy, Caesarism and nationality, Italy's strivings towards independence and unity, the like impulse towards unity in Germany, the gigantic struggles of the Germans and the French for the right of national reorganization, perhaps for the hegemony of Europe—all these ideas, tendencies, necessities and antagonisms of history, interwoven in the past, we have seen burst in a storm that shook the world, in the great drama of our times. From this hurricane Germany issued with the political reformation, the necessary outcome of the ecclesiastical. After an interregnum of sixty-four years the imperial authority was restored in the Protestant house of Hohenzollern; the German Empire arose as a national empire severed from the ancient political ties to Rome and Italy. Italy herself, which, owing to mediaeval dogmas, had for centuries been a fief of the German Empire, and which from the time of Charles V was to suffer the foreign rule of Spain and Austria, became entirely independent, and with the sanction of Europe was enabled to work out her national reconstruction without difficulty. For the first time since the days of the Gothic king Theodoric, she became once more a united kingdom. Italy and Germany, the two sisters linked together by fate, though at enmity with one another, from whose reciprocal connection in the Middle Ages European culture had arisen, were now divided and at last reconciled by freedom.

In the midst of these convulsions was accomplished the fall of the papacy, which had been erected on a new political foundation by Julius II, and recognized by Charles V. It fell at the time when Pius IX, the pope who had longest filled the chair of Peter, had completed the twenty-fifth year of his reign. The overthrow of the oldest, and, in the eyes of many, the most revered power of Europe, the power which had survived the countless revolutions of a thousand years, is the great tragedy of modern times. This power itself was the historic product of the political and ecclesiastical constitution of Europe, and had been created, preserved and combated by the ideas and necessities of the time. It fell in our own days amid the storm of the world's history, its grave surrounded by wars of races and events no less great and

459

stirring than those witnessed by the weak and unfortunate Clement VII. Its funeral knell was the thunder of terrible battles, battles such as history has but seldom seen, and the downfall of an empire. It perished owing not only to the destructive power of the entirely changed ideas of mankind, but also owing to the inflexibility of its own principle. For, as always in similar shipwrecks of history, the survival of a principle of rigid immobility becomes an evil of tragic import in the pressure of the advancing current of life. The political form of the papacy became an anachronism and an anomaly in the reconstituted world. Its fall was the sentence pronounced by history itself.

After the Counter-Reformation, which killed the spirit of the Renaissance, the declining papacy, devoid of rejuvenating vitality, still fighting for its existence, remained at ever-increasing antagonism to European culture. This culture, the result of universal progress, is nevertheless in great part the product of the Christian church. At impotent discord with progress, which in its timidity it longed to arrest, opposed to the freedom of states and peoples and to the advance of science, the development of which it repudiated the papacy—which owing to its rigidity and torpor had scarcely any history—sought its salvation in the revival of the mediaeval ideal of Gregory VII. The violent proclamation of papal absolutism, for which in its actual state the European intellect no longer possessed either the faith or the need, was in the immediate past the most lamentable, the most insolent, and the most despairing protest of the papal power against its own overthrow—that is to say, against the inevitable transformation demanded by history. It was at the same time the dogmatic keystone of the Gregorian church, above which, naturally, no superstructure is possible. The colossal pyramid of the Roman papacy was completed on July 18, 1870.

It will remain a historic monument visible to all future time, even when other equally great forms of the past have vanished from the sight of men. And even if it be a mausoleum for the now decrepit form of the papacy, history nevertheless does not possess a sufficient number of heroic titles to inscribe upon it, and with them even approximately record the all-embracing energy, the great creative achievements and the imperishable glory of the popes.

When in a future century the passionate struggles with the hierarchy—in which we are still engaged—have ceased, or when the popes themselves have become mere names and figures of the past, then only will mankind award full recognition to their memory, and the long series of pontiffs will form a system in the heaven of the history of civilization, that must far outshine every other line of princes and potentates.

A future historian of the fall of the papacy will linger with astonishment on the fact that the successor of St. Peter, in that same hour in which he mounted to the giddy and dazzling height of his dogmatic omnipotence, and in which he ventured to bury the Church's inner life and capacity for development in the dogma of infallibility, as it were in a sarcophagus, witnessed the falling away of all temporal conditions, and suffered the loss of the material foundations of his spiritual power, the possession, namely, of the city of Rome and the State of the Church, which had been his for a thousand years. He will then probably proceed to show that this coincidence of facts, the violent destruction of the ancient constitution of the church through the papacy, and the collapse of its temporal sovereignty, were a historic necessity; that the one was demanded by the other.

On September 20, 1870, the Italians became masters of Rome. A long chain of causes and effects extending from the Lombard King Desiderius down to Victor Emmanuel led to this event, which we spectators scarcely yet seem able to grasp. And as it was conditioned by the past of Italy, so is it also linked with the change in the fundamental ideas of the constitution of Europe. I speak of the entire collapse of that universal ideal of the Christian republic, which was expressed in the universal system of the church and the empire, until the rise of the modern monarchies and the German Reformation began to destroy this theory. From the year 1806 onwards, when the Roman-German imperium expired, Europe beheld first the fall of the Napoleonic universal

461

empire, then the withdrawal of Austria—on which a reflex of the ancient imperial idea still rested—from all its historic relations with Italy, finally the fall of the second Napoleonic empire, the last protector of the political papacy. True, that Germany (whence through the Reformation had proceeded the destruction of the universal church) restored the empire, but she only restored it within the narrow confines of nationality. Within these limits the ancient idea of empire held by Dante has receded and practically vanished from the Europe of the present.

Rome, the historic source of this cosmopolitan ideal, remained naturally the last stronghold of the theory of the universal Christian republic, the banner of which, abandoned by the empire, was here displayed in tragic and self-incurred loneliness by Pius IX. In this history I have described how, from the time of Charles the Great to that of Charles V, the historic system of the papacy remained inseparable from that of the empire, how one presupposed and upheld the other, how even their very conflict only increased their mutual energies, while neither disputed the principle of the other, and how the ruin of one necessarily entailed that of its rival. Perhaps we may even now say that had the papacy shown itself in its ideal greatness, the habitual reverence of nations for an exalted tradition would have demanded or at least desired that Rome—secularized indeed—should have continued her existence as a free Italian city. But at a terrible crisis the papacy, with a frankness hitherto unknown to history, avowed itself as an enemy on principle to modern culture and to all its possessions most cherished by educated nations, and the history of the last Vatican council, as of all the ecclesiastical acts of Pius IX that preceded it, clearly explains the entire alienation of races, states and governments from the papacy, as also its inevitable fall.

As a natural result of the ruin of the imperial idea, and of the collapse of the universal ideals which we have described, the Italians, without protest from Europe, nay, rather supported by public opinion, forcibly dethroned the pope, put an end to conditions in Rome that had become intolerable, and made the

462

ancient cosmopolitan city the capital of the young national kingdom. A future historian will have to describe the effects of this
unparalleled act, and the transformation to which it will necessarily subject the church, Italy and the city of Rome. No mortal
can read the Sibylline books of the future fortunes of Rome, no
prophet foretell whether Alma Roma will henceforth survive like
other capitals, simply as the fortunate capital of the fairest of
kingdoms and of a noble nation, or whether, if the universal requirements of the world demand it, once more in times to come
she may become the receptacle—consecrated by centuries—for
that idea of the federation and unity of the human race which
never vanishes from history and which is to be more perfectly
realized in the future. But if those ideals, which have given Rome
this unique position in the world, have already faded with the
past, and if the nations of Europe in their onward progress to
greater liberty no longer require an international center, the
great memories and monuments of history will ever preserve the
ties which bind Rome to the human race.

The Italians received Rome as the sacred bequest of history,
and while perhaps on no nation has ever been bestowed a like
exalted seat of government, on none has been laid a more difficult task or a more serious duty—the duty, that is to say, of acting as the heir and restorer of the city of Rome, of becoming once
more great through her greatness, of healing the terrible breach
between the church and nation by a moral reform.

Fourteen hundred years after the fall of the ancient Roman
Empire a united and free people entered Rome, not because they
stormed the outworn walls of Aurelian, but because behind these
walls the aged and decaying papacy was ready to fall, while
around it the changed and changing world was in part responsible for the causes of its decrepitude. For only when the idea of
the church was full of vigor and ruled the world were the popes
(almost always defenseless and often reduced to sore straits in
the past) able to defend Rome and themselves. Without claiming the prophetic gift, we may predict that the era of papal rule
over Rome is for ever ended, and that never again will an em-

peror cross the Alps to reerect the overturned throne of the Vatican priest-kings. For its fall marks a new and important phase in the development of the European mind, and the courageous revolution by which it was accomplished is protected by the principles—recognized by the educated world—of national right and of civil and religious freedom, whose banner the Italians planted on the ruins of the Roman papal kingdom.

The sight of the fall of an ancient and revered power may stir the tranquil spectator of history to pursue those reflections on the vicissitudes of all earthly greatness, with which at the beginning of our history we contemplated the fall of the Roman empire. For the city of Rome has evidently now reached another like epoch of her historic life; now also there is a fall and an uprisal, an inward and an outward metamorphosis in process of development. After the Romans, as this history has shown, have for centuries been condemned to sacrifice their own nature as citizens to the power of the papacy, they are at length released from this proscription. And only now, when by means of Italy they have been reinstated in their independence and manly dignity, and in many other rights and privileges of civilization which have hitherto been denied them, and have been awakened to a new life, only now can be laid to rest those tragic shades of history, whose series extends from Crescentius to Henry IV the penitent at Canossa, from Arnold of Brescia and the Hohenstaufens, to Dante, Cola di Rienzo, Petrarch and Machiavelli, and down to our own days.

For almost twenty years I was a spectator of the final struggles, by means of which the city of Rome uprose again with a population of free citizens. I was at the same time steeped in the past of the city; I examined into the fortunes and the vicissitudes of Rome, the great deeds and the great errors of the popes during a course of eleven centuries. I described the most eventful and moving tragedy in the history of the world; I traced the constantly recurring conflicts and sufferings of Rome and Italy, ever revolving round the same center, and the fateful part which since Gothic times Germany had been called to play. Precisely on this account I deem myself happy in that the history of the city of

Rome has found its true close. For it was no common fortune that allowed me not only to write and finish this history in Rome, but while engaged on its concluding pages to witness the final expiation of those very fortunes and sufferings of Rome, Italy and Germany which are recorded in these volumes.

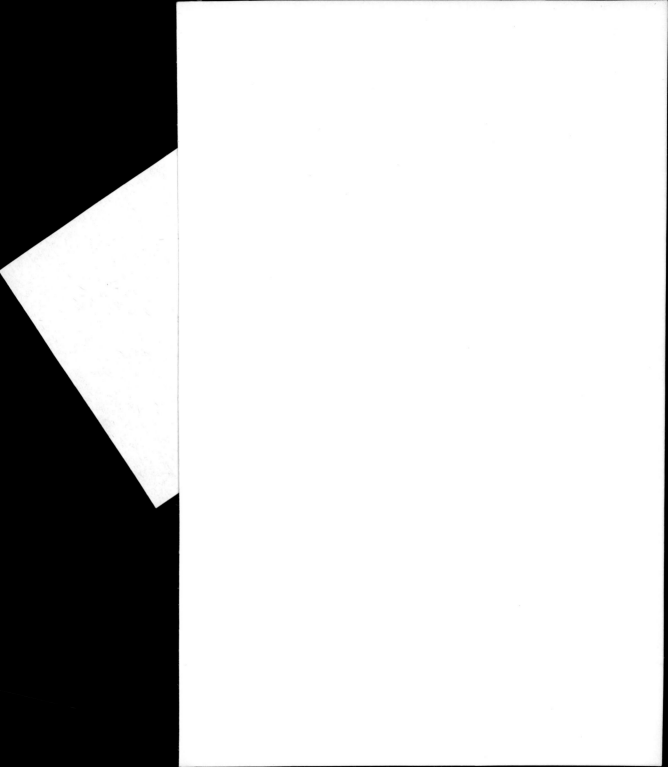

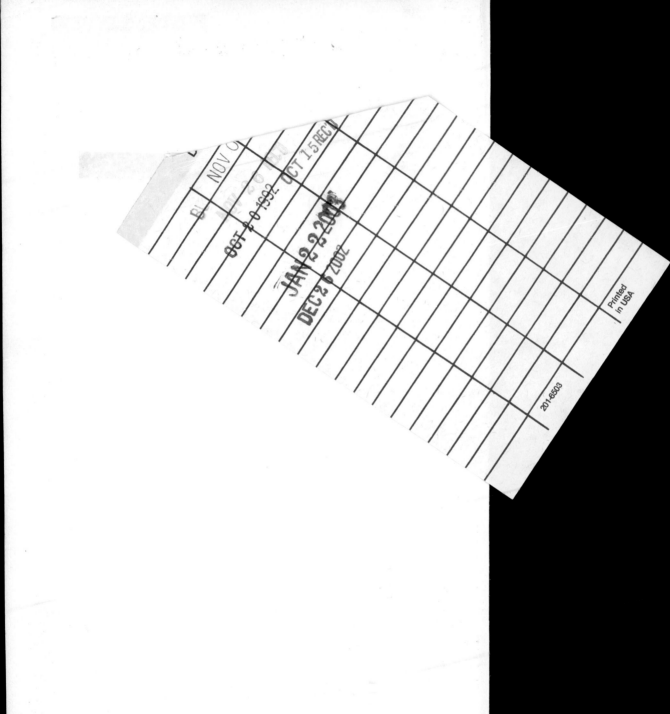